*Disability* KEY ISSUES AND FUTURE DIRECTIONS

# EDUCATION

# The SAGE Reference Series on Disability: Key Issues and Future Directions

*Series Editor: Gary L. Albrecht*

*Arts and Humanities*, by Brenda Jo Brueggemann
*Assistive Technology and Science*, by Cathy Bodine
*Disability Through the Life Course*, by Tamar Heller and Sarah Parker Harris
*Education*, by Cheryl Hanley-Maxwell and Lana Collet-Klingenberg
*Employment and Work*, by Susanne M. Bruyère and Linda Barrington
*Ethics, Law, and Policy*, by Jerome E. Bickenbach
*Health and Medicine*, by Ross M. Mullner
*Rehabilitation Interventions*, by Margaret A. Turk and Nancy R. Mudrick

*Disability* KEY ISSUES AND FUTURE DIRECTIONS

# EDUCATION

Cheryl Hanley-Maxwell
*University of Wisconsin–Madison*

Lana Collet-Klingenberg
*University of Wisconsin–Whitewater*

SERIES EDITOR
Gary L. Albrecht
*University of Illinois at Chicago*

Los Angeles | London | New Delhi
Singapore | Washington DC

Los Angeles | London | New Delhi
Singapore | Washington DC

FOR INFORMATION:

SAGE Publications, Inc.

2455 Teller Road

Thousand Oaks, California 91320

E-mail: order@sagepub.com

SAGE Publications Ltd.

1 Oliver's Yard

55 City Road

London EC1Y 1SP

United Kingdom

SAGE Publications India Pvt. Ltd.

B 1/I 1 Mohan Cooperative Industrial Area

Mathura Road, New Delhi 110 044

India

SAGE Publications Asia-Pacific Pte. Ltd.

33 Pekin Street #02-01

Far East Square

Singapore 048763

Publisher: Rolf A. Janke

Acquisitions Editor: Jim Brace-Thompson

Assistant to the Publisher: Michele Thompson

Project Development, Editing, & Management: Kevin Hillstrom,
    Laurie Collier Hillstrom

Production Editor: Jane Haenel

Reference Systems Manager: Leticia Gutierrez

Reference Systems Coordinator: Laura Notton

Typesetter: C&M Digitals (P) Ltd.

Proofreader: Ellen Howard

Indexer: Michael Ferreira

Cover Designer: Gail Buschman

Marketing Manager: Kristi Ward

Printed in the United States of America

Library of Congress Cataloging-in-Publication
Data

Hanley-Maxwell, Cheryl.

Education / Cheryl Hanley-Maxwell, Lana
Collet-Klingenberg.

p. cm. — (The Sage reference series
on disabiity; 2)
Includes bibliographical references and index.

ISBN 978-1-4129-8690-8 (hardback)

1. Special education—United States—History.
2. Children with disabilities—Education—
United States—History. 3. Children with
social disabilities—Education—History.
4. Educational equalization—United States—
History. I. Collet-Klingenberg, Lana. II. Title.

LC3981.H354 2011
379.2'60973—dc23          2011019176

11 12 13 14 15 10 9 8 7 6 5 4 3 2 1

# Contents

# Series Introduction

The SAGE Reference Series on Disability appears at a time when global attention is being focused on disability at all levels of society. Researchers, service providers, and policymakers are concerned with the prevalence, experience, meanings, and costs of disability because of the growing impact of disability on individuals and their families and subsequent increased demand for services (Banta & de Wit, 2008; Martin et al., 2010; Mont, 2007; Whitaker, 2010). For their part, disabled people and their families are keenly interested in taking a more proactive stance in recognizing and dealing with disability in their lives (Charlton, 1998; Iezzoni & O'Day, 2006). As a result, there is burgeoning literature, heightened Web activity, myriad Internet information and discussion groups, and new policy proposals and programs designed to produce evidence and disseminate information so that people with disabilities may be informed and live more independently (see, for example, the World Institute of Disability Web site at http://www.wid.org, the Center for International Rehabilitation Research Information and Exchange Web site at http://cirrie.buffalo.edu, and the Web portal to caregiver support groups at http://www.caregiver.com/regionalresources/index.htm).

Disability is recognized as a critical medical and social problem in current society, central to the discussions of health care and social welfare policies taking place around the world. The prominence of these disability issues is highlighted by the attention given to them by the most respected national and international organizations. The *World Report on Disability* (2011), co-sponsored by the World Health Organization (WHO) and the World Bank and based on an analysis of surveys from over 100 countries, estimates that 15% of the world's population (more than 1 billion people) currently experiences disability. This is the best prevalence estimate available today and indicates a marked increase over previous epidemiological calculations. Based on this work, the British medical journal *Lancet* dedicated an entire issue (November 28, 2009) to disability, focusing attention on the salience of the problem for health care systems world-wide. In addition, the WHO has developed community-based rehabilita-tion principles and strategies which are applicable to communities of diverse cultures and at all levels of development (WHO, 2010). The World Bank is concerned because of the link between disability and poverty (World Bank, 2004). Disability, in their view, could be a major impediment to economic development, particularly in emerging economies.

Efforts to address the problem of disability also have legal and human rights implications. Being disabled has historically led to dis-crimination, stigma, and dependency, which diminish an individual's full rights to citizenship and equality (European Disability Forum, 2003). In response to these concerns, the United Nations Convention on the Rights of Persons with Disabilities (2008) and the European Union Disability Strategy embodying the Charter of Fundamental Rights (2000) were passed to affirm that disabled people have the right to acquire and change nationalities, cannot be deprived of their ability to exercise liberty, have freedom of movement, are free to leave any coun-try including their own, are not deprived of the right to enter their own country, and have access to the welfare and benefits afforded to any citi-zen of their country. As of March 31, 2010, 144 nations—including the United States, China, India, and Russia—had signed the U.N. Conven-tion, and the European Union Disability Strategy had been ratified by all members of the European Community. These international agreements supplement and elaborate disability rights legislation such as the Amer-icans with Disabilities Act of 1990 and its amendments, the U.K. Disabil-ity Discrimination Act of 1995, and the Disabled Person's Fundamental Law of Japan, revised in 1993.

In the United States, the Institute of Medicine of the National Academy of Sciences has persistently focused attention on the medical, public health, and social policy aspects of disability in a broad-ranging series of reports: *Disability in America* (1991), *Enabling America* (1997), *The Dynamics of Disability: Measuring and Monitoring Disability for Social Security Pro-grams,* (2002), *The Future of Disability in America* (2007), and *Improving the Presumptive Disability Decision-Making Process for Veterans* (2008). The Cen-ters for Disease Control have a long-standing interest in diabetes and obe-sity because of their effects on morbidity, mortality, and disability. Current data show that the incidence and prevalence of obesity is rising across all age groups in the United States, that obesity is related to diabetes, which is also on the rise, and that both, taken together, increase the likelihood of experiencing disability (Bleich et al., 2008; Gill et al., 2010). People with diabetes also are likely to have comorbid depression, which increases their chances of functional disability (Egede, 2004).

Depression and other types of mental illness—like anxiety disorders, alcohol and drug dependence, and impulse-control disorders—are more prevalent than previously thought and often result in disability (Kessler & Wang, 2008). The prevalence of mental disorders in the United States is high, with about half of the population meeting criteria (as measured by the *Diagnostic and Statistical Manual of Mental Disorders*, or DSM-IV) for one more disorders in their lifetimes, and more than one-quarter of the population meeting criteria for a disorder in any single year. The more severe mental disorders are strongly associated with high comorbidity, resulting in disability.

Major American foundations with significant health portfolios have also turned their attention to disability. The Bill and Melinda Gates Foundation has directed considerable resources to eliminate disability-causing parasitic and communicable diseases such as malaria, elephantiasis, and river blindness. These efforts are designed to prevent and control disability-causing conditions in the developing world that inhibit personal independence and economic development. The Robert Wood Johnson Foundation has a long-standing program on self-determination for people with developmental disabilities in the United States aimed at increasing their ability to participate fully in society, and the Hogg Foundation is dedicated to improving mental health awareness and services. Taken in concert, these activities underscore the recognized importance of disability in the present world.

## Disability Concepts, Models, and Theories

There is an immense literature on disability concepts, models, and theories. An in-depth look at these issues and controversies can be found in the *Handbook of Disability Studies* (Albrecht, Seelman, & Bury, 2001), in the *Encyclopedia of Disability* (Albrecht, 2006), and in "The Sociology of Disability: Historical Foundations and Future Directions" (Albrecht, 2010). For the purposes of this reference series, it is useful to know that the World Health Organization, in the *International Classification of Functioning, Disability and Health* (ICF), defines disability as "an umbrella term for impairments, activity limitations or participation restrictions" (WHO, 2001, p. 3). ICF also lists environmental factors that interact with all these constructs. Further, the WHO defines impairments as "problems in body function or structure such as significant deviation or loss"; activity limitations as "difficulties an individual may have in executing activities"; participation as "involvement in a life situation"; and environmental factors as those components of "the physical, social and attitudinal environment in which people live and conduct their lives" (WHO, 2001, p. 10). The U.N. Convention on the Rights of Persons with Disabilities, in turn, defines disability as including "those who have long term physical, mental, intellectual or sensory impairments which in interaction with various barriers may hinder their full and effective participation in society on an equal basis with others." In the introduction to the *Lancet* special issue on disability, Officer and Groce (2009) conclude that "both the ICF and the Convention view disability as the outcome of complex interactions between health conditions and features of an individual's physical, social, and attitudinal environment that hinder their full and effective participation in society" (p. 1795). Hence, disability scholars and activists alike are concerned with breaking down physical, environmental, economic, and social barriers so that disabled people can live independently and participate as fully as possible in society.

## Types of Disability

Interest in disability by medical practitioners has traditionally been condition specific (such as spinal cord injury or disabilities due to heart disease), reflecting the medical model approach to training and disease taxonomies. Similarly, disabled people and their families are often most concerned about their particular conditions and how best to deal with them. The SAGE Reference Series on Disability recognizes that there are a broad range of disabilities that can be generally conceived of as falling in the categories of physical, mental, intellectual, and sensory disabilities. In practice, disabled persons may have more than one disability and are often difficult to place in one disability category. For instance, a spinal-cord injured individual might experience depression, and a person with multiple sclerosis may simultaneously deal with physical and sensory disabilities. It is also important to note that disabilities are dynamic. People do experience different rates of onset, progression, remission, and even transition from being disabled at one point in time, to not being disabled at another, to being disabled again. Examples of this change in disability status include disability due to bouts of arthritis, Guillain-Barré Syndrome, and postpartum depression.

## Disability Language

The symbols and language used to represent disability have sparked contentious debates over the years. In the *Handbook of Disability Studies* (Albrecht, Seelman, & Bury, 2001) and the *Encyclopedia of Disability* (Albrecht, 2006), authors from different countries were encouraged to use the terms and language of their cultures, but to explain them when necessary. In the present volumes, authors may use "people with disabilities" or "disabled people" to refer to individuals experiencing disability. Scholars in the United States have preferred "people with disabilities" (people-first language), while those in the United Kingdom, Canada, and Australia generally use "disabled people." In languages other than English, scholars typically use some form of the "disabled people" idiom. The U.S. version emphasizes American exceptionalism and the individual, whereas "disabled people" highlights the group and their minority status or state of being different. In my own writing, I have chosen "disabled people" because it stresses human diversity and variation.

In a recent discussion of this issue, DePoy and Gilson (2010) "suggest that maintaining debate and argument on what language is most correct derails a larger and more profound needed change, that of equalizing resources, valuation, and respect. Moreover, . . . locating disability 'with a person' reifies its embodiment and flies in the very face of the social model that person-first language is purported to espouse. . . . We have not heard anyone suggest that beauty, kindness, or even unkindness be located after personhood." While the debate is not likely over, we state why we use the language that we do.

# Organization of the Series

These issues were important in conceiving of and organizing the SAGE Reference Series on Disability. Instead of developing the series around specific disabilities resulting from Parkinson's disease or bi-polar disorder, or according to the larger categories of physical, mental, intellectual, and sensory disabilities, we decided to concentrate on the major topics that confront anyone interested in or experiencing disability. Thus, the series consists of eight volumes constructed around the following topics:

- Arts and Humanities
- Assistive Technology and Science
- Disability Through the Life Course
- Education
- Employment and Work
- Ethics, Law, and Policy
- Health and Medicine
- Rehabilitation Interventions

To provide structure, we chose to use a similar organization for each volume. Therefore, each volume contains the following elements:

Series Introduction

Preface

About the Author

About the Series Editor

Chapter 1. Introduction, Background, and History

Chapter 2. Current Issues, Controversies, and Solutions

Chapter 3. Chronology of Critical Events

Chapter 4. Biographies of Key Contributors in the Field

Chapter 5. Annotated Data, Statistics, Tables, and Graphs

Chapter 6. Annotated List of Organizations and Associations

Chapter 7. Selected Print and Electronic Resources

Glossary of Key Terms

Index

## The Audience

The eight-volume SAGE Reference Series on Disability targets an audience of undergraduate students and general readers that uses both academic and public libraries. However, the content and depth of the series will also make it attractive to graduate students, researchers, and policymakers. The series has been edited to have a consistent format and accessible style. The focus in each volume is on providing lay-friendly overviews of broad issues and guideposts for further research and exploration.

The series is innovative in that it will be published and marketed worldwide, with each volume available in electronic format soon after it appears in print. The print version consists of eight bound volumes. The electronic version is available through the SAGE Reference Online platform, which hosts 200 handbooks and encyclopedias across the social sciences, including the *Handbook of Disability Studies* and the *Encyclopedia of Disability*. With access to this platform through college, university, and public libraries, students, the lay public, and scholars can search these interrelated disability and social science sources from their computers or handheld and smart phone devices. The movement to an electronic platform presages the cloud computing revolution coming upon us. Cloud computing "refers to 'everything' a user may reach via the Internet, including services, storage, applications and people" (Hoehl & Sieh, 2010). According to Ray Ozzie (2010), recently Microsoft's chief architect, "We're moving toward a world of (1) cloud-based continuous services that connect us all and do our bidding, and (2) appliance-like connected devices enabling us to interact with those cloud-based services." Literally, information will be available at consumers' fingertips. Given the ample links to other resources in emerging databases, they can pursue any topic of interest in detail. This resource builds on the massive efforts to make information available to decision makers in real time, such as computerizing health and hospital records so that the diagnosis and treatment of chronic diseases and disabilities can be better managed (Celler, Lovell, & Basilakis, 2003). The SAGE Reference Series on Disability provides Internet and Web site addresses which lead the user into a world of social networks clustered around disability in general and specific conditions and issues. Entering and engaging with social networks revolving around health and disability promises to help individuals make more informed decisions and provide support in times of need (Smith & Christakis, 2008). The SAGE Reference Online platform will also be configured and updated to make it increasingly accessible to disabled people.

The SAGE Reference Series on Disability provides an extensive index for each volume. Through its placement on the SAGE Reference Online platform, the series will be fully searchable and cross-referenced, will allow keyword searching, and will be connected to the *Handbook of Disability Studies* and the *Encyclopedia of Disability*.

The authors of the volumes have taken considerable effort to vet the references, data, and resources for accuracy and credibility. The multiple Web sites for current data, information, government and United Nations documents, research findings, expert recommendations, self-help, discussion groups, and social policy are particularly useful, as they are being continuously updated. Examples of current and forthcoming data are the results and analysis of the findings of the U.S. 2010 Census, the ongoing reports of the Centers for Disease Control on disability, the World Health Organization's *World Report on Disability* and its updates, the World Bank reports on disability, poverty, and development, and reports from major foundations like Robert Wood Johnson, Bill and Melinda Gates, Ford, and Hogg. In terms of clinical outcomes, the evaluation of cost-effective interventions, management of disability, and programs that work, enormous attention is being given to evidence-based outcomes (Brownson, Fielding, & Maylahn, 2009; Marcus et al., 2006; Wolinsky et al., 2007) and comparative effectiveness research (Etheredge, 2010; Inglehart, 2010). Such data force a re-examination of policymakers' arguments. For example, there is mounting evidence that demonstrates the beneficial effects of exercise on preventing disability and enhancing function (Marcus et al., 2006). Recent studies also show that some health care reform initiatives may negatively affect disabled people's access to and costs of health care (Burns, Shah, & Smith, 2010). Furthermore, the seemingly inexorable rise in health care spending may not be correlated with desirable health outcomes (Rothberg et al., 2010). In this environment, valid data are the currency of the discussion (Andersen, Lollar, & Meyers, 2000). The authors' hopes are that this reference series will encourage students and the lay public to base their discussions and decisions on valid outcome data. Such an approach tempers the influence of ideologies surrounding health care and misconceptions about disabled people, their lives, and experiences.

SAGE Publications has made considerable effort to make these volumes accessible to disabled people in the printed book version and in the electronic platform format. In turn, SAGE and other publishers and vendors like Amazon are incorporating greater flexibility in the user interface to improve functionality to a broad range of users, such as disabled people. These efforts are important for disabled people as universities, governments, and health service delivery organizations are moving toward a paperless environment.

In the spirit of informed discussion and transparency, may this reference series encourage people from many different walks of life to become knowledgeable and engaged in the disability world. As a consequence, social policies should become better informed and individuals and families should be able to make better decisions regarding the experience of disability in their lives.

# Acknowledgments

I would like to recognize the vision of Rolf Janke in developing SAGE Publications' presence in the disability field, as represented by the *Handbook of Disability Studies* (2001), the five-volume *Encyclopedia of Disability* (2006), and now the eight-volume SAGE Reference Series on Disability. These products have helped advance the field and have made critical work accessible to scholars, students, and the general public through books and now the SAGE Reference Online platform. Jim Brace-Thompson at SAGE handled the signing of contracts and kept this complex project coordinated and moving on time. Kevin Hillstrom and Laurie Collier Hillstrom at Northern Lights Writers Group were intrepid in taking the composite pieces of this project and polishing and editing them into a coherent whole that is approachable, consistent in style and form, and rich in content. The authors of the eight volumes—Linda Barrington, Jerome Bickenbach, Cathy Bodine, Brenda Brueggemann, Susanne Bruyère, Lana Collet-Klingenberg, Cheryl Hanley-Maxwell, Sarah Parker Harris, Tamar Heller, Nancy Mudrick, Ross Mullner, and Peggy Turk—are to be commended for their enthusiasm, creativity, and fortitude in delivering high-quality volumes on a tight deadline. I was fortunate to work with such accomplished scholars.

Discussions with Barbara Altman, Colin Barnes, Catherine Barral, Len Barton, Isabelle Baszanger, Peter Blanck, Mary Boulton, David Braddock, Richard Burkhauser, Mike Bury, Ann Caldwell, Lennard Davis, Patrick Devlieger, Ray Fitzpatrick, Lawrence Frey, Carol Gill, Tamar Heller, Gary Kielhofner, Soewarta Kosen, Jo Lebeer, Mitch Loeb, Don Lollar, Paul Longmore, Ros Madden, Maria Martinho, Dennis Mathews, Sophie Mitra, Daniel Mont, Alana Officer, Randall Parker, David Pfeiffer, Jean-François Raveau, James Rimmer, Ed Roberts, Jean-Marie Robine, Joan Rogers, Richard Scotch, Kate Seelman, Tom Shakespeare, Sandor Sipos, Henri-Jacques Stiker, Edna Szymanski, Jutta Traviranus, Bryan Turner, Greg Vanderheiden, Isabelle Ville, Larry Voss, Ann Waldschmidt, and Irving Kenneth Zola over the years contributed to the content, logic, and structure of the series. They also were a wonderful source of suggestions for authors.

I would also like to acknowledge the hospitality and support of the Belgian Academy of Science and the Arts, the University of Leuven, Nuffield College, the University of Oxford, the Fondation Maison des Sciences de l'Homme, Paris, and the Department of Disability and Human Development at the University of Illinois at Chicago, who provided the time and environments to conceive of and develop the project. While none of these people or institutions is responsible for any deficiencies in the work, they all helped enormously in making it better.

Gary L. Albrecht
*University of Illinois at Chicago*
*University of Leuven*
*Belgian Academy of Science and Arts*

# References

Albrecht, G. L. (Ed.). (2006). *Encyclopedia of disability* (5 vols.). Thousand Oaks, CA: Sage.

Albrecht, G. L. (2010). The sociology of disability: Historical foundations and future directions. In C. Bird, A. Fremont, S. Timmermans, & P. Conrad (Eds.), *Handbook of medical sociology* (6th ed, pp. 192–209). Nashville, TN: Vanderbilt University Press.

Albrecht, G. L., Seelman, K. D., & Bury, M. (Eds.). (2001). *Handbook of disability studies*. Thousand Oaks, CA: Sage.

Andersen, E. M., Lollar, D. J., & Meyers, A. R. (2000). Disability outcomes research: Why this supplement, on this topic, at this time? *Archives of Physical Medicine and Rehabilitation, 81*, S1–S4.

Banta, H. D., & de Wit, G. A. (2008). Public health services and cost effectiveness analysis. *Annual Review of Public Health, 29*, 383–397.

Bleich, S., Cutler, D., Murray, C., & Adams, A. (2008). Why is the developed world obese? *Annual Review of Public Health, 29*, 273–295.

Brownson, R. C., Fielding, J. E., & Maylahn, C. M. (2009). Evidence-based public health: A fundamental concept for public health practice. *Annual Review of Public Health, 30*, 175–201.

Burns, M., Shah, N., & Smith, M. (2010). Why some disabled adults in Medicaid face large out-of-pocket expenses. *Health Affairs, 29*, 1517–1522.

Celler, B. G., Lovell, N. H., & Basilakis, J. (2003). Using information technology to improve the management of chronic disease. *Medical Journal of Australia, 179*, 242–246.

Charlton, J. I. (1998). *Nothing about us without us: Disability, oppression and empowerment*. Berkeley: University of California Press.

DePoy, E., & Gilson, S. F. (2010) *Studying disability: Multiple theories and responses*. Thousand Oaks, CA: Sage.

Egede, L. E. (2004). Diabetes, major depression, and functional disability among U.S. adults. *Diabetes Care, 27*, 421–428.

Etheredge, L. M. (2010). Creating a high-performance system for comparative effectiveness research. *Health Affairs, 29*, 1761–1767.

European Disability Forum. (2003). *Disability and social exclusion in the European Union: Time for change, tools for change*. Athens: Greek National Confederation of Disabled People.

European Union. (2000). *Charter of fundamental rights.* Retrieved from http://www .europarll.europa.eu/charter

Gill, T. M., Gahbauer, E. A., Han, L., & Allore, H. G. (2010). Trajectories of disability in the last year of life. *The New England Journal of Medicine, 362*(13), 1173–1180.

Hoehl, A. A., & Sieh, K. A. (2010). *Cloud computing and disability communities: How can cloud computing support a more accessible information age and society?* Boulder, CO: Coleman Institute.

Iezzoni, L. I., & O'Day, B. L. (2006). *More than ramps.* Oxford, UK: Oxford University Press.

Inglehart, J. K. (2010). The political fight over comparative effectiveness research. *Health Affairs, 29,* 1757–1760.

Institute of Medicine. (1991). *Disability in America.* Washington, DC: National Academies Press.

Institute of Medicine. (1997). *Enabling America.* Washington, DC: National Academies Press.

Institute of Medicine. (2001). *Health and behavior: The interplay of biological, behavioral and societal influences.* Washington, DC: National Academies Press.

Institute of Medicine. (2002). *The dynamics of disability: Measuring and monitoring disability for social security programs.* Washington, DC: National Academies Press.

Institute of Medicine. (2007). *The future of disability in America.* Washington, DC: National Academies Press.

Institute of Medicine. (2008). *Improving the presumptive disability decision-making process for veterans.* Washington, DC: National Academies Press.

Kessler, R. C., & Wang, P. S. (2008). The descriptive epidemiology of commonly occurring mental disorders in the United States. *Annual Review of Public Health, 29,* 115–129.

Marcus, B. H., Williams, D. M., Dubbert, P. M., Sallis, J. F., King, A. C., Yancey, A. K., et al. (2006). Physical activity intervention studies. *Circulation, 114,* 2739–2752.

Martin, L. G., Freedman, V. A., Schoeni, R. F., & Andreski, P. M. (2010). Trends in disability and related chronic conditions among people ages 50 to 64. *Health Affairs, 29*(4), 725–731.

Mont, D. (2007). *Measuring disability prevalence* (World Bank working paper). Washington, DC: The World Bank.

Officer, A., & Groce, N. E. (2009). Key concepts in disability. *The Lancet, 374,* 1795–1796.

Ozzie, R. (2010, October 28). *Dawn of a new day.* Ray Ozzie's Blog. Retrieved from http://ozzie.net/docs/dawn-of-a-new-day

Rothberg, M. B., Cohen, J., Lindenauer, P., Masetti, J., & Auerbach, A. (2010). Little evidence of correlation between growth in health care spending and reduced mortality. *Health Affairs, 29,* 1523–1531.

Smith, K. P., & Christakis, N. A. (2008). Social networks and health. *Annual Review of Sociology, 34,* 405–429.

United Nations. (2008). *Convention on the rights of persons with disabilities.* New York: United Nations. Retrieved from http://un.org/disabilities/convention

Whitaker, R. T. (2010). *Anatomy of an epidemic: Magic bullets, psychiatric drugs, and the astonishing rise of mental illness in America.* New York: Crown.

Wolinsky, F. D., Miller, D. K., Andresen, E. M., Malmstrom, T. K., Miller, J. P., & Miller, T. R. (2007). Effect of subclinical status in functional limitation and disability on adverse health outcomes 3 years later. *The Journals of Gerontology: Series A, 62,* 101–106.

World Bank Disability and Development Team. (2004). *Poverty reduction strategies: Their importance for disability.* Washington, DC: World Bank.

World Health Organization. (2001). *International classification of functioning, disability and health.* Geneva: Author.

World Health Organization. (2010). *Community-based rehabilitation guidelines.* Geneva and Washington, DC: Author.

World Health Organization, & World Bank. (2011). *World report on disability.* Geneva: World Health Organization.

# Preface

Education for children and adults with disabilities in the United States is rooted in a 200-year history, with a clear marker being the establishment in 1817 of the first school for persons with disabilities. In the decades since, societal attitudes about people with disabilities have been reflected in the availability and types of care and services offered to them, often varying dramatically with the type of disability and the prevailing religious, cultural, and political beliefs of the times. Today, widely available educational opportunities mask the historical struggles that children and adults with disabilities experienced in gaining access to educational systems. For more than 150 years, American public schools maintained a legal right to segregate and/or exclude some children with disabilities. Children with disabilities did not gain the legally mandated right to a free and appropriate education in the United States until 1976.

Historic and current factors that justify inclusion, exclusion, or segregation generally focus on two issues: (1) the purpose of education in the United States; and (2) perceptions of whether or not students with disabilities can benefit from the educational opportunities provided in public schools and institutions of higher education. These issues of purpose and benefit become especially salient when educational resources are scarce, and they are firmly grounded in the perceptions of power brokers, educators, and the general public about the nature of disability and the associated value of the person with disabilities. In this book, we have attempted to convey how responses to these issues over time have affected access to education, as well as the type and quality of educational services provided.

Chapters 1 and 2 lay the foundations and give depth of information that other chapters in the book add to or build on. These chapters provide a detailed history of education for children and adults with disabilities and explore themes and controversies that have defined the educational structures and opportunities from their earliest incarnations.

In Chapter 1, Lana Collet-Klingenberg and Cheryl Hanley-Maxwell discuss the details of the most salient events in the history of the field. They also provide an overview of the impact of key people and groups, federal legislation, social movements, and litigation on today's educational opportunities for individuals with disabilities. The emphasis in this chapter is on social and moral movements intended to address the educational needs of Americans in general, including those with disabilities, delinquent adolescents, and immigrants. Historically, much of this education for children and youth with disabilities took place in segregated settings, initially in institutions and later in segregated schools and classrooms. This situation began to change in the early years of the 20th century, when the ongoing growth of the social welfare movement and the workforce pressures of the newly industrializing nation encouraged state and federal governments to mandate and expand educational opportunities for marginalized children and adults, including those with disabilities (as well as veterans from the World Wars who returned from service with disabilities). These periods of progress were often interspersed with major setbacks, as evidenced by events such as the rise of the eugenics movement, which vilified the poor, immigrants, African Americans, and people with disabilities and contributed to a shift in emphasis toward protecting society from these people and justifying segregation and institutionalization. The outcomes of these competing pressures led to conditions and events that unfolded during the 1950s and beyond. As revealed in Chapter 1, the initial civil rights litigation, the social movements that followed that litigation, world events, and political upheaval led to a rapid unfolding of legislation and litigation that culminated in legally mandated access to educational opportunities for children and youth with disabilities in the mid-1970s.

In Chapter 2, Hanley-Maxwell and Collet-Klingenberg build on the foundation established in Chapter 1 by revealing the issues and controversies that lie beneath many of the events described in that chapter. Chapter 2 highlights a few of the most controversial issues in education today and demonstrates how those issues reflect enduring historical disagreements and cycles of change. Most of the controversies focus on the education rights of children and youth, rather than adults. It should be noted, though, that these cycles of change have also brought about increasing educational opportunities for adults with disabilities. Chapter 2 begins with a broad overview of issues and then tackles specific controversies. The chapter is structured to provide a look at the educational issues from early childhood through adulthood. It describes how the meaning of disability affects educational access, placement, and services, as well as the disproportional representation of students from historically underserved groups (e.g., Native Americans, African Americans, children who live in poverty, and children who are English language learners) in special education. It also addresses controversies related to instruction and interventions, including the use of applied behavior analysis (ABA) for children with Autism Spectrum Disorders, inclusive education, eligibility determination (especially using Response to Intervention as a way to determine if a child has specific learning disabilities), participation in high-stakes assessments, and inequitable education and post-secondary outcomes. Chapter 2 concludes with a discussion of issues related to secondary special education, post-school outcomes, and post-secondary education.

Chapters 3, 4, and 5 support and enhance the depth of the discussions in the first two chapters by providing additional detail regarding the time line of historical events (Chapter 3), biographies of some of the field's most influential people (Chapter 4), and statistics and data that reflect the constitution of the field today (Chapter 5). Specifically, in Chapter 3, Mary-Elizabeth Glass, Chen-chen Cheng, Hanley-Maxwell, and Collet-Klingenberg provide a broad historical overview with a timeline of critical events, starting with the 1817 opening of the Connecticut/American Asylum for the Education and Instruction of Deaf and Dumb Persons and ending with the 2010 passage of the Preventing Harmful Restraint and Seclusion in Schools Act (H.R. 4247) by the U.S. House of Representatives. Key contributors identified in earlier chapters, along with other important persons related to education and disability, are described in the biographies presented in Chapter 4. These 41 individuals have created and/or substantially shaped the face of special education and post-secondary opportunities for youth and adults with disabilities.

In Chapter 5, Amy C. Stevens Griffith and Hanley-Maxwell provide the data that reflect historical trends and changes, demonstrating how the patterns and controversies identified in Chapters 1 and 2 have played out in the lives of children and adults. This chapter depicts changes in eligibility for special education, service delivery patterns, and school and post-secondary outcomes for students who are provided with special education services. It also provides the data that illustrate the concept of overrepresentation introduced in Chapter 2, including differences in disciplinary actions based on race/ethnicity and disability category. Chapter 5 concludes with data that provide insight into student perceptions about school, their personal connections, and post-secondary aspirations, as well as the actual post-secondary outcomes.

The last two chapters of the book provide additional information and resources related to education for persons with disabilities. In Chapter 6, Michelle Raasch, Minyoung Kim, Collet-Klingenberg, and Hanley-Maxwell provide current information about grassroots groups and governmental agencies (some of which were introduced in Chapter 1 or highlighted in Chapter 3). Additionally, they introduce other groups, organizations, and governmental entities that continue to affect educational opportunities for children, youth, and adults with disabilities. Contact information is provided for each of the entries to enable further exploration of specific topics or areas of interest. Finally, in Chapter 7, Sharon M. Kolb and Collet-Klingenberg provide resources to assist in future research and exploration. These resources augment those identified in the reference lists in the preceding chapters. This final chapter is composed of annotated listings of selected print and electronic resources that have been included based on their relevance to educational issues discussed throughout the book.

In writing this book, we have tried to help you, the reader, understand the complexities of the meaning of disability as it relates to identifying students with educational disabilities in schools, as well as its impact on access to educational opportunities. Inevitably, this discussion returns to societal perceptions of the value of persons with disabilities within American life, as well as to the purpose of schooling in America today and in the past. Even as we write this preface, world events and economic pressures continue to push public schools to improve the outcomes for all students, including those with disabilities. The desired outcomes are that all people receive the education they need to obtain meaningful and economically viable employment, participate in our democracy, and become valued members of our communities. In the end, the fight for equitable and effective educational opportunities for persons with disabilities is a fight for social justice. We feel fortunate to have been part of that effort and hope that this book provides you with the insight and impetus needed to participate in that fight.

*Cheryl Hanley-Maxwell*
*Lana Collet-Klingenberg*

# About the Authors

**Cheryl Hanley-Maxwell, Ph.D.,** is a Professor in Rehabilitation Psychology and Special Education and an Associate Dean in the School of Education at the University of Wisconsin–Madison. As Associate Dean, she is primarily responsible for teacher education and related initiatives. In her faculty position, she teaches courses in special education. Her research and scholarly interests include secondary special education, reform and inclusion in secondary education, transition from school to adult roles for all individuals with disabilities, and community employment for people with severe disabilities. Dr. Hanley-Maxwell has authored more than 80 publications, including 60 journal articles and book chapters. Her work has appeared in the top journals in her areas of interest, including *Exceptional Children, Rehabilitation Counseling Bulletin, Review of Educational Research,* and the *Journal for the Association of Persons with Severe Handicaps.* In addition to her written work, she has provided more than 80 presentations and workshops, including invited peer-reviewed presentations and keynotes. She has directed or co-directed more than $5.5 million in grants focusing on research and personnel preparation. She has also served on the editorial boards for the *Journal of Vocational Rehabilitation, Rehabilitation Counseling Bulletin, Journal of Disability Policy Studies,* and *Review of Educational Research* and provided guest reviews for many other special education and rehabilitation-related journals. In addition to her scholarship, Dr. Hanley-Maxwell has provided public service to school districts, families of children with disabilities, and community organizations. She has also provided consultative services at the local, regional, state, and national levels, working with public school systems, state-level task forces and committees, advocacy groups, and professional organizations throughout the country. She earned her bachelor's, master's, and doctoral degrees in Special Education from the University of Illinois–Urbana/Champaign.

**Lana Collet-Klingenberg, Ph.D.,** is an Assistant Professor in Special Education at the University of Wisconsin–Whitewater. In this role she teaches many courses in the undergraduate teacher-preparation curriculum. She also coordinates the graduate Transition Certificate program and a freshman learning community for future educators. Research and scholarly interests include teacher education and professional development, secondary special education, school reform, transition from school to adult life, evidence-based practice and autism spectrum disorders, and service learning. Dr. Collet-Klingenberg has authored or coauthored more than 20 publications, including journal articles, book chapters, and online modules. This work has appeared in journals such as *Exceptional Children* and *Preventing School Failure*. Her most recent work with the National Professional Development Center on Autism Spectrum Disorders appears on the Ohio Center for Autism and Low Incidence (OCALI), Autism Internet Modules Web site (http://www.autisminternetmodules.org). Dr. Collet-Klingenberg has worked on a variety of federally funded grants in the areas of personnel preparation, professional development, and research, and has successfully written grants with awards totaling over $50,000. She has also served on the editorial board for *Career Development for Exceptional Individuals* and acted as a guest reviewer for *Review of Educational Research* and the *American Journal on Intellectual and Developmental Disabilities*. She is also a reviewer for the National Council for Accreditation of Teacher Education (NCATE). In addition to this scholarship and service, she has also presented at a variety of local, state, and national conferences in peer-reviewed forums as well as invited addresses and keynotes. She has also worked as an advocate for families in local school districts and as an education consultant at the local and state levels. She earned her bachelor's and master's degrees in Special Education from the University of Illinois-Urbana/Champaign, and her doctoral degree in Special Education from the University of Wisconsin–Madison.

# About the
# Series Editor

**Gary L. Albrecht** is a Fellow of the Royal Belgian Academy of Arts and Sciences, Extraordinary Guest Professor of Social Sciences, University of Leuven, Belgium, and Professor Emeritus of Public Health and of Disability and Human Development at the University of Illinois at Chicago. After receiving his Ph.D. from Emory University, he has served on the faculties of Emory University in Sociology and Psychiatry, Northwestern University in Sociology, Rehabilitation Medicine, and the Kellogg School of Management, and the University of Illinois at Chicago (UIC) in the School of Public Health and in the Department of Disability and Human Development. Since retiring from the UIC in 2005, he has divided his time between Europe and the United States, working in Brussels, Belgium, and Boulder, Colorado. He has served as a Scholar in Residence at the Maison des Sciences de l'Homme (MSH) in Paris, a visiting Fellow at Nuffield College, the University of Oxford, and a Fellow in Residence at the Royal Flemish Academy of Science and Arts, Brussels.

His research has focused on how adults acknowledge, interpret, and respond to unanticipated life events, such as disability onset. His work, supported by over $25 million of funding, has resulted in 16 books and over 140 articles and book chapters. He is currently working on a longitudinal study of disabled Iranian, Moroccan, Turkish, Jewish, and Congolese immigrants to Belgium. Another current project involves working with an international team on "Disability: A Global Picture," Chapter 2 of the *World Report on Disability*, co-sponsored by the World Health Organization and the World Bank, to be published in 2011.

He is past Chair of the Medical Sociology Section of the American Sociological Association, a past member of the Executive Committee of the Disability Forum of the American Public Health Association, an early member of the Society for Disability Studies, and an elected member of the Society for Research in Rehabilitation (UK). He has received the Award for the Promotion of Human Welfare and the Eliot Freidson Award for the book *The Disability Business: Rehabilitation in America*. He also has received a Switzer Distinguished Research Fellowship, Schmidt Fellowship, New York State Supreme Court Fellowship, Kellogg Fellowship, National Library of Medicine Fellowship, World Health Organization Fellowship, the Lee Founders Award from the Society for the Study of Social Problems, the Licht Award from the American Congress of Rehabilitation Medicine, the University of Illinois at Chicago Award for Excellence in Teaching, and has been elected Fellow of the American Association for the Advancement of Science (AAAS). He has led scientific delegations in rehabilitation medicine to the Soviet Union and the People's Republic of China and served on study sections, grant review panels, and strategic planning committees on disability in Australia, Canada, the European Community, France, Ireland, Japan, Poland, Sweden, South Africa, the United Kingdom, the United States, and the World Health Organization, Geneva. His most recent books are *The Handbook of Social Studies in Health and Medicine*, edited with Ray Fitzpatrick and Susan Scrimshaw (SAGE, 2000), the *Handbook of Disability Studies*, edited with Katherine D. Seelman and Michael Bury (SAGE, 2001), and the five-volume *Encyclopedia of Disability* (SAGE, 2006).

# *One*

# Introduction, Background, and History

Lana Collet-Klingenberg and
Cheryl Hanley-Maxwell

*History of special education and a history of exceptionality are not
the same. One deals with educational and institutional arrangements
first formally established in the eighteenth century, the other, with
people who have been present in society since its beginnings. Never-
theless, the histories are inextricably meshed, and the essential theme
of both is the varying treatment afforded the disabled population*

—Winzer, 1993, p. 3

**A**s stated so eloquently by Margret Winzer (1993), the events of history related to disability and the education of children with disabilities (a.k.a., special education) are closely intertwined. On a larger scale,
the history of access to education for individuals with disabilities reflects

1

political and social conditions, as well as religious tenets and beliefs about what constitutes humanness.

Prior to the 18th century, few, if any, cultures tolerated individual deviation of any kind (social, political, religious, intellectual, or physical). Those who differed from societal mores and expectations were treated with indifference at best, but were more likely to face abandonment, isolation, or death. Abandonment and isolation included confinement to psychiatric hospitals and institutions (Paul, French, & Cranston-Gingras, 2001). The treatment of people with disabilities in the United States typically mirrors that of the world at large. At certain times, however, such as the return of soldiers following the two World Wars, society has identified veterans with disabilities as heroes and as people in need of support as they attempt to re-enter their communities. The history of education for children and adults with disabilities reflects these same extremes.

The roots of education for individuals with disabilities in the United States began in the early 1800s, with institutions for children who were deaf, mute, and/or blind. Children with other disabilities were not provided any educational opportunities until many years later. The advent of public education for children with disabilities in the United States came sometime between the 1840s, when common schools were introduced (Karier, 1986), and 1918, when compulsory education was required, first by local communities, then by all states (Richardson, 1999; Ysseldyke & Algozzine, 1984).

Residential schools for students with disabilities also arose during this time period. The purpose of these small schools was to provide compensatory, time-limited training to enable the students to return to their communities as self-sufficient citizens. The creation of residential schools began more than 120 years of exclusion and/or segregation of children with disabilities (Galloway, 1980) by placing them in institutions, separate schools, and separate classrooms.

What later became known as the discipline of special education began to emerge as early as the 1920s, with the development of proven methods of teaching individuals with disabilities (Osgood, 2008). Because of the rapid expansion of special classes immediately following World War II, many urban school districts included special education programs by 1950. Between 1950 and 1970, special education services evolved into a continuum. The most restrictive forms of special education took place in institutions, while the least restrictive included special schools, special classes, and a combination of special classes and general education. Despite the growth of special education services, many students with disabilities continued to be excluded from public schools (Powell, 1994).

Judicial approval of exclusion started very early. For example, in an 1893 case, a Massachusetts court found in favor of a school that had expelled a child because he could not care for himself (*Watson v. City of Cambridge*, 1893; Yell, 1998). In 1919, the Wisconsin Supreme Court supported a school's expulsion of a student who had already attended public school through fourth grade because his condition was reported to be nauseating to other students and teachers, and he required too much time from the teacher (*Beattie v. Board of Education*, 1919; Yell, 1998). In another instance, the Cuyahoga County Court of Appeals ruled that the Ohio Department of Education had the authority to exclude students as necessary, even though compulsory attendance was a state law (Winzer, 1993).

Between 1827 and 1981 there were over 200 laws enacted that somehow related to disability in the United States (Ballard, Ramirez, & Weintraub, 1982). Furthermore, from 1966 to 1974, a series of federal laws were enacted and a series of court cases decided that spotlighted the rights of children with disabilities (Gartner & Lipsky, 1992). However, it was not until 1975 that centuries of significant historical events related to the treatment and education of individuals with disabilities culminated in the passage of the first federal law insuring educational opportunity for children with special needs, Public Law (P.L.) 94-142, the Education for All Handicapped Children Act. Since that time, amendments to P.L. 94-142, parallel legislation, and additional judicial action have guided and altered education for children and adults with disabilities.

Although education for individuals with disabilities in the United States has been evident since the early 1800s, organized efforts to educate all children and youth with disabilities have arisen fairly recently. The comparatively brief history of these efforts is replete with significant events and watershed moments and is documented thoroughly in educational literature. For this chapter on the history of education and disability, we present the highlights of that history by elucidating the historical figures who provoked change. Next, we describe efforts that started toward the end of the 1800s that led to the creation of special classes in public schools. Moving on, we also address the changes that took place in America during the 1940s through the 1960s that set the stage for critical legislation. We then provide a chronological look at landmark legislation and litigation that paved the way for today's education for individuals with disabilities, from early childhood through post-secondary education.

This chapter also includes a discussion of civil rights litigation and legislation as they relate to disability and education. As it is impractical to include all of the related litigation, the cases included in this chapter are only a sample of the many court cases that have been filed and tried. They have been included because they exemplify the major issues that have been contested in court, and they relate directly to current aspects of federal law regarding special education.

This focus on the legal aspects of special education provides a foundation critical to understanding the field, from its earliest beginnings to its ever-shifting ideologies and implementation in the present day. Without the federal funding allocated by legislation, the additional costs associated with educating children with disabilities may have deterred states and school districts from ensuring educational access for some children with disabilities. Furthermore, without litigation and subsequent legislation, the extent and quality of the education provided to children with disabilities would have depended on the willingness of school districts to provide appropriate—and sometimes more expensive—services. As a result, federal legislation and litigation created current educational access and services for children with disabilities, and thus help tell the story of special education. The cause and effect of litigation and law continually shape the field of special education, reflecting the emerging knowledge base and society's beliefs and desires regarding how best to educate individuals with disabilities (and, more subtly, the value society places on such individuals).

To facilitate understanding of the complex relationship between litigation and legislation, we organize the remaining parts of the chapter into four major sections: legislation prior to 1975, litigation prior to 1975, legislation and litigation 1975 and later, and the current state of the field and future directions of special education law. (For the reader who wishes to learn more about disability-related legislation and litigation, or who would like to stay current with the most recent legal developments related to special education, we recommend the use of an Internet search engine designed specifically for research specific to law, such as LexisNexis® Academic [2011].)

In this chapter, we refer to education for children with disabilities (ages 3 through 21) as special education. We use the term special education to encompass the broader concept of the education of children with disabilities, as reflected in the field and discipline of special education, and not just the service delivery system evident in public schools. Most of the chapter will focus on special education in the public schools, because this history is more evident and dynamic than that of early intervention (birth to 3) and post-secondary education. However, early intervention and post-secondary education also are addressed within the context of historical events and legislation.

# People Provoking Change: Foundational Contributors

Key people have contributed to the eventual establishment of special education as it exists in the 21st century. The earliest examples, which arose in European countries, formed the basis for later thinking and practice in the United States. In this section, in chronological order, we introduce the reader to those individuals who helped build the foundation for special education (Pinel and Itard, Gallaudet, Howe, Seguin, and Dix) and who created the first college-level program for persons with disabilities (Kendall).

In the late 18th century, the French physician Phillipe Pinel (1745–1826) worked to develop and promote humane care of psychiatric patients. His treatment style, which became known as "moral treatment," replaced shackles with straightjackets; provided regular meals, clothes, and beds; and removed physical punishments such as whipping. Pinel's work recognized the humanness of persons with disabilities and the possibilities associated with the learning potential of human beings (as opposed to animals). Because of his work, Pinel took an interest in examining the Wild Boy of Aveyron, a young man reportedly found living in the woods who was assumed to have lived in solitude for many years. Unfortunately, Pinel saw no learning potential in the young man and declared him hopeless (Gaynor, 1973). Jean-Marc Gaspard Itard (1775–1838), a French medical student who was part of the audience that witnessed Pinel's declaration, offered to continue working with the young man, whom he later named Victor.

Itard's interest in working with Victor was not surprising given that Victor did not speak, and Itard's main interests included studying and teaching individuals who were both deaf and mute. Itard worked with the boy for over five years, focusing on social, environmental, cognitive, and communication outcomes. Some scholars attribute the foundations of modern special education and the use of individualized education programs to these first attempts (Gaynor, 1973). It is also notable that Itard was the first physician on record to argue that environmental enrichment could ameliorate developmental delays (French, 2000).

A prominent American to positively impact the development of treatment (and later education) options for persons with disability was Reverend Thomas Hopkins Gallaudet (1787–1851). Gallaudet opened the first school for children with disabilities in the United States, the Asylum for the Deaf in Hartford, Connecticut, in 1817 (Osgood, 2008). He is reported to have traveled in Europe to learn more about teaching those who were deaf, recruit teachers for the school, and raise money.

Another early American leader in the field of disability education was Samuel Gridley Howe (1801–1876). Howe was born and raised in Boston, graduating with a medical degree from Harvard Medical School. In 1829, one of his friends, John Fisher, incorporated a school for the blind. Howe agreed to become its director in 1831 and opened the doors of the New England School for the Blind (now Perkins School for the Blind) the following year. During his 44 years as head of the school, Howe worked successfully with a girl named Laura Bridgman, who was both deaf and blind. His success not only led to improved education for individuals who were blind and/or deaf, but also directly influenced the later work of Annie Sullivan with Helen Keller.

In 1848, Howe also served as the director of the first public residential institution for the "idiotic," the Experimental School for Teaching and Training Idiotic Children at the Perkins Institute. Although the term "idiotic children" may be roughly translated to mean children with mental retardation, training schools of this era only served children who were thought to be able to return their communities and be self-sufficient. These schools were not for children with medical, physical, emotional, or intellectual disabilities that would not allow them to be self-sufficient in an inflexible society. In fact, Howe specifically said that these schools were not for incurables (Galloway, 1980).

Edward Seguin (1812–1880), one of Jean Itard's more famous students, immigrated to the United States in 1850. He initially took a job at Samuel Gridley Howe's school in Boston and then left to work at what would eventually be known as the Syracuse State School (Simpson, 1999). Seguin became known for his work with persons having mental retardation. He believed that these individuals could be trained successfully to take care of themselves and do meaningful work (Osgood, 2008). He held this belief in direct opposition to the prevailing view of the day that "idiocy" could not be cured or even made better (Richardson, 1999). Seguin helped found an organization that led to the development of the American Association on Intellectual and Developmental Disabilities (Gargiulo, 2009).

Seguin, Howe, and others in the early to mid-19th century laid the groundwork for another reformer, Dorothea Dix (1802–1887), to make huge advances for those considered to be second-class citizens in the United States. Dix was the single most influential and important reformer of both the mental illness and prison systems in the United States, as well as in Europe. Dix's advocacy and work focused on the humane treatment of inmates in prisons and patients in institutions who were mentally ill or mentally retarded. She changed the face of U.S. institutions, and her success formed the basis of later arguments that led to deinstitutionalization and the creation of special education. Perhaps lesser known is the fact that Dix spearheaded a drive to convince the federal government to set aside millions of acres of land to build facilities for the treatment of persons with mental illness and other impairments. The bill was passed by Congress, but it was vetoed by President Franklin Pierce.

Finally, in 1857, Amos Kendall founded what was eventually to become the first U.S. college for young adults with disabilities. The Columbia Institution for the Instruction of the Deaf and Dumb and the Blind was created to provide primary, secondary, and college education to academically able students with sensory and communication impairments. Through various changes over the next two decades, the Columbia Institution became the National Deaf-Mute College, which focused on college education for deaf-mute students. Subsequently, the National Deaf-Mute College was renamed Gallaudet College and eventually became the world-renowned Gallaudet University.

## Advances in the Late 19th and Early 20th Centuries

During the end of the 19th century and the first part of the 20th century, a number of events converged to lead to significant advances in the field of special education. The disciplines of anthropology, psychology, and sociology saw tremendous growth and raised awareness of the study of humans and human systems. In the early 1900s, for instance, the behaviorism movement introduced by John Watson in 1913 and supported by the work of Pavlov and Skinner emerged in psychology as a dominant and substantive field of study. Interestingly, much of the evidence-based research seen today in the field of special education is rooted in behavioral science as well as in medicine (Buysse & Wesley, 2006; Cutspec, 2003). In the fields of anthropology and sociology, influential schools of thought formed as well. Indeed, anthropology was just emerging as an academic discipline during this time period, as was sociology. The emergence and dominance of these fields of study served to keep the treatment of marginalized citizens at the forefront of the American mind.

The manner in which these emerging fields affected the education of children and adults with disabilities depended on the types or categories of disability. Within a few years of the founding of the Asylum for the Deaf, for example, public pressure was mounting to establish day schools for deaf and hard-of-hearing children. As oralism (an educational philosophy that teaches deaf children to communicate through spoken language and lip-reading) gained pre-eminence over manualism (an educational philosophy that teaches deaf children to communicate through sign language), proponents stressed the need for deaf children to have contact with the speaking world. Living in residential schools was incompatible with the goals of oralism. In 1869, the first two day schools for the deaf were established: the Western Pennsylvania School for the Deaf and the Boston School for Deaf-Mutes. Bowing to pressure from parents who wished to keep their children home, Ohio was the first state to mandate day classes for the deaf; other states quickly followed suit. Support for day schools and day classes did not come from deaf persons, who largely advocated for residential programs. Instead, day schools and day classes arose from parents' wishes as well as from the shortcomings of residential programs, which failed to serve more than 50% of the eligible children and refused to admit children under the age of 10 or 12. In addition to these factors, emerging transportation options made it possible to provide community-based school programs at centralized sites (Safford & Safford, 1998).

While strides were being made toward educating persons with disabilities, other events occurred in the late 1800s and early 1900s that negatively affected public attitudes toward those with disabilities. One of the most important events of this period was the introduction and proliferation of the concept of intelligence as a fixed and measurable trait, as revealed in the IQ test (Schlinger, 2003).

The first IQ test, the Simon-Binet Scale, was created in the early 1900s to help French schools identify incoming children who needed specialized help. The screening function of the Simon-Binet Scale caught the attention of H. H. Goddard, research director of the Vineland Training

School in New Jersey. He saw the test as a useful tool and imported it to the United States for use in sorting and classifying people. Unlike Binet, who believed intelligence was not a fixed trait and warned against using his IQ test as a measure of learning capacity, Goddard believed IQ was a fixed and hereditary trait. His advocacy for its utility—along with the work of Lewis Terman, who revised and re-normed the Simon-Binet Scale using an American sample (and renamed it the Stanford-Binet Intelligence Scale)—ensured the place of IQ testing in America. As it evolved from a screening instrument used to identify children in need of specialized service to a test used to measure the fixed and hereditary trait of intelligence, the IQ test grew into a tool used for repression and segregation. Goddard and Terman's supposedly scientific research linked mental deficiency with race, increased crime, and poverty, as well as advanced the dubious findings that mental retardation could be passed on from parent to child. These findings resulted in a 50-year period during which huge numbers of persons with disabilities were segregated into separate tracks, classes, programs, schools, and institutions and nearly 30,000 Americans with disabilities were sterilized. These practices continued for decades despite the fact that the foundation on which they were built was refuted by later research (Kode, 2002).

From the late 1880s through the first decades of the 1900s, public education for American children became increasingly common, with the purpose of education being the preparation of good citizens (Dewey, 1916). Large cities developed metropolitan school districts and compulsory attendance laws. Compulsory attendance laws reflected the government's interest in preparing educated citizens to participate in their governance, a growing public awareness of the need to create a skilled and educated workforce, and the progressive movement's goals of increasing self-sufficiency and improving the human condition. For children and adults with disabilities, efforts to create a skilled, self-sufficient workforce resulted in the development of residential training schools, and later special schools and classes. Parallel efforts focused on vocational education for students without disabilities and for disabled veterans returning from World War I.

## From Training Schools to Special Classes

Prior to gaining access to public education, children with disabilities were often served in special residential schools called training schools, such as the Industrial School for Crippled and Deformed Children, which opened in 1893 with the intent to make "cripples" self-supporting (Abt, 1924). The best known of these schools was the Vineland Training School, which was established in 1888 and formerly known as the New Jersey Home for the Education and Care of Feebleminded Children. These residential schools were by no means public schools, however, as they were often available only to families of wealth and influence and provided little more than warehousing of individuals with special needs (Gargiulo, 2009).

Closer to the end of the 19th century, special day schools and special classes began to appear. In the late 1890s, special programs for "backward children" formed in Providence, Rhode Island (1896), and Boston, Massachusetts (1899), were beginning to offer special day classes for "feebleminded" children." At the same time, Chicago, Illinois (1899), began providing the first public school classes for children with physical disabilities (Safford & Safford, 1998). As described above, public schools also began offering special classes for the deaf. Additionally, in 1910, Chicago began to offer speech correction programs in the public schools. Unfortunately, children with health impairments such as epilepsy were segregated into institutions, if they received any services at all. However, children with tuberculosis began receiving treatment in "out-of-door" schools that focused on rest and care, with education being an afterthought (Safford & Safford, 1998). These schools created individualized, medically related treatment programs that included instructional routines that placed fewer physical demands on the children, forming a clinical model. The use of this model in special classes or day schools resulted in the inclusion of many children with health impairments who would have been excluded otherwise (Safford & Safford, 1998).

Services for children who were blind were very limited. Special schools for the blind existed but, like schools for the deaf, they did not admit children under the age of 10 or 12 years old. Furthermore, access to these schools was very restricted. Advocates pushed public schools to create day classes to educate the large number of children who were blind or had visual impairments (resulting from childhood diseases) and who were not served by special schools. Still, by 1910, day classes served a very small percentage of children with visual impairments and blindness (Safford & Safford, 1998).

During this time period, Elizabeth Farrell (1870–1932) began her groundbreaking work. Farrell became a teacher at the Henry Street Settlement School (Public School Number One) on the Lower East Side of New York City in 1899. Under the supervision of the superintendent of schools, she worked to develop classes for students who had been removed from regular classes or whose learning needs were not being met through the traditional school programming. Over the course of a decade, Farrell developed a program of ungraded classes in the New York school system (Kode, 2002). These classes were held in regular schools (as Farrell did not believe in separate schools) and included remedial academic instruction as well as a life-skills focus. Farrell publically refuted Goddard's claims about mental deficiency. She also made it clear that the purpose of ungraded classes was to return students to mainstream classes, not to serve as a stepping stone to institutionalized care (Kode, 2002).

Interestingly, Farrell faced an early challenge concerning how to assess students for inclusion in the ungraded classes. Originally, students were referred for not passing or not contributing in the regular classroom. As the program grew, however, teachers struggled to find objective ways to identify which students were appropriate for the ungraded class program. One popular idea was to administer intelligence tests—a practice advocated by Henry Goddard—but Farrell fought this idea. Thus, while intelligence testing enjoyed some success in the city schools, it was never formally endorsed by the district as an appropriate way to determine eligibility for admittance to ungraded classes. Unfortunately, the problem of how to determine student eligibility never went away and became a major issue in the development of federal law some decades later (Kode, 2002).

One of Farrell's greatest achievements was to professionalize special education. Through her work in the New York schools, she moved from teaching ungraded classes to hiring, training, and supervising other teachers as the Inspector of the Ungraded Department. In this role, between 1906 and 1921, Farrell went from supervising 14 classes to over 250 classes (Kode, 2002). In 1912, Farrell established a department to train teachers for students with intellectual disabilities at the Brooklyn Training School for Teachers. Its function was to better prepare teachers to teach in ungraded classrooms.

Following the development the training program for teachers of students with intellectual disabilities, Farrell turned her attention to the now emerging field of special education. The first journal devoted to the field was titled *Ungraded*. As an associate editor, Farrell used it not only as a platform for disseminating curricular material, but also as a means of sharing research being conducted within the ungraded classrooms in the New York City schools (Kode, 2002). It was here that she began to legitimize the profession of special education. Farrell went on to join the faculties at both

New York University (1913–1916) and Columbia University (1915–1932), teaching classes that focused on curriculum and instruction, as well as classes geared toward those aspiring to school administration (Kode, 2002).

Farrell played a key role in the development of the Council for Exceptional Children, the first unifying organization structure for special education at the national level, in 1922. Prior to this time, Farrell was involved in the American Psychological Association and the New York State Association of Consulting Psychologists. Additionally, sometime between 1916 and 1918, she became the president of the Department of Special Education of the National Education Association, an organization founded by Alexander Graham Bell in 1897 (Kode, 2002). These activities, coupled with all of her early work as teacher and administrator, created the image of Elizabeth Farrell as both a practitioner and a visionary. She is remembered for her leadership and ingenuity in development of the field of special education.

Another leader in advancing special education emerged from the famous Kennedy family. Eunice Kennedy Shriver (1921–2009), sister to President John F. Kennedy, became prominent in the field of intellectual disabilities in the 1950s. In 1957, she and her husband, Sargent Shriver, became responsible for running the Kennedy Foundation's new program for prevention of mental retardation (Braddock, 2010). That program became the National Institute on Child Health and Human Development (NICHD), established within the National Institutes of Health (NIH). It is now considered the leading research enterprise of its kind. In 2008, NICHD was renamed after Eunice Kennedy Shriver (Braddock, 2010). Beginning with her involvement in the NICHD, Shriver contributed to the field of special education in many ways. In the early 1960s, she started a summer day camp at her home for children and adults with intellectual disabilities (McCallum, 2008). Her purpose was to explore the capabilities of persons with mental retardation in the area of sports and recreation (Smith, 2009). Shriver's summer camp soon evolved into the Special Olympics, a series of athletic competitions for persons with disabilities. In 1968, the first International Special Olympics Summer Games were held in Chicago, Illinois, with participation by 1,000 athletes from 26 states in the United States and Canada (McCallum, 2008). Since then, the Special Olympics have become world-renowned, both for the athletic events and as an organization that supports disability rights and promotes aware-ness. Although not directly related to education, Shriver's work in this area brought greater attention to people with intellectual disabilities. Her work also demonstrated that opportunity and support influenced the capabilities of those individuals.

## Parallel Vocational Efforts

Vocational education and vocational rehabilitation eventually converged with efforts to prepare children with disabilities for employment and create access to higher education for adults with disabilities. Understanding the history of education for individuals with disabilities requires a general awareness of efforts in both of these areas. The 1917 passage of the Smith-Hughes Act required states to establish vocational education programs. This act resulted in the development of vocational education programs that combined vocational preparation with academic instruction. Vocational rehabilitation was born in 1918 with the passage of the Smith-Sears Veterans Vocational Rehabilitation Act, which reflected the nation's obligation to address the needs of its disabled veterans, and later (1920) its civilians. Vocational rehabilitation initially focused on preparing individuals with disabilities for work, including post-secondary and later secondary education (Szymanski, Hanley-Maxwell, & Asselin, 1990). Around the same time that the U.S. Supreme Court upheld the forced sterilization of people with disabilities in *Buck v. Bell* (1927), the federal government continued to expand services to disabled veterans by reauthorizing and expanding vocational rehabilitation legislation, and by passing legislation to provide financial assistance to the elderly, the blind, and children with disabilities (i.e., the Social Security Act, 1935).

# A Changing America: The 1940s, 1950s, and 1960s

The contributions of Elizabeth Farrell and others marked the beginnings of the groundswell of events that occurred in the mid-20th century and culminated in major education-related changes for persons with disabilities. Attention to the needs of disabled veterans from two World Wars, the GI Bill, and the changing social and political landscapes of the 1950s and 1960s added to the work started by those earlier pioneers and led to the significant educational changes seen in the decades that followed. Beginning with meeting the needs of veterans and ending with key events that put a spotlight on the often inadequate and sometimes inhumane treatment of children and adults with disabilities, this section traverses the social movements and groups that have shaped contemporary educational services and opportunities for individuals with disabilities.

## Higher Education for Individuals With Disabilities

The GI Bill, which offered World War II veterans government-subsidized access to higher education, led to the development of the prototype for disabled student services programs in higher education. The Rehabilitation Services program was originally established in 1948 at the University of Illinois' Galesburg campus. When it moved to the Urbana-Champaign campus the following year, it became the first official program supporting students with physical disabilities in higher education and formed the foundation for independent living centers. Within two years of the inception of this program, funding from the 1950 Vocational Rehabilitation Act Amendment was used to establish more than 100 other rehabilitation-related programs at universities across the country, greatly expanding access to higher education for adults with various types of disabilities.

The development of vocational rehabilitation reflected the growing awareness that persons with disabilities were entitled to the same rights and services available to their non-disabled counterparts. This growing awareness was echoed by the actions and advocacy of post–World War II grassroots groups related to disability.

## Grassroots Groups

During the 1940s, 1950s, and 1960s, a number of grassroots disability groups began to take shape, adding to the voice of established groups such as the Council for Exceptional Children. These groups would do much to support families in seeking educational rights for children with disabilities. They would also create a public forum that facilitated acceptance of people with disabilities as individuals, thus giving them a voice.

The Association for Retarded Citizens, now known as The Arc, was one of the earliest groups to form. With a history of organized action dating back to the 1930s, The Arc was formally established as a national organization in 1950. From its earliest days, The Arc worked to educate the public about the potential of persons with mental retardation and to obtain day-care, education, and work programs for individuals with intellectual disabilities. Along with the National Foundation for Cerebral Palsy, founded in 1949 (and later renamed the United Cerebral Palsy Associations, Inc.),

The Arc helped to establish and drive the parents' movement. Other parentally organized and driven groups formed during the 1950s, 1960s, and 1970s as well. The Council of World Organizations Interested in the Handicapped (CWOIH) formed in 1953 and later became the International Council on Disability (ICOD). Two parental groups focused on learning disabilities formed in the mid-1960s: the Learning Disabilities Association (LDA) in 1964 and the Association of Children with Learning Disabilities (ACLD, later known as ACLD, Inc.) in 1966. The Autism Society of America (ASA) was also formed around this time (1965). These are just a few of the most prominent groups. The parents' movement initially gave rise to schools and classrooms for excluded children with disabilities, but later was a major force in the passage of P.L. 94-142, the Education for All Handicapped Children Act (Gargiulo, 2009).

Many other groups have been created by and for people with disabilities. For example, the National Federation of the Blind (NFB) has been in existence since the 1940s, and the World Federation of the Deaf (WFD) was established in 1951. In 1975, an organization called the American Association for the Education of the Severely/Profoundly Handicapped (AAESPH) was formed. AAESPH was subsequently renamed The Association for the Severely Handicapped (TASH) and eventually dropped the extended name, becoming simply TASH. Last, in 1977, the Association of Higher Education and Disability was established, supporting the inclusion of individuals with disabilities in higher education.

Today, hundreds of disability-associated groups exist. Some of these groups focus on disability rights, others on raising awareness and/or money for research and treatment. Still other groups work to increase educational, vocational, residential, and community opportunities for persons with disabilities.

## Social Change and Disability Specialization

As education for individuals with disabilities continued to evolve in the 1950s, 1960s, and 1970s, the United States experienced a time of broader social change when the lives and treatment of marginalized people received greater attention. Social change was particularly evident as presidential, judicial, and legislative attention turned to discrimination and deinstitutionalization. As both society and government gave increased attention to the rights and needs of minorities, the poor, and people with disabilities, new terms and philosophies related to disability emerged.

## Discrimination

The civil rights movement came to the forefront of American life in 1954 with the U.S. Supreme Court's decision in *Brown v. Board of Education*, which outlawed racial segregation in the nation's public schools and declared that all children had a right to an equal education (this court case is discussed in the next section of the chapter). The effects of this court decision extended far beyond education and affected government policy-making in a variety of areas for many years to come. For example, President Lyndon B. Johnson built upon the work of the civil rights movement when he declared a War on Poverty in 1964. As part of the War on Poverty, the Head Start program was created to help children overcome the difficulties associated with poverty by providing them with opportunities to learn foundational skills prior to entering kindergarten. The creators believed that this early learning would enhance later school outcomes, possibly prevent school failure, and ultimately derail the cycle of poverty. At the program's inception, serving children with disabilities was not a specific goal. However, Public Law (P.L.) 92-424, the Economic Opportunity Act Amendments of 1972, specified that 10% of the children served in Head Start must have disabilities.

Some of the social welfare legislation created during Johnson's presidency marked a continuation of social policies championed by President John F. Kennedy. Kennedy's social policies focused increased federal attention on institutional conditions, mental retardation, and the educational needs of children with disabilities. In 1961, Kennedy established the Panel on Mental Retardation. This panel included many world-renowned scientists, doctors, and educators and informed the White House Statement on Mental Retardation delivered by Kennedy later that same year:

> The manner in which our Nation cares for its citizens and conserves its manpower resources is more than an index to its concern for the less fortunate. It is a key to its future. Both wisdom and humanity dictate a deep interest in the physically handicapped, the mentally ill, and the mentally retarded. Yet, although we have made considerable progress in the treatment of physical handicaps, although we have attacked the problems of mental illness, although we have made great strides in the battle against disease, we as a nation have for too long postponed an intensive search for solutions to the problems of the mentally retarded. That failure should be corrected. (President's Panel on Mental Retardation, 1962, p. 196)

The President's panel delivered its final report in the fall of 1962. A notable theme of the report was its insistence that services and supports for people with mental retardation be provided as closely as possible to the individual's home and community, rather than in institutional settings that were often located quite distantly (Braddock, 2010). This theme was timely with regard to increasing public awareness of the continuing problems with inhumane treatment in institutional settings. This theme would also factor into legislation regarding the education of children with disabilities, reinforcing the argument in favor of these children attending neighborhood schools with same-age peers.

## Deinstitutionalization

Calls for deinstitutionalization and return to home and community grew louder as the conditions in institutions for children and adults with disabilities were increasingly exposed. In 1966, Burton Blatt and Fred Kaplan published a photographic essay called "Christmas in Purgatory" revealing the horrid living conditions and inhumane treatment endured by people living in institutions for persons with mental illness and mental retardation. That same year, Senator Robert Kennedy denounced the living conditions at Willowbrook State School in New York City. The facility had been built to house 4,000 people, but an investigation found that it was housing over 6,000 and that the persons living there were treated inhumanely (Kaser, 2005). Despite public outrage over such injustices, little was done in way of improvement. Indeed, some seven years later, journalist Geraldo Rivera released the documentary film titled *Willowbrook: The Last Great Disgrace*, just as the deinstitutionalization movement was getting underway (Primo, 1972).

In the 1970s, deinstitutionalization took hold and greatly influenced society's view of persons with disability, especially those with mental retardation and mental illness. It also created pressure on public schools to develop programs to serve children who previously had been institutionalized, as well as children who, up to that time, probably would have been institutionalized.

The deinstitutionalization movement reflected concerns about the personal and social costs related to institutions, as well as the size of the public expenditures. Most institutions were large, public facilities and/or campuses. The size of these institutions meant they were extremely expensive to operate and maintain. Despite the enormous amount of money spent on institutions, as described above, residents received unacceptable or barely acceptable care. Furthermore, they received inadequate services that produced little to no learning (see the discussion of *Wyatt v. Stickney* in this chapter). As a result, there was no possibility that residents could acquire the skills and behaviors that would allow them to return to their families and communities. Instead, they became passive, dependent individuals. In addition to the unacceptable conditions and learning environments of most public institutions, the locations and structures of the institutions meant that residents often were disconnected from their families, essentially eliminating familial ties and supports.

Proponents of deinstitutionalization not only cited social and moral reasons for deinstitutionalization, they also addressed the financial and efficacy issues. Supported by early research, they claimed that providing services and supports through existing or emerging community service networks (including schools) would enable children and adults with disabilities to live with their families or in more personalized, smaller residential options in their home communities. Furthermore, they claimed that utilizing school and community-level programs would reduce costs and redirect money to services that would produce better outcomes for these individuals, their families, and the communities in which they lived.

While the outcomes of the deinstitutionalization movement have been called into question, especially for adults with mental illness, there is little doubt that children with disabilities have benefitted from the movement. (See Braddock and Parrish [2001] for a comprehensive examination of the history of institutionalization and persons with disabilities.)

Perhaps the most important education-related legacies of deinstitutionalization grew out of court decisions that found institutionalization to be a violation of constitutional rights guaranteed under the 5th, 8th, and 14th amendments. Both the 5th and 14th amendments guarantee all citizens due process, or fair and equal treatment, under the law. The 14th amendment also guarantees all citizens equal protection under the law. Finally, the 8th amendment prohibits cruel and unusual punishment. As laws related to education for persons with disabilities were created and modified, these amendments formed their constitutional foundation.

## New Terms and Philosophies

New terms and philosophies related to the education and treatment of persons with disabilities began to emerge in the 1960s and 1970s. In 1969,

Bengt Nirje of the Swedish Association of Mentally Retarded Children introduced the concept of normalization (Nirje, 1969). Nirje described normalization as "making available to the mentally retarded patterns and conditions of everyday life which are as close as possible to the norms and patterns of the mainstream of society" (Nirje, 1969, p. 181). During the 1970s, Wolf Wolfensberger refined the principle of normalization to include "establish[ing] and/or maintain[ing] personal behaviors which are as culturally normative as possible" (Wolfensberger, 1972, p. 28). Since that time, the fields of special education and disability rights have used these concepts to create curricular content, provide the rationale for educating students with disabilities in general education settings, and promote self-advocacy and self-determination (Gargiulo, 2009).

Disability terms also changed as researchers explored new explanations for the causes of disability. At a parent-organized conference titled "Exploration into the Problems of the Perceptually Handicapped Child" held in Chicago in 1963, Dr. Samuel Kirk shared the term "learning disabled," which he had coined in an earlier publication, in an effort to organize a number of disability labels into a commonly understood grouping (Hallahan & Mock, 2003). Although Dr. Bernard Rimland did not invent the term "autism," he brought much attention to the disorder when he published his book *Infantile Autism: The Syndrome and Its Implications for a Neural Theory of Behavior* in 1964. Leo Kanner, the person who did coin the term, wrote the foreword to the book, thus giving it credibility. Interestingly, at that time the prevailing (and unfounded) theory regarding autism was that it was caused by cold and unloving parents, i.e., "refrigerator mothers." Rimland's book marked the beginning of an eventually successful effort to discredit University of Chicago professor Bruno Bettelheim's assertion that emotionally detached mothers produced children with autism (Pollak, 1997). Since this time, new disability categories have been identified and added to the array of disabilities covered by federal law.

The period from the mid-1940s through 1970s was a time of dramatic change in American culture. Longstanding problems of racism and classism were beginning to be addressed, and disability issues became more prominent in public discourse. These changes coalesced and formed the foundation for establishing the right of all children with disabilities—ages 3 through 21—to a free and appropriate public education (FAPE), as well as the right of adults with disabilities to reasonable accommodations in higher education. While this section of the chapter has highlighted some of the key factors involved in this cycle of progress, it should be noted that other events, such as the 1960s and 1970s antiwar movement and increasing civil rights actions—and related media coverage—most certainly had an impact as well. Some of the themes that emerged from this time period include humanity, dignity, privacy, and individualization. Many of these themes emerged in conversations that happened in a public venue, as part of litigation or as part of legislation.

## Civil Rights

As previously described, the civil rights movement had a deep influence on education for people with disabilities. The 1954 Supreme Court case that sparked the civil rights movement, *Brown v. Board of Education*, began the modern era of legislation and litigation related to disability and education. Although the Court's decision did not apply directly to persons with disabilities, it provided the constitutional principles that framed later legislation and litigation related to disability. These principles also served as the foundation for Section 504 of the 1973 Rehabilitation Act Amendments, which is considered the first civil rights legislation related to disability.

### Brown v. Board of Education

One of the most important catalysts for the civil rights movement, and precursors of educational reform for children and adults with disabilities, was the 1954 decision of the United States Supreme Court in the case of *Brown v. Board of Education* (347 U.S. 483). The question at the heart of this landmark case concerned the legality of the practice of educating children in racially segregated public schools. The Supreme Court determined that public schools that segregated students by the color of their skin were inherently unequal and deprived African American students of their constitutional right to equal protection of the law. Invoking the equal protection clause of the 14th amendment of the United States Constitution, the Court wrote:

> It is doubtful that any child may reasonably be expected to succeed in life if he is denied the opportunity of an education. Such an opportunity, where the state has undertaken to provide it, is a right which must be made available to all on equal terms. We come then to the question presented: Does segregation of children in public schools solely on the basis of race, even though the physical facilities and other "tangible" factors may be equal,

deprive the children of the minority group of equal educational opportunities? We believe that it does. (Supreme Court of the United States, *Brown v. Board of Education*, 347 U.S. 483 [1954])

The Court went on to quote an earlier Kansas decision that gave a detailed description of the negative impact of racial segregation on the children:

Segregation of white and colored children in public schools has a detrimental effect upon the colored children. The impact is greater when it has the sanction of the law; for the policy of separating the races is usually interpreted as denoting the inferiority of the negro group. A sense of inferiority affects the motivation of a child to learn. Segregation with the sanction of law, therefore, has a tendency to [retard] the educational and mental development of negro children and to deprive them of some of the benefits they would receive in a racial[ly] integrated school system. (Supreme Court of the United States, *Brown v. Board of Education*, 347 U.S. 483 [1954])

Although the *Brown v. Board of Education* decision applied only to race, the Court's determination that all children were entitled to equality in education was soon applied to children with disabilities. Using the constitutional principles cited in *Brown v. Board of Education*, parents of children with disabilities and their advocates began to bring lawsuits asserting these children's right to an education. The Court opinions were invoked again later as parents and advocates challenged the parallel but separate general and special education systems.

## Section 504 of the 1973 Rehabilitation Act Amendments

P.L. 93-112, the Rehabilitation Act Amendments, was a civil rights bill signed into law by President Richard Nixon in 1973, after he twice vetoed similar bills. Section 504 of P.L. 93-112 protects eligible children and adults with disabilities from discrimination on the basis of their disabilities. Specifically, the law sets parameters that prohibit discrimination based on disability when applied to programs, services, and entities that receive any form of federal funding (What every teacher needs to know, 1997). Provisions in the law state that (a) programs and services must be equally accessible to persons with disabilities; (b) it is illegal to prevent people with disabilities from participating in activities and benefiting from programs; and (c) persons with speech, hearing, vision or physical disabilities must be provided with adaptations, accommodations, and services to assist in their access and participation. Section 504 qualified the extent of accommodations, adaptations, and services by stating that these must be reasonable accommodations. Unfortunately, the law failed to provide a definition of reasonable accommodations. As a result, litigation was used to determine what was reasonable and what was not.

Section 504 is applied at all levels of education. It protects a variety of children, including, but not limited to, children with disabilities identified under the Education for All Handicapped Children Act (EHA, see below) and de-certified EHA students, obese students, students with mental health or physical health issues who are not EHA eligible (e.g., depression, anxiety, allergies/asthma, temporary disabilities), and parents with disabilities (Gargiulo, 2009).

At the post-secondary level, Section 504 prohibits discrimination against a qualified person with a disability in any aspect of the institution (whether or not the institution receives federal funding), including recruitment, admissions, housing, transportation, financial aid, counseling, academics, research, physical education, athletics, and employment assistance (Discrimination in Post-Secondary Education, 2010). Section 504 made post-secondary education more accessible to students with disabilities.

Combined with EHA and its subsequent amendments and reauthorizations, Section 504 provides a safety net for educational services for children with disabilities. Because Section 504 has a functional model for determining a disability, more individuals are eligible for coverage under Section 504 than under EHA (Gargiulo, 2009). Section 504 defines a qualified person with a disability as an individual who has a physical or mental impairment which substantially limits one or more life activities, has a record of such impairment, or is regarded as having such an impairment by others. This definition has resulted in accommodations and services for students who have not otherwise qualified as a student with a disability under EHA. Unfortunately, the Rehabilitation Act Amendments provide no funds to schools to help them accommodate the needs of students with disabilities.

## Americans with Disabilities Act of 1990

Signed into law by President George H. W. Bush in 1990, the Americans with Disabilities Act (ADA), or P.L. 101-336, is often described as the most comprehensive law for people with disabilities and the most significant civil rights law since the Civil Rights Act of 1964. Using the same definition of disability as Section 504 of the Rehabilitation Act, ADA provides protection against discrimination on the basis of disability in both the public and private sectors in the areas of employment, transportation, public accommodations, and telecommunications. ADA applies to adults with disabilities in post-secondary settings, children with disabilities in school settings, and disabled parents of children with disabilities in school settings (Gargiulo, 2009; Yell, 1998). The ADA also extends the Section 504 definition of who is eligible for protection under the law to include persons with HIV/AIDS, cosmetic disfigurements, and those who have successfully completed substance abuse programs.

Much legislation related to persons with disabilities preceded the sweeping civil rights legislation of Section 504 and the ADA. The next section describes a number of laws that contributed to the establishment of educational rights for children and adults with disabilities. Subsequently, the provisions found in Section 504 and the ADA further refined education law and practice as related to persons with disabilities.

# Setting the Stage for Special Education: Legislation Prior to 1975

The watershed moment in the creation of special education occurred in 1975 with the passage of the Education for All Handicapped Children Act (EHA). However, EHA is built on legislation and litigation that preceded its passage. This section examines key pieces of legislation that led to increased federal involvement in public schools. It also covers the Elementary and Secondary Education Act, the Handicapped Children's Early Education Assistance Act, and the Vocational Education Act.

## Federal Involvement in Education

The events that began to unfold in the 1950s heralded a new level of federal involvement in education. To understand the magnitude of this change, it is helpful to understand the constitutional boundaries related to education. Constitutionally, the federal government cannot mandate public education or the right to education. Education of the populace is the right and responsibility of individual states. However, Congress can pass legislation related to taxing and spending. As a result, federal involvement in education mostly takes the form of legislation related to spending authority. States that comply with the policy and procedural regulations associated with a particular piece of legislation have access to the funding authorized in that legislation. In turn, school districts have access to the federal dollars that flow through the states by complying with the states' policy and procedural requirements. In some cases, education-related legislation has also included provisions that deny states access to *all* federal funding if the states' educational policies and procedures do not comply with the regulations set forth in the legislation. This system of federal incentives and punishments has created historic and contemporary controversies surrounding the legality of federal involvement in education that date back to the actions taken during the 1950s and 1960s.

Given the lack of constitutional authority, the federal government had little comprehensive involvement in public education prior to the 1950s. In the late 1950s and early 1960s, however, Congress responded to pressures from advocacy groups, questions about the nation's technological superiority following the Soviet Union's successful launch of the satellite *Sputnik*, and rising public concerns for the welfare of fellow citizens by taking three actions that set the course for future federal involvement in public education.

In 1958, advocacy on the part of parent groups brought about the first legislation associated with teacher-training programs in special education, the Expansion of Teaching in the Education of Mentally Retarded Children Act (P.L. 85-926). P.L. 85-926 appropriated funds for the education of teachers to work with students having intellectual disabilities. The law's enactment came at the end of a decade in which the number of children enrolled in special education programs increased by 150% (Boggs, 1971). In 1961, the Teachers of the Deaf Act (P.L. 87-276) authorized training for teachers of students who were hard of hearing or deaf. In 1963, P.L. 85-926 was expanded to include children with other disabilities, supplementing the Elementary and Secondary Education Act (see below).

Also in 1958, Congress passed the National Defense Education Act (P.L. 85-864). This legislation was inspired by the Soviet Union's successful launch of *Sputnik*, the world's first artificial satellite, the previous year. It provided federal funding to improve math and science education in the United States in order to restore the nation's technological leadership. Although it did not directly address the education of students with disabilities, this law set an important precedent for federal involvement in public education (Martin, Martin, & Terman, 1996) and opened the door for special education authorization and funding.

The third congressional action of this era was the passage of the Economic Opportunity Act of 1964 (P.L. 88-452). P.L. 88-452 emerged from

President Lyndon Johnson's War on Poverty. The law launched Head Start, a preschool development program that was initially intended for low-income children but today includes children at risk for school failure due to a disability or having a parent with a disability (Barker, Solomon, & Anderson, 1998). This early law demonstrated the use of federal funds for public education purposes.

## Elementary and Secondary Education Act, 1965

Building upon the thinking behind P.L. 88-452, the 1965 Elementary and Secondary Education Act (ESEA; P.L. 89-10) and its 1965 amendments (P. L. 89-313) funded programs for economically disadvantaged children and children with disabilities in both elementary and secondary schools. ESEA is best known for its grant initiative, Title I, which aimed to develop educational programs and curriculum materials to better serve these children (Yell, 1998). Like Head Start, Title I programs recognized the link between poverty and poor school performance, and thus targeted students who were both disadvantaged and low achieving. Through the 1990s, this program was the largest single source of federal education aid and accounted for over 20% of the budget of the U.S. Department of Education (1993). In 2001, ESEA was reauthorized as No Child Left Behind (see below).

In addition to ESEA's effects through Title I, Title VI of the law mandated the creation of the Bureau for the Education of the Handicapped in the U.S. Office of Education. In 1969, the ESEA amendments relevant to children with disabilities became known as the Education of the Handicapped Act of 1970 (P.L. 91-230). Among other things, this act created the federal definition of learning disabilities and consolidated all other legislation related to children with disabilities, including the Handicapped Children's Early Education Assistance Act (Yell, 1998).

## Early Childhood Education for Children With Disabilities

Following along the same lines as the Economic Opportunity Act of 1964, which created Head Start, the Handicapped Children's Early Education Assistance Act of 1968 (P.L. 90-538) focused on preschool programs, including preschool programs for children with disabilities. This act led to the Handicapped Children's Early Education Program, one of the first examples of early childhood special education, and demonstrated the federal government's continued commitment to the support and oversight of educational programs (Gallagher, 2000). In the early 1970s, Congress passed several more laws that strengthened Head Start regulations and focused on the inclusion of children with disabilities (Braddock, 1987).

## Vocational Education Act

At the same time as Congress passed laws related to early childhood education and educational services for children with disabilities, it also passed laws related to vocational education. These laws, and their later amendments, also affected education for children and adults with disability. The primary purpose of the 1963 Vocational Education Act (P.L. 88-210) was to expand vocational education to greater numbers of youth and adults. The 1968 amendment to this act (P.L. 90-576) made appropriate training for work accessible to all persons. This law appropriated millions of dollars to vocational education and was the first such law to specify that funds could be used for persons with mental retardation, hearing impairments, or other disabilities (Gordon, 2003).

# Setting the Stage: Litigation Prior to 1975

Despite legislative advances, millions of children with disabilities continued to be excluded completely from public schools prior to the 1970s, and even more did not receive appropriate educational services (Martin et al., 1996). A number of court cases arose during this time to contest the fact that children were being excluded from school through the denial of special education services, or the fact that students were being assigned to special education classrooms against their parents' wishes, via discriminatory assessment and questionable placement procedures.

## Hobson v. Hansen (1968)

The 1968 District of Columbia case *Hobson v. Hansen* was one of the first to raise questions regarding how schools identified children as being in need of special education. At issue was whether students could be tracked into specific programs based on IQ tests. In 1969 the court found that it was unconstitutional to use test scores, specifically IQ tests, to group students into levels or tracks of education because such practices discriminated against those who were poor and those who were Black (Ballard et al., 1982).

## Diana v. California (1970)

The 1970 case *Diana v. California* also questioned the use of IQ testing due to testing bias. However, in this case, the challenge was based on whether the language of the tests must match the primary language of the child. The student in question was a native Spanish-speaker, with limited English proficiency, who had been given an IQ test in English. Based on her low IQ score, she was placed in a special education classroom for students with mental retardation. The court ruled in favor of the plaintiff, determining that children must be tested (or retested) in their primary language in order to avoid inappropriate educational placements (Ballard et al., 1982).

## Larry P. v. Riles (1972)

The 1972 case *Larry P. v. Riles* further refined what was considered appropriate assessment for determining whether to place a child in special education. The case concerned the disproportionate number of African American students who were placed in special education classes on the basis of standardized tests. Finding in favor of the plaintiffs, the court once again clearly stated that schools must use unbiased assessments that do not discriminate against students based on their race (Gargiulo, 2009).

## PARC v. Commonwealth of Pennsylvania (1972)

While some parents were trying to prevent their children from being wrongly placed in special education classes, others were trying to gain access to public schools and special education for their children. The Pennsylvania Association for Retarded Citizens (PARC) filed a lawsuit against the state of Pennsylvania, challenging the constitutionality of a state law that allowed schools to deny services to children with disabilities. The plaintiff also argued that the education provided to students with disabilities in public schools was not appropriate for them. The two sides signed a consent agreement in which the state affirmed that children with disabilities had the right to a free and appropriate public education, and that the denial of this right constituted a violation of the constitutional guarantee of procedural due process (Martin et al., 1996; Yell, 1998).

## Mills v. District of Columbia Board of Education (1972)

Like *PARC*, the 1972 case *Mills v. District of Columbia Board of Education* focused on the legality of denying education services to children with disabilities. This civil class action suit was brought by parents of children with special needs who were excluded from public education in the District of Columbia. The plaintiffs argued that the District of Columbia School District could not deny children with disabilities access to a public education. The school board argued that the children's special needs could not be met in a regular school and that the cost of providing alternative, private school services was prohibitive. Joseph Waddy, the sitting judge in this bench trial case, found in favor of the plaintiffs. He determined that the needs of the individual student, not the cost, would determine the educational services provided by the public school (Yell, 1998). Since this case was decided, schools have been prohibited by law from placing students in special education programs in advance of the eligibility and planning meeting that prepares what is now known as the Individualized Education Program, IEP (Martin et al., 1996).

## Wyatt v. Stickney (1972)

The 1972 case *Wyatt v. Stickney* pursued educational access in an institutional setting. In this right-to-treatment case, the judge decided that individuals living in a state institution had the legal right to be treated appropriately. The case established minimum standards for appropriate treatment, which included access to education. The ruling stated that the withholding of education, even in an institutional setting, could be considered unlawful detention because it reduced the opportunity for the individuals in question to be habilitated (Gargiulo, 2009).

By 1973, in excess of 30 federal court decisions had upheld the principles set by the courts in all of these cases. The principles described in the *PARC v. Commonwealth of Pennsylvania* and *Mills v. Board of Education* cases (Martin et al., 1996) were especially important because they applied and extended the constitutional arguments of *Brown v. Board of Education* to children with disabilities, setting the stage for EHA.

# Legislation and Litigation, Post 1974

Although the Education for All Handicapped Children Act (EHA) seems straightforward, understanding its wide-ranging effects on educational services for children with disabilities requires an understanding of the initial act, related litigation, and subsequent amendments. Consequently, in this section, we introduce the initial law and explain each of its subsequent amendments. Within the major sections covering EHA and its amendments, we weave discussion of related influential litigation and also describe parallel legislation in the areas of vocational education and vocational rehabilitation that occurred during the time immediately following each act. Finally, we address No Child Left Behind and its impact on special education.

## Education for All Handicapped Children Act of 1975

Arguably the most important piece of legislation ever passed concerning the education of children with disabilities, the Education for All Handicapped Children Act (EHA; P.L. 94-142) was signed into law by President Gerald Ford in 1975. Extending states' right-to-education laws, this federal law firmly established the principle of a free and appropriate public education for all children ages 6 to 21 years with disabilities (Gallagher, 2000). More important, the law combined this assurance with the promise of federal funds to state education authorities (Yell, 1998). Children qualified for special education services under the law because they were identified as having mental retardation, hearing impairment, deafness, speech impairment, visual handicap, serious emotionally disturbance (including mental illness), orthopedic impairment, other health impairments, deafblindness, multi-handicaps, or specific learning disabilities.

Reflecting the litigation that preceded its passage, EHA contained six mandated rights for qualifying students with disabilities: (a) zero reject and child find, (b) nondiscriminatory or unbiased evaluation, (c) individualized and appropriate education, (d) least restrictive environment, (e) procedural due process, and (f) participatory democracy for educational decision making (Gargiulo, 2009). Each right has been critical in the implementation of the education for children with disabilities, and each deserves individual attention.

The six rights contained in EHA guarantee that no child may be denied an education, regardless of the type or severity of disability (zero reject). Indeed, educational authorities are required to seek children in need of a special education (child find). Every child identified as possibly being in need of special education must receive an appropriate, nondiscriminatory assessment. This means that only qualified evaluators who use a variety of instruments and procedures that reflect the culture and language of the child can perform an assessment and determine the disability label given to the child (nondiscriminatory evaluation). Based on the evaluation, a multi-disciplinary team develops an Individualized Education Program (IEP) to ensure that each eligible child receives an individualized and appropriate education. Each IEP must describe the child's current level of functioning, state the annual learning objectives for the child, explain the services that will be provided to assist the child in reaching the annual goals, and include the location of those services. Eligible children should receive their education in settings that allow them greatest access to their peers and the educational opportunities enjoyed by their peers. However, those settings must also provide the supports and services needed to assist eligible children in reaching their annual goals (least restrictive environment) (Gargiulo, 2009).

Parents are also guaranteed due process in relation to their child's participation in special education. Procedural due process requirements cover multiple areas, including evaluation, disability identification, and educational placement. For instance, a school district must obtain parental permission before conducting any evaluation to determine a child's initial or continuing eligibility for special education and/or the services the child will receive. In addition, a school district must give parents written notice before it begins providing special education services, changes a student's placement, or denies services. School personnel are also required to obtain parental approval before making any changes to an IEP between meetings. Parents also must be given access to all information used to make evaluation or educational decisions, and school districts are required to consider independent evaluation information provided by parents at the IEP meeting. Additionally, parents have the right to protest school district decisions by using a legal process that culminates in a due process hearing (Gargiulo, 2009).

Finally, P.L. 94-142 requires participatory democracy for educational decision making. Participatory democracy means shared decision making in which parents receive understandable explanations and translations of any materials used in IEP meetings and have the opportunity to participate in a meaningful way (Gargiulo, 2009). This right also requires school districts to allow parents an appropriate amount of time to read and respond to school materials pertaining to their child. Participatory democracy results in home–school communication prior to development of the IEP document.

P.L. 94-142 also identified a list of related services that may be used to assist eligible students in accessing or benefiting from their education (e.g., school psychology, school counselor, occupational therapist, speech and language therapist, physical therapist). Finally, EHA contained enforcement provisions. The federal funds allocated to administer special education programs could be withdrawn from state and/or local educational agencies that failed to comply with the law's requirements.

### Litigation

Litigation continued to occur after the enactment of P.L. 94-142 as the courts struggled to clarify the limits of special education law. The cases covered in this section demonstrate the gradual shift in legal interpretation of EHA from securing the right to education to further defining an appropriate education. Some of the issues addressed by these cases include what constitutes a change of placement, what qualifies as a related service, what determines the appropriate length of the school year, and whether providing services in the general education setting constitutes the least restrictive environment. Last, the passage of P.L. 94-142 raised legal issues concerning who was financially responsible for a child's education and for the costs associated with parents exercising their due process rights.

**Stuart v. Nappi (1978).** *Stuart v. Nappi* was one of the earliest cases to test the meaning of educational placement under EHA. This case challenged disciplinary procedures as they applied to students with disabilities and specifically addressed the expulsion of students with disabilities from school. The court ruled that expulsion is effectively a change of placement, and thus requires that due process procedures be followed. The outcome of this case meant that a school may suspend a student with a disability for disruptive behavior, but due process must be followed in order to assure that the student's right to a free and appropriate education is not violated. The basis for this ruling was the "stay-put" provision incorporated in the Education of the Handicapped Act in 1970 (Gargiulo, 2009; Skiba, 2002). The stay-put provision prohibited schools from changing the educational placement of children with disabilities until the review procedures associated with due process had been completed.

**Armstrong v. Kline (1979).** Originating in Pennsylvania, *Armstrong v. Kline* was the first significant case concerning the provision of extended school year services to children with disabilities. It resulted in specific guidelines regarding the relationship between length of school year and appropriate education. The judge concluded that the 180-day school year mandated by the school district violated the right of children with severe and profound impairments or severe emotional disturbance to a free and appropriate public education (FAPE) (Kraft, 1999). The court determined that schools may need to provide education that exceeds 180 days in order to meet the unique needs of a child with a disability (as established in *Mills*, 1972).

*Tatro v. State of Texas* **(1984).** Another significant legal case examined what services a school must provide to allow a student to access and/or benefit from education. *Tatro v. State of Texas* focused on whether or not medical services could be specified as a related service in the Individualized Education Program. The U.S. Supreme Court ruled that catheterization qualified as a related service because it allowed the student in question to benefit from special education. The decision went on to state that some medical procedures were exempt because they must be performed by a trained medical professional. Catheterization did not fall under this category, however, because it could be performed by a trained school nurse, nurse's aide, or health care worker (Gargiulo, 2009).

*Board of Education v. Rowley* **(1982).** This U.S. Supreme Court case was the first to interpret what constituted an appropriate education in regard to the extent of benefit a child must derive from the services provided. Lawyers for Rowley maintained that the child with a hearing impairment at the center of the suit should be provided with a sign-language interpreter to allow her to benefit maximally from her education. The Court found that the services already being provided by the school district to the child in question were reasonable and ensured that the child was benefitting from her education (Martin et al.,1996). In other words, the Court ruled that the school district did not necessarily have to maximize the potential benefit to the child in order to provide an appropriate education.

### Parallel Legislation

In the decade following the passage of P.L. 94-142, parallel legislation concerning vocational education focused on the needs of persons who have barriers to employment. In 1982, the Job Training Partnership Act (JTPA; P.L. 97-300) replaced the Comprehensive Employment and Training Act programs (P.L. 93-203). This act funded programs that provided job training to individuals who were economically disadvantaged and faced barriers to employment (Gordon, 2003). Because many of these individuals also had disabilities and were still in school, special education and vocational education teachers were able to use JTPA funds to find and support work experiences for students. Through the 1992 Job Training Reform Amendments (P.L. 102-367), JTPA was expanded to include individuals with disabilities specifically, including students who met economic criteria (Hanley-Maxwell, Owens-Johnson, & Fabian, 2004).

In addition to JTPA, the Carl D. Perkins Vocational Education Act of 1984 (P.L. 98-524) amended the Vocational Education Act of 1963 and its 1976 amendment. The Perkins Act established economic and social goals related to improving labor force skills and equalizing opportunities for adults (Gordon, 2003). As one of its social goals, Perkins facilitated the provision of services to at-risk populations, which included students with disabilities.

## Education of the Handicapped Amendments of 1986

P.L. 99-457, the Education of the Handicapped Amendments (EHA), extended the age of children served under EHA, specifying that children with disabilities become eligible at age 3 (Yell, 1998). It also provided incentives to states to adopt special education programs aimed at infants and toddlers, an age group previously omitted from the federal law (Martin et al., 1996). This section of EHA, titled Part H, effectively changed the age range of entitlement from 6 to 21 years to birth to 21 years for children who qualified as having a disability (Yell, 1998). Additionally, EHA strengthened the "stay-put" provision first articulated in 1970. The stay-put provision mandated that when a change of educational placement was considered for children with disabilities, these children should remain in their current educational placement until the review procedures associated with due process were completed (or until all parties agreed to the change) (Martin et al., 1986; Skiba, 2002).

## Handicapped Children's Protection Act of 1986

In addition to broadening the scope of eligibility for special education services, Congress created legislation meant to clarify the intent of EHA. Following a series of court cases concerning the parental right to recover litigation costs, the Handicapped Children's Protection Act of 1986 (P.L. 99-372) provided for the payment of attorney fees and court costs to parents who won lawsuits while exercising their due process rights under P.L. 94-142 (Yell, 1990).

## Litigation

Litigation in the late 1980s continued to focus on defining what constituted an appropriate education. Echoing themes from earlier litigation, plaintiffs continued to try to establish the right to an education for all children with disabilities. For instance, they fought to ensure that school districts followed due process procedures when suspending students for extended periods. They also sought to ensure that all children received an education that was appropriate for their needs and was delivered in the least restrictive, most effective environment, whether in the general education classroom or in a private program paid for by the public school.

***Garland Independent School District v. Wilks* (1987).** The *Garland Independent School District v. Wilks* case extended what was meant by "benefit" in the Supreme Court's finding in the *Rowley* case, which said that an education is appropriate if the student benefits from it. In this case, the child was not benefitting from the services provided. The child in question had been placed in a private, extended-day program, as well as in public school with a traditional six-hour day. The child's behavior regressed so severely in the public school program that he became dangerous to himself and others and had to be restrained. Consequently, his behavior prevented him from succeeding in the public school setting. To ensure the child's educational progress, he was enrolled in an after-school program, the tuition for which his mother sought reimbursement. The court found in favor of the respondent, upholding the right of a child to receive a district-funded extended-day program (Martin et al., 1996).

***Honig v. Doe* (1988).** *Honig v. Doe* was the first Supreme Court case to address disciplinary measures for students in special education. In this case, the school district had suspended two students who received special education services for violent and disruptive behavior. The suspensions were indefinite, pending the completion of expulsion hearings. The issue in question was whether the school district had the right to suspend the students with disabilities if their inappropriate behaviors were manifestations of their disabilities (Bartlett, 1989; Yell, 1998).

As the lower court did in *Stuart v. Nappi*, the Supreme Court justices cited the stay-put rule stating that suspending students with disabilities for more than 10 consecutive days amounted to a change in placement. As such, the students were entitled to remain in their current educational placement (i.e., the school with special education services) until any disputes over the change of placement had been resolved or the decision had been made in accordance with procedural due process safeguards (Barlett, 1989). This case helped to establish procedural due process requirements for schools to determine whether or not the behavior responsible for the expulsion action is a manifestation of the student's disability. If it is, then the school is prohibited from expelling the student (Yell, 1998). This and related court cases established manifestation determination as a legal requirement. The manifestation issue would be specifically addressed in the 1997 amendments to IDEA.

Honig argued that the stay-put provision of EHA was not intended to deprive schools of their authority to decide if a child exhibiting dangerous behavior could be returned to the classroom. The court disagreed, stating that the intent of the stay-put provision was to prevent schools from making unilateral decisions to exclude children with disabilities. Consequently, school districts had to adhere to a literal interpretation of the stay-put provision, regardless of the child's behavior (Yell, 1998).

The Court went on to say that schools were entitled to use normal disciplinary procedures, specifically identifying study carrels, time out, detention, withholding of privileges, and suspensions up to 10 days. The justices noted that the 10-day suspension limit continued to protect students and staff and gave the district sufficient time to follow appropriate procedures related to finding an interim placement (Yell, 1998). This ruling created significant controversy and paved the way for future amendments (IDEA 1997 and 2004) to change the restrictions on schools related to disciplining children with disabilities.

*Timothy W. v. Rochester School District* **(1989).** *Timothy W. v. Rochester School District* is another case where access to education in the public school was denied to a student with disabilities. In this right-to-education suit, filed in New Hampshire, the First Circuit Court of Appeals found that all children, regardless of the severity of their disabilities, retain the right to a free and appropriate public education. The court also specified that the student and the student's family did not bear the burden of demonstrating that the student could benefit from education in order for him to be entitled to it. This finding provided a legal affirmation of the concept of zero reject (Gargiulo, 2009).

*Daniel R.R. v. State Board of Education* **(1989).** In addition to more general questions involving access to public education, parents and advocates also pursued litigation to determine whether education in a segregated classroom denied access, thus probing the legal meaning of the least restrictive environment (LRE). The *Daniel* case, decided in the Fifth Circuit Court of Appeals, resulted in clarification of the LRE. Plaintiffs in this case appealed an earlier finding that a segregated special education classroom was the appropriate placement for a student with cognitive disabilities. Although the court upheld the earlier decision, it also established a two-part rule for determining compliance with LRE. The first part of the rule assesses whether, with modifications and supplementary services, the student is making satisfactory progress in the general education classroom. The second part determines whether the student has been included with typical peers to the maximum extent possible (Martin et al., 1996).

This early litigation related to the meaning of LRE marked the beginning of a groundswell that continued to build during the 1990s and culminated in a push to educate all students in the general education classroom, known as the inclusion movement. Parents, researchers, and advocates increasingly questioned the efficacy of segregated special education. Ironically, they asked the same questions Lloyd Dunn, a prominent special education researcher, had asked prior to the passage of EHA (Dunn, 1968). The intensifying pressure for inclusion resulted in later IDEA amendments that placed an emphasis on the general education setting and curriculum.

## Individuals with Disabilities Education Act of 1990

During the last decade of the 20th century, the Education for All Handicapped Children Act was renamed the Individuals with Disabilities Education Act, or IDEA (P.L. 101-476). This legislation also changed the name of the Handicapped Children's Early Education Program (HCEEP) to the Early Education Program for Children with Disabilities (EEPCD). In addition to name changes, the new law incorporated a number of major changes, including the use of person-first language throughout, the addition of transition planning for students aged 16 years and older, the creation of two new categories of disability (autism and traumatic brain injury), and the addition of new related services (e.g., rehabilitation counseling). Another important change introduced in IDEA was an emphasis on the importance of providing assistive technology access to children with disabilities (Martin et al., 1996). IDEA also established the legal definition of disability used today in special education law:

The term "child with a disability" means a child—(i) with mental retardation, hearing impairments (including deafness), speech or language impairments, visual impairments (including blindness), serious emotional disturbance (referred to in this title as "emotional disturbance") [including mental illness], orthopedic impairments, autism, traumatic brain injury, other health impairments, or specific learning disabilities; and (ii) who, by reason thereof, needs special education and related services.

The introduction of transition requirements and rehabilitation counseling as a related service in these amendments reflected the growing concern about the vocational outcomes for students with disabilities. Following research that showed high rates of unemployment and underemployment for former students with disabilities, Madeline Will, the Assistant Secretary of the Office of Special Education and Rehabilitative Services in the U.S. Department of Education, identified school-to-work transition as an area needing attention. In her 1984 paper "OSERS Programming for the Transition of Youth with Disabilities: Bridges from School to Working Life," she described the need to build a bridge between secondary education and post-secondary education. This bridge would help students and their families navigate the change from a world of entitled educational services to an adult world of limited services based on eligibility and vacancies, no services, or services in segregated settings (Will, 1984). Although these concerns are echoed in other laws that cover all students, as we will show in the discussion of parallel legislation from this time, IDEA introduced the specific requirements related to transition assessment, planning, and services for students with disabilities. These requirements would change in subsequent amendments, but would remain an important part of the law.

## Litigation

The court cases described below led to clearer definitions of what constitutes an appropriate education, considering such requirements as least restrictive environment, extended school year, and due process. Other court cases honed in on inclusive education from the perspective of what constitutes educational progress as it relates to FAPE and location of education services.

*Florence County School District Four v. Carter* **(1993).** In 1991, the Fourth Circuit Court of Appeals heard the case of *Carter v. Florence County School*

*District Four.* At issue was a lower court's ruling that the child in question's IEP goals and services were inadequate to ensure her educational progress, and therefore that the school district had failed to meet FAPE requirements. The appeals court supported the lower court's ruling. In addition, it found that the school district's failure to meet FAPE requirements obligated the district to pay for the expenses incurred when the child's parents withdrew her from public school and placed her in a private school. The case was eventually heard by the U.S. Supreme Court in 1993. The Supreme Court decision established a precedent that a school district's failure to comply with IDEA could render it financially responsible if a student was then enrolled in a private school, as long as that school was providing an appropriate education (Yell, 1998).

**Sacramento City School District v. Rachel H. (1994).** *Sacramento City School District v. Rachel H.* was a groundbreaking case in the promotion of inclusive education. In this case, the school district appealed an earlier ruling ordering it to educate a child with significant cognitive disabilities in a regular classroom. The district court upheld the earlier finding, ruling that the LRE was indeed the regular classroom for this student and that providing instruction in the regular education setting did not place an undue financial burden on the school district (Martin et al., 1996).

This case also resulted in an expansion of the standards for appropriate placement set in *Daniel R.R. v. State Board of Education* (1989). The judges in the *Sacramento* case named four factors they considered in determining whether the placement was appropriate for this student. First, the court considered the educational benefits available to the child in the regular classroom, with appropriate services, as compared with the benefits available in the special education classroom. The court found that the child's IEP goals could be achieved in the general education classroom and that the child was making adequate progress in that setting. Second, the court considered the non-academic benefits that the student received through participation in the general education classroom with her non-disabled peers. In relation to this factor, the court considered the student's communication and social skill development. Once again, the court found evidence that the general education setting benefited the development of the child. The remaining two factors considered by the court posed a potential threat to the intentions of IDEA (Martin et al., 1996). The third factor was the effect of the child's presence on the teacher and peers, and the fourth factor was the costs associated child's presence in the general education classroom. IDEA specifies that the effect of the child with disabilities on others in the setting is only relevant in determining placement if the student is so disruptive that teaching time is lost. Furthermore, earlier court rulings in cases such as *Mills v. District of Columbia Board of Education* (1972) established the fact that the educational needs of the student came before the cost to the school district (Yell, 1998). In short, the third and fourth factors the court considered stood in opposition to earlier rulings, making their inclusion in the *Sacramento* decision problematic.

*Oberti v. Board of Education of the Borough of Clementon School District* **(1993).** Like the *Sacramento* case, *Oberti v. Board of Education* resulted in a clear judicial preference for education in general classrooms over education in separate special education classrooms. In this case, the court determined that the LRE was the general education classroom. It also found that the school must provide supplementary aids and services in the general education classroom, and document the fact that these services are inadequate in addressing the child's needs, before placing a child into a more segregated setting (Gargiulo, 2009). Taken together, *Oberti* and *Sacramento* formed a firm foundation of support for inclusive education. The preference for general education settings became law in future amendments to IDEA.

The preference for placing students with disabilities in general education classrooms (sometimes called full inclusion) stands in opposition to the preference for providing a continuum of services (from fully included to completely segregated). Opponents to full inclusion voiced concerns that if a full continuum of services was not available, individual student needs may not be met. They argued that the preference for the general education setting put ideology above individual child needs (Lieberman, 1996). These concerns continue today as school districts, parents, and advocates seek the setting that best meets the educational (academic and non-academic) needs of children with disabilities while capitalizing on their strengths. We will address this issue more fully in Chapter 2.

### Parallel Legislation

As described in the earlier discussion about transition, American society showed increasing concern in the 1990s about preparing students to enter the world of work and adult life after secondary education, either immediately or after post-secondary education. The concern was particularly worrisome in relation to students with disabilities. Consequently, the

1992 amendments to the Vocational Rehabilitation Act included a provision to address the vocational preparation of students with disabilities that paralleled transition requirements in the 1990 amendments to IDEA. Among other things, this amendment directed state vocational rehabilitation counselors to work with public schools in preparing youth with disabilities for post-school life (Hanley-Maxwell et al., 2004).

Concern about all students' career preparation and academic advancement was evident in two other pieces of legislation: the Goals 2000: Educate America Act of 1994 (P.L. 103-227) and the School to Work Opportunities Act of 1994 (P.L. 103-239). Both of these acts sought to establish structures and standards/goals that would improve students' post-school outcomes through the development of skills necessary for employment (Hanley-Maxwell & Collet-Klingenberg, in press). Goals 2000 created a framework to support increased student learning by including the preparation of students for employment among its eight goals (Sec. 2, Purpose, 2010). The School to Work Opportunities Act was more specific. The intent of this act was to create educational programs that would ensure that all children were prepared to be successful in employment. This act focused on connecting academics and school-based learning with occupational and work-based learning, and on creating partnerships between secondary and post-secondary education and between education and business (Ordover & Annexstien, 1999). Both pieces of legislation covered students with and without disabilities.

## Individuals with Disabilities Education Act of 1997

In the late 1990s, IDEA was reauthorized as P.L. 105-17. This incarnation of P.L. 94-142 featured the most significant changes to the law since its original passage. Critics of the prior legislation charged that there was too much paperwork associated with implementation, that low achievement expectations for children with disabilities was the norm, and that not enough emphasis was placed on the translation of research into practice (Yell, 1998). Thus, the authors of the reauthorization bill condensed the original eight parts into four and made some significant changes in the language that strengthened the role and importance of the individual and the family. The amendments also required school districts to give students with disabilities greater access to the general education environment, curricula, and performance assessment; expanded transition services down to students age 14; and altered the way in which goals are written and measured in the Individualized Education Program. The 1997 amendments continued to require school districts to incorporate assistive technology and allowed Orientation and Mobility (for students with visual impairment and blindness) as a related service. Other changes to the legislation concerned conflict mediation, discipline, and funding (Gargiulo, 2009; Yell, 1998).

Disciplinary changes in the 1997 amendments reflected the frustrations of parents, advocates, and school personnel (all for different reasons) when it came to disciplining students with disabilities. As described above, prior to these amendments the courts established that schools could not suspend students with disabilities for longer than 10 days or expel them without following due process procedures. Nor could school districts expel students for behaviors resulting from their disabilities (Skiba, 2002).

Establishing whether the behavior was a manifestation of the disability was difficult and contentious, and the law provided little guidance regarding the process to be followed. Additionally, parents and advocates contended that school districts frequently suspended students with disabilities for short periods that did not meet the 10-day limit instead of providing them with appropriate behavioral interventions. Simultaneously, school officials argued that the law placed too many restrictions on what they could do to intervene in relation to inappropriate behavior (other than weapons violations) (Skiba, 2002).

The 1997 amendments eased the restrictions on when suspension could be used, allowing schools to suspend a child for violating any school rules as long as the suspension lasted no more than 10 days and was not part of a pattern of suspensions. Additionally, schools are not required to provide services during the first 10 days (total, meaning cumulative days out of school) of suspension. After the first 10 days, schools must provide services that are in keeping with the student's IEP goals. The amendments also expanded schools' authority in dealing with weapons and drug violations, if the child posed a danger to himself or others. However, the amendments also strengthened the protections for students by prohibiting long-term suspensions and expulsion when the behavior was a manifestation of the child's disability, unless services were continued in an alternative setting. Furthermore, when students are suspended for behavior not related to their disabilities, schools must provide alternative services, identified by the IEP team, which will enable those students to progress on their IEP goals. Additionally, suspensions or expulsion cannot occur without the school creating and implementing a behavior intervention plan or reviewing an existing behavior intervention plan to determine if changes are needed. Finally, manifest determinations are required if the disciplinary action constitutes a change in placement. To make a manifest determination, members of the IEP team must conduct a functional behavioral assessment (FBA) to understand the function of and factors influencing the behavior, and to describe the behavior as precisely as possible (Alberto & Troutman, 2006; Skiba, 2002).

### Litigation

Litigation during 1997 and following passage of the 1997 IDEA amendments challenged existing restrictions and reaffirmed some earlier decisions. Two important cases during this period focused on special education in private schools and what constitutes related services.

*Agostini v. Felton* **(1997).** In *Agostini v. Felton,* the U.S. Supreme Court reversed a previous ruling that banned the use of public funds to provide educational support and services for students with disabilities being educated in private schools. This monumental reversal resulted in the provision of special education services to children in parochial and other private schools (Gargiulo, 2009).

*Cedar Rapids Community School District v. Garret F.* **(1999).** Similar to *Tatro v. State of Texas* (1984), this U.S. Supreme Court decision clarified what qualifies as a related service in an Individualized Education Program. The ruling affirmed the use and support of intensive, ongoing health care services if necessary to keep a student in school. It made a distinction, however, based on whether those medical services could be provided by trained school staff or required the skill of a physician (Gargiulo, 2009).

### Parallel Legislation

Throughout the 1990s and into the 2000s, much of the legislation related to schools has focused on improving achievement and post-school outcomes for all students, including those with disabilities. The 1997 IDEA amendments shared this focus with their emphasis on inclusive education and attention to transition. This period also saw the passage of legislation aimed at improving education and employment outcomes for a broader scope of people, including children and youth with disabilities. This legislation included the Workforce Investment Act of 1998 (WIA; P.L. 105-220) and its amendments, as well as the 1998 amendments to the Carl D. Perkins Vocational and Applied Technology Education Amendments (Perkins Act) of 1984.

WIA was designed to consolidate and coordinate employment, training, literacy, and vocational rehabilitation programs. Because vocational rehabilitation was part of the consolidation, this act contained the Rehabilitation Act Amendments of 1998 (P.L. 105-220) as Title VI. WIA targeted the creation of accessible job services and employment training for adults and youth by providing a variety of services, including assessment, academic skill instruction and support, occupational training, and work experiences. As one of its initiatives, the WIA mandated the creation of One-Stop Job Centers that would coordinate access to job services and employment training. The One-Stop Job Centers blended state agencies that focused on employment. WIA also provided an array of services designed to prepare youth for post-secondary education and employment. Because the legislation required that 5% of students served in these youth programs come from high-need categories other than income, which included students with disabilities, WIA offered opportunities to develop inclusive employment preparation programs (Hanley-Maxwell et al., 2004; National Center on Secondary Education and Transition, 2002).

Originally passed in 1984, the Carl D. Perkins Vocational and Technical Education Act was amended in 1990 to include a greater focus on the integration of academic and vocational skills. The 1998 Perkins Act amendments placed additional emphasis on academic standards and accountability. In particular, the 1998 amendments targeted student achievement in academics and technical skills, post-secondary employment or education, and preparation for nontraditional careers. This act also required support services for students from special populations (including students with disabilities) to increase their access to and achievement in these programs. It is important to note that the Perkins Act provided specific assistance for post-secondary vocational education, in addition to secondary vocational education. Consequently, this act greatly expanded secondary and post-secondary education options for youth and adults with disabilities. When the act was amended again in 2006, the authors changed terminology from vocational education to career and technical preparation to better reflect the content of the programs and increased accountability measures. They also added a requirement that secondary and post-secondary programs be connected to assist students in identifying crosscutting programs of study (Carl D. Perkins Vocational and Technical Education Act of 2006, 2010). This change had the potential to make a positive impact on students, including students with disabilities, by giving students and families more information to better inform their secondary and post-secondary program and planning decisions.

## No Child Left Behind, NCLB (2001)

A reincarnation of the Elementary and Secondary Education Act of 1965, No Child Left Behind (NCLB; P.L. 107-110) was reauthorized by Congress in 2001. In keeping with the accountability theme of the late 1990s and early 2000s, this act aimed to enact educational reform and increase accountability of schools to the federal government. As a result, NCLB has been controversial from its inception. Briefly stated, this law requires all students (including students in special education) to demonstrate proficiency in reading, math, and science beginning in third grade and continuing through eighth grade, with at least one additional assessment in Grades 10 through 12. Schools are required to report to the state educational authority (SEA) and demonstrate adequate yearly progress (AYP) toward a goal of 100% proficiency of all tested students by 2014 (Gargiulo, 2009). NCLB requires testing for most of the school population, with the exception of a small percentage of students in special education having disabilities severe enough to exclude them (these students take an alternative assessment that in most states is measured via the Individualized Education Program).

The thinking underlying NCLB was that in order to demonstrate AYP, schools would be forced to provide improved instruction to all students and instructional accommodations for those with disabilities, resulting in a service delivery system that was more closely aligned than the traditional regular-versus-special-education service delivery found in public education (Salend, 2008). Potential implications of this thinking, and the resulting high-stakes testing, include curricula that "teaches to the test," academic achievement as the sole outcome, and IEP goals that are aligned with general education content standards. Good or bad, NCLB has changed the face of education, both general and special, in the United States.

## Individuals with Disabilities Education Improvement Act of 2004

In the fall of 2004, Congress once again passed legislation reauthorizing the Individuals with Disabilities Education Act (IDEA). Shortly thereafter, President George W. Bush signed into law P.L. 108-446, the Individuals with Disabilities Education Improvement Act (IDEIA). Some of the revisions made in IDEIA were intended to better align IDEA requirements with NCLB requirements. Like IDEA 1997 and NCLB, these revisions addressed concerns about the achievement, or lack thereof, demonstrated by students with disabilities.

IDEIA added Attention Deficit Hyperactivity Disorder (ADHD) to the category of Other Health Impairments (OHI). This addition legitimized ADHD as a disability separate from learning disabilities or emotional and behavioral disabilities. However, some people were disappointed by the fact that the legislation did not identify ADHD as its own category, distinct from OHI (Hallahan, Kauffman, & Pullen, 2009).

The amendments also required schools to use Functional Behavioral Assessment (FBA) for developing Behavior Intervention Plans (BIP) for learners with significantly problematic behavior, or behavior that could result in the removal of the student from his or her current educational placement. FBA provided a means for objectively and systematically assessing all aspects of problem behavior. The BIP was intended to prevent unnecessary exclusion by creating and implementing interventions designed to eliminate or reduce the targeted behavior (Gargiulo, 2009).

Other changes to the law affected how IEPs were developed and monitored. Some of the changes included the following:

- Short-term objectives or benchmarks were no longer a mandated part of the IEP except for students who required alternate forms of achievement testing (such as that required for NCLB).
- IEP teams were allowed to convene via telephone or video conference.
- Established IEPs could be modified with parental consent via written documentation without reconvening the team and re-writing the entire IEP.
- With the consent of parents, multiyear (up to three years) IEPs could be developed and implemented.
- The age for required transition planning was moved from 14 to 16 years, and transition goals were required for the areas of post-secondary education and/or training, employment, and independent living (Hallahan et al., 2009).

Finally, this incarnation of IDEA reflected the federal trend toward school accountability, which was evident in No Child Left Behind. The language of both laws strongly promoted the use of research-based or evidence-based practice in education. This emphasis was apparent in sections of the law that directly impacted the student—for example, by specifying types of services, curricula, and instruction provided—as well as in sections delineating the standards set for highly qualified teachers (Individuals with Disabilities Education Improvement Act, 2004).

## The State of the Field and Future Directions in Special Education Law

Taken together, the laws and court cases reviewed in this section of the chapter have made a huge impact on the relatively young field of special education. Many of the laws have affected the rights of all people with disabilities, in school and beyond. There is common agreement regarding the life-span coverage provided by three of the most sweeping laws (IDEA, the Rehabilitation Act, and ADA) when considered in concert. IDEA addresses the educational rights of children with disabilities from birth to age 21 in the categories of autism, deaf-blindness, deafness, emotional disturbance, hearing impairment, mental retardation, multiple disabilities, orthopedic impairment, other health impairments, specific learning disability, speech or language impairment, traumatic brain injury, or visual impairment (including blindness). For students who do not meet the stringent definitions of disability found in IDEA, there is the safety net of Section 504 of the Rehabilitation Act of 1973. The Rehabilitation Act also protects adults with disabilities by prohibiting discrimination in any facility or program that receives federal funds. The Americans with Disabilities Act of 1990 provides the final layer of protection against discrimination. This act extends coverage from federally funded facilities and programs to any public program or venue, including post-secondary education settings.

Outcomes for children with disabilities were addressed in legislation such as the Civil Rights Act of 1964, the Economic Opportunity Act of 1964, the Elementary and Secondary Education Act of 1973, the Education for All Handicapped Children Act of 1975, the Comprehensive Employment Training Act of 1973, and the Vocational Act of 1976 (Gordon, 2003). However, the federal government focused little attention specifically on post-secondary outcomes for children with disabilities until 1984, when Madeline Will launched the federal transition initiative. Will defined transition as

> an outcome oriented process encompassing a broad array of services and experiences that lead to employment. Transition is a period that includes high school, the point of graduation, additional post secondary education or adult services, and the initial years of employment. Transition is a bridge between the security and structure offered by the school and the risks of life. (Will, 1984, p. 1)

The Individuals with Disabilities Education Act of 1990 reflected this new focus on post-high school outcomes for individuals with disabilities. Transition planning became an integral part of the law. The law specified that transition plans must align the individual child's program of study with post-school plans and make connections with adult services and post-secondary education providers. Although the IDEA amendments have waffled on when transition planning must start—first by age 16, then by age 14, and finally by age 16 or 14 when necessary—the laws have never wavered on the importance of this process (Hanley-Maxwell et al., 2004). The emphasis on transition planning marks a striking contrast from the days less than three decades earlier when children with disabilities might not even be allowed in the doors of a school.

The Individuals with Disabilities Education Improvement Act, signed into law by President George W. Bush on December 3, 2004, is the most comprehensive version yet of the original Education for All Handicapped Children Act (P.L. 94-142). In its more than three decades of existence, this law has grown from one that ensured the right to a free and appropriate education for children with disabilities to one that works to promote maximum achievement in school and into young adulthood. Through this and other legislation, such as Section 504 and the ADA, lawmakers have responded to the public outcry for equality of people with disabilities.

Some critics argue, however, that the intersection of No Child Left Behind with IDEA has created a system that is actually going backward in terms of educating persons with disabilities. Indeed, many of these same critics argue that these two laws have hurt all students, not just those with disabilities. The focus on high-stakes testing has led many Individualized Education Programs to become more academic (and less life-skill focused) in nature as teams work to improve achievement scores across the board and demonstrate AYP.

The right to a free appropriate public education, due process, unbiased assessment, and extended school year were also pursued via federal court actions during the 1970s and the decades that followed. The interaction between legislation and litigation reveals the effect litigation has on interpreting legislation and shaping future amendments. It is important to note that this process continues in the 21st century. The 2005 case of *Schaffer v. Weast* offers an example of how litigation serves to interpret legislation. The question raised in this case concerned who bears the burden of proof in a due process hearing to decide whether or not an IEP is appropriate. The Supreme Court ruled that the burden of proof rests with the party seeking relief, which in this case was the parents who claimed that their child's IEP was inappropriate (Gargiulo, 2009). Similarly, in *Winkelman v. Parma City School District* (2007) the U.S. Supreme Court ruled that parents have the right to represent the interests of their child in court, thus they are not required to have legal representation (Wright & Wright, 1999–2010). And in *Forest Grove School District v. T.A.* (2009) the U.S. Supreme Court found legal grounds in IDEA to allow financial reimbursement for private education of a child with a disability, even when the student had not been served previously in special education in a public setting (Wright & Wright, 1999–2010). It remains to be seen how this and other litigation will influence the next round of legislation.

## Conclusion

We have reviewed highlights of the history of special education from the early 1800s to the present day and have touched on its connections with world and U.S. history. The pioneers of special education shaped the field with a constant eye toward the fair and humane treatment of individuals with disabilities, as present-day families and practitioners continue to do. Indeed, the loudest voices in the fight for educational rights have often been those of parents and of teachers.

What have our forebears achieved, and for what do we continue to strive? A system of education that coexists, often via inclusive classrooms, with general education, and that emphasizes the strengths of the individual working toward interdependence, provides accommodations to assist the learner rather than demanding readiness to be included, and teaches/ supports the individual to make choices and live in a self-determined manner. Service delivery within this system is team driven and focused on the needs and preferences of the individual with disabilities and his or her family.

Historical movements, legislation, and litigation have raised many issues and debates across the years. These issues remain with us in various forms today and continue to inform the debates and controversies as they relate to education for individuals with disabilities. We will revisit some of the historical issues and debates, and introduce other issues, in Chapter 2 as we discuss the persistent problems and controversial issues in the field today.

The remainder of this book will provide further information needed to understand the history of education for persons with disabilities as we look to the future. Building upon the history presented in this chapter, Chapter 2 provides a look at the problems, controversies, and solutions related to education and disability. It also fills in the backstory of historical events and trends. While Chapters 1 and 2 provide the overview and foundation, Chapters 3 through 5 provide additional details and add depth to the information presented in the first two chapters. Chapter 3 expands on the history described in Chapter 1 by presenting a chronology of events related to education for individuals with disabilities. Chapter 4 contains short biographies of 41 key people who have influenced special education and higher education services for youth and adults with disabilities. Chapter 5 provides annotated data, statistics, tables, and graphs related to the education of children and adults with disabilities. As such, this chapter offers evidence that supports the information contained in Chapters 1 and 2. The remaining two chapters make available sources of information to aid in further study. Chapter 6 provides a list of relevant organizations and associations, annotated with descriptions and contact information. It is organized to assist the reader in identifying and contacting organizations of interest. Finally, in Chapter 7 we employ the same structure as in Chapter 6 to provide annotated listings of selected print and electronic resources. These resources have been selected based on their relevance and scope to assist in additional research.

# References

Abt, H. (1924). The care, cure, and education of the crippled child. Retrieved from http://www.disabilitymuseum.org/lib/docs/1449.htm?page=1

Agostini v. Felton , 521 U.S. 203 (1997).

Alamo Heights Independent School District v. State Board of Education, 790 F .2d 1153 (5th Cir. 1986). *Education for the Handicapped Law Report*, 554 (315)

Alberto, P., & Troutman, A. (2006). *Applied behavior analysis for teachers* (7th ed.). Upper Saddle River, NJ: Pearson Education.

Americans with Disabilities Act, 42 U.S.C.A. § 12101 *et seq.* (1990).

Arc of the United States. The ARC. Retrieved from http://www.thearc.org/NetCommunity/Page.aspx?pid=1386

Armstrong v. Kline, 476 F.Supp. 583 (E.D. Pa. 1979).

Association on Higher Education and Disability. (2010). About AHEAD. Retrieved from http://www.ahead.org

Ballard, J. B., Ramirez, B. A., & Weintraub, F. J. (Eds.). (1982). *Special education in America: Its legal and governmental foundations.* Reston, VA: Council for Exceptional Children.

Barker, L. T., Solomon, D., & Anderson, M. (1998). *Access to Head Start programs for families with disabled parents.* Oakland, CA: Berkeley Planning Associates.

Bartlett, L. (1989). Disciplining handicapped students: Legal issues in light of *Honig v. Doe. Exceptional Children, 55*, 357–366.

Beattie v. Board of Education, 172 N.W. 153 (Wis. 1919).

Blatt, B., & Kaplan, F. (1966). *Christmas in purgatory: A photographic essay on mental retardation.* Boston: Allyn & Bacon.

Board of Education v. Rowley, 458 U.S. 176; 102 S. Ct. 3034; 73 L. Ed. 2d 690 (1982).

Boggs, E. (1971). Federal legislation 1966–71. In J. Wortis (Ed.), *Mental retardation, an annual review* (pp. 103–127). New York: Grune & Stratton.

Braddock, D. (1987). *Federal policy toward mental retardation and developmental disabilities.* Baltimore, MD: Brookes.

Braddock, D. (2010). Honoring Eunice Kennedy Shriver's legacy in intellectual disability. *Intellectual and Developmental Disabilities, 48*(1), 63–72.

Braddock, D. L., & Parrish, S. L. (2001). An institutional history of disability. In G. L. Albrecht, K. D. Seelman, & M. Bury (Eds.), *Handbook of Disability Studies* (pp. 11–68). Thousand Oaks, CA: Sage.

Brown v. Board of Education, 347 U.S. 483 (1954). Retrieved from http://www .nationalcenter.org/brown.html

Buysse, V., & Wesley, P. W. (2006). Evidence-based practice: How did it emerge and what does it really mean for the early childhood field? In V. Buysse & P. W. Wesley (Eds.), *Evidence-based practice in the early childhood field* (pp. 1–34). Washington, DC: ZERO TO THREE Press.

Carl D. Perkins Vocational and Technical Education Act, 20 U.S.C. §2380 *et seq.* (1984).

Carl D. Perkins Vocational and Technical Education Act, 20 U.S.C. §2301 *et seq.* (1998). Retrieved from http://www2.ed.gov/offices/OVAE/CTE/legis.html

Carl D. Perkins Vocational and Technical Education Act, 20 U.S.C. §2301 *et seq.* (2006). Retrieved from http://frwebgate.access.gpo.gov/cgi-bin/getdoc .cgi?dbname=109_cong_bills&docid=f:s250enr.txt.pdf

Carter v. Florence County School District Four, 950 F .2d 156 (4th Cir. 1991).

Cedar Rapids Community School Dist. v. Garret F. (96–1793), 526 U.S. 66 (1999) 106 F.3d 822, affirmed.

Civil Rights Act, 42 U.S.C. §2000d *et seq.* (1964).

Comprehensive Employment and Training Act, 29 U.S.C. § 801, *et seq.* (1978).

Cutspec, P. A. (2003). *Evidence-based medicine: The first evidence-based approach to best practice.* Paper prepared for the Center for Evidence-Based Practices, Research and Training Center on Early Childhood Development, Orlena Puckett Institute, Asheville, NC.

Daniel R.R. v. State Board of Education, 874 F.2d 1036 (5th Cir. 1989).

Dewey, J. (1916). *Democracy and education: An introduction to the philosophy of education.* New York: Macmillan.

Diana v. State Board of Education, C.A. No. 70–37 (N.D. Cal. 1970).

Discrimination in post-secondary education. (2010). Retrieved from http://www .disabilityrightsnc.org/pages/148/discrimination-post-secondary-education

Dorothea Dix. (2010). Retrieved from http://www.museumofdisability.org/ original_pantheon_dix.asp

Dunn, L. M. (1968). Special education for the mildly retarded—is much of it justifiable? *Exceptional Children, 35,* 5–22.

Economic Opportunity Act, 42 U.S.C. § 2701 (1964).

Economic Opportunity Act Amendments, 42 U.S.C. § 2701 (1972).

Education for All Handicapped Children Act, 20 U.S.C. § 1401 *et seq.* (1975).

Education of Mentally Retarded Children Act, U.S. Statutes at Large 72, 1777 (1958).

Education of the Handicapped Act, § 601–662 (1970).

Education of the Handicapped Amendments, 20 U.S.C. § 1401 *et seq.* (1986).

Elementary and Secondary Education Act, 20 U.S.C. § 6301 *et seq.* (1965).

Elementary and Secondary Education Act [No Child Left Behind], 20 U.S.C. § 7980 *et seq.* (2001).

Expansion of Teaching in the Education of Mentally Retarded Children Act, 72 Stat. 1777 (1958).

Florence County School District Four v. Shannon Carter, 510 U.S. 7, 114 S.Ct. 361(1993).

Forest Grove School Dist. v. T. A. (No. 08–305), __ U.S. __ (2009). Retrieved from http://www.supremecourt.gov/opinions/08pdf/08-305.pdf

French, J. E. (2000). Jean-Marie-Gaspard Itard. In A. E. Kazdin (Ed.), *Encyclopedia of psychology* (Vol. 4, pp. 377–378). Oxford, UK: Oxford University Press.

Gallagher, J. J. (2000). The beginnings of federal help for young children with disabilities. *Topics in Early Childhood Special Education, 20*(1), 3–6.

Galloway, C. (1980). *The roots of exclusion.* Paper prepared for California on Human Services and the California Department of Rehabilitation, Sacramento, CA.

Gargiulo, R. M, (2009). *Special education in contemporary society: An introduction to exceptionality* (3rd ed.). Thousand Oaks, CA: Sage.

Garland Independent School District v. Wilks, 657 F. Supp. 1163 (N.D.Tex. 1987).

Gartner, A., & Lipsky, D. K. (1992). Beyond special education: Toward a quality system for all students. In T. Hehir, & T. Latus (Eds.), *Special education at the century's end: Evolution of theory and practice since 1970* (pp. 123–157). Cambridge, MA: President and Fellows of Harvard College.

Gaynor, J. F. (1973). The "failure" of M. H. G. Itard. *Journal of Special Education, 7*(4), 439–445.

Goals 2000: Educate America Act, 20 U.S.C. §§ 5801 *et seq.* (1994).

Gordon, H. R. D. (2003). *The history and growth of vocational education in America* (2nd ed.). Long Grove, IL: Waveland Press.

Hallahan, D. P., Kauffman, J. M., & Pullen P. C. (2009). *Exceptional learners: An introduction to special education* (11th ed.). Boston: Allyn & Bacon.

Hallahan, D. P., & Mock, D.R. (2003). A brief history of the field of learning disabilities. In H. L. Swanson, K. R. Harris, & S. Graham (Eds.), *Handbook of learning disabilities.* New York: Guilford Press.

Handicapped Children's Early Education Assistance Act, 20 U.S.C. 621 *et seq.* (1968).

Handicapped Children's Protection Act, 20 U.S.C. § 1401 *et seq.* (1986).

Hanley-Maxwell, C., & Collet-Klingenberg, L. (in press). Preparing students for employment. In P. Wehman & J. Kregel (Eds.), *Functional curriculum for elementary, middle, and secondary age students with special needs* (3rd ed.). Austin, TX: Pro-Ed.

Hanley-Maxwell, C., Owens-Johnson, L., & Fabian, E. (2004). Supported employment. In E. M. Szymanski & R. M. Parker (Eds.), *Work and disability: Issues and strategies in career development and job placement* (2nd ed., pp. 273–406). Austin, TX: Pro-Ed.

Head Start, background and history. (2010). Retrieved from http://sitemaker .umich.edu/356.bell/background_history

History of Gallaudet University (2009). Retrieved from http://aaweb.gallaudet .edu/About_Gallaudet/History_of_the_University.html

Hobson v. Hansen, 267 F. Supp. 401, 320 F. Supp. 409, 320 F. Supp. 720, 327 F. Supp. 844, 44 FRD 18 (1968).

Honig v. Doe, 484 U.S. 305, 322–23 (1988).

Howe, Samuel Gridley. (2008). *The Columbia encyclopedia* (6th ed.). Retrieved from http://www.encyclopedia.com/doc/1E1-Howe-Sam.html

Individuals with Disabilities Education Act, 20 U.S.C. § 1400 *et seq.* (1990).

Individuals with Disabilities Education Act Amendments, 20 U.S.C. §1400 *et seq.* (1997).

Individuals with Disabilities Education Improvement Act, 20 U.S.C. §1400 *et seq.* (2004).

Job Training Partnership Act (PL 97–300), 19 U.S.C. § 1501 *et seq.* (1982).

Job Training Partnership Act Amendments (PL 102–367), 29 USC §§ 1577 *et seq.* (1992).

Karier, C. J. (1986). *The individual, society, and education: A history of American educational ideas* (2nd ed). Urbana/Chicago: University of Illinois Press.

Kaser, J. (2005). *A guide to Willowbrook State School resources at other institutions.* The College of Staten Island, CUNY, Archives & Special Collections Library, 1L-216, Staten Island, NY.

Kode, K. (2002). *Elizabeth Farrell and the history of special education.* Arlington, VA: Council for Exceptional Children.

Kraft, R. (1999). Extended school year services (ESY)—What the courts have said. *ParenTalk, 19*(1).

Larry P. v. Riles, 343 F. Supp. 1306 (N.D. Cal. 1972), *aff'd* 502 F.2d 963 (9th Cir. 1974).

LexisNexis Academic (2011). Retrieved from http://www.lexisnexis.com/hottopics/lnacademic/?

Lieberman, L. M. (1996). Preserving special education . . . for those who need it. In W. Stainback & S. Stainback (Eds.), *Controversial issues confronting special education* (pp. 16–27). Boston: Allyn & Bacon.

Martin, E. W., Martin, R., & Terman, D. L. (1996). The legislative and litigation history of special education. *The future of children: Special education for students with disabilities, 6*(1), 25–39.

McCallum, J. (2008, December 8). Small steps, great strides. *Sports Illustrated, 109*(22). Retrieved from http://sportsillustrated.cnn.com/vault/article/magazine/MAG1149366/index.htm

Mills v. Board of Education of the District of Columbia, 348 F. Supp. 866 (D.D.C. 1972).

National Center on Secondary Education and Transition. (2002, December). Youth with disabilities and the Workforce Investment Act of 1998. *Policy Update: Summarizing Recent Laws and Federal Regulations, 1*(2). Minneapolis: Institute on Community Integration, University of Minnesota.

Nirje, B. (1969). The normalization principle and its human management implications. In R. Kugel & W. Wolfensberger (Eds.), *Changing patterns in residential services for the mentally retarded* (pp. 179–195). Washington, DC: President's Committee on Mental Retardation.

No Child Left Behind Act of 2001, 20 U.S.C. § 6319 (2008).

Oberti v. Board of Education, 995 F.2d 1204 (3rd Cir. 1993).

Ordover, E., & Annexstein, L. (1999). *Disabilities in school-to-work systems: A guide to federal law and policies*. Minneapolis: National Transition Network, Institute on Community Integration, University of Minnesota.

Osgood, R. L. (2008). *The history of special education: A struggle for equality in American public schools*. Westport, CT: Praeger.

Paul, J., French, P., & Cranston-Gingras, A. (2001). Ethics and special education. *Focus on Exceptional Children 34*(1), 1–16.

Pennsylvania Association for Retarded Citizens (PARC) v. Commonwealth of Pennsylvania, 343 F. Supp. 279 (E. D. Pa 1972).

Phillipe Pinel. (2010). Retrieved from http://www.museumofdisability.org/original_pantheon_pinel.asp

Pollak, R. (1997). *The creation of Dr. B: A biography of Bruno Bettelheim*. New York: Simon & Schuster.

Powell, D. R. (1994). Head start and research: Notes on a special issue. *Early Childhood Research Quarterly, 241*.

President's Panel on Mental Retardation. (1962). *National action to combat mental retardation*. Washington, DC: Government Printing Office.

Primo, A. T. (Producer), & Rivera, G. (Reporter). (1972). *Willowbrook: The last great disgrace* [Documentary film]. U.S.A.: WABC.

Rehabilitation Act Amendments, 29 U.S.C. § 701 *et seq.* (1973).

Rehabilitation Act Amendments, 29 U.S.C. § 798 *et seq.* (1998).

Richardson, J. G. (1999). *Common, delinquent, and special*. New York: Psychology Press.

Rimland, B. (1964). *Infantile autism. The syndrome and its implications for a neural theory of behavior*. East Norwalk, CT: Appleton-Century-Crofts.

Sacramento City School Dist. v. Rachel H., 14 F.3d 1398 (9th Cir. 1994).

Safford, P. L., & Safford, E. J. (1998). Visions of the special class. *Remedial and Special Education, 19*, 229–238.

Salend, S. (2008). *Creating inclusive classrooms* (6th ed.). Upper Saddle River, NJ: Pearson Education.

Schlinger, H. D. (2003). The myth of intelligence. *The Psychological Record, 53*, 15–32.

School to Work Opportunities Act, 20 U.S.C. § 6101 *et seq.* (1994).

Section 504 of the Rehabilitation Act, 29 U.S.C. § 794 *et seq.* (1973). Retrieved from http://www.dol.gov/oasam/regs/statutes/sec504.htm

Shaffer v. Weast, 546 U.S. 49 (2005).

Simpson, M. K. (1999). The moral government of idiots: Moral treatment in the work of Seguin. *History of Psychiatry, 10*(38), 227–243.

Skiba, R. (2002). Special education and school discipline: A precarious balance. *Behavioral Disorders, 27*(2), 81–97.

Smith, J. Y. (2009, August 12). The Olympian force behind a revolution [Special section]. *Washington Post*.

Smith-Hughes National Vocational Education Act, P.L. 64-347 § 103 (1917).

Smith-Sears Veterans' Rehabilitation Act, P.L. 65-178 (1918).

Stuart v. Nappi, 443 F. Supp. 1235 (D. Conn. 1978).

Szymanski, E. M., Hanley-Maxwell, C., & Asselin, S. (1990). Rehabilitation counseling, special education, and vocational special needs education: Three transition disciplines. *Career Development for Exceptional Individuals, 13*, 29–38.

Tatro v. The State of Texas, 625 F.2d 557 (CA5 1980), 703 F.2d 832 (5th Cir. 1983), *aff'd*, 468 U.S. 883 (1984).

Teachers of the Deaf Act, 20 U.S.C. § 1411 *et seq.* (1961).

Timothy W. v. Rochester, New Hampshire, School District, 875 F.2d 954 (1st Cir. 1989).

Vocational Education Act, 20 U.S.C., Chapter 32 (1963).

Vocational Education Act, 20 U.S.C., Chapter 32 (1968).

Watson v. City of Cambridge, 32 N.E. 864 (Mass. 1893).

What every teacher needs to know: A comparison of Section 504, ADA, and IDEA. (1997). *CEC Today, 4*(4), 1, 5, 15.

Will, M. (1984). *OSERS programming for the transition of youth with disabilities: Bridges from school to working life.* Washington, DC: Office of Special Education and Rehabilitation Services, U.S. Office of Education.

Winkelman v. Parma City School District, 550 U.S. 516 (2007).

Winzer, M. A. (1993). *The history of special education: From isolation to integration.* Washington, DC: Gallaudet University Press.

Wolfensberger, W. (1972). *Normalization: The principle of normalization in human services.* Toronto, ON: National Institute on Mental Retardation.

Workforce Investment Act, 29 U.S.C. § 2801 *et seq.* (1998).

Wright, P. W. D., & Wright, P. D. (1999–2010). Special education case law. Retrieved from www.wrightslaw.com/caselaw.htm

Wyatt v. Stickney, 344 F. Supp. 373, 379 (M.D. Ala. 1972).

Yell, M. L. (1990). The handicapped children's protection act of 1986: Time to pay the piper? *Exceptional Children, 56*(5), 396–407.

Yell, M. L. (1998). *The law and special education.* Upper Saddle River, NJ: Prentice-Hall.

Ysseldyke, J. E., & Algozzine, B. (1984). *Introduction to special education.* Boston: Houghton Mifflin.

# Two

# Current Issues, Controversies, and Solutions

Cheryl Hanley-Maxwell and
Lana Collet-Klingenberg

The history of American education parallels and reflects America's changing social values and economic needs. In the 20th and 21st centuries, American educational systems have been challenged to respond to issues of equality and achievement, as Americans have sought to live up to the democratic ideals on which this nation was formed, as well as meet ongoing economic and defense needs (Benner, 1998). From the change to an industrial economy in the early 20th century to the emerging information and technological economy of the 21st century, American schools have been the primary mode for the transmission of cultural values and the preparation of children for adult roles as responsible citizens and workers. As described in Chapter 1, events such as the Soviet Union's 1957 launch of *Sputnik* and President Lyndon Johnson's War on Poverty have influenced the curricular content and structure of American education. Additionally, the social changes represented in the *Brown v. Board of Education* decision, the Education for All Handicapped Children Act (and subsequent amend-ments), and the Americans with Disabilities Act have affected access and equity in American schools and institutions of higher education. Most recently, questions regarding national defense and economic health have added new layers of complexity to American education.

Concerns about American education have led to a variety of actions, including federal mandates to demonstrate instructional efficacy through high-stakes testing; emphases on curriculum, instruction, and assess-ments that help students acquire 21st-century skills; and creation of com-petition (e.g., school choice, vouchers, charter schools) to motivate improvement in public schools. Additionally, overall student perfor-mance and achievement gaps among various groups of students have resulted in questions regarding teacher quality. Such questions, along with severe teacher shortages in math, science, special education, and English as a Second Language/Bilingual Education, have led to an increased focus on the preparation of teachers, including alternative paths to licensure and questions about how to best prepare teachers. In short, American rhetoric at the beginning of the 21st century centers around three questions: (1) Are American schools preparing children to be com-petitive in a worldwide economy? (2) Are sufficient numbers of teachers adequately prepared to ensure that all children have equitable educa-tional outcomes? (3) What should be done about schools and teachers who are failing to prepare our children? Given the lack of success of American schools in educating children with disabilities, these broad questions set the backdrop for many of the issues in education for individ-uals with disabilities.

From the very beginning, education for individuals with disabilities has been fraught with controversies, including perceptions of what constitutes disability, the relative value of individuals with disabilities, reasons to educate persons with disabilities, and moral and financial imperatives as they relate to educational access. The federal law guaran-teeing equal access to a free and appropriate public education has gener-ated even more questions related to the provision of education for persons with disabilities—questions about assessment, instruction, and efficacy. These issues, juxtaposed with groundbreaking but vague laws, have fueled ongoing debates and created new controversies in education. The focus has gradually shifted from gaining access to educational ser-vices (first in institutions, then in private and public schools) to achieving excellence in service provision for persons with disabilities. While the specifics of the controversies have changed over time, the basis of the controversies has not changed in nearly fifty years!

In this chapter, we introduce a variety of issues and then address some of the most prominent issues in education for students with disabilities. We address these issues in three major sections related to the age of learners with disabilities: (1) early intervention/early childhood, (2) elementary and secondary education, and (3) post-secondary education. To ground these discussions, we provide a brief overview of the educational services offered at each level. Because the majority of controversies reside in elementary and secondary education, this section comprises the bulk of the chapter. Although federal law refers to special education as part of the elementary and secondary public school systems, scholars and advocates often use the term special education to refer to lifelong educational services, from infancy through adulthood. In this chapter, we will distinguish between educational age/grade levels (early childhood intervention, elementary and secondary education, and post-secondary education) by primarily using special education to refer to educational services for children ages 3 through 21. Our discussion begins with a brief overview of issues that cross age/grade boundaries.

## What Are the Issues?

Various sources identify what are considered the most important issues in special education. For example, in 2007 the Representative Assembly of the Council for Exceptional Children (CEC) published a list of important issues in special education that included the following (Council for Exceptional Children, 2010):

1. National special education policy

2. Funding

3. Professional development

4. Staff shortage

5. Practice

6. Research

7. National general education policy

8. Paperwork

9. Inclusion

10. Disproportional representation in special education

Similar to this list, a variety of special education texts over the past 20 years have identified controversies and issues that extend beyond research, although that topic inevitably finds its way into the texts as well because of the extensive amount of research that grounds special education practice and conflict.

Although specific topics vary from text to text and topical nuances change as special education conceptualizations change, the topics cluster around a common core. This core includes the philosophical and theoretical underpinnings of special education, the organization and delivery of special education services, problems related to classification and labeling, the content and delivery of instruction, and classroom management. It also covers questions surrounding who should collaborate with whom, personnel preparation and continuing professional development, the impact of federal actions (law, policy, funding), school outcomes, transition, technology, and gifted education. It is a matter of concern that the issues raised in the texts from the early 1990s could be easily repackaged and slightly updated and remain relevant today. Very recent issues texts (e.g., Byrnes, 2007; Taylor, 2006) focus on disability-specific and systems controversies described above, as well as how medical and technological developments intersect with education (with resulting ethical questions). Controversies swirl around disability identification and definitions, instructional and intervention planning and implementation, general and special education policies, and structural constraints such as availability of funding and qualified personnel. Some of the difficult questions raised by these controversies include:

- Why are there increasing numbers of children being diagnosed with Attention Deficit Hyperactive Disorder (ADHD) and Autism Spectrum Disorders?
- Is it possible to prevent emotional and behavioral disorders and some learning disabilities?
- What is the best way to identify children with learning disabilities?
- Why do children from historically oppressed groups (i.e., minority cultures such as African American and Native American), English language learners, and boys continue to be overrepresented in special education?
- Are residential schools better than neighborhood schools for deaf children?
- Should deaf children be taught oral versus manual communication, or both?
- What are the best interventions for children with Autism Spectrum Disorders?

- What are the best instructional approaches for students with learning disabilities?
- How should students with disabilities be educated in general education settings?
- Should all children be required to learn general education curriculum content, meet general education standards, and participate in high-stakes assessments related to learning in the general education curriculum?
- What role does technology play in the instruction and assessment of students with identified disabilities?
- What role should paraprofessionals play in the education of children with identified disabilities?
- What should be done about persistent teacher shortages in special education?
- Are teachers adequately prepared to instruct students with disabilities? Are teachers adequately prepared in general?
- Why do students served in special education continue to have poor in-school and post-school outcomes?
- How should children and youth with disabilities be included in school discipline policies and procedures?
- What roles do medical advances (e.g., neuroscience of learning, cochlear implants, medications to control behavior) play in education?
- Will adequate funding for early childhood intervention, schools, and special education in particular improve outcomes for children and youth with identified disabilities?

Related questions address the reasons why the laws pertaining to early childhood intervention, special education, and post-secondary access were created. In general, we expect education to socialize children in relation to cultural rules, structures, and expectations; and to prepare children and youth for employment. We do this to improve the security of the nation's economic base by developing its primary resource (people) into consumers and taxpayers, and thereby reducing its social burden (financial and other support programs). When educational systems fail to meet the goal of producing graduates who become consumers and taxpayers and do not rely on social supports, questions are raised, structures are changed, and policies are created. Data on poor school performance and post-school outcomes for individuals with disabilities incite additional and ongoing concerns regarding the effectiveness of educational services for students with and without disabilities. Frustrations related to these outcomes are mounting because the results of years of research have informed legislative changes, but they have yet to substantially transform classroom practices.

As discussed in detail in Chapter 1, special education grew out of the failure of general education to meet the needs of all learners. Among the assumptions that undergirded its creation was the belief that general education could not be shaped or would not change to meet the needs of all learners. Consequently, special education grew as a parallel system of education, distinct from general education—so distinct, in fact, that some states administered special education programs through agencies that were not state departments of education and maintained separate funding streams, with special education being grouped with welfare programs.

Although these conditions eventually changed, with special education becoming nested within general education for administrative, financial management, and regulatory purposes, it continued to operate as a separate program with its own spaces, teachers, materials, methods, curricula, and (additional) federal funding streams. The historic separateness of special education makes it easy to forget that special education is part of the public schools, and that children receiving special education services are, for the most part, students in the public schools. As such, educational programs and services provided to these children are bound by the same local, state, and federal regulations as general education programs and services, and children with disabilities have the right to the same educational opportunities as their peers without disabilities.

While the federal funds allocated to special education provided additional resources needed to create and deliver educational programs tailored to the learning needs of individual children with disabilities, it also served as a means to remove children who presented academic or behavioral challenges to general education teachers from the general education setting. Unfortunately, race, ethnicity, gender, and language became primary—if unplanned—factors in determining which persons required special education. Consequently, while operating as a separate system intended to ensure that all children had access to an education that met their learning needs, special education grew into a system that created and maintained inequities in schooling (Florian, 2007).

Questions related to who receives service in early intervention, special education, and post-secondary education programs, as well as where and how instruction is provided, have been raised since the inception of educational services for children considered to have disabilities. Although current conceptions of education for children, youth, and adults with disabilities are changing, these issues remain a relevant underpinning for both longstanding and new controversies in the field. They have become even more important in light of poor in-school and post-school outcomes for students with disabilities. The remainder of this chapter will discuss some of these issues in greater depth and introduce additional issues and controversies in education, across age/grade levels. These issues include concerns uncovered and described by special education researchers (e.g., early intervention and special education outcomes, use of suspension and expulsion as disciplinary measures for disability-related behaviors, lack of access to general education curricula and expectations) and interventions developed to address the identified concerns (e.g., Functional Behavioral Assessment, Response to Intervention, transition planning). Most of this research has occurred within the context of educational settings in schools and communities, and it has created effective instructional programs, curricula, behavioral interventions, and service delivery systems. Yet the results of this research have failed to make lasting changes to the services and programs provided in public schools, and students with disabilities continue to experience poor outcomes. As a result, in recent years, federal research-funding emphases have focused on "scaling up," translating research-validated practices into applied practices within public schools. The issues described in the remainder of this chapter reflect problems uncovered through this research and/or the interventions developed to ameliorate the identified problems.

# Early Childhood Intervention: Birth to Kindergarten

Research has unequivocally shown that early intervention plays a critical role in improving early development and positively affecting long term outcomes for children at risk for learning problems (Bruder, 2010; Fowler, Ostrosky, & Yates, 2007). Some children in need of intervention are identified at birth, or soon after, by medical personnel. Other children are identified during the early childhood, preschool years when they fail to meet cognitive, motor, communication, or adaptive behavior developmental milestones or exhibit behaviors that are not in keeping with typical development (Bruder, 2010). These children may be identified by a variety of people, including parents, medical personnel, family members, neighbors, childcare providers, and teachers in early childhood (EC) programs that serve a broad base of children (e.g., Head Start). Other children are "caught" during early childhood screenings conducted by public school districts as part of Child Find, a component of the Zero Reject aspect of the Individuals with Disabilities Education Act (IDEA). When children are identified as potentially being in need of early childhood intervention services, they are referred to early intervention (EI) programs or early childhood (EC) programs (Fowler et al., 2007). EI programs target children from birth to 3 years old. EC programs target children between the ages of 3 and 5 (Bruder, 2010).

EI and EC programs typically provide family-centered services to eligible children and their families, with services designed to improve the children's developmental, social, and learning outcomes. The type, frequency, intensity, focus, and goals of those services vary based on the needs of the child and family, but often include speech and language therapy, physical therapy, occupational therapy, and social work. Medical and developmental professionals (e.g., therapists, educators, and other professionals who work with young children) are also active service providers for many children receiving EI or EC services (Fowler et al., 2007).

Establishing eligibility and planning for services occurs during the Individualized Family Service Plan (IFSP) process coordinated by EI and EC professionals. Using the strengths and needs of the child as the basis, an IFSP is created to provide services intended to support families and aid in improving the child's physical, cognitive, social, and emotional growth (Gallagher, 2006) and, more recently, school readiness. The natural environments of homes, childcare centers, and pre-kindergarten programs typically are the service provision locations (Fowler et al., 2007). Variations in service provision are based on availability of local services, geographic location of the child's home in relationship to the location of available services, and the ability of the family to access/utilize services (Hallahan, Kaufman, & Pullen, 2009).

Controversies and concerns related to early intervention and early childhood special education focus on systems and program issues: the disparate availability and effectiveness of services, the challenge of adapting services to the unique needs of each family, and the problem of declining resources (Fowler et al., 2007). Additional controversy surrounds the use of applied behavior analysis (ABA) as an early intervention (Prizant, 2009; Simpson, 2001) for young children diagnosed with autism. Proponents of ABA argue that it is the only evidence-based practice available for work with very young learners. Opponents argue that it is an intervention that involves meaningless repetition and teaches skills that do not generalize to natural settings.

## Systems and Program Issues

Best practice in early childhood intervention dictates that all programs must be family-centered, delivered in natural environments, and created in close collaboration with families. However, considerable variation along these dimensions exists in early childhood intervention services. This variation is due to several factors. First, governance issues confound the creation and regulation of systems and programs related to early intervention. Early intervention programs and services covering children from birth to age 3 are permissive, not mandated, so individual states create their own service systems that comply with federal regulations in order to gain access to federal funding for these programs. Federal law mandates early childhood services for children ages 3 to 6. These systems and services fall within the broader category of education, however, so states make their own decisions about eligibility criteria, service coordination, and lead agency selection. State decision-making results in variations not only in who get services, but also in who provides services and the qualifications of those providers. Second, young children and their families are very diverse. The variance in needs and complexity of problems these children and their families exhibit increase the variability and, some would argue, the quality of services (Bruder, 2010).

Service variations would not be problematic if there was evidence to prove that the services provided were effective. Unfortunately, there is growing evidence that program providers are not utilizing the practices that research has identified as most effective, and that these practices often are not included in personnel preparation programs. Furthermore, service providers and states have not demonstrated the efficacy of their services. In fact, accountability data that would provide evidence of efficacy are often absent or inadequate, or have revealed that early childhood intervention programs are producing no positive effects (a finding contrary to research results) (Bruder, 2010). As a result, IDEA now requires states to collect data showing that programs are effective in improving child outcomes in the development of social/emotional skills, behavior, and "acquisition and use of knowledge and skills (including early language/communication and early literacy)" (Bruder, 2010, p. 346). States must also demonstrate that families knowledgably participate in early childhood intervention, which involves parents knowing their rights, being conversant in relation to their children's needs, and having the skills to actively participate in activities designed to improve the learning and development of their children. Although this data requirement is a positive step in improving early childhood intervention services, concerns exist in relation to the reliability, validity, and variation in the way states choose to collect and report the results (Bruder, 2010).

Bruder (2010) recommends changes in early childhood services that encompass the individual child, program, and policy levels. At the individual program level, she recommends that providers examine the relationship between attainment of IFSP/IEP (Individualized Education Program) goals and the interventions provided. In keeping with this recommendation, she advocates for research to continue identifying effective practices and to ensure that these practices are incorporated into personnel preparation programs and service provision. Recognizing that it is often difficult to translate research to practice, Bruder further recommends that technical assistance and professional development programs be revitalized. In an effort to monitor the effectiveness of programs, she recommends creating transparent accountability systems that meet psychometric requirements and are comprehensive enough to include data about cost, personnel qualifications (i.e., professional standards), types of services provided, collaboration to improve the transition to school-based services, use of research-based practices, and responsiveness to the unique needs of families. Finally, Bruder recommends coordinating programs and combining funding streams across various types of early childhood programs, education, and other child and family services/support programs to enhance and leverage existing resources.

## Effective Interventions for Children on the Autism Spectrum

An extremely controversial topic in early childhood intervention, as well as in school-age programs, involves determining what interventions are the most effective and should be funded/supported by EC/EI programs. This topic is particularly controversial in regard to children who are diagnosed with Autism Spectrum Disorders (ASD). Until recently, little was known about the effectiveness of the most popular interventions for children with ASD. However, popular interventions and components of comprehensive programs represent well-researched practices (Callahan, Shukla-Mehta, Magee, & Wie, 2010). Applied behavior analysis (ABA) is an approach, a theory, and a group of interventions that utilizes such evidence-based practices. However, clouding discussion of effective practices related to ABA is confusion surrounding the meaning of the term. Specifically, some laypeople refer to a particular intervention that is only peripherally related to the field of ABA as "ABA." Thus, issues and controversies abound related to the accuracy of the term ABA as well as its implementation and efficacy claims.

## What Is ABA?

The popularly used term "ABA" is an imprecise representation of an intervention method that is more accurately known as discrete trial training (DTT). Although DTT falls within the umbrella of ABA, it is only one of many ABA instructional/intervention methods. Furthermore, in addition to referring to a broader class of behaviorally based methods, the term ABA also refers to a research approach. As a result, the ABA acronym may refer to many different things (Prizant, 2009). When used in relation to instruction or intervention, ABA is a general term that applies to data-based methods which utilize behavioral principals related to the events or circumstances that precede behavior (antecedents), and the events or circumstances that follow behavior (consequences). These methods include careful analysis of the behavior (or its absence) and its context in order to identify relationships between its antecedents and its consequences. Analyses are used to create systematic plans to teach new behavior or modify existing behavior (Simpson, 2001). Behavioral methods used in instructional programs typically include manipulating the antecedents through increasingly intrusive levels of assistance (e.g., verbal hints, pointing, physical touch, hand-over-hand guidance) to obtain correct responses, and then systematically reducing (or fading) levels of assistance. Consequences that increase the likelihood the behavior will occur again, reinforcement, and error correction are also used (Alberto & Troutman, 2006). Teachers, parents, therapists, and others may use ABA within the context of formal instructional programs, as part of incidental learning, or in response to the occurrence of behavior. It may be used to teach steps in a complex task, simple skills, or complex skills/tasks in natural settings or controlled settings (Simpson, 2001).

As indicated above, the term "ABA" is also used to refer to an instructional method that uses an errorless learning approach involving systematic, repeated trials of instruction called discrete trial training (DTT). In this method, tasks and skills are broken into their component parts for teaching and for data collection. Specially trained (and certified) therapists teach these components individually, or individually within the total task, using a highly regimented, one-on-one instructional program. Within this type of ABA/DTT instruction, the learning setting is carefully controlled, and instruction often occurs in a small room that contains few distractions (e.g., pictures, other learners). Data related to skill acquisition are collected daily and are used to inform further instruction. Consequently, it is a highly accountable intervention. It is important to note that

ABA/DTT targets discrete skill acquisition rather than broad, integrated, and complex skills. As mentioned earlier, those who oppose the use of ABA/DTT argue that the skills learned do not readily generalize to non-instructional settings or even to situations where people other than the therapist do the DTT instruction (Prizant, 2009).

## What Are the Controversies Related to ABA?

Not only does ABA (applied behavior analysis) have multiple meanings within the context of intervention for children with ASD, its effectiveness as an educational tool has been called into question. Proponents of ABA/DTT claim that it is the best and only way to achieve improvement in the development of children with ASD. Furthermore, advocates of ABA/DTT claim that children need to receive these services from specially trained therapists in highly controlled, low-stimulation environments for a specific amount of time each week, often 40 hours per week (Prizant, 2009; Strain, 2001). Proponents also claim that to receive maximal benefit from this intervention, and maybe even cure autism, children must receive this intervention during early childhood, preferably before age 5 (Prizant, 2009; Vismara & Rogers, 2010).

Other researchers and professionals challenge the validity of these claims (Callahan et al., 2010; Prizant, 2009). They also note that ABA/DTT is not consistent with the National Research Council (NRC) recommendations for effective interventions for children with ASD (NRC, 2001). Based on a comprehensive review of the research, the NRC recommends that children with ASD be in intervention programs that provide active engagement for at least 25 hours per week. It suggests that such programs focus on

(a) functional, spontaneous communication;
(b) social instruction in various settings . . . ;
(c) teaching . . . play skills focusing on appropriate use of toys and play with peers;
(d) instruction leading to generalization and maintenance of cognitive goals in natural contexts;
(e) positive approaches to . . . problem behaviors; and
(f) functional academic skills when appropriate (Prizant, 2009, pp. 29–30).

Although ABA/DTT meets the NRC's guideline of active engagement for at least 25 hours per week, it fails to meet all the other guidelines. It focuses on a narrow scope of discrete skills rather than broader, more complex skills typically found in communication and social relationships. Additionally, it is delivered in a single, highly controlled setting, the therapist works in a cue–response mode that does not include peers or family members, and it does not attend to generalization and maintenance issues.

Regardless of the accuracy of the ABA/DTT name or the method's adherence to NRC guidelines, proponents claim that young children who receive this intervention typically make significant gains in all areas of development and, in some cases, are cured. Claims that ABA/DTT can cure autism are based on studies that examined the trajectories of 19 children who, as young children, participated in an ABA/DTT intervention program. The results of these studies indicated that, at follow-up, approximately 50% of the children were "cured," or found to be "indistinguishable" from other same-age children (Lovaas, 1987; McEachin, Smith, & Lovaas, 1993). Given these startlingly hopeful outcomes, it is unfortunate that other researchers have been unable to replicate the results. These results and their lack of replication have led to highly charged interactions around the use of ABA/DTT. Proponents use the original research to support their claims for its effectiveness, while opponents focus on the weaknesses of the original research, including the inability of other researchers to replicate (and thus verify) its results, to cast doubt on its effectiveness as a cure (Prizant, 2009).

The debates regarding the effectiveness of ABA/DTT often overshadow research that has demonstrated that many effective programs use general ABA principles as part of their foundation (Simpson, 2001). Furthermore, research has suggested that early, intensive ABA-based interventions that commence before age five, include 20 hours or more per week of intervention, last at least two years, and follow NRC guidelines appear to yield positive results. These results suggest that children experience "accelerated gains, including increased scores in IQ and other standardized tests; enhanced communication, cognition, and social-emotional functioning; and mainstreamed school placements" (Vismara & Rogers, 2010, p. 460) through such interventions. Thus, it is important to note that while research indicates early intervention and use of ABA principles appear to be factors in effective programs for children with ASD, there is no reliable evidence to support the use of ABA/DTT only or the claim that ABA/DTT can cure autism. However, the effectiveness and popularity of ABA intervention with young children with ASD have convinced some states to provide funding for ABA intervention for qualified young children.

Researchers and practitioners express additional concerns about interventions using ABA/DTT only. These concerns arise from research indicating that limitations related to communication and social development are inherent in the methods used (Koegel & Koegel, 1995, 2006; Strain, McGee, & Kohler, 2001). Because ABA/DTT relies on methods in which the therapist carefully controls the antecedents, using only adult request/direction-response instruction, the possibilities of child-initiated behavior or spontaneity are severely reduced. As a result, typical reciprocal communication, spontaneous or self-initiated communication or behaviors, and the development of normal social relationships with adults and other children are limited or nonexistent. Given that these are areas in which children with ASD have particular difficulty, opponents find their absence in this approach to instruction to be dismaying. Furthermore, as mentioned earlier, skills learned in ABA/DTT programs may not generalize to "independent use in daily interactions and activities" (Prizant, 2009, p. 29).

Issues related to ABA, as discussed above, focus on its use as an effective early childhood intervention. However, the controversies related to this intervention extend into kindergarten and beyond. Simpson (2001) provides a hypothetical scenario that captures how requests for ABA/DTT intervention commonly play out in public schools. In his scenario, parents—supported by advocates, their home therapy team, and research results—arrive at an IEP meeting stating that they want ABA/DTT used at school. They specify that they want the instruction to be provided in a separate room, for a minimum of 40 hours per week (6 to 8 hours per day, 6 days a week). These demands are incompatible with most schools' structures and personnel allocations. Meeting these demands requires school personnel to find space for the individualized instruction in schools that typically do not have unused, dedicated space. Additionally, because the instructional schedules for other students to not match those requested by the parent, school personnel assignments have to be extended or changed, usually at an additional cost to the school district. In Simpson's scenario, the parents also demand that the school personnel who will deliver the instruction to their child be trained by their home therapy team to ensure that the program is delivered as designed. Furthermore, they demand that the program be supervised and coordinated by a "behavior analyst of their choosing . . . hired by the school district" (Simpson, 2001, p. 69). In addition to monitoring and supervising program, the behavior analyst will collect data and design and conduct program evaluation. Finally, they indicate that they expect the behavior analyst to coordinate weekly meetings at which the parents, school personnel, and the home intervention team will analyze program data to assess whether the student is progressing as expected and alter programs as necessary to achieve the desirable outcomes. Weekly meetings such as these place additional time demands on school personnel and could result in the need to frequently reconvene IEP teams. As Simpson notes, although this scenario demonstrates a high degree of parental participation in the program design and decision-making processes (a highly desirable outcome), it also demonstrates how demands for the ABA/DTT services conflict with school policies, practices, and settings.

Clearly, the issues related to the exclusive use of ABA/DTT—including the effectiveness of the intervention, the appropriateness of the skill focus, the structure of the program, infrastructure needs, and personnel issues (Simpson, 2001)—take on new meaning when considered in light of K–12 education. The demands of ABA/DTT complicate other issues facing K–12 education, including how to determine eligibility, what constitutes an appropriate education, how to meet staffing needs in times of economic hardship, and how to respond to federal policies. At the heart of the never-ending debate over ABA is not the question of whether it is a proven instructional approach, but questions about the boundaries of its use and whether it is implemented with fidelity. The bigger and certainly more important issue is what constitutes evidence-based or research-based practice, and how to support teachers in identifying and applying such practices in the instructional setting.

# Special Education: Kindergarten Through Secondary Education

Since the inception of special education, the number of children served by the program has increased dramatically. In the 30 years that span 1976–1977 to 2006–2007, the number of children and youth between the ages of 3 and 21 served in the public schools has nearly doubled, from approximately 3.7 million (8% of children and youth in public schools) to 6.7 million (13.5%) (National Center for Education Statistics, 2010b). In addition to increases in the total number children served in special education, five disability categories (multiple disabilities, deaf-blindness, autism, traumatic brain injury, and developmental delay) have been added to the original eight categories. The categories of specific learning disabilities, other health impairments (including ADHD), autism, multiple disabilities, and developmental delays account for the largest increases in the number of children served. Although the number of children identified as having intellectual disabilities (i.e., mental retardation) decreased during this period, those reductions occurred when the categories of autism, multiple disabilities, and developmental delays were added (National Center for Education Statistics, 2010b). This suggests that some children who previously would have been identified as having intellectual disabilities are now identified as having one of these other disabilities. Spiraling increases in children identified with autism as well as ADHD have led to questions related to the diagnoses of these disabilities.

In addition to significant increases in the overall number of children identified as having disabilities that entitle them to special education, demographic patterns reveal concerns about who is identified as having a disability. In 2004, 9.2% of all school-age children from 6 to 21 were served in special education, with variations in the percentage of students served within individual race/ethnicity groups. Children served under the categories of specific learning disability, speech or language impairment, intellectual disability/mental retardation, and emotional disturbance comprised the vast majority of these students. The distribution of students within special education reveals demographic patterns of over- and underrepresentation, where the percentage of students included in the disability categories exceed or lag behind their percentage of the total school population. African Americans, Native Americans, and boys, for instance, tend to be overrepresented in special education programs (see Chapter 5 for more data).

While the popularity and use of preschool programs and 4-year-old kindergarten are on the rise, some children with disabilities begin their educational experiences with kindergarten. In addition, as described in Chapter 1, all children with disabilities are entitled to continue to receive educational services until age 22 or high school graduation, whichever comes first. During this time, eligible children receive instructional services, supports, and related services intended to enhance their development and improve their learning and schooling outcomes (Gallagher, 2006).

Although special education services vary from child to child and school district to school district, all school districts must provide eligible children with services identified through the Individualized Education Program (IEP) process. This process includes identification and referral of potentially eligible children, eligibility assessment, program planning, program implementation, and ongoing evaluation in relation to continuing eligibility and program effectiveness monitoring. The IEP process includes input from special and general educators, the students and their parents or guardians, appropriate related service professionals, school district administrators (Gallagher, 2006), and sometimes advocates and other community and family members.

The term "special education" encompasses a variety of meanings. It refers to places, services, curricula, methodologies, and, in its totality, programs that differ from those used in general education. There are many controversies surrounding special education, including questions related to who, what, where, why, and how. This section addresses these controversies by beginning with a broad discussion of issues related to who is identified as having an educational disability. This discussion sets the stage for four additional topics: assessment (who and why), placement (where), curriculum (what), and instruction (how). The section closes with a discussion of secondary special education.

## Who Has an Educational Disability?

Determining who has an educational disability and who needs special education services is fraught with controversy. The question is difficult to address because the point at which learning or behavior differences become disabilities is entangled in student, family, peer, teacher, classroom, school, community, state, national, and cultural variables. The point at which difference intersects with special education by becoming disability reflects persistent concerns about the definition or meaning of disability and about disproportional representation.

### Meaning of Disability

As described in Chapter 1, the meaning of disability and the understanding of its origins have changed through the centuries, reflecting changing cultural beliefs, social values, and scientific knowledge. Disability has been viewed as disease, deviance, and more recently, difference. As difference, it is similar to other human characteristics that vary naturally. As deviance or disease, disability is something to cure, control, avoid, or punish. At various points in history, persons with disabilities were considered deviant to greater or lesser degrees. In 1972, Wolfensberger described eight roles ascribed to persons with intellectual disabilities: (1) subhuman organism, (2) menace, (3) unspeakable object of dread, (4) object of pity,

(5) holy innocent, (6) diseased organism, (7) object of ridicule, and (8) eternal child. In all eight roles, the individual with a disability is deviant or diseased, less than and distinct from "normal" individuals. Even when considered as a "holy innocent," these persons were lacking some part that all other (normal) human beings had. As such, treating them differently than other children and adults was justified, resulting in their being hidden, infantilized, neglected (Wolfensberger, 1972), and often subjected to abuse and degradation (Blatt & Kaplan, 1966).

Deviance is culturally determined, setting specific, and often includes irrelevant characteristics that make the person different from the predominant standard in that environment. Unfortunately, perceptions of deviance often result in stereotyping (i.e., generalizing conceptions and beliefs about groups of people based on erroneous or overly simplified assumptions) and labeling. All this affects how children and adults with disabilities are viewed vis-à-vis education. Even if educators do not subscribe overtly to one of the above roles, beliefs about disability and the models used to construct the meaning of disability affect their practices. For example, a young adult who is viewed as an eternal child will receive an education commensurate with young children as opposed to an education that is in keeping with her/his chronological age. In educational terms, this individual will receive a developmental education versus a functional education. An example of this type of educational practice is a 17-year-old with severe autism whose reading instruction is limited to books targeted for preschoolers (e.g., *Sesame Street, Bob the Builder*) rather than focused on learning to read signs in the community and sight words for work. Thus, educational practices reflect vestiges of Wolfensberger's eight roles.

Some educational practices today are still based in deficit beliefs that certain degrees of intellectual, physical, sensory, social, or affective variations must be cured, changed, controlled, or contained. From this perspective, disability is identified as a problem within the individual as opposed to a socially created situation (Valle & Connor, 2010). Locating disability within the student often results in behavioral assessments that target only the student with a disability for evaluation and eligibility assessments, behavior management practices that externally control rather than teach, pedagogies that are not designed to capitalize on the student's previous learning or learning strengths, and separate classrooms. However, recent moves toward inclusive education for students with disabilities, ecological assessment, and universal design demonstrate that educational systems are beginning to move from a deficit model to a social model (Valle & Conner, 2010). These changes could result in students with disabilities, along with their nondisabled peers, having access to the same curriculum at levels that best match their learning needs, learning and being assessed in ways that best match their individual learning and performance styles, using materials that are universally accessible, and perhaps achieving learning outcomes that are more equitable. Unfortunately, until education systems move away from the expert/professional approach that relies on diagnosis (e.g., eligibility determination and assignment of label) and treatments designed to "fix" students with disabilities rather than improve their environments or their access to their environments, the move from the deficit model to the social model cannot be completed.

The disability rights movement has undoubtedly influenced progress in education toward a more social model of disability. Although the initial purpose of the movement was to secure the rights of individuals with disabilities to access and participate in the same settings and activities as individuals without disabilities, the movement also sought respect for the individuality and humanity of persons with disabilities. The movement has grown to include activism promoting the acceptance of disability as a natural human variation or as a positive characteristic, one that does not need to be "fixed" (Disability Rights Education and Defense Fund, 2008).

The disability rights movement is particularly active in the Deaf community. It is reflected in the Deaf opposing cochlear implants, resisting oral communication, and objecting to education that results in deaf children growing up in only hearing environments. Many Deaf individuals believe that their deafness separates them so entirely from the hearing world that deafness constitutes a culture. In viewing deafness as a culture, Deaf individuals stress that they have their own language, literature, and cultural behaviors or rituals. Deaf individuals who see deafness as a separate culture often advocate for residential schools for the deaf, in which children who are deaf are educated with other children who are deaf and can learn their cultural traditions. For some Deaf activists, the current movement directed at eliminating separate schools and separate classrooms is seen as cultural genocide, a way for the hearing culture to prevent the Deaf culture from passing on its traditions (MSM Productions, Ltd., 2004–2010).

## Disproportional Representation

Representation of various groups of individuals in special education in general and in specific disability categories provides clear examples of the social construction of disabilities. Which differences are attributed to disability or deviance reflects social values and beliefs. When these differences are associated with some groups of students more than others, it often results in these groups of students being overrepresented in programs that focus on remediating their deficits, in specific disability categories, and in special education in general, and being underrepresented in programs that focus on their strengths.

Over- or underrepresentation is determined in multiple ways. In one explanation, if the probability of receiving a specific disability category label can be predicted using a demographic characteristic or combination of characteristics, that characteristic or combination of characteristics are disproportionally represented in the disability category associated with that label (Oswald, Coutinho, Best, & Singh, 1998, as cited in Artilles, Kosleski, Trent, Osher, & Ortiz, 2010). When disproportional representation occurs, demographic data reveal that some groups of students are represented in greater percentages in special education, and in specific categories, than they are in the total school population (Harry, 2007). African Americans, Native Americans, English language learners (ELL), students from low socioeconomic status (SES) households, as well as boys historically are overrepresented in the high-incidence categories of special education (specific learning disabilities or SLD; emotional behavioral disabilities or EBD; mild intellectual disabilities) and underrepresented in gifted and talented programs (Artilles et al., 2010).

Artilles et al. (2010) refer to these racial and ethnic minorities and low-SES students as historically underserved groups, because education history suggests that the overrepresentation of these groups is tied directly to how power, privilege, and cultural dominance play out in public schools to deny some children equitable educational opportunities. Furthermore, there is evidence that when structural factors are altered, large-scale reforms are implemented, and school cultures are changed, the effect of these demographic variables on student learning and behavior change. Additionally, patterns of overrepresentation vary with the demographic characteristics of the communities in which these students live, particularly as they relate to income level and minority composition. Finally, it is important to note that patterns of overrepresentation are most closely associated with the high-incidence, mild-disabilities categories. These categories are highly dependent on subjective professional judgment to determine eligibility, and the differences between the categories and between low achieving and disability are unclear (Harry, 2007). Unfortunately, issues related to English language learners further cloud the picture.

English language acquisition patterns mirror the language difficulties experienced by students with specific learning disabilities in reading. The overlap is so significant that it is often difficult to determine whether English as a Second Language (ESL) students have learning disabilities.

The percentage of students in the low-incidence disability categories of visually impaired/blind, hearing impaired/deaf, and orthopedic impairment within each ethnic group closely mirrors the group's representation in the total school population. On the other hand, representation in high-incidence disability categories varies greatly across race/ethnicity. African American, American Indian/Alaskan Native, and to some extent White students are overrepresented in special education, while Asian/ Pacific Islanders and Hispanic students are underrepresented. However, a careful look at individual categories reveals other race/ethnicity based patterns. The percentage of Black students identified with intellectual disabilities is nearly double their percentage of the total school population, and the proportion identified with emotional behavioral disability is more than 10% higher. The proportion of American Indian/Alaskan Native students in the developmental delay category is more than double their percentage of the school population. The percentage of White students in the other health impaired category, which includes ADHD, is nearly 13% higher than the percentage of these students in the total school population, while the proportion identified as having an emotional behavioral disability is 8% lower. Students who are Asian/Pacific Islander appear to be significantly underrepresented in the emotional behavioral disability, other health impaired, and specific learning disabilities categories, while Hispanic students are significantly underrepresented in the categories of developmental delay, other health impaired, and emotional behavioral disability (Data Accountability Center, 2010; National Center for Education Statistics, 2010a).

Overrepresentation in special education is problematic because of the degree of stigma attached to each disability label, the poorer school and post-school outcomes associated with students in special education, and the fact that students with certain disability labels tend to be excluded from general education classrooms more often and for greater lengths of time. A lower degree of stigma is associated with learning disabilities and speech or language disabilities, while a higher degree of stigma is associated with intellectual disabilities and emotional behavioral disabilities. Students with intellectual disabilities or emotional behavioral disabilities are more likely to be educated in segregated settings than are students with other disability labels. This exclusion, whether it consists of full-time special classes or separate schools, effectively segregates these students. This segregation, along with disproportional representation, suggests that special education has been used to continue race-based segregation that denies equal access to educational opportunities (Artilles et al., 2010).

Artilles et al. (2010) describe the paradox of special education as it relates to the complexity of disproportional representation. They say it is puzzling "how policy and programmatic resources (i.e., special education) created to address the civil rights of a marginalized group (i.e., students with disabilities) can constitute an index of inequality for other marginalized groups (i.e., students form historically underserved groups)" (p. 281). The reasons lie in historical contexts, societal actions, cultural assumptions, and their interactions with disability definitions in special education.

Historic views of special education justify disproportional representation with three factors: poverty, special education as a safety net, and special education as a "value added" service (Artilles et al., 2010, p. 282). Using poverty as a justification for disproportional representation involves arguments that children from low-income families are exposed to more risk factors that are correlated to learning risks than children from higher income families. The fact that these children happen to come from historically underserved/oppressed groups is seen as an artifact related to poverty. Although it is true that children from low-income families are exposed to greater health risks and are less likely than middle- to upper-income children to receive health care, poverty alone cannot account for the differences in educational achievement and incidence of educational disability in this group of children, particularly African American children. In fact, recent research calls into question the degree to which poverty contributes to overrepresentation. What this research suggests is that race is not an incidental factor in this equation; rather, race is a primary factor that shows historic patterns of discrimination and exclusion (Harry, 2007).

## Assessment

Assessment in special education has historically served two primary purposes: (1) establishing eligibility; and (2) planning instruction, intervention, and services based on the needs and assets of individual students. Current best practice and federal legislation (IDEA; No Child Left Behind, NCLB) also call for the use of assessment data to monitor student and school progress, and to examine student responses to intervention so as to guide continued program adjustment. These purposes result in assessments that differ from general education assessments in their forms (e.g., performance as opposed to written assessments, observational assessments) and types (e.g., ecological assessments, functional analyses of behavior). Assessments related to students with disabilities have become increasingly complex and contentious as the field of special education moves into more inclusive environments. Assessment controversies surround the purposes of assessment, who is assessed, what is assessed, how it is assessed, and who conducts the assessment (Bourke & Mentis, 2007). However, the primary controversies center on eligibility determinations and the role of assessment in planning and progress monitoring. More recently, because of increasing alarm concerning the achievement gap and research demonstrating poor outcomes for students with disabilities, standards and accountability measures have taken center stage.

### Eligibility

Assessment for eligibility is problematic. One primary concern is that determining eligibility results in affixing categorical labels to children, and thus publicly naming what are assumed to be deficits within the child. The obsession with categorizing and sorting people is not unique to special education. However, its presence in education and its often devastating effects raise red flags about the assigning of labels and the processes used to determine eligibility and subsequently assign labels. This concern is particularly evident in relation to children identified as having specific learning disabilities (SLD) and those identified as having attention deficit hyperactivity disorder (ADHD). Exponential growth in the number of children identified as having SLD and/or ADHD has raised significant questions about the processes used to determine eligibility and has resulted in the exploration of alternative ways to identify who needs special education versus who needs better general education instruction. This discussion of eligibility begins with a discussion of labeling, and then addresses the processes used to assess children for eligibility. It ends with a more in-depth look at the particular problems associated with the identification of children with specific learning disabilities.

### Labeling

The meaning of disability often is communicated in the labels associated with those who are identified as having disabilities; as such, labeling is not a politically or socially neutral activity. Labeling can be used to categorize and separate people in ways that denigrate or harm the labeled individuals. Labels can also enable individuals to access services or resources that require eligibility. A commonly named benefit to labeling in education is that labels can help educators identify children in need of specific instructional approaches or possible adaptations and accommodations. However, in education practice, there is little difference in the curriculum, instructional methods, and behavioral interventions for students who have high-incidence disabilities (i.e., specific learning disabilities, emotional behavioral disabilities, mild intellectual disabilities) (Harry, 2007). Furthermore, in inclusive education settings, labeling has lost even more meaning. Labels increasingly are not being used to group students, and special educators are increasingly serving a broad array of students, sometimes including students without disability labels, in general education classrooms.

Disability labels represent deficits or deviances. As a result, they justify the use of different allocations of resources, services, curricula, and settings. Furthermore, they often are used to explain why some children are not benefitting from their educations. Failure and limitations are attributed to the disability (and indirectly, though not subtly, to the child), rather than the setting, services, or people who deliver the services. Consequently, labels exert considerable power over those who receive them and communicate the relative social value of the labeled individual.

The power of labels can be readily seen in language changes that incorporated medical labels into common terminology used to diminish an individual or to create humor that assures the inferiority of the labeled individual. Medical labels for people with intellectual disabilities are excellent examples of this phenomenon. Researchers and physicians originally referred to all individuals with intellectual disabilities as idiots, but they eventually felt that the category of idiot was too broad. As a result, they decided to refer to individuals who had lesser degrees of intellectual disability as feebleminded, reserving idiot for those with more severe intellectual disabilities. Subsequently, in the early 1900s, researchers and physicians felt the broad label feebleminded was still inadequate in describing this group of people. As a result, they began using a more refined system of labeling that further reflected the degree of retardation. The once feebleminded became known as imbeciles and morons, with moron referring to mild intellectual disability. These terms, along with idiot, are commonly used on today's playgrounds when children are teasing or bullying someone.

"Enlightened," educationally based terms for individuals labeled as moron, imbecile, and idiot began to be used in the second half of the 20th century. Such terms included educable mentally handicapped/retarded, trainable mentally handicapped/retarded, and custodial. These terms referred to the learning capacity of the individual and identified what type of education, if any, was appropriate for the labeled person: public school with watered-down academics; separate training school focused on vocational, self-care, and home-living skills; or minimal training and lifelong care only. Because of the inherent problems of a classification schema that puts such obvious limits on the learning potential of the individual student, the terms were later changed to reflect "level of functioning," becoming mildly, moderately, and severely mentally retarded, and later replacing mental retardation with intellectual disability. And, as mentioned above, when the medical terms became commonly recognized and used in everyday conversation, often in a derogatory or demeaning manner, professional communities would replace them with new terminology. In all cases, through labeling, the disability became the person rather than a reference to a characteristic of the person, and the label was used to determine and then rationalize the educational services provided to that person. This tendency of medical or educational terms to become commonplace and be used in a derogatory manner has led to efforts to create social awareness about the inappropriate use of such terms. A case in point is the recent effort by Special Olympics to eliminate the use of the word retarded in everyday language. This movement, called "The R-Word Campaign," has enjoyed great success on college campuses, on the Internet, and within the social influences of Special Olympics (see http://www.r-word.org).

In the late 20th century, language changed once again. This time the emphasis became "person first," to acknowledge the individual first, followed by the disability label. Subsequently, individuals with specific disabilities have been referred to as students with learning disabilities, students with intellectual disabilities, or students with visual disabilities. The only exception is the deaf, many of whom, as previously stated, believe they represent a separate culture. As a result, just as a speaker would describe an American student using the cultural modifier referring to a country (e.g., American) first, followed by the noun referring to the person (student), the cultural modifier for the Deaf comes first and the person second, as in Deaf student (MSM Productions, Ltd., 2004–2010). Although this language change could signal changing attitudes and beliefs, language changes alone cannot address the problems inherent in a system that separates children based on labels and requires labels to provide access to the services and supports intended to enhance their learning.

### Processes for Eligibility Determination

Determining which label to affix to a student is sometimes merely a best guess. The process of determining eligibility involves looking for a fit between the student's learning and behavioral characteristics, as represented in assessments, classroom performances, professional judgment, and the federal disability definitions. In fact, there are very few disabilities for which there are truly objective measures that can be used to classify or name the disability (Artilles et al., 2010). Consequently, serious questions have been raised about eligibility assessments, including the reliability and biases of information obtained as well as their lack of utility in program planning.

The ubiquitous use of IQ scores as criteria for eligibility in many of the disability categories ignores the controversies that surround the conception of IQ and its utility in education. IQ tests provide only static measures of knowledge and skill, and they provide little information that can be used to create instructional programs or understand the particular student's learning difficulties. Furthermore, IQ testing is often used, inappropriately, to predict the learning capacity of the individual. There is no evidence that suggests such use is valid (Bourke & Mentis, 2007). Debates that surround the use of IQ assessment focus on the "what" of assessment, how it reflects system and social biases. Criticisms of other aspects of the eligibility assessment process echo these same concerns. Special education eligibility assessments extend beyond students' performance on IQ tests and often include results of achievement testing, assessments of language and reading, and other measures. The intention is to create as full a picture as possible before making eligibility decisions. The importance of developing a clear understanding of students' strengths and weaknesses means that the information gathered must also include student products (e.g., tests, projects, assignments), student observations, and checklists related to student behavior or skills. However, this process still primarily focuses on determining children's deficits in order to demonstrate the degree to which students deviate from culturally determined norms.

Although eligibility assessments typically focus only on the student, research has pointed to the role of the environment in student learning and behavior. Consequently, high-stakes decisions such as eligibility are beginning to include ecological assessments, which involve examining the contexts in which the learning or behavior problems occur. One of the most controversial ecological assessments is the Functional Behavior Assessment (FBA). The controversy that surrounds the FBA is not eligibility determination per se, but rather its role in maintaining eligibility.

As described in Chapter 1, the Individuals with Disabilities Education Act (IDEA) requires that FBAs precede most behavior-based decisions related to a change of placement for students in special education. The intent of this requirement is hold school personnel more accountable for the provision of services to students with disabilities, even if they are suspended or expelled. FBAs are also part of Manifest Determinations that ascertain whether students' behaviors are substantially related to their disabilities. If the behaviors in question arise from inappropriate placements or inadequate educational programs, or are a manifestation of their disabilities, students cannot be suspended from school for more than 10 days or expelled. Instead, schools must provide alternative programs that protect the education entitlement rights of these students. The FBA provides educators with the information needed to understand students' behaviors, the function(s) those behaviors serve, the conditions under which they occur and reoccur, and the consequences that maintain or increase them (Bourke & Mentis, 2007). This information comes from observations, interviews (with teachers, parents, other family members, the student, and sometimes peers), record reviews, rating scales, and formal assessments. The results of an FBA determine if the dangerous behavior exhibited by the learner with a disability is related to his or her disability. For example, a child with an intellectual disability—of which gullibility is a frequent trait—might bring a weapon to school not with the intent to harm others, but because a sibling or peer suggested it. Or a child with an emotional behavioral disorder—which often involves impulse control problems— might threaten to kill a classmate during an altercation. If it is determined that the behavior can be attributed to the disability, the school may still remove the child from the regular school setting in order to ensure the safety of that student and others. However, the school is still responsible for meeting the educational needs of the child. This responsibility may be met by providing educational services in another setting (Skiba, 2002).

In addition to determining, documenting, and sometimes influencing a change of educational placement, Functional Behavioral Assessment results inform the creation of Behavioral Intervention Plans (BIPs). BIPs are plans for the implementation of interventions designed to address the needs of students whose behavior impedes their learning, or who have been referred to alternative placement, suspended for more than 10 days, or placed in alternative settings for weapon or drug offenses (Gargiulo, 2009).

## Identification of Children With Specific Learning Disabilities (SLD)

Approximately 4 to 5% of school-age children are identified as children with specific learning disabilities (SLD). They account for more than 50% of all children served in special education (Gargiulo, 2009). The identification of students with specific learning disabilities has been problematic from the start. Educational researchers looking for the source of learning and performance difficulties experienced by a subgroup of children noted similarities with those experienced by adults who had sustained head injuries. These researchers hypothesized that children who exhibited these difficulties must have sustained undetected brain damage. Further study did not support this line of thinking but led to the creation of a broad disability category called learning disabilities (Harry, 2007).

Children in this category do not have intellectual disabilities; in fact, most of these children have normal IQs. Yet there is a severe discrepancy between expected child performance based on IQ and actual child achievement. These children's learning difficulties are not attributable to behaviors associated with emotional behavioral disabilities, sensory deficits, health or physical factors, or social and environmental factors (Gargiulo, 2009). Although no organic factors have been identified as the source of the problems these children experience, researchers and practitioners continue to attribute the difficulties to intrinsic factors, and the search for organic differences that create learning disabilities continues. Most recently, advances in brain imaging have allowed researchers to compare the brain activity of children who are good readers to that of children who are poor readers. These imaging studies indicate that there are differences in brain activity between the two groups. However, there is no evidence yet to establish a cause-and-effect relationship or to identify which way the relationship goes. The question that remains is whether differences in brain activity contribute to reading difficulties or reading difficulties contribute to differences in brain activity. Early research suggests that intensive reading instruction can alter brain activity, but it is too soon to know how to use this information (Harry, 2007).

Because of the difficulties associated with identifying learning disabilities, discussions of SLD must start with the federal definition. Problems with the federal definition and assessment processes have led to the development of an alternative method of identifying children with learning disabilities, Response to Intervention (RTI). Each is discussed below.

### IDEA

According to IDEA, a specific learning disability is

a disorder in one or more of the basic psychological processes involved in understanding or in using language, spoken or written, that may manifest itself in an imperfect ability to listen, think, speak, read, write, spell, or to do mathematical calculations, including conditions such as perceptual disabilities, brain injury, minimal brain dysfunction, dyslexia, and developmental aphasia. . . . The term does not include learning problems that are primarily the result of visual, hearing, or motor disabilities, of mental retardation, of emotional disturbance, or of environmental, cultural, or economic disadvantage. (Code of Federal Regulations, 2005)

As can be seen, this definition relies heavily on exclusion. An unfortunate artifact of this is that the definition rules out children whose environments are thought to contribute to their learning problems (i.e., children from low-income families). Consequently, low-income children who experience learning difficulties are more likely to be identified as having mild intellectual disabilities than to be placed in the more acceptable category of learning disabilities (Harry, 2007).

Eligibility for services under the category of SLD has traditionally been determined through IQ testing, achievement testing, curriculum-based assessments, observations, and portfolio assessments. To be eligible for services, children must have normal intelligence and, over time, exhibit patterns of severe learning problems in information processing, including severe difficulties in acquisition, storage, organization, retrieval, manipulation, and expression of information. One criticism to this process of determining eligibility has been that, because of the need to exhibit patterns of learning problems, it requires the child to have demonstrated repeated failure before being identified as a child in need of special education (Gargiulo, 2009).

Another common criticism is that the discrepancy analysis conducted under IDEA fails to distinguish learners who are low achieving because of a true learning disability from those whose difficulties stem from not being properly instructed and supported. Because of these concerns, a new, more functional definition has emerged that focuses on the impact of good and/or different instruction prior to referring the child for special education (Gallagher, 2006). Gallagher notes that this type of definition moves the focus from the etiology of the disability to its functional effect and directs attention to types of interventions. This new definition, known as Response to Intervention (RTI), has resulted in the birth of the tiered version of eligibility assessment.

### Response to Intervention (RTI)

Although the number of children identified as having learning disabilities has decreased, experts still worry that far too many children are identified inappropriately (Gallagher, 2006). The 2004 amendments to IDEA addressed this concern by introducing Response to Intervention (RTI) as an alternative approach for identifying students with learning disabilities.

The Individuals with Disabilities Education Improvement Act (IDEIA) of 2004 required states to specify whether they would mandate or permit school districts to use RTI as a method to qualify students as learning disabled, and whether they would prohibit or allow the continued use of severe discrepancy between expected child performance based on IQ and actual child achievement as a method to qualify students. States were also allowed to use an alternative approach to eligibility determination. However, the selected approach had to be research-based. State responses have varied, with 12 states requiring RTI and most of the remaining states permitting use of both RTI and discrepancy analysis. Some states have also decided to include an alternative, research-based option. As a result, in all but 12 states, school districts may still choose how they qualify students for special education services because of learning disabilities (Zirkel, 2010).

RTI employs a three-tiered approach to eligibility determination which measures children's responses to increasingly intensive levels of intervention. Some special education researchers recommend a highly structured process in which special educators play an active role, research-based curricula are used, and evidenced-based practices are employed throughout. Others view RTI as a more informal process that relies on experience, innovation, and problem solving to create differentiated programs in Tier 1, and then adds the expertise of behavioral consultants in Tiers 2 and 3 (Fuchs, Fuchs, & Stecker, 2010). Consequently, the controversies surrounding RTI are not related to its use as a pre-referral process, but rather to the implementation of the process itself (Vaughn, Wanzek, & Denton, 2007). These concerns center around how RTI can be used with older students, and whether educators have sufficient knowledge in diagnostic and formative assessment and research-based interventions to fully implement interventions at the various tiers. However, Vaughn et al. (2007) note that this approach to eligibility assessment has several benefits associated with it, including providing immediate interventions. They state that, as a result, it "eliminates the [current] 'wait to fail' [requirement] . . . and provides a prevention model with early identification of students at risk for academic and/or behavior problems" (pp. 363–364).

A large number of special education researchers who focus on instructional interventions for students with learning disabilities favor a more structured, three-tiered model that has specific procedural criteria embedded in each tier. Tier I in this model focuses on improving instruction for all students. It includes frequent screening for learning difficulties, use of flexible grouping, decision-making based on data derived from benchmark assessments given throughout the year, and high-quality, well-researched instruction and intervention. Because this level refers to the practices used with all students, general educators are the source of instruction and intervention. To ensure that educators are well informed, ongoing professional development is required to assist educators in learning how to use evidence-based practices and in remaining current on emerging practice changes (Vaughn et al., 2007).

Students who do not respond to Tier I instruction or intervention are moved into the supplemental services provided in Tier II. Tier II includes small group instruction that is added to the general classroom instruction; specialized, evidence-based instruction and intervention; and more frequent, regular monitoring of progress (e.g., semi-monthly). Interventions and supplemental instruction may or may not be provided by the general educator, and may or may not occur in the general education classroom. A small percentage of students will not respond as well as they need to at this level. These students will then enter Tier III interventions. This supplemental instruction and intervention increases in intensity and duration (Vaughn et al., 2007).

In addition to broad classroom instruction and intervention, students at Tier III receive even more highly individualized instruction or intervention. Instruction is provided in very small groups, and progress on specific target skills/behaviors or sets of skills/behaviors is monitored frequently. Tier III services typically are provided by specialists who carefully implement all aspects of the selected research-based practices. Like Tier II, instruction may or may not be delivered in the general education classroom. Students who do not respond adequately to Tier III interventions are referred to special education (Vaughn et al., 2007). Concerns related to this approach to RTI include equal access to appropriately trained personnel, the professional development needs of general educators, conflicting philosophies of educators, a lack of resources, and the potential for stigmatization of students removed from the classroom for Tier II and III instruction (Vaughn et al., 2007).

Researchers who favor a more embedded, grassroots model describe the practices and interventions of each tier differently. In this model, Tier I includes differentiated instruction and intervention, universal design, attention to learning styles, flexible grouping, varied pace of instruction, and varied assessments, keeping "students' experiences, interest, learning styles and readiness levels" in mind (Fuchs et al., 2010, p. 312). In Tier II and III, as in the structured model, outside specialists are brought in to consult with teachers on assessment and development of instructional and intervention strategies, with alternative instruction or intervention delivered by specialists in Tier III. Concerns related to this model include access to appropriately trained personnel, the professional development needs of general educators, conflicting philosophies of education, resources, and evidence that general educators will not faithfully implement the needed changes in Tiers I and II. However, it is possible that greater attention to school and teacher accountability measures would create conditions that could address some of these concerns (Fuchs et al., 2010).

## Planning and Progress Monitoring

Assessment in special education sometimes includes formative and summative assessments. Formative assessments are used prior to, during, and at the conclusion of instruction. They may also be used later to determine whether the students have maintained their learning. Summative assessments are always used at the end of instruction.

Formative assessments are used to evaluate a variety of skills, from academics to self-help skills. They may be tightly tied to a specific curriculum, lesson, unit, or particular skill, or they may provide a broad base of information that encompasses a larger array of skills in which the new learning is to be embedded. Finally, they may focus on knowledge and/or performance.

When used prior to instruction, formative assessments provide baseline data about student knowledge and skill levels. This data includes skills and knowledge the student has mastered or partially mastered, and skills and knowledge the student has not mastered. This information is then used to create an individualized instructional program, determine where a student's instruction should begin in the scope and sequence of an existing curriculum, or determine if a student needs specialized instruction or support in only some aspects of the lesson or unit. When used during instruction, formative assessments monitor students' learning progress. This information can and should be used to determine if the instructional program needs to be changed or if there are areas in need of additional instruction. When used at the conclusion of instruction, formative assessment once again provides the data needed to determine the next instructional steps. Curriculum Based Measures (CBM) are commonly used formative assessments (Alonzo, Ketterlin-Geller, & Tindal, 2007). These measures provide specific information about the knowledge or skills of students in specific curricular areas (e.g., reading). Functional assessments are also a type of formative assessment.

Functional assessment refers to assessing actual task performances. It typically involves identifying the steps required in the activity and the sequence or order in which the steps must be performed (depending on the needs of the individual). Functional assessment is often associated with the performance of "functional skills," or those applied skills needed in current and/or future environments. Although these assessments are often used with students with severe disabilities, functional assessment can be used to assess any person's performance on any task (e.g., the driving test required to get a driver's license).

Assessments used for formative purposes may also be used for the summative purposes of documenting the level of learning at the completion of a program, unit, or semester. When used in this manner, the assessments can increase accountability by providing information about student achievement across classrooms, schools, districts, states, and the nation (Bourke & Mentis, 2007).

Although not yet implemented on a large scale, momentum is gaining to develop formative assessments, such as curriculum-based measures, that align with summative, accountability measures (Rouse & McLaughlin, 2007). The potential for the use of structured formative assessments is enormous. They are low-stakes assessments that can be locally adapted to inform instructional decisions at the classroom level. Furthermore, they are critical to the effective implementation of RTI.

Dorn (2010) suggests that cumulative formative assessment and a record of the instructional changes made in light of the results could form the basis for informed decisions about teacher and administrator quality. This potential application creates one of the barriers to the regular use of structured formative assessments. Another challenge is that, in general, formative assessments are viewed as less rigorous than high-stakes summative assessment. Additionally, widespread use of cumulative formative assessment would raise concerns over the capacity of organizations to implement them, as it would require a large investment of staff time and support (Dorn, 2010) to administer the assessments, interpret the results, and alter or individualize the instruction as necessary.

When used appropriately, as in the case of formative measures, assessments can provide educators with the information needed to develop individualized instruction and behavior programs, to monitor students' progress and adjust programs to better meet students' needs, to identify adaptations and accommodations needs, and to assess the effectiveness of those supports. However, assessment is a politically charged activity that exerts the assessor's power over the individual being assessed, whether it is to determine grades, evaluate a teacher's effectiveness, or provide accountability data. These authors feel very strongly that if used properly, assessment can be a positive learning opportunity for both teachers and students.

One way to derive more benefit from assessment is to teach students to self-assess. Supporting students in learning how to set their own goals, determining how to measure their progress, assessing their own progress, and making adjustments to their learning or behavior as needed creates a learning atmosphere that transfers responsibility and power to students (Bourke & Mentis, 2007) and more fully engages students in the learning process. It also addresses the concern of implementation cost, as students share responsibility and time in developing and completing assessment measures. More engaged and committed learners improve learning outcomes. Furthermore, teaching students to self-assess ensures that assessment is relevant to the learner. Finally, it teaches students valuable skills. Recent emphases on teaching students self-determination skills include teaching the skills needed for self-assessment in the belief that these skills are critical to adult functioning. Research clearly indicates that students can accurately assess their own instructional levels, performance, and behavior, and collect their own data (Alberto & Troutman, 2006). In fact, research has shown that individuals who self-assess and monitor their own performance are more likely to make changes in the desired direction, including skill acquisition and behavioral change (Hanley-Maxwell & Collet-Klingenberg, in press).

### Standards and Accountability

Achievement test data, high dropout rates, employer dissatisfaction with employee skills, and other sources of feedback reveal that American schools are not doing a good job in educating students. This failure is especially obvious when looking at the achievement gap, as measured in district-wide assessments, between White students and students who are minorities, have limited English proficiency, live in poverty, or have disabilities, along with the high dropout rates associated with these groups of students. The No Child Left Behind (NCLB) legislation included provisions to address these historic and persistent inequities (Gallagher, 2006; Rouse & McLaughlin, 2007).

NCLB is part of a larger, standards-based reform movement. The intent of this movement is to improve the educational outcomes for all students. Advocates cite the poor academic performance of American students in comparison to students from other developed countries and argue that this poor performance is due, in part, to the lack of accountability and high-quality performance standards in American education (Rouse & McLaughlin, 2007). Consequently, NCLB directed state and local education agencies to "ensure that [all] students are prepared to enter college and the workforce with the skills to succeed" (Hanley-Maxwell & Izzo, in press) by providing them with instruction based in standards that emphasize academic proficiency.

To accomplish the goal of improving education for all students, NCLB created an accountability structure designed to monitor and enforce improvements in educational outcomes, especially for students in the targeted groups. To ensure quality instruction, the law required every school district to be staffed with "highly qualified" personnel. Furthermore, school districts must show adequate yearly progress (AYP) in minimizing the performance gaps that currently exist and in meeting specific standards/goals articulated at the federal, state, and local levels. One of the primary mandates relates to standardized testing of "all" students (a small number of students, usually those with the most severe disabilities, are tested using alternative formats, as designated in their IEPs). As such, NCLB dictates more frequent grade-level testing, currently at Grades 3 through 8 and once during high school, using a minimum of three levels of performance: basic, proficient, and advanced. If a school or district fails to meet AYP, that school or district is more closely monitored in terms of testing outcomes over the next few years, and close scrutiny is given to corrective actions taken to try to meet AYP. Cumulative failure to show AYP across the board opens the door for corrective action at the state and then the federal level (Gallagher, 2006; Rouse & McLaughlin, 2007).

One of the enforcement options included in NCLB involves enhancing parents' voices in their children's educational outcomes. With the new reporting measures, parents of children in "nonperforming schools" have the option of asking for and receiving tutoring or other special programs for their children, or of moving their children to a school where AYP is being demonstrated. Other enforcement options include requiring failing schools to restructure, converting them to charter schools, or subjecting them to state takeover (Rouse & McLaughlin, 2007).

The federal government emphasized the importance of the NCLB mandates for students with disabilities by explicitly aligning IDEA with NCLB through the 2004 amendments. Recent research reveals that including students with disabilities in high-stakes standardized tests improves their performance on these assessments. Unfortunately, inclusion in these assessments has not reduced the achievement gap between students with and without disabilities. As a result, the use of standardized tests as accountability measures for students with disabilities is still controversial. Proponents say that these measures are necessary to ensure educational equity, while opponents say that the format of standardized testing disadvantages students with disabilities. Additional controversies surrounding accountability assessment for students with disabilities include the use of alternative assessments (who receives alternative assessments), the use of adaptations and accommodations (whether they invalidate the results), and data sharing and reporting (exclusion of data related to students with disabilities because of the use of adaptations and accommodations or low numbers of students in a given category). Critics raise concerns that these three aspects subvert the purpose of accountability assessment (Rouse & McLaughlin, 2007). Finally, concerns about the focus and content of standards for students without disabilities may overshadow the learning needs of students with disabilities. The academic content focus of high-stakes testing may result in teachers excluding content and instruction in areas of vital importance to post-school success, such as social skills, vocational skills, and community living skills. Although alternative exams may include this content, the number of students who are approved to participate in alternative assessment is extremely small. The number of students who have IEP goals in these areas is likely to be larger than the number who participate in alternative assessment. For these students, the emphasis on meeting academic standards may result in lopsided instruction that focuses solely on academic goals, thus meeting only part of their needs (Gallagher, 2006). A related issue that is impacted by testing for accountability has to do with the location of instruction for learners with IEPs.

# Placement: Inclusion Versus Continuum

Today, special education services are provided in a variety of environments, from general education classrooms to separate public or private schools, including schools for the deaf, to correctional institutions (National Center for Educational Statistics, 2010a). Locations may also include homes, community settings, and places of employment. Significant controversy has surrounded the conception of special education as a place. As early as the 1960s, prior to the creation and implementation of the landmark Education for All Handicapped Children Act (EAHCA), Lloyd Dunn (1968) questioned the efficacy of segregated special education programs for children with mild intellectual disabilities. Dunn saw special education as a program that used highly effective instructional strategies in separate settings to fix these children so that they could return to the general education classrooms, able to learn commensurately with their non-disabled peers. He questioned the viability of these separate programs because they were not living up to their original intent; most students with mild intellectual disabilities were not returning to general education, and those few who did were still unable to learn equally with their general education peers. Although other researchers agreed with Dunn that special education programs should include potent instructional strategies, they believed that using its best practices would not be enough for some children, and that these children would always need specialized programs in separate spaces. To that end, Evelyn Deno (1970) advocated for a continuum of service alternatives that spanned separate special education settings (including the highly restrictive settings or residential schools and hospitals) to general education classrooms.

The "place" controversy has taken many forms in the years since Dunn and Deno's work, including mainstreaming, the Regular Education Initiative, and full inclusion. The vagueness of IDEA's requirement that special education services be provided in the Least Restrictive Environment has fueled the debate, and subsequent reauthorizations of IDEA have only added to the controversies. Today's controversies of place are reflected in previous discussions related to disproportional representation, labeling, and Response to Intervention (RTI). They are also reflected in discussions to come in the areas of curriculum, instruction, and secondary special education. Furthermore, some of the issues that ground these controversies are beginning to play out in post-secondary education. Regardless of the controversy, data reveal that a large percentage of students with disabilities are being educated in general education settings for the vast majority of their instruction days (Sullivan & Kozleski, 2009, as cited in Artilles et al., 2010). For example, data from 2006 indicate that nearly 54% of students with disabilities spend more than 80% of their days in general education. However, this same data set reveals significant differences among the disability categories. Students with speech or language impairments are most likely to spend more than 80% of their days in general education, whereas students with intellectual disabilities or multiple disabilities are highly unlikely to spend this amount of time in general education. In fact, over 40% of students with intellectual disabilities or multiple disabilities spend less than 40% of their school day in general education settings (National Center for Educational Statistics, 2010a).

Since its inception, special education has had an unsettled relationship with general education. While most educators agree that students with disabilities learn valuable skills in general education settings, they do not agree on whether effective instruction can be provided in the general education classroom. Proponents of doing away with special education as a place call for educating all students with disabilities in general education classrooms, with supports and services provided in a manner consistent with those provided to students without disabilities. Proponents of maintaining special education as a place, on the other hand, advocate for a continuum of services that includes both general education classrooms and specialized settings.

Researchers, scholars, educators, and parents who advocate for special education as a continuum of services that includes separate settings ground their argument in the history of education for children with disabilities, noting general education's failure to educate all children effectively. Furthermore, they cite research that describes undesirable conditions for students with disabilities in general education classrooms. These proponents of a separate, though loosely related system of special education also cite the following criticisms of general educators: unfavorable attitudes toward students with disabilities; reluctance to utilize differentiated instruction; and lack of knowledge related to effective interventions for students with disabilities. They argue that students with disabilities need specialized instruction and/or curricula, and that many evidence-based practices are incompatible with general education structures, resources, and philosophies (Fuchs et al., 2010; Gallagher, 2006).

Proponents of a dual education system argue that if general educators are to be effective with students with disabilities, they must be prepared to teach all students, including those with special needs. However, it is not feasible and may not be desirable to prepare all teachers to teach all children. While they acknowledge that outcomes for students with disabilities have been poor, they claim that these outcomes are not due to structural problems, but rather are primarily the result of a lack of implementation of best practices. Proponents of special education as a continuum also express concern that if special education loses its separate identity, it will also lose its special budget allocations and focus on personnel. They worry that merging two historically distinct systems of education will result in the extinction of special education, and that, consequently, the unique needs of students with disabilities will not be addressed (Gallagher, 2006). They believe that the only way to ensure that students with disabilities get the appropriate, individualized education to which they are entitled is to provide a continuum of services to accommodate the range of needs students have.

Proponents of educating students with disabilities only in general education settings (sometimes called full inclusion) also ground some of their arguments in the rights of students with disabilities get an appropriate, individualized education. However, they argue that providing this education in separate settings denies these students access to the same educational opportunities as their peers without disabilities have. They cite poor outcome data and disproportional representation as symptoms of the structural problems related to maintaining special education as a separate setting. Furthermore, they argue that the methods used to identify children with disabilities are invalid, unreliable, and stigmatizing, and that they reify a flawed conception that equates all difference with deficit. They state that full inclusion is necessary to provide all students, regardless of their disabilities, with an appropriate education free of stigma or discrimination (Florian, 2007). "Proponents of inclusive education believe . . . that access to challenging curriculum, higher expectations, and interactions with peers without disabilities [are] compelling reasons for students with disabilities to be educated in general education classrooms" (Hanley-Maxwell & Bottge, 2006, p. 176). Finally, proponents of single location, general education believe that the integration of the two systems will result in the creation of a more flexible and responsive system that will meet the needs of all students, and will perhaps better address the needs of learners who are considered to be at-risk but do not currently qualify for special education.

Beyond the debate about whether or not students with disabilities should receive all or most of their education in general education classrooms, questions have been raised about the capacity of general education to ensure successful outcomes for all learners. For inclusive education to be successful, school cultures must change. Administrators must actively support inclusive education by creating an atmosphere in which inclusive education is expected. They must also provide general and special education teachers with enough time to collaboratively create differentiated instruction (by developing curricular and instructional accommodations) and universally designed lessons and assessments, as well as with the freedom to explore new roles and partnerships, the professional development they need, and additional resources as necessary.

Secondary schools pose special challenges to inclusive education. In addition to placing increased demands on student independence and responsibility, the structure of secondary schools is less flexible than that of elementary schools. Instructional time often is governed by set schedules, the emphasis is on curricular content rather than learning processes and instructional supports, and the varying purposes of secondary education (e.g., college preparation, vocational preparation) begin to come in conflict. The inflexible structure, levels of content knowledge, increasingly disparate needs of students with disabilities, and overreliance on large group instruction at the secondary level make successful inclusive environments more difficult to create and sustain (Hanley-Maxwell & Bottge, 2006).

## Curriculum

The content of curriculum has been debated in all of education (Rose, 2007). Employers decry the fact that schools fail to provide necessary employment skills, and politicians express concerns that American children are not being prepared to compete in global markets (Hanley-Maxwell & Izzo, in press). Regardless of the specific criticism, most experts agree that American schools are not successful in preparing all children for adult life. These issues are magnified in special education, where curriculum is supposed to be matched to the needs of individual students. This match is intended to improve the cognitive, social, developmental, and functional outcomes for these students (Rose, 2007), and yet long-term outcome data for students in special education does not paint a positive picture (Newman, Wagner, Cameto, & Knokey, 2009).

Curriculum in special education has focused on identifying student deficits and then creating instructional programs to address those deficits. This deficit focus reflects the pervasive medical/deficit model of special education. Another major theoretical underpinning of special education, behavioral psychology, focuses on observable and measurable behavior (Rose, 2007). Many special education curricula reflect this underpinning, resulting in curricula that include general education content with different instructional methods (i.e., differentiated instruction); adapted general education content; or content that deviates from or supplements the general education content. Deviations and supplements have included a focus on applied content in the areas of work, independent living, leisure and recreation, self-care and community use, social skills, communication, and more recently, learning strategies and self-determination (e.g., self-assessment, self-monitoring, self-instruction, self-management, self-advocacy, problem solving, choice and decision making, goal setting and attainment). The curriculum for students with emotional and behavioral disabilities was and is especially problematic in segregated special education settings. This curriculum tends to be void of academics, instead focusing on behavior management (Harry, 2007) and social skills. In general, special education curricula have been criticized for their reduced focus on academic knowledge and low academic expectations for students.

As students with disabilities spend more time in general education settings, participate in high-stakes assessment, and are held to the same academic standards as their non-disabled peers, increasingly they will be exposed to general education curriculum content (Rose, 2007). Some professionals and researchers fear that this will result in failure to meet the spectrum of needs of individual students (Rose, 2007). Their fears about the general education curriculum include a greater concern for group achievement than individual student achievement, a reduced focus on the development of support and process skills (e.g., self-determination, learning strategies), and the loss of instructional time and space needed to help students acquire critical functional skills. Curricular issues are especially problematic at the high school level, where professionals and parents must make decisions about the value of students' participation in content classes that far outstrip their knowledge and skills and possibly limit attainment of functional life skills.

## Instruction and Intervention

Instructional strategies used by special educators have often been different from those used by general educators. Instruction may be provided using traditional instructional approaches (e.g., whole and small group) or alternative instructional approaches (e.g., individual, collaborative groups, peer tutoring, project based, computer assisted, applied learning). Special education instruction often uses direct instruction strategies that employ principles of applied behavior analysis (ABA). Behavioral interventions and classroom management strategies also typically apply principles of applied behavior analysis to increase desirable and decrease undesirable behavior.

Controversies in instruction often center on the needs of students with learning disabilities, reflecting concerns about the increasing trend toward educating students with disabilities in general education classrooms, as well as rapidly changing knowledge bases. Researchers in the area of learning disabilities have built an extensive and impressive database related to effective instructional practices for most students with learning disabilities, especially in the area of reading instruction. This research clearly indicates that the most effective instruction for students with learning disabilities explicitly teaches all steps in a task and systematically controls the difficulty of the task to allow the student to build on previous learning (i.e., scaffolding). It also provides many and varying opportunities for student practice, coupled with immediate, corrective feedback. Finally, teachers must continuously monitor progress and make instructional decisions based on data obtained (Vaughn et al., 2007). This method of instruction requires significant teacher time and attention, and thus it is clearly not applicable to large group instruction or pedagogy that focuses on students constructing their own learning through interacting with the instructional materials. Consequently, proponents of this approach believe that students with learning disabilities cannot be adequately served in fully inclusive educational settings, and instead advocate for the continuation of alternative settings, as needed.

Other issues in instruction relate to the changing roles of professionals and paraprofessionals. These roles are changing in response to inclusive education. These roles are also changing as school districts contend with declining budgets and serious shortages of trained special educators, at a time when special education enrollments are climbing. Proponents of inclusive education see this constellation of issues as one more reason why all students should be served in general education settings, allowing special educators to take on other roles.

Today, special educators or related service professionals may provide indirect supports to students. These supports include collaborating with general educators to create universally designed lessons and activities that allow all students to access, participate, and perform without modifications or adaptations. They may also work with general educators to create differentiated lessons and activities by adapting or modifying instruction, materials, level or depth of content, learning performances and products, and assessments to meet the learning and/or performance needs of individual students (with or without disabilities). They may help general educators interpret results from assessments that are part of RTI, and they may coach general educators in providing interventions to students at risk for or experiencing learning difficulties. Finally, special education professionals may provide indirect support by working with general educators to design and implement behavioral interventions and supports in general education classrooms and other school settings (Vaughn et al., 2007).

In an inclusive model, special educators, paraprofessionals, and related service providers may also provide direct services. Related service professionals may provide their intervention in separate settings, such as speech and language therapy rooms, or within the context of the students' instructional environments. Special educators may co-teach or team teach with general educators in general education classrooms, and they may provide supporting or alternative instruction in a variety of settings (e.g., general education classrooms, special education classrooms, community settings, places of employment) (Vaughn et al., 2007).

## Secondary Special Education

Despite changes in American society over the years, the primary purpose of education has remained the same: to create an educated workforce of adults prepared for roles and responsibilities as citizens in a democracy. In recent years, preparation for employment has moved to the forefront of this overarching purpose. The rationales for this move include the need to keep America economically strong by preparing workers who will be innovative, productive, and competitive in a worldwide economy, as well as the need to keep America and Americans safe and healthy through advances in science and technology (Hanley-Maxwell & Izzo, in press). As such, education is seen as the vehicle with which Americans can eliminate barriers to earning a living wage, thus reducing dependence on public assistance programs and broadening adult options. In other words, education is intended "to prepare youth to become productive members of society [by] maintaining employment, being good citizens, paying taxes, and contributing to our economy" (Hanley-Maxwell & Izzo, in press).

If schools are to prepare youth for future adult roles as workers, citizens, and family members, teachers and administrators must be concerned with what students learn, how content is presented to ensure learning, and how material learned in school applies to real life. Furthermore, because job skills and related roles and functions are continuously evolving, schools need to prepare students to be flexible, lifelong learners so that they can adjust to these changes by learning new skills as needed. Since the publication of *A Nation at Risk* in 1983 (U.S. National Commission on Excellence in Education), concerns have been raised about the success of schools in meeting these goals. More recently, the efficacy of American education has been questioned as it relates to preparing children to be productive societal members who can successfully compete in a global economy, especially in the areas of high skills and high wages (Hanley-Maxwell & Izzo, in press). Although these issues have implications for all levels of schooling, they acquire a sense of urgency at the secondary education level, as school leaving becomes imminent. Unfortunately, at this level, education for youth with disabilities becomes more complex, and the need to address student-related issues (e.g., truancy, drug use, need for increased self-management) becomes more urgent.

Secondary special education is a layered system. Some students remain in school until age 22, while others exit at different ages and in different ways. School services for young adults with disabilities who remain in the K–12 school system after age 18 vary. Some youth continue to work toward their diplomas by completing the general education curriculum in regular school or alternative settings. For others, the primary focus of their education has shifted to the development of functional living and vocational skills. These students receive instruction in independent living (e.g., home living, self-care, money management, cooking), community access and participation (e.g., grocery shopping, using mass transit, leisure and recreation, voting), and employment (e.g., job seeking, job skills) in the appropriate corresponding settings. They also continue to work on functional academic skills (e.g., reading, math) and social-interpersonal skills (e.g., self-management, self-advocacy) (Hanley-Maxwell & Collet-Klingenberg, in press).

Regardless of age, youth and young adults with disabilities have several ways to exit from high school. These include dropping out, receiving a certificate (e.g., locally offered, completion via attendance, course completion requirements, Pre-GED/Skills Option), or receiving a standard or differentiated/modified diploma (e.g., high distinction, honors, standard basic, IEP, occupational, Alternative Adult [GED], advanced studies, modified standard, alternate completion). These and other variations exist because state laws related to high school completion vary. In some states, the state government sets the criteria and names the options; in other states, local school boards set the criteria and name the options. Criteria for diplomas and certificates include Carnegie unit completion (class credits in specific content areas), exit or competency exams, standards achievement, advanced coursework, and grade point average (Johnson & Thurlow, 2003).

Controversies and issues abound in relation to high school completion and secondary education in general, and more specifically for youth ages 18 to 22 who are still being served in the K–12 systems. Parents and advocates express concerns about how students with disabilities exit high school and what they receive at the point of school leaving, because these factors affect post-secondary opportunities and outcomes. For example, students who drop out of high school earn significantly less than their peers with diplomas (Hanley-Maxwell & Izzo, in press). Similarly, access to post-secondary education may be limited or students may be required to complete remedial coursework as a result of receiving a non-standard diploma, and employers may view students with non-standard diplomas as less qualified (Johnson & Thurlow, 2003).

Because of the issues related to exiting and the post-school implications, all the problems in general and special education come to the forefront when children with disabilities enter high school. Missed learning opportunities, lack of educational achievement, and dramatically different school structures collide with the thorny issues of adolescence and dwindling years of educational entitlement to create especially intractable problems.

Research reveals a myriad of problems related to secondary education for students with disabilities. These students are less likely than their non-disabled peers to complete a full academic curriculum in high school, especially in the areas of math and science, and more likely to have taken remedial course work. They are also likely to have lower grade point averages and lower SAT scores. Furthermore, many never finish high school, opting instead to drop out. Studies of high school IEPs reveal that students with disabilities rarely participate in extracurricular activities, enrichment programs, or community-based youth programs, which affects their friendships and other social connections while in high school and after high school.

The National Longitudinal Transition Study (NLTS I and II) has gathered data on students with disabilities since the early 1990s. Recent analyses (Wagner, Newman, & Cameto, 2004) provide a snapshot of how students with disabilities are faring in high schools. The grades of high school students with disabilities have improved over the past decade, with most students receiving at least passing grades and many moving from Cs to As and Bs. Access to academic courses in general education classrooms increased by more than 20%, with approximately 30% of these students taking courses in math, science, social studies, and foreign languages. Adaptive technology, curricular and instructional supports, and social supports such as mental health, social work, and health services are more readily available. Furthermore, more students with disabilities are succeeding socially, following the rules and getting along with their teachers and peers. Finally, in recent years, students with disabilities have been more likely to be both employed and attending school during their high school years.

Despite these positive patterns, a closer look at secondary classrooms revealed continuing academic and social problems. Approximately 25% of the general education teachers noted that students with disabilities experienced problems in keeping up in their work and being engaged in academic class activities and assignments. This may have been due in part to the students being far below grade level in math and reading, as well as being absent more frequently. Students with disabilities also experienced social problems resulting in school disciplinary actions, arrests, and job terminations, and these social problems were associated with lower grades. Furthermore, although the students received higher grades than their counterparts in the previous decade, these grades did not coincide with improved academic achievement, as measured by standardized achievement tests (Newman, 2006). Finally, dropout rates for students with disabilities remained distressingly high. For example, in 2001–2002, two-thirds of students identified as having emotional disabilities and one-third of students identified as having learning disabilities or mild intellectual disabilities dropped out of school.

In-school problems and dropout statistics reveal only part of the problem. Studies also show that only 45% of youth with disabilities participate in post-secondary education, compared to 53% of their peers without disabilities (Newman et al., 2009). Although these data reflect improvements, results from a 2004 Harris survey show there are still large gaps between students with and without disabilities in terms of college completion. Only 12% of students with disabilities finish college, versus 23% of their nondisabled counterparts (as cited in Hanley-Maxwell & Izzo, in press). In total, this picture suggests that few youth with disabilities are getting the education needed to compete for better-paying jobs (Hanley-Maxwell & Izzo, in press). Furthermore, rates of post-secondary unemployment and underemployment are high. For example, the National Longitudinal Transition Survey (NLTS-2) reported the results of follow-up contact with former students with disabilities. The survey found that while 66% of youth had jobs, only 53% of youth with disabilities were working (Hanley-Maxwell & Izzo, in press). Additionally, the 2009 Annual Disability Statistics Compendium (as cited in Hanley-Maxwell & Izzo, in press) reported that employment rates for adults living in the community were approximately 75% for those without disabilities and only 36.2% for those with disabilities. These poor employment and post-secondary education rates may reflect the fact that students with disabilities are not reaching secondary education with the skills they need to succeed and flourish, and may indicate that secondary schools are not providing access to curricula and experiences that prepare these students for employment and further education (Hanley-Maxwell & Izzo, in press).

What is even more distressing is that these conditions still exist after nearly 35 years of federally mandated public education and 20 years of federally mandated transition planning. Clearly, students with disabilities are still not achieving equitable outcomes. The current environment—with competing mandates of high-stakes testing, inclusion, and vocational/life preparation—will undoubtedly continue to confuse high school educators as they attempt to meet the needs of students with disabilities. Fortunately, there are some promising high school reform efforts that hold great promise for students with disabilities, including those focusing on employment preparation for all students and using applied or blended curricular approaches (Wills, 2008).

## Post-Secondary Education

Historically, after high school most students with disabilities have not continued into post-secondary education. However, in recent years, more students with disabilities have accessed post-secondary education after completing their K–12 education (Newman et al., 2009). Students with disabilities can choose from a variety of post-secondary options, which include colleges and universities, vocational and technical schools, and community colleges, with community colleges currently being the preference for most students with disabilities (Shaw, 2007). Students with disabilities have a right to access post-secondary education programs and services, and to access accommodations within those settings. As described in Chapter 1, these rights were established by Section 504 of the Rehabilitation Act of 1973, and later by the Americans with Disabilities Act of 1990 (ADA). Section 504 and ADA apply to students at all levels of education (and beyond education).

However, with high school graduation, the entitlements of IDEA cease, because IDEA applies only to the K–12 education system. What this means is that the K–12 responsibility for identifying students with disabilities, assessing those students, and planning for (via the IEP) and delivering their services does not exist at the post-secondary level. Instead, post-secondary education institutions have to guarantee equal access to their programs and services (e.g., to instruction, assessment, clubs, events, athletics, financial aid, housing) by providing reasonable accommodations to eligible students (i.e., those who have a documented disability as defined in Section 504 or the ADA) (see Chapter 1; Shaw, 2007). Despite these legal requirements, youth with disabilities who want to continue their education in post-secondary settings face challenges related to access and accommodations. This section describes those challenges and introduces the most recent trend in post-secondary education: post-secondary programs for young adults with severe disabilities.

## Access and Accommodation in Post-Secondary Education

Students with disabilities who are admitted to a university/college or a specific program are admitted only because they have met typical entrance requirements. Colleges and programs do not have to alter admissions requirements to make access easier for individuals with disabilities. After they are admitted to regular college programs, students with disabilities have to identify themselves to the disability service provider (DSP) and provide disability documentation that meets specific requirements. The documentation must (a) come from an appropriate and qualified professional (e.g., psychiatrist), (b) confirm the existence of an appropriately verified disability, (c) describe the functional limitations created by the disability, (d) describe the impact of the disability on the student (especially as it relates to the academic setting—if possible), and (e) suggest accommodations.

High schools can help make this process smoother. One way to do this is to understand the documentation differences between what is required for the IEP and what is required for the specific institution in which the student hopes to enroll. Most students who have IEPs have the beginnings of the basic documentation required to access post-secondary disability service. However, the documentation may not be sufficient, and not all students with IEPs will be eligible for post-secondary services. Furthermore, some post-secondary students who were not eligible under IDEA will be eligible under Section 504/ADA (Sitlington & Clark, 2005). Consequently, students with disabilities and their secondary education teachers need to check with the institution that the student wants to attend to find out what its specific requirements are in terms of content and form of the documentation.

Information sharing related to disability and accommodation needs is trickier in post-secondary settings because of confidentiality requirements. Consequently, it is important that students with disabilities understand the differences between the K–12 system and post-secondary systems. Both systems must abide by Family Educational Rights and Privacy Act (FERPA) regulations. But because the student in post-secondary education is over age 18, and college programs are not viewed as one unified system, post-secondary institutions comply with FERPA requirements differently than K–12 school systems. At the post-secondary education level, students must initiate sharing information about their disability with the DSP; there is no case manager to do this for them, and parents may not act in their stead without explicit written permission. Furthermore, unlike what happens in the K–12 system, the DSP cannot share any disability-related information with faculty/instructors unless the student has signed a release. Even then, it is still up to the student to contact instructors to self-identify and discuss accommodations. Instructors may not share any information they receive about the student with anyone else, including parents, without the student's explicit permission (U.S. Department of Education, Office for Civil Rights, 2007).

After being found eligible for services by the DSP, typically students are provided with "accommodations verifications" that certify they are entitled to receive specific types of accommodations. These verifications must then be communicated to the instructors of each of the courses the student takes. How these accommodations are provided varies from institution to institution, and sometimes from program to program within an institution. It is important to stress that at the post-secondary level, students are responsible for initiating the process of becoming eligible for services and for following through on institutional requirements to obtain those services (Shaw, 2007).

Although accommodations vary at the post-secondary level, there are some common accommodations provided that go beyond guaranteeing physical access to building, activities, or housing. These include testing accommodations such as providing extended time on tests (double or 1.5 times the regular amount), taking tests/exams in a room with reduced distractions, and supplying a scribe and/or reader for the test taker. Other common accommodations include improving access to text by providing alternative media formats (e.g., large print or Braille, digital audio CD in an MP3 format, audio cassette, e-text, Kurzweil Reader software) and in-class accommodations (e.g., note takers, sign language interpreters, preferential seating, food and/or beverages permitted in classes, assistive technology in labs). Other often-provided accommodations include reduced course loads, waivers of content requirements not critical to the degree (e.g., foreign language classes), assistive technology (e.g., software programs, text readers), and priority course registration.

The typical accommodations are provided at no extra cost to eligible students. Some universities/colleges offer other services through a fee-based system. Such services might include specialized transportation, tutors, summer support programs, and diagnostic services. For example, the University of Connecticut (Beyond Access Services, 2010) offers four fee-based programs that target the needs of students with Asperger's, learning disabilities, ADHD, and psychiatric disabilities:

1. Strategic Education for Students with Autism Spectrum Disorder (SEAD) provides support and training in academic and social skills for students with Asperger's.

2. Building Opportunities for Students with Learning Disabilities (BOLD) focuses on creating a supportive learning environment and training students in the use of study skills and assistive technology.

3. Tutoring PLUS provides individualized support and tutoring services to students with learning disabilities, ADHD, and/or psychiatric disabilities.

4. Focused Academic Skill Training (FAST), open to all students, targets the development of study skills, time management, test taking, problem solving, and self-advocacy, and includes group workshops and weekly meetings with a strategy instructor.

Finally, some universities/colleges are designed for students with specific disabilities. For example, Gallaudet University is internationally known for its liberal arts education for deaf and hard-of-hearing undergraduate students, and its graduate programs for deaf, hard-of-hearing, and hearing students. The university is a fully accessible campus that provides instruction and other interpersonal communication bilingually, in American Sign Language and English (About Gallaudet, 2010).

There are also limits to what accommodations post-secondary institutions are expected to provide. All accommodations at this level must be reasonable accommodations, as described in Section 504 and the ADA. Accommodations may not create an excessive financial burden on the institution; cause health or safety risks to faculty, staff, or students; or go against established codes of conduct. Furthermore, as Patricia Sitlington and Gary Clark (2005) explain, reasonable accommodations must not "result in unfair advantage, require significant alteration to the program or activity, [or] result in lower academic or technical standards" (p. 225). Thus, the process of accessing reasonable and appropriate accommodations must be student initiated, and those accommodations are typically limited to supplemental services, environmental changes, and supplemental "tools" (Sitlington & Clark, 2005).

Because high schools and colleges are very different systems, all students must understand the differences—and teachers must prepare them to deal with the differences—if they are going to be successful in the post-secondary setting. Low college-completion rates may indicate that students with disabilities are not being adequately prepared to adjust to the structure and format, as well as the social requirements (with the onus being on the student), associated with post-secondary education. Additionally, it is critical that students understand that colleges/universities have continuation criteria (e.g., grade point average) that must be met if the student is to keep his/her place in the program (Sitlington & Clark, 2005).

As referred to above, a major change for many students with disabilities involves who leads service provision and management. In the K–12 system, a case manager coordinates and oversees services. In post-secondary education (and most other adult service systems), the person with a disability is expected to be self-determined and self-managed, and thus in charge of his or her service needs. Students with disabilities exiting high school are often not prepared with the skills or expectations to effectively manage their own case. Furthermore, some students arrive in colleges and universities with continuing skill development needs in the areas of organization, study skills, and test preparation. Some colleges/universities recognize that many students arrive on campus with these skill development needs and offer short courses and other support services to assist students. Additionally, disability service providers may offer supplemental programs and services to provide more intense or ongoing support for students whose disabilities include deficits in these areas. However, as stated earlier, ultimately it is up to the student to determine his or her own success in post-secondary education (Sitlington & Clark, 2005).

## Post-Secondary Programs for Individuals With Significant Disabilities

Recently, some universities/colleges have begun offering programs that include accommodations and adaptations specifically for students with significant disabilities (including intellectual and multiple disabilities) who previously have not been eligible for college. REACH and Cutting Edge are two examples of these programs. The University of Iowa offers REACH: Realizing Education and Career Hopes (REACH, 2010). This program is a two-year, residential, on-campus program designed to improve the employment readiness, independent living, and community participation of its students. To graduate, REACH students complete a liberal arts curriculum that is similar to the undergraduate curriculum, and participate in extensive career exploration, including job-getting skills and career internships. Additionally, they must participate in activities that focus on developing independent living and working skills. REACH students also participate in other collegiate activities (e.g., events, intramural sports, residence hall activities, student organizations). Graduates of the two-year program earn a certificate (REACH, 2010).

The Cutting-Edge Program at Edgewood College in Madison, Wisconsin, is a one-year program designed to meet the needs of individual students. Some coursework is designed to meet individualized independent living and working goals. Other coursework targets skills building in common areas of community safety, social relationships and social skills, and community participation. Additionally, Cutting-Edge students explore potential careers through short work experiences, job shadowing, and tours; and learn job-getting skills (e.g., developing a resume). Students who live on-campus also learn independent living skills, such a self-care, money management, and interpersonal communication. All students must complete an internship that specifically focuses on developing vocational skills and social skills, and a summer outreach project that focuses on developing independent living skills—including home living, community use, and interpersonal relationships in residential settings—in an intensive one-week residential experience (Cutting-Edge Program, 2010).

For all post-secondary learners, the issues and controversies at this level of education include the definition of disability, what constitutes reasonable accommodation, how accommodations and adaptations affect program standards and expectations, and universal design. Other issues focus on increasing post-secondary education participation, assisting students with disabilities in the transition from high school to college, and improving the graduation rates for students with disabilities. As stated above and worth stating again, the teaching of skills related to self-determination and self-advocacy is a critical component of post school success! Continuing retention issues suggest that students with disabilities lack adequate academic and support skill preparation for higher education (Sitlington & Clark, 2005).

## Conclusion

We began this chapter by listing some of the many questions raised during the decades-long struggle for educational equality in this country. Throughout the chapter, we explored these questions and related issues in relation to service provision across age/grade levels. We placed particular emphasis on the historical and current tensions inherent in both labeling learners (and disproportional representation) and in the language used to describe interventions (i.e., ABA and RTI). We also presented a brief discussion of the controversy surrounding the high-stakes testing that has emerged since the passage of NCLB in 2001.

Controversy has been an indelible aspect of special education since its inception. While some lament the ongoing debates and often heated discussions, perhaps it is for the best that we do not settle for a system of education that has not yet satisfactorily answered the questions of whether children are prepared for adult life, whether teachers are adequately prepared, and how best to improve post-school outcomes. Interestingly, the cyclical nature of controversy closely parallels the cycles of progress and setback discussed in Chapter 1. For sure, controversy incites change. Regardless of the side they take in any of the arguments, most stakeholders would agree that the status of special education should not remain static. It is through intelligent and respectful conversations and research about the disparities within the field of special education—and with regard to the perspectives of all involved, most especially individuals with disabilities and their families—that we will continue to shape a better educational future for all individuals.

# References

About Gallaudet. (2010). Retrieved from http://aaweb.gallaudet.edu/About.xml

Alberto, P., & Troutman, A. (2006). *Applied behavior analysis for teachers* (7th ed.). Upper Saddle River, NJ: Pearson Education.

Alonzo, J., Ketterlin-Geller, L. R., & Tindal, G. (2007). Curriculum-based measurement in reading and math: Providing rigorous outcomes to support learning. In L. Florian (Ed.), *The Sage Handbook of Special Education* (pp. 307–318). London: Sage.

Artilles, A. J., Kozleski, E., Trent, S., Osher, D., & Ortiz, A. (2010). Justifying and explaining disproportionality, 1968–2008: A critique of underlying views of culture. *Exceptional Children, 76,* 279–299.

Benner, S. M. (1998). *Issues in special education within the context of American society.* Belmont, CA: Wadsworth.

Beyond Access Services. (2010). Retrieved from http://www.csd.uconn.edu/beyond_access.html

Blatt, B., & Kaplan, F. (1966). *Christmas in purgatory: A photographic essay on mental retardation.* Boston: Allyn & Bacon.

Bourke, R., & Mentis, M. (2007). Self-assessment as a lens for learning. In L. Florian (Ed.), *The Sage Handbook of Special Education* (pp. 319–330). London: Sage.

Bruder, M. B. (2010). Early childhood intervention: A promise to children and families for their future. *Exceptional Children, 76,* 399–355.

Byrnes, M. (2007). *Taking sides: Clashing views on controversial issues in special education.* Columbus, OH: Dushkin/McGraw-Hill.

Callahan, K., Shukla-Mehta, S., Magee, S., & Wie, M. (2010). ABA versus TEACCH: The case for defining and validating comprehensive treatment models in autism. *Journal of Autism and Developmental Disorders, 40,* 74–88.

Code of Federal Regulations. (2005, December). Title 34: Education. Retrieved from http://cfr.vlex.com/vid/75–105-annual-priorities-19756233

Council for Exception Children (CEC). (2010). CEC identifies critical issues facing special education. Retrieved from http://www.cec.sped.org/AM/Template.cfm?Section=Home&CONTENTID=8598&TEMPLATE=/CM/ContentDisplay.cfm

Cutting-Edge Program. (2010). Retrieved from http://www.edgewood.edu/prospective/undergraduate/cuttingEdge/default.aspx

Data Accountability Center. (2010). *Table 1–16. Students ages 6 through 21 served under IDEA, Part B, by race/ethnicity and state: 2004.* Retrieved from https://www.ideadata.org/arc_toc6.asp#partbCC

Deno, E. (1970). Special education as developmental capital. *Exceptional Children, 37(3),* 229–237.

Disability Rights Education and Defense Fund. (2008). Retrieved from http://www.dredf.org/about/index.shtml

Dorn, S. (2010). The political dilemmas of formative assessment. *Exceptional Children, 76(3),* 325–337.

Dunn, L. E. (1968). Special education for the mentally retarded: Is much of it justifiable? *Exceptional Children, 35,* 5–22.

Florian, L. (2007). Reimagining special education. In L. Florian (Ed.), *The Sage Handbook of Special Education* (pp. 7–20). Thousand Oaks, CA: Sage.

Fowler, S. A., Ostrosky, M. M., & Yates, T. J. (2007). Teaching and learning in the early years. In L. Florian (Ed.), *The Sage Handbook of Special Education* (pp. 349–359). Thousand Oaks, CA: Sage.

Fuchs, D., Fuchs, L. S., & Stecker, P. M. (2010). The blurring of special education in the new continuum of general education placements and services. *Exceptional Children, 76,* 301–323.

Gallagher, J. (2006). *Driving change in special education.* Baltimore, MD: Brookes.

Gargiulo, R. M. (2009). *Special education in contemporary society: An introduction to exceptionality* (3rd ed.). Thousand Oaks, CA: Sage.

Hallahan, D. P., Kauffman, J. M., & Pullen, P. C. (2009). *Exceptional learners: An introduction to special education* (11th ed.). Boston: Allyn & Bacon.

Hanley-Maxwell, C., & Bottge, B. (2006). Reconceptualizing and recentering research in special education. In C. Conrad & R. Serlin (Eds.), *Handbook on research in education: Engaging ideas and enriching inquiry* (pp. 175–196). Thousand Oaks, CA: Sage.

Hanley-Maxwell, C., & Collet-Klingenberg, L. (in press). Curricular choices related to work. In P. Wehman & J. Kregel (Eds.), *Functional curriculum for elementary, middle, and secondary age students with special needs* (3rd ed.). Austin, TX: Pro-Ed.

Hanley-Maxwell, C., & Izzo, M. (in press). Employment skills instruction. In M. Wehmeyer & K. Webb (Eds.), *Handbook of transition for youth with disabilities.* New York: Routledge, Taylor & Francis.

Harry, B. (2007). The disproportionate placement of ethnic minorities in special education. In L. Florian (Ed.), *The Sage Handbook of Special Education* (pp. 67–84). Thousand Oaks, CA: Sage.

Individuals with Disabilities Education Improvement Act, 20 U.S.C. §1400 *et seq.* (2004).

Johnson, D. R., & Thurlow, M. L. (2003). *A national study on graduation requirements and diploma options for youth with disabilities* (Technical Report 36). Retrieved from http://education.umn.edu/NCEO/OnlinePubs/Technical36.htm

Koegel, R., & Koegel, L. (Eds.). (1995). *Teaching children with autism.* Baltimore, MD: Brookes.

Koegel, R., & Koegel, L. (Eds.). (2006). *Pivotal response treatments for autism: Communication, social, and academic development.* Baltimore, MD: Brookes.

Lovaas, O. I. (1987). Behavioral treatment and normal educational and intellectual functioning in young autistic children. *Journal of Consulting and Clinical Psychology, 55,* 3–9.

McEachin, J. J., Smith, T., & Lovaas, O. I. (1993). Long-term outcome for children with autism who received early intensive behavioral treatment. *American Journal on Mental Retardation, 97,* 359–372.

MSM Productions, Ltd. (2004–2010). *What is deaf culture?* Retrieved from http://www.deafculture.com/definitions

National Center for Education Statistics. (2010a). *Table 7.2: Percentage distribution of public elementary and secondary students, by region, state, and race/ethnicity: 2004.* Retrieved from http://nces.ed.gov/pubs2007/minoritytrends/tables/table_7_2.asp

National Center for Education Statistics. (2010b). *What percentage of students with disabilities are educated in regular classrooms?* Retrieved from http://nces.ed.gov/fastfacts/display.asp?id=59

National Research Council. (2001). *Educating children with autism.* Washington, DC: National Academy Press.

Newman, L. (2006). *Facts from NLTS2: General education participation and academic performance of students with learning disabilities.* Retrieved from http://ies.ed.gov/ncser/pdf/20063001.pdf

Newman, L., Wagner, M., Cameto, R., & Knokey, A. M. (2009). *The post-high school outcomes of youth with disabilities up to 4 years after high school. A report of findings from the National Longitudinal Transition Study-2 (NLTS2). (NCSER 2009–3017).* Menlo Park, CA: SRI International. Retrieved from www.nlts2.org/reports/2009_04/nlts2_report_2009_04_complete.pdf

Oswald, D. P., Coutinho, M .J., Best, A. M., & Singh, N. N. (1998). Ethnicity in special education and relationships with school related economic and educational variables. *Journal of Special Education, 32,* 194–206.

Prizant, B. M. (2009, Spring). Treatment options and parent choice. Is ABA the only way? *Autism Spectrum Quarterly,* 28–32.

REACH. (2010). REACH: Reaching Educational and Career Hopes. Retrieved from http://www.education.uiowa.edu/reach

Rose, R. (2007). Curriculum considerations in meeting special educational needs. In L. Florian (Ed.), *The Sage Handbook of Special Education* (pp. 295–306). Thousand Oaks, CA: Sage.

Rouse, M., & McLaughlin, M. J. (2007). Changing perspectives of special education in the evolving context of educational reform. In L. Florian (Ed.), *The Sage Handbook of Special Education* (pp. 85–103). Thousand Oaks, CA: Sage.

Shaw, S. F. (2007). Post-secondary education. In L. Florian (Ed.), *The Sage Handbook of Special Education* (pp. 390–401). Thousand Oaks, CA: Sage.

Simpson, R. L. (2001). ABA and students with autism spectrum disorders: Issues and considerations for effective practice. *Focus on Autism and Other Developmental Disabilities, 16*(2), 68–71.

Sitlington, P., & Clark, G. (2005). Transition to post-secondary education. In *Transition education and services for students with disabilities* (pp. 204–232). Boston: Pearson.

Skiba, R. (2002). Special education and school discipline: A precarious balance. *Behavioral Disorders, 27*(2), 81–97.

Strain, P. (2001). ABA and students with autism spectrum disorder. *Focus on Autism and Other Developmental Disabilities, 16*(2), 68–71.

Strain, P., McGee, G., and Kohler, F. (2001). Inclusion of children with autism in early intervention settings. In M. Guralnick (Ed.), *Early childhood inclusion. Focus on change* (pp. 337–363). Baltimore, MD: Brookes.

Sullivan, A. L., & Kozleski, E. B. (2009). *State profile of efforts to create culturally responsive educational systems: North Carolina* (State Profile Series). Tempe, AZ: NCCRESt. Retrieved from http://www.nccrest.org

Taylor, G. (2006). *Trends in special education: Projections for the next decade.* Lewiston, NY: Edwin Mellen Press.

U.S. Department of Education, Office for Civil Rights. (2007). *Students with disabilities preparing for postsecondary education: Know your rights and responsibilities.* Washington, DC: Author.

U.S. National Commission on Excellence in Education. (1983). *A nation at risk: The imperative for educational reform. A report to the nation and secretary of education.* Washington, DC: U.S. Department of Education. Retrieved from http://www2.ed.gov/pubs/NatAtRisk/index.html

Valle, J. W., & Connor, D. J. (2010). *Rethinking disability: A disability studies approach to inclusive practices.* New York: McGraw-Hill.

Vaughn, S., Wanzek, J., & Denton, C. A. (2007). Teaching elementary students who experience learning difficulties. In L. Florian (Ed.), *The Sage Handbook of Special Education* (pp. 360–377). Thousand Oaks, CA: Sage.

Vismara, L. A., & Rogers, S. J. (2010). Behavioral treatments in autism spectrum disorder: What do we know? *Annual Review of Clinical Psychology, 6,* 447–468.

Wagner, M., Newman, L., & Cameto, R. (2004). *Changes over time in the secondary school experiences of students with disabilities. A report of findings from the National Longitudinal Transition Study (NLTS) and the National Longitudinal Transition Study-2 (NLTS2).* Menlo Park, CA: SRI International. Retrieved from http://www.nlts2.org/reports/changestime_report.html

Wills, J. (2008). *Preparing all youth for academic and career readiness.* Washington, DC: National Collaborative on Workforce and Disability for Youth, Institute for Educational Leadership. Retrieved from http://www.ncwd-youth.info/assets/reports/preparing_all_youth_for_academic_and_career_readiness.pdf

Wolfensberger, W. (1972). *Normalization: The principle of normalization in human services.* Toronto, ON: National Institute on Mental Retardation.

Zirkel, P. A. (2010, May/June). The legal meaning of specific learning disability for special education eligibility. *Teaching Exceptional Children,* 62–67.

# *Three*

# Chronology of Critical Events

## Mary-Elizabeth Glass, Chen-chen Cheng, Cheryl Hanley-Maxwell, and Lana Collet-Klingenberg

The events of history related to disability and the education of children with disabilities (a.k.a. special education) are closely intertwined This chapter presents a chronology of some of the major milestones in those histories.

### 1817

The Connecticut/American Asylum for the Education and Instruction of Deaf and Dumb Persons (later referred to as the American Asylum) opens as the first permanent school for individuals with disabilities.

### 1822

The American Asylum introduces trade teaching as part of its curriculum on April 15.

## 1832

The New England Asylum for the Blind begins instruction and becomes known for its educational successes with blind students, the most famous of whom are Laura Bridgman and Helen Keller. The school is currently known as the Perkins School for the Blind.

## 1837

Laura Bridgman enrolls at the New England Asylum for the Blind in October and becomes the first deaf and blind person educated in America. Her success helps develop understanding of the value of educating individuals with disabilities.

## 1838

"Intermediate schools" and "schools for special instruction" form in Boston serving students who are struggling academically or behaviorally. The schools are opened to improve outcomes for all students and to lighten teachers' workloads.

## 1840s

Common schools are revitalized as socializing agencies to ensure all students learn core American values. The schools also emphasize moral and vocational education for individuals with disabilities because of their need for charity and their perceived lack of cultural and moral values.

## 1843

The American Asylum selects a small group of deaf students to receive the first oral language instruction in the United States.

## 1847

The *American Annals of the Deaf and Dumb* (currently the *American Annals of the Deaf*) begins publishing information about instructional aids to teachers of the deaf. It also promotes societal understanding of the deaf.

## 1848

The Experimental School for Teaching and Training Idiotic Children opens in a wing of the Perkins Institute for the Blind as the first public residential institution in America focused on individuals with intellectual disabilities.

## 1850s

Samuel Gridley Howe and Edward Seguin replace the term "idiot" with "feebleminded" because they believe it is a gentler way of classifying this type of disability.

## 1850

Frenchman Edward Seguin immigrates to America. An advocate for improving the education and treatment of children with disabilities, Seguin creates the physiological method, a structured, multi-sensory program using positive reinforcement to develop life skills. This method becomes the foundation for institutional training programs for individuals with intellectual disabilities.

## 1852

Massachusetts becomes the first state to require compulsory school attendance. By 1909 six states pass attendance laws for children who are deaf, blind, or have mild disabilities.

## 1857

Amos Kendall founds the Columbia Institution for the Instruction of the Deaf and Dumb and the Blind, the first U.S. college dedicated to individuals with disabilities. In 1986 the Education of the Deaf Act (P.L. 99-371) renames the institution Gallaudet University.

## 1859

The Missouri School for the Blind starts using Braille and officially adopts it in 1860. This reading and writing system for the blind is widely adopted in other American schools by 1892.

## 1864

President Abraham Lincoln signs the Enabling Act authorizing the granting of college degrees to graduates of the Columbia Institution for the Instruction of the Deaf and Dumb and the Blind. The act allows the school to confer the same degrees that other colleges grant.

## 1867

Clark School for the Deaf opens as the first U.S. residential school to focus on using oral instruction to teach semi-deaf and semi-mute children to speak and read lips. Harriett Rogers and Alexander Graham Bell help shape the school's development, instruction, and philosophy; and the school's success leads to increased use of oral instruction in other institutions.

## 1868

The first Conference of American Principals votes to expand oral and articulation departments to all schools for the deaf. However, manual language instruction continues as the primary method for educating individuals classified as congenitally deaf.

## 1869

The School for Deaf-Mutes (later the Horace Mann School for the Deaf) opens as the first public day school for children with disabilities. The subsequent opening of the Western Pennsylvania School for the Deaf reflects the rising popularity of day schools and day classes for students with disabilities.

## 1871

Schools in New Haven, Connecticut, open some of the first ungraded classes for academically and behaviorally struggling students of various ages, ability levels, and backgrounds—an early example of student segregation.

## 1876

Edward Seguin begins serving as the first president of the Association of Medical Officers of American Institutions for Idiotic and Feebleminded Persons, which is created to encourage superintendents to share their experiences educating individuals with intellectual disabilities. This group eventually becomes the American Association on Intellectual and Developmental Disabilities.

## 1877

*The Jukes: A Study in Crime, Pauperism, Disease and Heredity,* by Richard Dugdale, notes links between environment and heredity when explaining an individual's behavior. Dugdale's findings are later manipulated to support the eugenics movement in America.

Education reformers drop "asylum" from the title of educational facilities for blind students, reflecting their belief that deaf and/or blind students are capable and deserving of an education in a school setting rather than in an institution or asylum. This evolution in perspective, however, does not extend to individuals with other types of disabilities.

## 1879

Segregated day classes for "feebleminded" students (students with intellectual disabilities) open in Cleveland, Ohio.

## 1870s-1880s

Juvenile reformatories in the United States undergo expansion and change. The number of facilities jumps from 19 to approximately 60. A large number of the reformatories expand their educational offerings to include trade and skill instruction to residents, many of whom would be identified today as having behavioral disabilities.

## 1880

The National Association of the Deaf (NAD) begins as a nonprofit, civil rights organization, created by and for the American deaf community to ensure representation of deaf and hard-of-hearing citizens in social and economic activities at the local and national level.

## 1884

Alexander Graham Bell introduces the concept of "special education" at a National Education Association (NEA) meeting.

## 1887

The Perkins Institution for the Blind responds to a national movement toward providing kindergarten and other forms of early childhood education by establishing the nation's first kindergarten for blind children at Perkins School.

## 1888

The Sarah Fuller Home for Little Children Who Cannot Hear opens as the first residential school to provide early oral instruction to deaf children considered too young to attend school.

The New Jersey Home for the Education and Care of Feebleminded Children opens and becomes widely recognized for its research on intellectual disabilities and intelligence testing. Increases in enrollments result in a relocation of the facility to Vineland philanthropist B. D. Maxham's estate, where it eventually becomes known as the Vineland Training School.

## 1893

The Industrial School for Crippled and Deformed Children opens in Boston as the first American school for students with physical disabilities. The primary goal of this school is to make students self-sufficient. Its opening coincides with the passage of some of America's earliest compulsory education laws.

In the case of *Watson v. City of Cambridge,* the Massachusetts Supreme Court determines that the Cambridge school district is justified in expelling a student because he could not care for himself. The decision establishes legal precedent for the exclusion of children with disabilities from educational programs.

In October the city of Providence, Rhode Island, opens three schools to work with children who are deemed to be difficult to manage, relieving general educators of the duty.

## 1896

The first psychological clinic in America opens as a private enterprise. Similar clinics soon begin appearing throughout the country and are quickly integrated within school support systems.

After finding that educating "mentally deficient" children in separate schools with children identified as difficult to manage is not effective, Providence, Rhode Island, opens the first public school class to educate children who are considered to be "feebleminded" or have other intellectual disabilities.

## 1899

As part of its plan to ensure that no child is excluded from some form of care, the Boston school district opens it first class for "feebleminded" children in January 1899. These small classes (no more than 15 students) emphasize working on tasks that require the use of hands to "arouse action in the brain," along with kindergarten-level work and games.

The Chicago Public Schools begins instructing "crippled children" (students with orthopedic disabilities) in the first public day-school program specifically designed for children with mobility and/or orthopedic disabilities.

Elizabeth Farrell, an educator in New York City's Public School No. 1, begins teaching at the Henry Street Settlement School. She creates a system of ungraded classes for students removed from the general education setting in order to remediate student deficiencies and return students to the general education setting.

## 1900

The Chicago Public Schools offers day classes for the blind and partially sighted, providing specialized instruction as well as socialization opportunities with non-disabled peers.

## 1903

The American Breeder's Association becomes the first national organization to promote the study of eugenic and genetic research in America. Proponents of the eugenics movement support the sterilization and segregation of individuals with disabilities and immigrants. The eugenics philosophy, as reflected in educational theories and practices, results in disproportionate placement of immigrant and minority children in separate and ungraded classes, thus linking "feeblemindedness" to race and cultural differences.

## 1905

Alfred Binet and Theodore Simon disseminate information about the Binet-Simon Intelligence Test in a widely read article that describes the development of a series of tests for identifying and determining varying degrees of mental retardation. Henry Goddard, a supporter of eugenics at Vineland, adapts and standardizes the test. The adapted test classifies individuals based on degrees of intelligence and provides a means of sorting them into educational or institutional placements.

## 1906

Elizabeth Farrell becomes the Inspector of the Ungraded Department of the New York City Public Schools. She professionalizes the field of special education, trains and supervises teachers of ungraded classes, and expands the number of ungraded classes from 14 to 250 classes by 1921.

## 1909

The first White House Conference on Children and Youth focuses on the care of dependent and neglected children. Conference outcomes include a general recognition of the need for remedial programming for children with special needs.

## 1910

The Chicago Public Schools hires ten speech correction teachers to work with students in the areas of articulation, disfluency, and other voice disorders.

## 1912

Elizabeth Farrell begins training instructors of students with intellectual disabilities at the Brooklyn Training School for Teachers. Her students participate in a three-month graduate course that includes training in various areas including psychology, physiology, and methods of instruction.

## 1913

J. B. Watson introduces behaviorism to the field of psychology. The guiding principles of behaviorism—observation as key to understanding human behavior and the belief that changes in the environment can influence and predict behavior—gain broad acceptance in the 1930s, significantly influencing subsequent educational research and methodology, especially as it relates to students with disabilities.

## 1916

In *The Jukes in 1915*, a follow-up study to Dugdale's 1877 work, Arthur Estabrook concludes that all individuals identified as "feebleminded" should be placed in permanent custodial care and sterilized to keep them from passing "undesirable" traits to their children.

Houghton Mifflin publishes Louis Terman's *The Measurement of Intelligence: An Explanation of and a Complete Guide for the Use of the Stanford Revision and Extension of the Binet-Simon Intelligence Scale*. Terman's revisions allow for testing across the full spectrum of ability levels.

## 1916–1918

Elizabeth Farrell becomes president of the Department of Special Education of the National Education Association. She brings together individuals from a variety of areas and disciplines, including state departments of education, hospitals, universities, clinics, and residential and day schools, to discuss educational needs of students in special education programs.

## 1917

President Woodrow Wilson signs the National Vocational Education Act (Smith-Hughes Act, P.L. 64-347) on February 23. This act enables states to receive matching federal money for vocational education programs and provides the foundation for later employment training programs for youth with disabilities.

## 1918

The Smith-Sears Veteran's Rehabilitation Act, also known as the Soldier's Rehabilitation Act (P.L. 65-178), is enacted on June 27. The measure creates a vocational rehabilitation program for disabled war veterans with the goal of returning them to civil employment after their discharge from the military. As amended in 1920, the act includes American citizens with disabilities and provides the groundwork for later programs designed to prepare youth with disabilities to move from school to employment.

## 1919

Industrial schools support the growing number of youth identified as vagrant, destitute, incorrigible, neglected, or homeless in urban areas. These schools act as a home, public educational institution, and training facility to many individuals who would now be identified as having an emotional disability.

In the case of *Beattie v. Board of Education*, the Wisconsin Supreme Court supports a school district's decision to deny an education to a student of average intelligence with physical disabilities because he has a depressing and nauseating effect on his teachers and fellow students.

## 1921

M. C. Migel starts the American Foundation for the Blind (AFB). The AFB influences the training and curriculum used in institutions of higher education, shapes how students with vision loss are taught in schools, and provides information and resources to professionals who work with individuals with vision loss.

## 1922

Elizabeth Farrell starts the International Council for Exceptional Children (CEC) in New York at the Columbia University Teachers College and becomes the organization's first president. CEC creates professional standards for special education teachers and disseminates ideas regarding the education of children with disabilities.

## 1923

A small group of psychiatrists form the American Orthopsychiatric Association. The organization's mission is to stimulate awareness of educational practices, treatment options, and therapeutic services to support students with learning and behavioral characteristics (which in the latter half of the 20th century will be identified as emotional behavioral disabilities).

## 1925

Samuel Orton identifies and describes "strephosymbolia" or twisted symbols, later known as dyslexia. Orton attributes the problems of children with reading difficulties to word and letter orientation problems. His later work with Anna Gillingham creates instruction designed to focus the learner's attention on recognizing and remembering appropriately oriented symbols (e.g., b versus d) by simultaneously engaging multiple senses as part of the learning process.

## 1930s

Albert Strauss and Heinz Werner provide insight into the field of learning disabilities as they investigate the concept of "brain injury," challenging the traditional—but inadequate—construct of mental deficiency related to some children's specific cognitive and performance deficits. Their work opens the door to the development of later descriptions of learning disabilities.

## 1930

President Herbert Hoover convenes the White House Conference on Child Health and Protection, which runs from November 19 to November 21. Participants create a report that includes analysis and recommendations for the education and treatment of children with disabilities. This report also analyzes how often children with disabilities are enrolled in special education programs and institutions.

## 1934

The International Council for Exceptional Children publishes its first official publication, the *International Council for Exceptional Children Review*. Now known as *Exceptional Children*, it is one of the leading journals in special education.

## 1940

The National Federation of the Blind (NFB) is founded on November 16. It grows to become the nation's largest organization for the blind, with affiliates in all 50 states. NFB provides access to various resources and services for the blind and educates the general public on issues concerning visual impairment and blindness.

## 1948

The University of Illinois, Galesburg, creates the nation's first disabled student services program to provide support for students with physical disabilities in higher education. This program helps lay the groundwork for the development of independent living centers.

## 1949

Dr. Samuel Kirk opens the first experimental preschool for children identified as having mental retardation. Kirk and colleagues study the effects of early intervention on 3- to 5-year-old children with intellectual disabilities. They also facilitate the development of specific diagnostic tests that can be used to guide instructional decisions.

The grassroots efforts of two prominent New York families result in the establishment of the National Foundation for Cerebral Palsy. Now known as United Cerebral Palsy (UCP), the organization's primary goals include increasing public awareness, identifying/creating opportunities and services for individuals with cerebral palsy and other disabilities, and providing support services for the families of individuals with cerebral palsy and other disabilities.

## 1950

A group of parents establishes the Milwaukee Society for Brain Injured Children to increase awareness of these children and their educational needs. Their work reflects efforts to seek the medical origin of learning difficulties and contributes to the growing practice of offering separate educational programs for children who would later be described as having learning disabilities.

Parents of children with intellectual disabilities establish the National Association of Parents and Friends of Mentally Retarded Children in May. This group, which is now known as The Arc, contributes to improvements in education, community involvement, and integration of individuals with intellectual disabilities.

## 1951

The World Federation of the Deaf (WFD) begins its work to increase recognition of sign language as a language, improve educational offerings to people who are deaf, promote access to information, and secure human rights for people around the world who are deaf or hearing impaired.

## 1954

On May 17 the U.S. Supreme Court hands down the landmark *Brown v. Board of Education* decision, which states that equality in education is impossible when separate facilities are maintained for White and Black students. This decision intensifies interest in examining exclusionary educational practices and drives a surge in equal rights cases involving children with disabilities in the 1960s and early 1970s. The *Brown* decision also influences future legislation regarding the education of children with disabilities.

President Dwight D. Eisenhower signs the Vocational Rehabilitation Act Amendments (P.L. 83-565) on August 3, expanding the federal government's level of involvement in vocational rehabilitation. The act significantly increases funding for services provided to individuals with intellectual disabilities and mental health needs, directs new monies to rehabilitation programs and facilities, provides funding for disability-related demonstration and research grants, and establishes a program of college and university grants for training rehabilitation counselors to work with individuals with disabilities. Finally, the amendments increase funding for rehabilitation-related programs at universities, ultimately resulting in the creation of more than 100 university-based disabled student services programs.

## 1958

Seymour Sarason and Thomas Gladwin publish *Psychological and Cultural Problems in Mental Subnormality: A Review of Research,* which describes the difference between "mental retardation" as a condition that develops as a result of environmental factors (disadvantage), and "mental deficiency" as an unchangeable cognitive condition (disability).

The Captioned Films Act of 1958 (P.L. 85-905) creates the federally funded Captioned Films for the Deaf, a loan service for captioned films.

President Eisenhower signs the National Defense Education Act (NDEA; P.L. 85-864) on September 2. This act promotes the security of the United States by providing increased educational opportunities to and developing the technical skills of American youth. The NDEA establishes a precedent for federal involvement in education that eventually leads to federal intervention in special education.

Passed on September 6, four days after NDEA, the Education of Mentally Retarded Children Act of 1958 (P.L. 85-926) provides federal funding to prepare teachers and researchers to improve the education of children with intellectual disabilities. It includes funding for personnel preparation programs at higher education institutions, as well as state and local teacher preparation and continuing professional development programs.

## 1960s

Oral instruction peaks as the dominant educational method for deaf children. At this time, most public and residential schools for the deaf do not employ deaf teachers or provide manual instruction to the students in attendance. The use of manual instruction (i.e., sign language) begins to rise as educational researchers demonstrate that children who use sign language achieve more academically.

## 1960

Founded by Eunice Kennedy Shriver, the Special Olympics holds its first international summer games at Soldier Field in Chicago, Illinois, on July 19 and 20. Since then, Special Olympics competitions at the local, national, and international level have provided opportunities for athletes with disabilities to train and participate throughout the year. These events are often carried out through partnerships with individual schools, school districts, and communities that encourage volunteerism and participation.

## 1961

Charles Ferster, an American behavioral psychologist, changes the way autism is conceptualized by advocating for an alternative instructional approach that uses a behavioral model of treatment. His work broadens autism research from a cure-oriented approach to one that recognizes that behaviors (including language, communication, and social skills) can be changed.

The Teachers of the Deaf Act (P.L. 87-276), which provides funding for the training of instructional personnel who work with children identified as deaf or hard of hearing, becomes law on September 22. The measure lays the groundwork for future legislation to support students with disabilities in school.

On October 11 the President's Panel on Mental Retardation issues three significant reports detailing recommendations for improving the experiences of individuals with intellectual disabilities in education, health care, legal rights, and societal acceptance. The panel's call for greater research within identified areas of need also results in increased awareness of intellectual disabilities as well as new legislation and federal and state funding of programs for individuals with intellectual disabilities.

## 1962

Maynard Reynolds develops an educational framework of a continuum of services for students with disabilities. The base level of the pyramid-like system is the general education classroom with various levels of supports and services. Reynolds states that all students with disabilities should start in general education first, moving up the pyramid to more restrictive settings only when necessary.

G. Orville Johnson's *Special Education for the Mentally Handicapped: A Paradox* challenges the practice of segregating students with disabilities from their peers by questioning the academic and social benefits received by students with intellectual disabilities when they are educated in segregated classes. Johnson also cites the importance of considering the monetary costs associated with segregation.

## 1963

Dr. Samuel Kirk first uses the term "learning disability" on April 6 at *Exploration Into the Problems of the Perceptually Handicapped Child,* a conference convened by parents of children with serious learning problems in school. Parents subsequently use this term in the title of a newly formed organization, the Association for Learning Disabilities of America, now known as the Learning Disability Association of America (LDA).

In August the National Association for Retarded Children (NARC), later known as The Arc, publishes a Bill of Rights for children with intellectual disabilities. In particular, it notes children's right to opportunities to reach their fullest potential, receive quality care from affectionate and understanding individuals, and receive a free public education from skilled teachers.

The Maternal and Child Health and Mental Retardation Planning Amendment to the Social Security Act (P.L. 88-156) becomes law on October 24. The legislation, a response to recommendations made by the President's Panel on Mental Retardation, earmarks money for increased maternal and child health services and research to prevent the occurrence of intellectual disabilities. The act also provides financial assistance to states to develop comprehensive state and community programs to improve student outcomes.

Passed into law on October 31, the Mental Retardation Facilities and Community Mental Health Centers Construction Act of 1963 (P.L. 88-164) provides state grants to (1) train teachers who work with students with intellectual and other disabilities and (2) develop research centers focused on individuals with intellectual disabilities and community mental health centers. The act also establishes the Division of Handicapped Children and Youth within the U.S. Department of Education.

The Vocational Education Act (P.L. 88-210), which becomes law on December 18, increases federal funding and support for the extension, development, and improvement of vocational education schools. The act allocates funding for research on vocational education and training and funds programs for individuals with disabilities.

## 1964

*Infantile Autism: The Syndrome and Its Implications for a Neural Theory of Behavior* by Dr. Bernard Rimland dispels theories that bad parenting or "refrigerator mothers" cause autism. It identifies autism as a biological disorder, altering societal views of the nature, causes, and treatment of autism.

Parents who attend the *Exploration Into the Problems of the Perceptually Handicapped Child* conference on April 6 create the Learning Disabilities Association of America (LDAA). The work of the LDAA influences educational legislation, policies, and practices related to improving services for individuals with disabilities. The organization is especially influential in changing federal regulations under the Individuals with Disabilities Education Act (IDEA) that relate to students with learning disabilities.

The Economic Opportunity Act (EOA) of 1964 (P.L. 88-452), passed on August 20, establishes programs to eliminate the causes of poverty by supporting job training centers and public and private nonprofit community action agencies and work-training programs, including Neighborhood Youth Corps, the Job Corps, and VISTA (Volunteers in Service to America). The act also supports education and training programs (e.g., work study programs at colleges and universities) that provide opportunities for underprivileged Americans to increase their marketable skills. Notably, EOA creates the Office of Economic Opportunity and Title II B grants for states to establish the first Adult Basic Education programs.

## 1965

Head Start launches early intervention programs targeting the cognitive and socio-emotional outcomes of low-income children. The policy that creates Head Start, however, is criticized for its lack of clear guidelines and inconsistent interpretation.

Senator Robert Kennedy condemns the inadequate treatment of individuals with intellectual disabilities at New York's Willowbrook State School, which is severely understaffed and overcrowded and denies residents access to education and other civil rights. Attention to these problems adds impetus to a movement in many local communities to expand educational offerings and other services to individuals with disabilities.

The Elementary and Secondary Education Act (ESEA; P.L. 89-10) allocates federal money to states and local school districts with high levels of poverty and large numbers of low-achieving students to develop effective interventions. Signed into law by President Lyndon B. Johnson on April 11, ESEA also includes funding for Head Start and Title I programs.

The National Society for Autistic Children, which becomes the Autism Society of America (ASA), organizes in November and begins providing information about education, treatment, and quality of life to individuals across the autism spectrum and their families. ASA also advocates for state and federal policy changes.

## 1966

Burton Blatt and Fred Kaplan's book *Christmas in Purgatory. A Photographic Essay on Mental Retardation* pictorially describes the inhumane treatment and atrocious living conditions in state mental institutions.

Convened on May 11, the President's Committee on Mental Retardation begins work on four priority goals, including the early recognition and treatment of intellectual disabilities and the provision of special education and habilitation services for individuals with intellectual disabilities. In 2003 the committee's name changes to the President's Committee for People with Intellectual Disabilities (PCPID).

The Elementary and Secondary Education Act Amendments of 1966 (P.L. 89-750), passed into law on November 3, create the Bureau of Education of the Handicapped (BEH). Its purposes are to bring together parents, professionals, and other interest groups; develop relationships with special education leaders and members of Congress; and identify shortcomings in special education and advance necessary reforms in educational policies and programming for children with disabilities.

## 1967

Signed into law on June 29, the Education Professional Development Act (EPDA; P.L. 90-35) provides federal funding to improve instruction for individuals with disabilities. The EPDA specifically targets teacher training and professional development for existing general education teachers and related personnel.

## 1968

Lloyd Dunn publishes "Special Education for the Mildly Retarded—Is Much of It Justifiable?" in the September issue of *Exceptional Children*. Dunn argues that segregated educational settings are inherently unequal, questions the effectiveness of segregated special education programs, and expresses concerns regarding the misidentification of minority and/or underprivileged students as having intellectual disabilities.

The Handicapped Children's Early Assistance Act (HCEA; P.L. 90-538), signed into law on September 30, creates funding for experimental programs to support young children with disabilities and ensure the availability of technical assistance and support. The subsequent success of these programs confirms the positive effects of early intervention services for students with disabilities and lays the foundation for legislation mandating early intervention services for children with disabilities, starting at birth.

On October 16, the Vocational Education Amendments of 1968 (P.L. 90-576) creates the National Advisory Council, which makes recommendations regarding improvements to vocational education programs and policies. The act also expands funding and support for vocational education programs to individuals with intellectual and sensory disabilities.

## 1969

Benget Nirje brings the principles of normalization and issues of self-determination for individuals with severe disabilities to America. Nirje supports the idea that, regardless of type or severity of disabilities, individuals should be physically and socially included in all parts of society.

Congress passes the Children with Specific Learning Disabilities Act of 1969. The act becomes Title VI-G of the Elementary and Secondary Education Act Amendments of 1970 (P.L. 91-230). This is the first federal law that requires public funding for remedial special education support services for students with learning disabilities.

In *Hobson v. Hansen*, District Court Judge J. Skelly Wright rules that tracking students into an educational program based on IQ testing discriminates against economically disadvantaged and minority students. The ruling reflects rising concerns about how schools identify students with disabilities.

## 1970

Title VI of the Elementary and Secondary Education Act Amendments of 1969 (P.L. 91-230), passed on April 13, combines several previously established federal programs for students with disabilities under one law and includes the definition of learning disabilities used in federal law.

The consent decree in *Diana v. California State Board of Education* states that children cannot be placed into special education services due to their performance on a culturally or a linguistically biased test. The ruling establishes that evaluation of children for placement in special education programs must include testing in the student's primary language.

## 1972

The U.S. District Court for the Northern District of California in *Larry P. v. Riles* rules that intelligence test results cannot be the sole reason for placing students into special education, and that tests used for referring students for special education services must be normed for use with students of that particular culture. On appeal, the same court affirms its ruling in 1974 and again in 1979. In 1984, the United States 9th Circuit Court of Appeals upholds the earlier decisions.

Wolf Wolfensberger's *Normalization: The Principle of Normalization in Human Services* extends Nirje's work by articulating the guiding principles of the normalization movement, examining how society values individuals with intellectual disability, and describing the ways in which labeling individuals adversely affects normalization.

Geraldo Rivera's exposé *Willowbrook: The Last Disgrace* brings national attention to continued mistreatment and unacceptable living conditions at Staten Island's Willowbrook State School, an institution for children with mental retardation. The scandal garners widespread public support for deinstitutionalization and alternative placement options for the school's residents.

The consent decree in *PARC (Pennsylvania Association for Retarded Children) v. Pennsylvania* states that all children with intellectual disabilities are entitled to a free public education and that educating students with disabilities in a general education classroom is preferable to doing so in a segregated setting. This ruling substantially influences future legislation on special education issues, particularly in relation to parental notification of educational placement changes.

Federal Court Judge Frank M. Johnson's March 2 ruling in *Wyatt v. Stickney* creates minimum standards of care, education, and treatment for individuals with mental retardation and mental illness.

In *Mills v. Board of Education of the District of Columbia*, a U.S. district court rules that children with disabilities should not bear the burden of the school district's financial constraints any more than children without disabilities. The August 1 ruling serves notice to districts around the country that funding problems are not a legitimate reason to withhold special education services to children who need them.

The Economic Opportunity Act Amendments (P.L. 92-424), passed in September, require Head Start centers to allocate 10% of their enrollments to students with disabilities.

## 1973

Marian Wright Edelman creates the Children's Defense Fund (CDF), an advocacy group for children. One of CDF's earliest reports reveals that certain groups of students, including children from minority groups and children with intellectual, physical, and emotional disabilities, are often excluded from schools because they place additional administrative and financial demands on schools.

Section 504 of the Rehabilitation Act Amendments of 1973 (P.L. 93-112) clearly delineates civil rights protections for individuals with disabilities, mandating that persons with disabilities cannot be denied participation in or benefits from publicly funded services, facilities, or activities solely because of their disability. Passed on September 26, This act also focuses attention on vocational rehabilitation services for individuals with significant disabilities.

## 1974

People First, founded on January 8, is one of the first self-advocacy groups organized around the principles of the self-determination movement. This group advocates the use of "people-first" language in legislation, education agencies and institutions of higher education, research journals, and conferences.

The President's Committee on Mental Retardation and the Association for Childhood Education International holds the Conference on Early Intervention for High Risk Infants and Young Children at the University of North Carolina beginning on May 5. One of the first conferences on early intervention, it focuses on the time lost between when young children demonstrate learning readiness and when educational intervention and mental stimulation begin by examining the impact of early intervention on learning and future outcomes. The conference helps to lay the foundation for nationwide early childhood intervention networks, new education models and practices, and legislation supporting the needs of infants and children and their families.

Passage of the Family Educational Rights and Privacy Act (FERPA) on August 21 expands the privacy and access rights of parents/guardians to records maintained by institutions and educational agencies that receive federal funding. The act mandates that parents/guardians have the right to review their students' educational records, request modification of records they believe are inaccurate or misleading, and, if necessary, request and receive a hearing when they desire changes to information found in the records. Finally, the law prevents institutions and educational agencies from releasing information about children without the written permission of their parents/guardians.

## 1975

The American Association for the Education of the Severely/Profoundly Handicapped (AAESPH), a volunteer-based grassroots organization, incorporates on April 4. This organization, currently known as TASH, quickly becomes an international leader in promoting inclusion of all individuals with disabilities—and particularly those with more significant needs—in educational settings, workplaces, and communities.

The Education for All Handicapped Children Act (EAHCA; P.L. 94-142) guarantees that all children with disabilities (from ages 6 through 21) receive a "free and appropriate public education" (FAPE). Under EAHCA, children with disabilities must be evaluated appropriately, given access to the least restrictive environments, and provided with Individualized Education Programs (IEPs) that are developed in conjunction with parents/guardians. The act expands parents'/guardians' rights, guaranteeing access to due process procedures and participation in all planning meetings. The passage of this act on November 29 significantly increases the number of students receiving publicly funded special education services.

## 1977

The Association of Higher Education and Disability (AHEAD) begins providing educational activities to promote and support higher education for individuals with disabilities.

## 1978

The U.S. District Court for Connecticut rules on January 4 in *Stuart v. Nappi* that expulsion of a student with disabilities on disciplinary grounds is equivalent to a change in educational placement and affects the student's right to a free and appropriate education in the least restrictive environment available. The ruling requires school districts to follow due process procedures prior to expelling students with disabilities.

## 1979

The *Armstrong v. Kline* decision by the U.S. District Court for Eastern Pennsylvania rules that when students with disabilities experience significant regression during school breaks, school districts must provide extended school year (ESY) services, based on individual student needs, at no additional cost to the students or their families.

## 1982

The U.S. Supreme Court decides that an "appropriate" education is determined by whether or not the student benefits from the education. This decision, rendered in *Board of Education v. Rowley,* limits the extent of the services that school districts are obligated to provide to students with disabilities.

The Job Training Partnership Act (JTPA; P.L. 97-300), passed on October 13, assists economically disadvantaged individuals who face barriers to employment by providing funding for job training programs. The act is later expanded to include students with disabilities who meet economic requirements.

## 1983

In April the U.S. Department of Education publishes *A Nation at Risk: The Imperative for Educational Reform.* This report raises concerns about the quality of public schools and details the need to improve American education via standard-based education and achievement assessment.

Amendments to the Education of the Handicapped Act (P.L. 98-199) require states to develop programs to assist students with disabilities in moving from school to work and to collect data on the number of students exiting special education services. The amendments also provide incentives to encourage states to provide early intervention services to children with disabilities up to age 5.

## 1984

Assistant Secretary of Education Madeline Will releases *Office of Special Education and Rehabilitation Services (OSERS) Programming for the Transition of Youth With Disabilities: Bridges From School to Working Life.* Will's report describes and analyzes high unemployment and underemployment rates for former students with disabilities. It details the need to assist students with disabilities and their families in managing the changes connected with moving from mandated educational services to eligibility-based adult services.

In its July 5 decision in *Tatro v. State of Texas,* the U.S. Supreme Court rules that school districts must provide all medical services necessary to ensure that students with disabilities can benefit from their special education. The ruling mandates that school health personnel be capable of performing all necessary medical services, and it rules that the plaintiff bears the burden of proof when questioning individualized education programs (IEPs).

The Carl D. Perkins Vocational Education Act (P.L. 98-524), which becomes law on October 31, focuses on improving labor force skills and access to vocational education programs for students with disabilities and other at-risk populations. The act authorizes the funding for vocational support services such as counseling and guidance, and vocational planning.

## 1986

Assistant Secretary of Education Madeline Will introduces the Regular Education Initiative (REI), which focuses on providing additional training to general educators in an effort to improve the identification and education of students with disabilities. REI emphasizes collaboration between general and special education teachers who share responsibilities for students with disabilities, and it provides funding to state educational agencies to train school personnel.

The U.S. 5th Circuit Court of Appeals in *Alamo Heights v. Board of Education* upholds the *Armstrong v. Kline* (1979) ruling related to providing extended school year (ESY) services to students with disabilities who experience academic regression during summer school breaks. The ruling also requires school districts to provide transportation services to children who receive ESY services.

Education of the Handicapped Act Amendments (P.L. 99-457) of October 8 require states to provide special education preschool services to 3- to 5-year-old children with disabilities and provides financial incentives to states to encourage the creation of comprehensive interdisciplinary service programs focused on infants and toddlers with disabilities and their families.

## 1987

Dr. O. Ivar Lovaas publishes research results indicating that children with autism can achieve normal functioning when provided with early, intensive, and highly structured one-to-one behavioral intervention. His findings lay the foundation for subsequent research related to behaviorally based interventions, as well as debates about appropriate treatment regimens for children with autism.

On April 13 the U.S. District Court for the Northern District of Texas rules in *Garland v. Wilks* that when a student is not benefiting from his or her public school program but is benefiting from a private extended-day program, the school district must pay for the extended-day programming.

## 1988

The Secondary Education and Transitional Service for Youth with Disabilities Program of the Office of Special Education and Rehabilitation Services (OSERS) begins the Self-Determination Initiative, a program designed to provide individuals with disabilities a greater voice in the decisions that affect their lives. The initiative funds 26 model demonstration projects to (1) identify and teach skills to support self-determination through development of assessment tools and curricula, and (2) support research about self-determination and secondary planning research.

In its January 20 decision in *Honig v. Doe*, the U.S. Supreme Court determines that a school district must conduct a manifest determination prior to suspending or expelling a student with disabilities to ensure that the student is not being penalized for behaviors related to his or her disability. Under this ruling, school districts must provide alternative services for students whose misconduct is a manifestation of their disabilities.

After students in the Deaf President Now movement (DPN) protest the appointment of a non-deaf president for Gallaudet University, the university appoints its first deaf president, Dr. I. King Jordan, in March.

The Technology-Related Assistance for Individuals with Disabilities Act (P.L. 100-407), which becomes law on October 6, supports developing assistive technology (AT) for children and adults with disabilities to create greater access to and involvement in their communities. Outcomes of these efforts include advances in technology and training and support activities, including early intervention, schools, community, and workplace supports.

## 1989

In *Timothy W. v. Rochester School District* the U.S. 1st Circuit Court of Appeals rules that entitlement to a free and appropriate education stands whether or not the parents can prove the child is benefiting from the education. Prior to this May 24 ruling, school districts had the power to deny an education to some children with severe disabilities because there was no proof they would benefit from their educations.

The U.S. 5th Circuit Court of Appeals June 12 ruling in *Daniel R. R. v. State Board of Education* establishes a two-part rule for determining compliance with least restrictive environment (the setting that provides greatest participation in the regular classroom while ensuring maximum educational benefit for the child with a disability): (1) determine if, with modifications and supplementary services, the student is making satisfactory progress in the general education classroom; and (2) determine if the student has been included with typical peers to the maximum extent possible, while meeting the first part of the rule. The court states that determining satisfactory progress includes examining academic, language, and social benefits. The court specifies that the least restrictive environment is typically the general education classroom with sufficient accommodations (e.g., supplemented or modified program, supplementary aids and services). However, teacher workload and the educational effect for children without disabilities may also enter into the determination.

## 1990

Douglas Biklen's *Communication Unbound: Autism and Praxis* introduces the concept of facilitated communication (FC) in the United States. FC subsequently becomes a popular method of communicating with individuals with autism. However, FC remains enormously controversial due to research studies that question the efficacy of the practice.

The Americans with Disabilities Act (ADA; P.L. 101-336) is signed into law on July 26, extending civil rights protections for individuals with disabilities to non-publicly funded settings and entities, including telecommunication, transportation, and employment arenas. ADA also requires public school districts to ensure students with disabilities have access to all programs and services within the most integrated setting that is appropriate and beneficial for them.

The Individuals with Disabilities Education Act (IDEA) Amendments of 1990 (P.L. 101-476) add autism and traumatic brain injury as disability categories and change the language used in the law from "handicapped" to "disability." The revised law also requires that all individualized education programs (IEPs) contain a transition service statement for all students who are at least 14 years of age and a transition plan for all students who are at least 16 years of age.

## 1992

The 1992 Amendments to the Vocational Rehabilitation Act (P.L. 102-569) create transition requirements that parallel those in IDEA. The amendments require state vocational rehabilitation counselors to work with public schools in preparing youth with disabilities for post-school life.

## 1993

The U.S. 3rd Circuit Court of Appeals May 28 ruling in *Oberti v. Board of Education of the Borough of Clementon School District* determines that the general education setting is preferable to separate special education classrooms for students with disabilities, and it further mandates the provision of supplementary aids and services for students with disabilities who are placed in the general education classroom.

On November 9 the U.S. Supreme Court issues a significant ruling in *Florence County School District Four v. Carter.* According to the ruling, when a school district fails to comply with "free and appropriate public education" (FAPE) guidelines (as evidenced by the child's level of achievement), the school district can be held financially responsible for paying the student's tuition at a specialized private school that provides appropriate, effective services.

## 1994

In *Sacramento City School District v. Rachel H.,* the U.S. District Court for Eastern California finds that the general education classroom is the least restrictive environment for a student with moderate intellectual disabilities and that the cost of providing instruction in the integrated setting does not create excessive financial hardship for the school district. On appeal, the decision is affirmed January 24, 1994.

The Goals 2000: Educate America Act (P.L. 103-227) becomes law on March 31. The legislation mandates academic standards for all students and stresses educational equity for children who have disabilities or are from traditionally underserved minority groups.

The School to Work Opportunities Act of 1994 (P.L. 103-239) is passed on May 4. It focuses on improving post-school employment outcomes for all students by creating structures and standards/goals for developing employment-related skills, connecting academics and school-based learning with occupational and work-based learning, and creating partnerships among secondary and post-secondary education and businesses.

## 1995

The U.S. Department of Labor launches its Workforce Recruitment Programs for College Students with Disabilities (WRP). The WRP recruits and connects post-secondary students and recent graduates with disabilities to summer and permanent federal employment opportunities.

Early Head Start begins offering services to low-income families, infants, toddlers, and pregnant women, addressing prenatal health of pregnant women, children's health, and family functions.

## 1996

On February 8 Congress passes the Telecommunications Act (P.L. 104-104), which mandates equal access to telecommunications services and equipment for all people with disabilities, regardless of age. This includes access to tele-communication-related learning and teaching materials (i.e., electronic media, audio-visual assistive equipment, and Internet resources in school settings) for students with disabilities. In addition, the legislation requires manufacturers to design and produce accessible and usable devices and equipment.

## 1997

The Individuals with Disabilities Act Amendments (P.L. 105-17), which become law on June 4, mandate greater access to general education for students with disabilities, including assistive technology and related services when needed. The age for transition services is extended downward to begin at age 14. A major change is authority given to schools for weapons and drug violations by students with disabilities, while ensuring that if behavior is determined to be related to disability, the students must be provided with an education, even if they are removed from the school setting.

The U.S. Supreme Court's June 23 ruling in *Agostini v. Felton* allows publicly funded special education services to be provided to students with disabilities in private schools.

## 1998

California voters pass the highly controversial English Language in Public Schools Initiative, also known as Proposition 227, on June 2. The measure requires all instruction in the state's public schools to be in English and it places new limitations on special classes for "limited English proficient" (LEP) students. The law allows waivers if school personnel and parents determine that the waiver will allow a student to learn English more quickly, the student is English proficient, or alternative instruction will be more beneficial. Because this law affects the language of instruction used for students with disabilities who are also English Language Learners, the law also allows waivers for students with disabilities.

The Workforce Investment Act (WIA) of 1998 (P.L. 105-220) becomes law on August 7. WIA combines vocational rehabilitation with other employment-related programs. It creates accessible One-Stop Job Centers to coordinate access to job services and employment training for adults and youth and provides services to prepare youth for post-secondary education and employment. These services include assessment, academic skill instruction and support, occupational training, and inclusive employment preparation programs.

The Rehabilitation Act Amendments become Title VI of Workforce Investment Act (P.L. 105-220).

The Amendments to the Carl D. Perkins Vocational and Technical Education Act (P.L. 105-332) passed on October 31 place emphasis on academic standards and accountability, targeting student achievement in academics and technical skills, post-secondary employment or education, and preparation for nontraditional careers. The amendments require that students from special populations (including students with disabilities) be supported in their access to and achievement in vocational programs. They also expand financial support to include post-secondary vocational education.

## 1999

On March 3 the U.S. Supreme Court affirms in *Cedar Rapids Community School District v. Garret F.* that intensive, ongoing health care services qualify as related services and must be provided if they are necessary to keep a student in school and can be provided by anyone other than a physician, regardless of cost.

## 2000

In May the U.S. Office of Special Education Programs (OSEP) convenes a planning committee to address pre-referral and identification issues for students with learning disabilities. This group initiates a coordinated effort to examine Response to Intervention (RTI) as a means of identifying students with learning disabilities and providing those students with academic intervention and support prior to their enrollment in special education programs. In follow-up, the OSEP funds the National Research Center on Learning Disabilities (NRCLD) to develop RTI and improve the identification of children with learning disabilities.

## 2002

The 2002 amendments to the Elementary and Secondary Education Act (P.L. 107-110)—better known as the No Child Left Behind Act (NCLB)—are signed into law on January 8 by President George W. Bush. The legislation holds schools, school districts, and states accountable for the academic achievement of all children. NCLB mandates standardized testing to measure academic achievement and requires accountability systems that track students' testing outcomes. The law mandates demonstrations of "adequate yearly progress" (AYP) for all students, including students with disabilities and students identified as having limited English proficiency. It also specifies penalties for schools failing to meet their AYP goals.

## 2004

On October 25 the reauthorization of the Assistive Technology Act (P.L. 108-364) expands assistive technology (AT) services to all persons who have federally defined disabilities for whom AT will increase or maintain their skills or functioning levels.

On December 3 the Individuals with Disabilities Education Improvement Act (IDEIA; P.L. 108-446) aligns IDEA with NCLB and requires states to report on the numbers of students who are assessed based on grade-level assessments, alternative assessment (for students with significant disabilities), and modified assessment criteria. It also adds Response to

Intervention (RTI) as an alternative process for identifying students with learning disabilities.

## 2005

On November 14 the U.S. Supreme Court rules in *Schaffer v. Weast* that the burden of proof in a due process hearing challenging an individualized education program (IEP) is with the contesting party (whether the disabled child, the parents, or the school district).

## 2006

The Combating Autism Act (P.L. 109-416) is signed into law on December 19. The first federal autism-specific law, the act provides funding for research, intervention, screening, and education related to Autism Spectrum Disorders.

## 2007

Responding to a suit brought under the Individuals with Disabilities Education Act, the U.S. Supreme Court rules in *Winkelman v. Parma City School District* on May 21 that parents have the right to represent the interests of their child in court and are not required to have legal representation.

## 2008

U.S. Secretary of Education Margaret Spellings speaks at the *2008 Global Summit on Education: Inclusive Practices for Students With Disabilities* in September. Spellings describes the positive outcomes of including students with disabilities in regular classrooms, calls for inclusive education worldwide, and announces grants that target assessment for students with disabilities and limited English proficiency in the United States.

## 2009

The American Reinvestment and Recovery Act (P.L. 111-5), which becomes law on February 17, provides over $90 billion to states and school districts and allocates more than $12.2 billion to special education —primarily for programs and projects covered under IDEA Part B for students ages 3 to 21 and Part C projects for infants and toddlers in early intervention services.

On June 22 the U.S. Supreme Court rules in *Forest Grove School District v. T.A.* that if a school district fails to provide a free and appropriate public education, the Individuals with Disabilities Education Act (IDEA) allows financial reimbursement for an appropriate private education of a child with a disability, even when the child has not previously received special education services in the public school setting.

## 2010

The U.S. House of Representatives passes the Preventing Harmful Restraint and Seclusion in Schools Act (H.R. 4247). This act prohibits the use of physical interventions that could create health or safety risks, specifies conditions under which restraint and seclusion are permitted in schools, encourages training for teachers and school personnel in relation to the use of restraint and seclusion, and requires schools to discuss uses of restraints and seclusion with parents.

# *Four*

# Biographies of Key Contributors in the Field

Cheryl Hanley-Maxwell and
Lana Collet-Klingenberg

A large number of individuals have made significant contributions to the development of special education for persons with disabilities. The biographical sketches in this chapter, presented in alphabetical order, profile some of those individuals and their contributions.

## Donald Baer (1931–2002)

*American founder of the discipline of applied behavior analysis*

Donald M. Baer was born in St. Louis, Missouri, on October 25, 1931, to George and Ida (Feldman) Baer, Jewish immigrants from Belorussia. Raised in Chicago, he earned both his bachelor's degree (in 1950) and his Ph.D. in experimental psychology (in 1957) from the University of Chicago. He then joined the faculty at the University of Washington, where he and colleague Sidney W. Bijou established the "behavior analysis" approach to child development, systematically analyzing child behavior. This work formed the foundation for the discipline of applied behavior analysis (ABA), which Baer created with Montrose Wolfe and Todd Risley after joining the faculty at the University of Kansas in the late

1960s. This discipline became a major approach to creating and applying research-driven interventions in treating children with autism and many other forms of developmental disability. Specifically, applied behavior analysis is predicated on teaching new behaviors or modifying inappropriate behavior through manipulating conditions or events that precede or follow targeted behavior. Baer's work in this area included improving the language, social skills, and "imitative" socialization skills of children with intellectual disabilities and other developmental disabilities.

Other significant areas of research undertaken by Baer included modification of problem behavior and generalization of the outcomes of those interventions and interventions for young children in preschool programs and other early education programs. His research also contributed to further development of applied research design and methods in the study of human behavior. During his lifetime, Baer produced hundreds of papers, books, and presentations on early childhood education, developmental disabilities and antisocial behavior in children, and intellectual disabilities. The most famous of these publications was a 1968 article, "Some Current Dimensions of Applied Behavior Analysis" (written with colleagues Todd Risley and Montrose Wolf), that appeared in the *Journal of Applied Behavior Analysis*. This piece continues to be regarded as the seminal description of the underpinnings of applied behavior analysis. Baer was also a key figure in the development of the Bureau of Child Research (now the Schiefelbusch Life Span Institute-LSI) at the University of Kansas. By the early 1970s, this research institution was widely recognized as a global center of applied behavioral analysis.

Baer died on April 28, 2002, of heart failure in Lawrence, Kansas. He was survived by his wife, Elsie Pinkston, and three daughters.

## Further Reading

University of Kansas Department of Applied Behavioral Science. (2002). Donald M. Baer, 1931–2002 [obituary]. Retrieved from http://www.absc.ku.edu/inmemory/baer.shtml

Wesolowski, M. D. (2002, Fall). Pioneer profiles: An interview with Donald Baer. *Behavior Analysis, 25*(2), 135–150.

# Alfred Binet (1857–1911)

*French psychologist who invented the Binet-Simon intelligence test*

Alfred Binet was born Alfredo Binetti on July 8, 1857, in Nice, France. The son of a physician father and artist mother, Binet grew up in Paris and graduated from law school in 1878. Shortly after graduating, however, his growing fascination with psychiatry led him to abandon his fledgling law career and instead embark on an extended course of private study into the era's most influential psychiatric texts. In 1883 he took a research position in the neurological department of the Salpêtrière Hospital in Paris, where he remained for the next seven years. During this time Binet experienced a brief fascination with the hypnosis theories of department director Jean-Martin Charcot, a source of later embarrassment to the psychiatrist.

In 1891 Binet moved on to Sorbonne University, where he worked as a researcher and associate director in its Laboratory of Experimental Psychology. In 1894 he co-founded *L'Annee Psychologique,* a major psychology journal. That same year he was promoted to director of the laboratory, a position he held until his death in 1911. It was in this capacity that Binet undertook his famous efforts to quantify children's intelligence levels. Binet's research in this area was already well underway in 1904, when the French government asked a society of child psychologists, La Société Libre pour l'Etude Psychologique de l'Enfant, to create an advisory commission on the education of children with intellectual disabilities. Specifically, French authorities wanted the commission to create a means for identifying children with special needs for alternative education.

Binet's appointment to the commission spurred him to collaborate with doctoral student Theodore Simon in the development of a series of tests—called a scale—designed to assess mental abilities. These tests emphasized attention, memory, and other cognitive functions rather than learned information. Once the tests were compiled, Binet and Simon devised performance measurements weighted in accordance with average children's abilities at different ages. The scale consisted of 30 tasks of increasing complexity designed to determine appropriate educational placement for all children who took the test. Test scores were reported as a mental age, ranging from 3 to 13 years. A test subject's mental age might match his or her chronological age, but a "mental age" score that was lower than chronological age was an indicator of possible intellectual disability (conversely, children who scored higher than their chronological age were designated as potentially gifted children).

Upon its unveiling in 1905, the so-called Binet-Simon Scale (which the creators revised twice, in 1908 and 1911) became a popular intelligence-measuring tool among school administrators in Europe as well as in the United States, where a revised scale created by Henry H. Goddard came into common usage. Goddard's version of the Binet-Simon intelligence test was further revised in 1916 by psychologist Lewis M. Terman of Stanford

University. Terman's version, known as the Stanford-Binet test, became the most popular intelligence test in the United States for the next several decades. Binet died in Paris on October 18, 1911.

## Further Reading

Fancher, R. E. (1985). *The intelligence men: Makers of the I.Q. controversy.* New York: Norton.
Wolf, T. H. (1973). *Alfred Binet.* Chicago: University of Chicago Press.

## Burton Blatt (1927–1985)

*American advocate for people with intellectual disabilities*

Burton Blatt was born in New York City on May 23, 1927. His parents were Abraham and Jennie Starr Blatt. Blatt served with the U.S. Navy during World War II, then returned to his hometown after the war, earning a bachelor of science degree from New York University in 1949. One year later he received a master's degree from Teacher's College, Columbia University. From 1950 to 1955, he taught children with intellectual disabilities in New York City. In 1955 he was awarded both a graduate scholarship and a teaching assistantship to Pennsylvania State University, from which he earned his doctorate in 1956.

After leaving Penn State, Blatt became an associate professor of special education at New Haven State Teachers College (later Southern Connecticut State College, now Southern Connecticut State University). In 1957 he and Yale University's Seymour Sarason collaborated to establish the first of three psycho-educational clinics (other clinics were later established at Boston University and Syracuse University). In 1959 he was promoted to professor and chair of the college's newly minted Special Education Department. In 1961 Blatt joined Boston University's School of Education as professor and chair of its Special Education Department.

By this time Blatt was already well-known for his expertise on mental health and retardation issues, as well as his passionate advocacy for the rights of people with intellectual disabilities. Much in demand as a lecturer on these subjects, he also frequently served as a consultant to a wide array of state and federal agencies, philanthropic organizations, universities, and associations for retarded citizens on policy issues related to intellectual disabilities. In 1966, though, Blatt became known far beyond the circles of academia and government with his groundbreaking book *Christmas in Purgatory,* an explosive and haunting exposé of what he termed "cruel and inhuman" living conditions in American mental institutions. The book, published with photographer Fred Kaplan, became a rallying cry for institutional reformers, who took aim at facilities charged with caring for children and adults with intellectual disabilities across the United States. In 1967 Blatt and Kaplan published a version of the exposé in *Look Magazine*, "The Tragedy and Hope of Retarded Children."

In 1969 Blatt moved on to Syracuse University, where he accepted a position as professor of education and director of the school's Division of Special Education and Rehabilitation. In 1971 he helped founded the Center on Human Policy, a research institution dedicated to advocacy on behalf of people with disabilities. Blatt was appointed dean of the Syracuse University School of Education and Rehabilitation in 1976. Three years later he published a sequel to his groundbreaking *Christmas in Purgatory* titled *The Family Papers: A Return to Purgatory*, in which he reiterated his calls for deinstitutionalization and his support for community living programs, family support services, and education programs for children and adults with severe intellectual disabilities. Blatt died on January 20, 1985, but his work lives on through Syracuse University's Burton Blatt Institute, a leading advocacy organization for the advancement of civic, economic, and social rights of persons with disabilities.

## Further Reading

Blatt, B. (1970). *Exodus from pandemonium: Human abuse and a reformation of public policy.* Boston: Allyn & Bacon.

Blatt, B. (1999). *In search of the promised land: The collected papers of Burton Blatt.* Washington, DC: American Association on Mental Retardation.

## Louis Braille (1809–1852)

*French inventor of the Braille system of reading and writing for blind people*

Louis Braille was born on January 4, 1809, in Coupvray, a small town outside of Paris, France. The son of Constance and Louis Braille Sr., a saddlemaker, young Braille was blinded at the age of 3, when he accidentally injured an eye while handling one of his father's leatherworking tools. The wound quickly became infected and spread to his other eye, a development that blinded him for the rest of his life. At age 10 Braille enrolled on scholarship at Paris's Royal Institution for Blind Youth (Institut National des Jeunes Aveugles), one of the first schools of its kind. But most instruction at the school was accomplished orally, as the only reading options for blind and visually impaired people of this era were limited edition books of huge size featuring raised letters that could only be deciphered with great difficulty by touch.

In 1821 a former French Army officer named Charles Barbier became acquainted with the director of the school. Upon learning that Barbier had developed a silent military communication system called "night writing," which blended raised dots and dashes on paper into a readable code, the director arranged a demonstration for his students. When Braille and other students touched the samples of night writing (which was never implemented for use by the French military), they appropriated the medium to send each other written messages. In addition, Braille began revising the code to make it easier to use, most notably by replacing Barbier's 12-dot system with a 6-dot system that was easier to read and use for message composition.

The Braille code proved enormously popular with students at the school, but the administration refused to incorporate it into its teachings. Faculty members expressed concern that implementation of Braille's innovative reading and writing system would further separate blind people from sighted people. Undaunted, Braille published the world's first book printed in Braille in 1827. The subject of the book was his tactile-based system of reading and writing. One year later, Braille accepted a teaching position at the Royal Institution for Blind Youth, from which he had recently graduated. He spent the rest of his life as an instructor at the school.

In his spare time, meanwhile, Braille continued to work on his coding system. In 1837 he unveiled symbols for mathematics and music, and in 1840 he collaborated with Pierre Foucault to develop a printing machine capable of creating Braille text. Braille died in Paris of tuberculosis on January 6, 1852. It was only after his death that his Braille system was broadly accepted. France officially recognized his system in 1854, and by the close of the 19th century, it was being used in many parts of the world.

## Further Reading

Mellor, C. M. (2006). *Louis Braille: A touch of genius*. Boston: National Braille Press.

Roblin, J. (1955). *The reading fingers: Life of Louis Braille, 1809–1852*. New York: American Foundation for the Blind. Retrieved from http://www.afb.org/roblinbiography/book.asp

# Lou Brown (1939– )

*American education reformer and advocate
for persons with disabilities*

Lou Brown began his college education at East Carolina University, where he earned a bachelor's degree in social studies in 1963 and a master's degree in clinical psychology in 1965. In 1969 he received a doctorate in special education and vocational rehabilitation from Florida State University. Upon graduating from Florida State he immediately joined the faculty of the University of Wisconsin–Madison's Department of Rehabilitation Psychology and Special Education. He remained at Wisconsin until his retirement in 2003.

During his 34 years in Wisconsin's Department of Rehabilitation Psychology and Special Education, Brown became one of the leading voices for special education reform and the rights of persons with disabilities in the United States. His outspoken criticisms of the longstanding segregationist orientation of educational and other social services were initially viewed in some quarters as extreme, but this perspective is today widely debated within special education and disability policy circles.

Brown has steadfastly argued that students and other individuals with disabilities are capable of becoming productive and fully integrated members of the broader society in which they live, but that their capacity to do so has been hampered by institutions such as group homes, special schools, classes, and workshops that segregate people with disabilities from non-disabled peers. Brown has repeatedly called for a much greater emphasis on community integration in educational, vocational, and recreational programs for people with disabilities. He argues that this can be accomplished by "developing service delivery models, curricula and values that prepare students with disabilities to live, work and play in integrated society."

## Further Reading

Lou Brown Home Page. Retrieved from http://rpse.education.wisc.edu/faculty/
     lbrown
Martin, T. J., & Toplis, R. M. (2007). Brown, Lou. In C. R. Reynolds & E. Fletcher-
     Janzen (Eds.), *Encyclopedia of special education* (3rd ed.). Hoboken, NJ: Wiley.

# William M. Cruickshank (1915–1992)

*American expert on special education and mental disabilities*

William M. Cruickshank was born in Detroit, Michigan, in 1915. He received a bachelor's degree from Eastern Michigan University in 1937 before enrolling at the University of Chicago, where he earned his master's degree in 1938. He served in the U.S. Armed Forces as a clinical psychologist from 1942 to 1945 and earned his doctorate from the University of Michigan in 1945.

Cruickshank's academic career began at Syracuse University in 1946 as a professor of psychology and education. In 1952 he was appointed dean of special services and distinguished professor of psychology and education at Syracuse, and he later became director of the school's Division of Special Education and Rehabilitation. In 1966 he, his wife, Dorothy (Wager) Cruickshank, and three daughters relocated to Ann Arbor, Michigan, where he accepted an appointment as director at the University of Michigan's Institute for the Study of Mental Retardation and Related Disabilities. He served in this position until 1980, when he stepped down (he remained a professor of psychology and education at Michigan until 1985). In 1976 he founded the International Academy for Research in Learning Disabilities (IARLD), an organization for which he also served as president and executive director.

Cruickshank's primary interest throughout his long and distinguished career was treatments for children with learning disabilities, including problems stemming from brain injuries as well as those with neurological, psychological, genetic, and neonatal origins. His most influential work in this regard included reforms of teacher preparation for working with children with disabilities; development of disability screening and assessment practices in early childhood; improvement of educational settings for children with disabilities (such as through the reduction of distracting environment stimuli and use of visually stimulating materials); and improvement of medical diagnostics in investigating learning disabilities. Cruickshank also traveled far and wide to increase awareness of programs and processes for children with learning disabilities, and he served as a consultant to approximately 30 foreign governments (as well as many state and provincial governments in the United States and Canada) during his long career. He also published widely in scholarly journals and served as an author or editor of more than 40 books. Cruickshank died of heart disease in Ann Arbor on August 13, 1992.

## Further Reading

Hallahan, D. P. (1993, Summer). A tribute to William M. Cruickshank (1915–1992). *Journal of Special Education, 27,* 247–250. doi:10.1177/002246699302700207

Weiss, M. P., & Lloyd, J. W. (2001). Structure and effective teaching. In D. P. Hallahan & B. K. Keogh (Eds.), *Research and global perspectives in learning disabilities: Essays in honor of William M. Cruickshank.* Mahwah, NJ: Lawrence Erlbaum.

# Lloyd Dunn (1917–2006)

*Canadian-American pioneer in developmental disability education and policy*

Lloyd M. Dunn was born in Saskatchewan, Canada, in 1917. After earning bachelor's and master's degrees from the University of Saskatchewan, Dunn worked as a principal and high school teacher in his home province until World War II, when he served as a radar officer for the British Royal Air Force. Dunn entered the University of Illinois at Urbana-Champaign after the war, and under the mentorship of renowned special education scholar Sam A. Kirk, he earned the first doctorate in special education and psychology ever bestowed by the school.

In 1953 Dunn began a 10-year stint as chair of the Department of Special Education at the George Peabody College for Teachers (now part of Vanderbilt University), and from 1963 to 1967, he served as director of Peabody's Institute on Mental Retardation and Intellectual Development. Dunn became an immensely influential special education scholar and policy consultant during these years at Peabody. He developed and published important developmental disability assessment tools such as the Peabody Picture Vocabulary Test, the Peabody Language Development Program, and the Peabody Individual Achievement Test during this time. In addition, from 1960 to 1964, he served on President John F. Kennedy's Panel on Mental Retardation, where he helped craft some of the earliest legislation benefiting people with disabilities. He also played a prominent role in the panel's decision to found a national network of 12 research facilities, including the John F. Kennedy Center for Research on Human Development at Vanderbilt University, for the study and treatment of people with developmental disabilities.

Profoundly influenced by the evolving civil rights movement and its condemnation of "separate but equal" rationalizations for segregation, Dunn also was at the vanguard of a group of education scholars who questioned whether children with mild mental and physical disabilities were being disadvantaged by their removal from general school populations into separate classrooms and courses of instruction. His 1968 paper on this subject, titled "Special Education for the Mildly Retarded: Is Much of it Justifiable?" was a major impetus for the "mainstreaming" of children with mild retardation into public school classrooms in the 1970s.

In the late 1960s, Dunn left Peabody for the University of Hawaii, where he worked for the next 30 years. During this time he continued to conduct research and campaign for reforms in public policy and special education related to people with intellectual disabilities and other developmental disabilities. In 1997 Dunn and his wife, Leota, who collaborated with him on much of his research, established the Dunn Family Chair of Educational and Psychological Assessment and a related research center at Vanderbilt Peabody College. Dunn died in Las Vegas, Nevada, on April 6, 2006.

## Further Reading

Dunn, L. M. (1968). Special education for the mentally retarded: Is much of it justifiable? *Exceptional Children, 35*, 5–22.

Osgood, R. L. (2005). *The history of inclusion in the United States.* Washington, DC: Gallaudet University Press.

# Siegfried Engelmann (1931– )

*American co-developer of the Direct Instruction (DI) program of educational instruction*

Siegfried E. "Zig" Engelmann was born on November 26, 1931, in Chicago, Illinois. In 1953 he married Therese Piorkowski, with whom he had four children. Two years later he earned a bachelor's degree in philosophy from the University of Illinois. Engelmann then worked for the next decade in a variety of fields, including jobs as an investment counselor and advertising executive.

In 1964 Engelmann accepted a position as an education specialist at his alma mater's Institute for Research on Exceptional Children in Champaign. He spent most of the next six years at the institute, during which time he directed a number of grant-funded projects on the subject of educational instruction for disadvantaged children, ranging from students from poor backgrounds to those with learning disabilities. He also collaborated with

Carl Bereiter during this time to launch the Bereiter-Engelmann Preschool Program, which touted the benefits of intensive instruction in cognitive performance among disadvantaged preschoolers.

In 1970 Engelmann took a faculty position in the University of Oregon's Department of Special Education (in 1974 he was made a full professor), and in the early 1970s he joined with Wesley Becker to roll out a program of educational instruction for disadvantaged children called the Direct Instructional System for Teaching and Remediation (DISTAR). This model of instruction, which was created within the framework of a federal effort called Project Follow Through to extend the national Head Start program, emphasized tightly scripted and fast-paced lesson plans, ability grouping, continuous monitoring/assessment of progress, and emphasis on the development of cognitive strategies.

Engelmann's profile in the special education community rose dramatically during the 1970s and 1980s, as empirical studies indicated that the Engelmann-Becker program, which came to be known as Direct Instruction (DI), and similar curricula were more effective than other models of teaching and development utilized in Project Follow Through. These results brought about increased implementation of Direct Instruction in schools and districts across the United States and Canada, especially in institutions charged with teaching disadvantaged children or children with learning disabilities.

Direct Instruction's strictly prescribed practices have been criticized by some educators as excessively "robotic" and hostile to teacher creativity and autonomy. But the outspoken Engelmann and many of his supporters assert that numerous studies conducted in the 1990s and 2000s continue to show the greater efficacy of direct instruction programs in spurring high academic achievement, including among developmentally disabled and other disadvantaged students. In 1997 Engelmann founded the nonprofit National Institution for Direct Instruction in Eugene, Oregon, to publicize, implement, and support DI programs.

## Further Reading

Marshall, K. J. (2010). Direct instruction. In T. C. Hunt, J. Carper, T. J. Lisley, & C. D. Raisch (Eds.), *Encyclopedia of educational reform and dissent.* Thousand Oaks, CA: Sage.

Siegfried Engelmann (b. 1931). Retrieved from http://psych.athabascau.ca/html/387/OpenModules/Engelmann/Engelmannbio.shtml

# Doug Fuchs (1949– ) and Lynn Fuchs (1955– )

*American leaders in the study of learning disabilities and developers of the Response to Intervention (RTI) program*

Lynn Fuchs was born in 1955 in New Jersey; her husband Doug Fuchs was born in 1949 in Brooklyn, New York. They both earned bachelor's degrees in 1972 from Johns Hopkins University in Baltimore, Maryland, the city where their lifelong interest in education first became evident. While in Baltimore, they joined with friends to establish a successful Saturday school for underprivileged students in their neighborhood. In 1973 they both earned master's degrees in elementary education from the University of Pennsylvania. In 1978 Doug Fuchs received his Ph.D. in educational psychology from the University of Minnesota, and Lynn Fuchs earned the same degree from Minnesota three years later.

In 1985 the Fuchses joined the faculty of Vanderbilt University's Peabody College. Lynn Fuchs worked prior to that at the University of Minnesota and Boston's Wheelock College, while Doug Fuchs taught at the University of Minnesota and Clark University in Worcester, Massachusetts. After arriving at Peabody (and subsequently joining the prestigious Vanderbilt Kennedy Center for Research on Human Development), they began a long and fruitful professional collaboration that has made them among the nation's foremost special education researchers.

Garnering research grants from places such as the National Institute of Child Health and Human Development (NICHD) and the U.S. Department of Education's Institute of Education Sciences (IES), the Fuchses have developed a variety of successful teaching strategies for students, including disadvantaged children and those with learning disabilities. Those strategies include student assessment tools like Curriculum-Based Measurement (CBM); and Peer-Assisted Learning Strategies (PALS), a program that pairs up students who tutor each other in research-based reading and math activities. Their research has also contributed significantly to the development of systematic strategies for RTI (Response to Intervention), a tiered program of intervention designed to identify academically "at-risk" students, diagnose the basis for their difficulties, and implement programs of small-group tutoring or individualized instruction to help them. They also co-direct the Vanderbilt Kennedy Center Reading Clinic with colleague Donald Compton.

Although the Fuchses maintain their own independent programs of research, they both play leading roles (along with Peabody colleagues

Donald Compton and Dan Reschly and Donald Deshler of the University of Kansas) in the research and administrative activities of the National Research Center on Learning Disabilities (NRCLD). Established in 2001 through a grant from the U.S. Department of Education, the center focuses on the study and dissemination of research related to RTI and effective interventions for students with specific learning disabilities. Located at Vanderbilt, the NRCLD conducts research on alternative methods of identification within the RTI framework, researches special education policies at the state and local levels, and assists states and school districts with RTI programs.

The Fuchses have won numerous honors and awards during their illustrious careers. Many of these honors were individual in nature, but others, including the 2003 Career Research Award from the Council for Exceptional Children and the 2005 Distinguished Researcher Award from the Special Education Research Special Interest Group (SIG) of the American Educational Research Association, were bestowed jointly on both members of the husband-and-wife team.

## Further Reading

Beckham, J. L. (2009, Spring). Double vision: Personalized strategies for children with learning disabilities add up to big benefits for everybody. *Vanderbilt Magazine, 90*(1). Retrieved from http://www.vanderbilt.edu/magazines/vanderbilt-magazine/2009/03/double-vision

Fuchs, D., Fuchs, L., & Vaughn, S. (2008). *Response to intervention: A framework for reading educators.* Newark, DE: International Reading Association.

## Thomas Hopkins Gallaudet (1787–1851)

*American educator who established the first American school for the deaf*

Thomas Hopkins Gallaudet was born in Philadelphia, Pennsylvania, on December 10, 1787. He graduated from Yale College (now Yale University) in 1805. Drawn to several different career paths, Gallaudet studied law, taught school, and worked as a salesman before deciding to enter the ministry. He received his divinity degree from Andover Theological Seminary in 1814 and became a minister.

While visiting his parents in Hartford, Gallaudet met Alice Cogswell, the nine-year-old daughter of his parents' neighbor, Dr. Mason Cogswell.

Alice was deaf, and Gallaudet, observing how isolated she was, became determined to help her learn to communicate. Encouraged by Dr. Cogswell to learn all he could about educating the deaf, Gallaudet traveled to England. There he met Abbe Sicard, head of the Royal Institute of Deaf-Mutes in Paris, and two teachers who were also deaf, Laurent Clerc and Jean Massieu. Gallaudet went to Paris to study at the Institute, where he learned the method of French sign language used by Sicard and his staff.

In 1816 Gallaudet returned to the United States with Clerc, who had agreed to help him found a school for the deaf. Together, they toured New England to raise funds for a school in Hartford, which would become known as the American School for the Deaf. It was the first school of its kind in the nation, and the first class included Alice Cogswell. From 1817 to 1830, Gallaudet was the principal of the school and was involved in every aspect of its development, including teaching, raising funds, and lecturing on behalf of deaf people. At that time, many people with hearing impairments were shunned by society and denied an education. Gallaudet helped to change that, promoting the benefits of education for deaf people and championing the communication method that would become known as American Sign Language, which he and Clerc developed. In 1821 he met and married Sophia Fowler, a deaf student at the American School; they eventually had eight children.

Gallaudet's health began to fail, and in 1830 he resigned from the American School for the Deaf. At that time, the school had 140 pupils and an international reputation, and it still educates deaf students today. After his retirement, Gallaudet wrote several books for children, including a speller, a dictionary, and volumes on religion. He also became the first professor of philosophy of education at New York University. Near the end of his life, Gallaudet became involved in the movement to reform the treatment of persons with mental illness in institutions. He died in Hartford on September 10, 1851.

Gallaudet is perhaps best known to Americans today for the famed school for the deaf that bears his name: Gallaudet University in Washington, D.C. Founded by his son Edward Gallaudet in 1864 as the National College for the Deaf and Dumb, the school was authorized by Congress and its charter was signed by President Abraham Lincoln. It was renamed Gallaudet College in 1894 and became Gallaudet University in 1986. It is considered the world leader in education for deaf and hard of hearing students.

## Further Reading

Kutler, S. I. (Ed.). (2003). Deaf in America. In *Dictionary of American History*. New York: Scribner.

The Legacy Begins. Retrieved from http://aaweb.gallaudet.edu/About_Gallaudet/History_of_the_University/The_Legacy_Begins.html

# Henry Herbert Goddard (1866–1957)

*American psychologist who popularized the Binet-Simon IQ test and helped draft the first laws mandating special education in the United States*

Henry Herbert Goddard was born on August 14, 1866, in Vassalboro, Maine, to Henry Clay Goddard and Sarah Winslow Goddard. Goddard received his bachelor's degree from Haverford College in 1887, his master's degree in mathematics from Haverford in 1889, and his Ph.D. in psychology from Clark University in 1899. He married Emma Florence Robbins in 1889; they had no children.

Goddard was a professor of psychology and education at a teacher's college in Pennsylvania from 1899 to 1906, then became the director of research at the Training School for Feeble-Minded Girls and Boys in Vineland, New Jersey. There, he began the first scientific research into intellectual disabilities.

Goddard traveled to Europe in 1908 to study the theories behind the Binet-Simon intelligence scale, the basis for IQ testing. He returned to the United States and translated Binet's scale into English, then used the tests to measure intelligence in the students at Vineland. Convinced of the test's ability to accurately measure intelligence, Goddard widely disseminated the test throughout the United States. In 1911 he used the results of tests given at Vineland and in the New York public schools to help the State of New Jersey draft the first U.S. law requiring that children who were blind, deaf, or mentally retarded be provided with special education in the public schools.

Controversially, Goddard also used his results to further his theories about inherited intelligence and eugenics. He believed that intelligence was an inherited trait, basing his theories on Mendelian genetics. He posited that "feeblemindedness," his term for intellectual disabilities, was the result of a recessive gene, and that intelligence was predetermined in an individual's genetic makeup. Using these theories, he researched two branches of a family, publishing the results in 1912 as *The Kallikak Family: A Study in the Heredity of Feeble-Mindedness* ("Kallikak" was a pseudonym, based on the Greek words for "good and bad"). Goddard described how the oldest ancestor in the study had fathered two families: a "bad" one, the result of an affair with a woman Goddard called "a feeble-minded tavern girl," which resulted in an illegitimate son and subsequent generations of retardation, alcoholism, illegitimacy, and other negative attributes; and a "good" one, the result of a marriage to a "normal" woman, which resulted in generations of people of normal intelligence and high achievement.

The Kallikak book received widespread praise and popularized Goddard's belief that mentally retarded people should be sterilized and isolated from the general public. These theories were popular among eugenicists and led to the passage of sterilization laws in many states. They also led to the screening of immigrants at Ellis Island for evidence of mental deficiency, and to the deportation of the "mentally deficient."

By the 1940s, Goddard's theories had become widely discredited, but they are not his only legacy. He used intelligence testing to advocate for special education in the public schools. Goddard was involved in preparing the Alpha and Beta intelligence tests of U.S. Army recruits in World War I, leading to their general acceptance in military and civilian life. Today, most contemporary intelligence tests are based in part on Goddard's methodology.

Goddard continued to teach until his retirement in 1938. He then moved to Santa Barbara, California, where he died on June 19, 1957. Still a controversial figure today, Goddard is remembered as the "father of intelligence testing" in the United States and for his advocacy of special education, as well as for his eugenicist beliefs.

## Further Reading

Fancher, R. E. (1985). *The intelligence men: Makers of the IQ controversy.* New York: Norton.

Zenderland, L. (1998). *Measuring minds: Henry Herbert Goddard and the origins of American intelligence testing.* Cambridge, UK: Cambridge University Press.

# Marc Gold (1931–1982)

*American educator and advocate for special education*

Marc Gold was born in 1931. He received his bachelor's degree from Los Angeles State College and became a special education teacher in East Los Angeles. After several years of teaching, Gold developed a radically different approach to special education. He believed that students with severe disabilities had been improperly labeled by society as unteachable. He believed that these students had more potential than anyone had thought, and that they could indeed learn, with the right teaching methods.

Gold went back to school at the University of Illinois at Urbana-Champaign and received his doctorate in experimental child psychology and special education in 1969. He was hired by the university to conduct research at the Institute for Child Behavior and Development. At that time, most professionals believed that students with low IQs were incapable of learning; Gold's research changed that thinking. Working with students with IQs assessed below 50, he demonstrated how they could learn to complete tasks while developing self help, mobility, vocational, and social skills. Based on his findings, Gold developed a teaching system he called Try Another Way that focused on task analysis, method, content, and process. In three-day workshops, he trained teachers and support staff in his system of instructional strategies for students with severe disabilities, which helped the students to learn and perform sophisticated and marketable tasks. In addition, Gold showed how these successful strategies improved students' sense of self, self-esteem, and sense of place within mainstream society.

Gold left teaching in the 1970s to devote himself to training full-time. He founded his own company, Mark Gold and Associates, which presented the Try Another Way approach to thousands of staff around the country, and many state educational agencies adopted his methods. He died of cancer in 1982.

Gold served on several boards and other governing councils related to people with disabilities. He was president of the Workshop Division of the Illinois Rehabilitation Association, a member of the Executive Board of the American Association of Education for the Severely/Profoundly Handicapped, vice president of the Vocational Rehabilitation Division of the American Association on Mental Deficiency, and on the editorial boards of *The American Journal of Mental Deficiency* and *Mental Retardation*.

## Further Reading

Perske, R. (1987). The legacy of Marc Gold. In C. S. Mcloughlin, J. B. Garner, & M. Callahan (Eds.), *Getting employed, staying employed: Job development and training for persons with severe handicaps* (pp. vi–xii). Baltimore, MD: Brookes.

Sands, D. J., & Wehmeyer, M. L. (Eds.). (1996). *Self-determination across the life span: Independence and choice for people with disabilities.* Baltimore, MD: Brookes.

# Daniel Hallahan (1944– )

*American professor of special education who focuses on learning disabilities in children*

Daniel P. Hallahan was born in 1944. He attended the University of Michigan, receiving his bachelor's degree in psychology in 1967 and completing a combined doctorate in education and psychology in 1971. Since that time he has taught at the University of Virginia, where he is currently the chairperson of the Department of Curriculum, Instruction, and Special Education in the university's Curry School of Education.

Hallahan is also a prolific researcher and writer, and has authored or co-authored several of the major textbooks in the field of special education, including *Psychological Foundations of Learning Disabilities* and *Exceptional Learners: Introduction to Special Education.* He has made seminal contributions to the field of special education, affecting the way children with learning disabilities are taught, as well as what they are taught. One of the most important features of his work is the emphasis on classroom practice. As one of the first researchers to identify processing deficits in children with learning disabilities, he created the techniques now widely used to help children with disabilities learn, applying self-monitoring, highlighting, and organizational training to academic learning.

In addition to his research interest in children with learning disabilities, Hallahan is involved in studies of attention deficit hyperactivity disorder (ADHD) and the history of special education. He has documented the issues and controversies that have arisen in the field of special education from the point of view of scholars, teachers, school districts, the public, and federal policymakers, noting how public and professional trends have changed over time to accommodate the evolving concept of learning disabilities in America.

Hallahan is the Charles S. Robb Professor of Education at the University of Virginia. He has been the principal or co-principal investigator on several federally funded research projects and was the founder and director of Virginia's Learning Disabilities Research Institute. Hallahan is the recipient of many awards, including the 2000 Council for Exceptional Children Special Education Research Award and the 2003 State Council of Higher Education for Virginia Outstanding Faculty Award. He was the founding editor of the journal *Exceptionality* and continues to serve on its board, as well as on those of *Learning Disabilities Research and Practice*, *Learning Disability Quarterly*, and the *Journal of Special Education*.

## Further Reading

Kauffman, J. M., & Hallahan, D. P. (2005). *Special education: What it is and why we need it*. Boston: Allyn & Bacon.

Spotlight on CEC special education research award recipient Daniel Hallahan. (2000, Fall). *Exceptional Children, 67*, 1.

## Andy Halpern (1939–2008)

*American academic researcher who specialized in the transition from adolescence to adulthood for people with disabilities*

Andrew Stephen Halpern was born on July 29, 1939, in Brooklyn New York, to Israel and Sylvia Halpern. He received his bachelor's degree from Carleton College, his master's degree from Yale University, and his doctorate from the University of Wisconsin–Madison's Department of Counseling and Behavioral Studies (now the Rehabilitation Psychology and Special Education Department). He married Elizabeth Paddock in 1966; they had two children, Stacey and Benjamin.

Halpern began his academic career in special education at the State University of New York at Buffalo. After continuing his research at the University of Texas, he completed his career in the College of Education at the University of Oregon. Specializing in the area of transition from adolescence to adulthood for people with disabilities, Halpern was the founding director of the Secondary Special Education and Transition research workgroup at Oregon. The unit was created in 1987 in response to the widely acknowledged need to improve the post-secondary outcomes of youth with disabilities. Under Halpern, the group expanded its research to include many issues in the field of transition, including accessing and completing post-secondary education, finding meaningful employment, developing social relationships, and living independently.

Of special interest to Halpern were quality of life issues, and he devoted much of his research to analysis, measurement, and development of programs to provide workable practices for youth with disabilities. In 1993, he developed a model for transition that included outcomes relating to employment, social networks, residential issues, and community concerns. He also focused his research on the challenges faced by young people with disabilities in post-secondary education, especially in the development of programs and policies to prevent young people from dropping out of college.

At the University of Oregon, Halpern helped develop the longest continuously operating training program on transition issues in the United States. The Secondary Special Education and Transition area focuses on such crucial areas as self-determination, career development, employment issues relating to gender, vocational rehabilitation, and the creation of collaborative programs across academic disciplines for young people with disabilities.

Halpern died of cancer on March 7, 2008, in Eugene, Oregon. He was the recipient of several awards, including the 2010 George Wright Varsity Award from the University of Wisconsin-Madison's Department of Rehabilitation Psychology and Special Education for "outstanding contributions to the fields of rehabilitation counseling and rehabilitation psychology."

## Further Reading

Halpern, A. (1990). Transition issues that affect research on evaluation. *Studies in Educational Evaluation, 16*(2), 297–318.

Halpern, A. (1993, May). Quality of life as a conceptual framework for evaluating transition outcomes. *Exceptional Children, 59*(6), 486–499.

# Norris Haring (1923– )

*American academic researcher specializing in children with learning and behavioral disabilities*

Norris Grover Haring was born on July 25, 1923, in Kearney, Nebraska, to Grover and Elsie Haring. He received his bachelor's degree from Nebraska State Teaching College in 1948, his master's degree from the University of Nebraska in 1950, and his Ed.D. from Syracuse University in 1956. He married Dorothy Borgens in 1950, and they had three children.

Haring began his career in education in 1956 as the director of special education for the Arlington County Public Schools in Arlington, Virginia.

After two years in that position, he became an associate professor and the coordinator of special education for the University of Maryland, where he worked for three years. In 1960 he joined the faculty of the University of Kansas Medical Center, where he served as professor of education and educational director of the Children's Rehabilitation Unit.

In 1965 Haring became professor of special education and director of research, grants, and contracts in special education at the University of Washington's College of Education, where he worked until his retirement in 1996. In his first year at Washington, Haring founded the university's Experimental Education Unit, which he directed for many years while continuing to produce research in his area expertise: developing strategies for children with learning and behavioral disabilities. Of particular importance to Haring are the necessity of early intervention, the benefits of tailoring instruction to the needs of individual children, and the advantages of providing inclusive educational resources to children with disabilities. A pioneer in the field of special education, he also developed a method of precision measurement, which he used to study the effectiveness of instructional methods in children with a wide range of disabilities, including those with severe disabilities, such as deaf blindness, autism, and Down syndrome.

In 2009 Haring and his wife, Dorothy, also a lifelong educator, founded the Norris and Dorothy Haring Center for Applied Research and Education at the University of Washington. Incorporating the Experimental Education Unit that he founded in 1965, the new Haring Center expanded to include an Applied Research Unit and a Professional Development Unit. It integrates the principles of Haring's Education Unit and implements its key missions of applied research into finding the best strategies to teach children with disabilities. It also offers courses and opportunities in professional development for educational staff, both within and outside the university. Funded through an endowment established by the Harings, the new center provides educational opportunities for graduate students, as well as support for students, families, and researchers in the field of disabilities.

## Further Reading

Haring, N., McCormick, L., & Haring, T. (1994). *Exceptional children and youth* (6th ed.). Englewood Cliffs, NJ: Prentice Hall.

Kelley, P. (2009, March 12). Experimental Education Unit to become research center with planned gift from founding director. *University of Washington News*. Retrieved from http://uwnews.org/uweek/article.aspx?id=47936

# Beth Harry (1944– )

*Jamaican-born American researcher focusing on the impact of special education on children from diverse backgrounds*

Elizabeth Harry was born on November 28, 1944, in Jamaica. She received her bachelor's degree in English from the University of Toronto in 1967, her master's degree in education from the Ontario Institute for Studies in Education in 1973, and her Ph.D. in special education from Syracuse University in 1989.

Harry began her teaching career in Canada, then moved to Trinidad in 1973, where she taught at the University of West Indies in Trinidad. While living there, she had her first child, Melanie. It was Melanie's birth that prompted Harry to focus on the field of special education. Melanie was born with cerebral palsy, and Harry, as her primary caregiver, was faced with the challenge of finding adequate medical care as well as appropriate educational placement for her daughter. When Melanie was three, Harry founded a nonprofit school in Trinidad for special-needs children, the first preschool of its kind in the island nation. The school continued operating after Melanie died at the age of five, and it has since expanded to become the Immortelle Children's Center in Port of Spain, serving more than 100 students.

After Melanie's death, Harry returned to graduate school to focus on special education. Her special area of research is the effect of special education on children and families who come from diverse cultural and linguistic environments. She taught at the University of Maryland for several years, then joined the faculty at the University of Miami in 1995. She is currently professor of special education, family and multicultural issues, in the Department of Teaching and Learning at the University of Miami's School of Education.

In her recent work, Harry has studied children with disabilities living in the United States from diverse backgrounds, including Puerto Rican, African American, and Hispanic American populations. Another focus of Harry's research is the disproportionate number of minority students in special education programs, and she has examined the topic as part of a National Academy of Science investigative panel. In 2003 she received a Fullbright award to study the educational and cultural issues confronting Moroccan children in Spanish schools.

Harry is the author of numerous articles and books, including *Why Are So Many Minority Students in Special Education?* and *Case Studies of Minority Student Placement in Special Education*. In 2010 she published a memoir,

*Melanie, Bird With a Broken Wing: A Mother's Story.* Harry is also a member of the National Association of State Directors of Special Education and a research fellow at the Center for Effective Collaboration and Practice.

## Further Reading

Harry, B., and Klingner, J. (2006). *Why are so many minority students in special education? Understanding race and disability in schools.* New York: Teachers College Press.

Veciana-Suarez, A. (2009, February 9). Author shares her experiences of mothering special-needs child. *Miami Herald.* http://www.deseretnews.com/article/705291046/Moms-Author-shares-her-experiences-of-mothering-a-special-needs-child.html?pg=1

## Samuel Gridley Howe (1801–1876)

*American physician, social reformer, and advocate for persons with disabilities*

Samuel Gridley Howe was born on November 10, 1801, in Boston, Massachusetts, to Joseph and Patty Howe. He graduated from Brown University in 1821 and received his M.D. from Harvard in 1824. After medical school, Howe traveled to Greece, where he served as a physician during Greece's war against Turkey.

Upon returning to the United States, Howe became involved in the education of the blind. He was named director of the New England Asylum for the Blind, which later became the country's first college for the blind. Howe traveled to Europe to learn the latest techniques of instruction for the blind, even creating a kind of raised-letter alphabet, similar to the one invented by Louis Braille later in the century. Using his own methods, Howe created books, maps, and other materials for his students.

Perhaps the most important of Howe's efforts had to do with his philosophy of persons with disabilities. At a time in history when most people believed that individuals with disabilities were intellectually inferior and unteachable, and should be isolated from society, Howe was convinced of their potential. He wrote and lectured on the subject, promoting the academic success of his students and convincing many in the medical and educational communities that people with disabilities needed education and opportunity, not pity and charity. An early advocate for what is now called inclusion, Howe organized schools that were designed to integrate people with disabilities into their communities.

Howe's early advocacy for the blind expanded over the years to include championing the rights of people with mental illness and developmental disabilities. Focusing on the inherent humanity of all people, he was also a prominent supporter of abolition and prison reform and advocate for the rights of African Americans and former convicts.

Now considered an early pioneer in the movement for disability rights, Howe is remembered today for his fervent belief in the abilities and rights of persons with disabilities. When he died on January 9, 1876, his work was continued by his wife, Julia Ward Howe, an equally fervent advocate for disability rights who is now best known as the author of "The Battle Hymn of the Republic."

## Further Reading

Meltzer, M. (1964). *A light in the dark: The life of Samuel Gridley Howe*. New York: Crowell.

Schwartz, H. (1956). *Samuel Gridley Howe: Social reformer, 1801–1876*. Cambridge, MA: Harvard University Press.

## Jean Itard (1775–1838)

*French physician who pioneered the education of deaf-mutes and people with mental disabilities*

Jean-Marc Gaspard Itard was born on April 24, 1775, in Oraison, France. Although he had no formal medical training, he served as an assistant in a military hospital during the French Revolution and learned enough to enter a surgical internship in 1796. In 1800 Itard was made the chief physician at the National Institution for Deaf-Mutes in Paris. Through his studies of the human ear, he founded the field of otolaryngology, writing a textbook on the subject and inventing the Eustachian catheter, called Itard's Catheter. Perhaps most importantly, his efforts to educate his most famous patient, the Wild Boy of Aveyron, led to Itard's being considered the "father of special education."

In 1799, a group of French hunters discovered a feral boy, about 11 or 12 years of age, living in a forest in southern France. Naked, filthy, and frightened of the men, the boy was unable to speak or communicate, and he escaped from the first home in which he was placed. He was eventually caught again and brought to Paris, where he was evaluated by doctors who were eager to examine a "human savage" in a near-primitive state. Most of them agreed with the famous psychiatrist Philippe Pinel, who declared that the boy wasn't "wild" but mentally deficient, an "incurable idiot," and incapable of learning.

Itard did not agree. He named the child Victor and proceeded to try to educate him. He developed a plan to teach Victor to speak, to communicate using signing and symbols, to engage with those around him, to become aware of his environment, and to respond to cultural and social stimuli. Itard based his approach on the concept that knowledge is sensory, and that since Victor could see and hear, he could also learn. After five years of instruction, Victor had indeed improved: he could speak using a limited vocabulary, read, and follow simple instructions. But he never made the kind of progress Itard had expected. It is not known whether Victor had a specific disability, although over the years many have speculated that he may had autism or had other mental or behavioral disabilities.

For his work with Victor, Itard is widely considered a pioneer in special education. He was the first doctor in history to propose using an enriched environment and a scientific approach to overcome delays in development. After Itard's death in 1838, his work lived on in his pupil Edouard Seguin, who did groundbreaking work with students with cognitive disabilities and influenced the work of physician and educator Maria Montessori.

## Further Reading

French, J. E. (2000). Itard, Jean-Marie Gaspard. In A. E. Kazdin (Ed.), *Encyclopedia of psychology* (pp. 377–378). Oxford, UK: Oxford University Press.

Gaynor, J. F. (1973). The "failure" of J. M. G. Itard. *Journal of Special Education, 7*(4), 439–445.

# James Kauffman (1940– )

*American academic researcher focusing on special education issues in children with behavioral disorders*

James Milton Kauffman was born on December 7, 1940, in Hannibal, Missouri. His parents were Nelson and Carol Kauffman. Nelson was a minister, and Carol was a novelist. Kauffman received his bachelor of science degree from Goshen College in 1962, his master's in education from Washburn University in 1966, and his Ed.D. from the University of Kansas in 1969.

Kauffman began his career at the Southard School of the Menninger Clinic in Topeka, Kansas, where he was a teacher of elementary-age children with severe behavioral disabilities. After two years at Menninger, he taught regular elementary students in Indiana and Kansas public schools as well as students with emotional disabilities in elementary and middle schools in Kansas. Following a year as an assistant professor of special education at Illinois State University in 1969, he joined the faculty of the Department of Special Education at the University of Virginia. Kauffman taught at Virginia from 1970 until his retirement in 2003, rising to become Associate Dean for Research, Chair of the Department of Special Education in the Curry School of Education, and Charles S. Robb Chair in Education. He is the author of hundreds of articles and several seminal books in the field of special education, including *Exceptional Learners: An Introduction to Special Education*, now in its 12th edition, which he co-authored with Daniel Hallahan, and *Characteristics of Emotional and Behavioral Disorders of Children and Youth*, now in its 9th edition, which he co-authored with Timothy J. Landrum.

Kauffman's areas of interest in special education include emotional and behavioral disorders and learning disabilities. He has also been involved in public policy as it pertains to education, and he has researched the history of special education. He is the recipient of numerous awards, including the Outstanding Service Award from the Midwest Symposium for Leadership in Behavioral Disorders in 1991, the Research Award from the Council for Exceptional Children in 1994, and the Outstanding Leadership Award from the Council for Children with Behavioral Disorders in 2002. He was a founding member of the International Academy for Research in Learning Disabilities, President of the Council for Children with Behavioral Disorders, and President of the Society for Learning Disabilities and Remedial Education. Now an Emeritus Professor at Virginia, Kauffman continues to research, write, and contribute to the field of special education.

## Further Reading

Crockett, J. B., Gerber, M. M., & Laundrum, T. J. (Eds.). (2007). *Achieving the radical reform of special education: Essays in honor of James M. Kauffman*. Mahwah, NJ: Lawrence Erlbaum.

Kauffman, J. M. (2010). *The tragicomedy of public education: Laughing and crying, thinking and fixing*. Verona, WI: The Attainment Company, Inc.

# Helen Keller (1880–1968)

*American writer and advocate for people who are blind or have other disabilities*

Helen Keller was born in Tuscumbia, Alabama, on June 27, 1880. Her parents were Colonel Arthur Keller, a former Confederate Army officer who worked as a newspaper editor, and Kate Keller. Healthy as an infant, Keller suffered an illness (possibly scarlet fever) that robbed her of her sight and hearing when she was 19 months old. Frustrated and unable to comprehend her world, Keller was a difficult, unmanageable child until teacher Anne Sullivan arrived in Tuscumbia in 1887. Sullivan employed a diligent approach of teaching Keller to associate objects with words, spelling the names of objects letter by letter via finger tracings on the palm of her student's hand while making Keller touch the objects. Sullivan's methods eventually took hold, and Keller eagerly learned countless words. In time she learned to read and write using both the regular alphabet and Braille, and she also set about learning to speak. With Sullivan as her constant companion, Keller attended school, where she proved to be spirited and intelligent. She was accepted at Radcliffe College in 1890, earning a bachelor's degree in 1894.

In 1903 Keller wrote and published her autobiography, *The Story of My Life*, the first of several works in which she conveyed her experiences and perceptions of the world as a person with deaf-blindness. Through her writing, lectures, and associations with prominent Americans of her era, she also became a devoted advocate for people with disabilities of all types and an outspoken proponent of other progressive social causes. However, her work on behalf of the blind, both in the United States and in other nations, proved to be her strongest calling. In 1915 she joined the board of the newly formed Permanent Blind War Relief Fund (eventually renamed Helen Keller International), and in 1924 she began an association with the American Foundation for the Blind, raising money for its Helen Keller Endowment Fund. Through her work on behalf of these organizations, she became an international figure, meeting with heads of state and travelling the world well into her 70s to inspire other people with disabilities and advocate for their needs. Sullivan remained at Keller's side until her death in 1936; after that, Keller benefited from the devoted assistance of Polly Thomson.

Keller earned worldwide respect as well as countless awards for her work, including the Presidential Medal of Freedom, the highest honor given to American citizens, in 1964. Other nations bestowed similar awards, and she was presented with numerous honorary degrees and association memberships. She retired from public life in 1961. The story of Keller's early association with Sullivan was captured in the play and Oscar-winning 1962 movie *The Miracle Worker*, and she was also the subject of an Oscar-winning 1955 documentary titled *Helen Keller in Her Story*. Keller died in Westport, Connecticut, on June 1, 1968.

## Further Reading

Helen Keller Biography. American Foundation for the Blind. Retrieved from
    http://www.afb.org/section.asp?SectionID=1&TopicID=129
Hermann, D. (1998). *Helen Keller: A life*. New York: Alfred A. Knopf .
Keller, H. (1903). *The story of my life*. New York: Doubleday, Page & Co.

# John F. Kennedy (1917–1963)

*American president who inaugurated federal legislation to fund special education and programs for people with disabilities*

John Fitzgerald Kennedy was born on May 29, 1917, in Brookline, Massachusetts, to Joseph Kennedy, a wealthy businessman, and Rose Fitzgerald Kennedy. Both of his parents were the products of powerful political families. John was the second of nine children in his family. His siblings included a younger sister, Rosemary, who was born with intellectual disabilities. Kennedy graduated from Harvard University in 1940 and, following the U.S. entry into World War II in 1941, joined the navy and served until 1945. He married Jacqueline Bouvier in 1953, and they had two children, Caroline and John Jr.

Kennedy entered national politics in 1946, with his election to the U.S. House of Representatives as a Democrat from Boston. In 1952 he was elected to the U.S. Senate, and in 1960 he was elected as the 35th president of the United States. As part of his domestic policy agenda, Kennedy was an outspoken advocate for people with intellectual disabilities. His parents had created a foundation to improve the lives of persons with intellectual disabilites, the Joseph P. Kennedy Jr. Foundation, which was directed by his sister Eunice Kennedy Shriver for many years. With her support, Kennedy endeavored to bring the issues surrounding intellectual disabilities "out of the shadows" and into the public sphere. "Mental retardation ranks with mental health as a major health, social, and economic problem in this country," he declared. "It strikes our most precious asset, our children."

Early in his administration, Kennedy established the National Institute of Child Health and Human Development, which still conducts research into intellectual disabilities. In October 1961, Kennedy appointed a panel of specialists to "prescribe a plan of action in the field of mental retardation." In February 1963, Kennedy presented a Special Message to the Congress on Mental Illness and Mental Retardation, in which he outlined the panel's recommendations to create community-centered agencies to replace mental hospitals; develop diagnostic, clinical, and treatment centers; and fund special education resources, including training and rehabilitative services.

In October 1963, Kennedy signed the first major federal legislation on mental illness and retardation, the Maternal and Child Health and Mental Retardation Planning Amendment to the Social Security Act. It was followed by another legislative act that implemented many of the panel's recommendations, including providing grants to the states to develop facilities and programs for individuals with intellectual disabilities, funding research centers to study and treat intellectual disabilities, and increasing funding to train special education teachers.

Kennedy was assassinated in November 1963. His successor, Lyndon B Johnson, was also a strong advocate for people with disabilities. Johnson continued Kennedy's President's Panel on Mental Retardation, making it an ongoing advisory group and changing its name to the President's Committee for People with Mental Retardation in 1966, a program that is still in existence today as the President's Committee on Intellectual Disabilities.

## Further Reading

Kennedy, J. F. (1963, October 24). Remarks on signing the Maternal and Child Health and Mental Retardation Planning Amendment to the Social Security Act. Retrieved from http://www.jfklibrary.org/Asset-Viewer/Archives/JFKPOF-047–038.aspx

O'Neill, W. L., & Jackson, K. T. (2003). John F. Kennedy. In *The Scribner encyclopedia of American lives thematic series: The 1960s*. New York: Scribner.

# Barbara Keogh (1925– )

*American academic researcher focusing on special education and early childhood development*

Barbara Keogh was born on January 1, 1925, in Glendale, California. She received her bachelor's degree in psychology from Pomona College in

1946, her master's degree in psychology from Stanford University in 1947, and her doctoral degree in psychology from Claremont Graduate School in 1963. She did her internship in clinical psychology at Stanford Medical School and was a postdoctoral fellow at the University of Birmingham, England, funded by the U.S. Public Health Department.

Keogh began her professional career as a clinical psychologist working for the Alameda County, California, juvenile court in 1949. She started working as a school psychologist in the San Francisco area in the 1950s, and in that position she assessed young children with learning problems, focusing on reading and spatial organization problems. The assessment tools she developed became the basis of her Ph.D. research and also led to further studies in examining and assessing developmental changes in children.

Keogh joined the faculty at the University of California Los Angeles in 1966 and continued her work researching the ways in which children learn. Her research led her to a career in special education, focusing on the early identification and prevention of learning and behavioral problems. As part of her research, Keogh was involved in clinical observations of exceptional children in school settings, where she developed her theories of how variations in temperament, or behavioral styles, affect children's learning abilities, as well as the ways in which they are perceived by teachers and members of their families.

These theories led Keogh to further research studies, including Project REACH, which was a longitudinal study of developmental problems of infants and children. This study was expanded and developed by Keogh and others in Project CHILD, in which both children and families were studied over a number of years.

In addition to her research in early childhood development, Keogh was a member of the National Advisory Committee on the Handicapped during the creation and passage of P.L. 94-142, the Education for All Handicapped Children Act of 1975, the landmark legislation that changed the way children with disabilities are educated in the United States. She was the recipient of the Council for Exceptional Children's Research Award in 1992 and, as a professor emerita at UCLA, continues to write and speak on issues regarding children with learning disabilities and special education.

## Further Reading

Keogh, B. K. (1999, Spring). Reflections on a research career: One thing leads to another. *Exceptional Children, 65*(3), 295–301.

Keogh, B. K., Bernheimer, L. P., Galllimore, R., & Weisner, T. (1998). Child and family outcomes over time: A longitudinal perspective on developmental delays. In M. Lewis & C. Feiring (Eds.), *Families, risk, and competence*. Mahwah, NJ: Lawrence Erlbaum.

## Samuel Kirk (1904–1996)

*American psychologist and educator*
*known as the "father of special education"*

Samuel Alexander Kirk was born on September 1, 1904, in Rugby, North Dakota, to Richard and Nellie Kirk, who were farmers. After receiving his bachelor's degree in psychology from the University of Chicago in 1929, he moved on to the University of Michigan, where he earned a master's degree in psychology in 1931 and a doctoral degree in psychology in 1935.

While completing his Ph.D., Kirk began working as a research psychologist at the Wayne County Training School in Northville, Michigan, where he was a counselor to teenage boys with intellectual disabilities. Working with these children, Kirk observed that education for mentally challenged youth at that time was limited to custodial care. From that point he focused his career on correcting that approach, developing both assessment tools and programs designed for children with a wide range of disabilities. His work helped him earn the title, "the father of special education."

During a career that spanned more than 60 years, Kirk became an international authority on special education, focusing on diagnosis, teacher training, and social policy. After receiving his doctorate, he joined the faculty of Milwaukee State Teachers College, where he was the director of the Division of Education for Exceptional Children until 1947. Then he became a professor at the University of Illinois at Urbana-Champaign, where he continued his pioneering work in special education and founded the Institute for Research on Exceptional Children. His accomplishments drew the attention of the Joseph P. Kennedy Jr. Foundation, an organization that works to improve the lives of people with intellectual disabilities.

At an academic conference in 1963, Kirk made education history as the first person to use and define the phrase "learning disabilities," thus providing a framework and language for a new academic field. He also developed one of the first assessment tools for learning disabilities, the Illinois Test of Psycholinguistic Abilities, which was widely used in the United States and around the world.

Also in 1963, Kirk's experience and expertise enabled him to play an influential role in public policy on the national level. President John F. Kennedy chose him to be the director of the Division of Handicapped Children in the U.S. Office of Education. In this role, Kirk persuaded the U.S. Congress to fund the training of teachers in special education, and he also helped establish the federal laws that require the nation's public schools to provide a free and appropriate public education (FAPE) for all children, including those with disabilities. In addition to his work on U.S. education policy, Kirk traveled widely, helping to establish programs in special education around the world.

After retiring from the University of Illinois in 1968, Kirk moved to Tucson, Arizona, where he joined the faculty of the University of Arizona and served as a professor of education until his death on July 21, 1996. In addition to his work as a teacher and policy specialist, Kirk wrote several major works in the field of special education, including *Educating Exceptional Children*, which has been published in many editions and translated into many languages. He was widely hailed for his contributions and received many awards for his work, including the Association for Children with Learning Disabilities Annual Award and the International Milestone Award from the International Federation on Learning Disabilities.

## Further Reading

Kirk, S. A. (1993). *The foundations of special education: Selected papers and speeches of Samuel A. Kirk*. Reston, VA: Council for Exceptional Children.
Minskoff, E. H. (1998). Sam Kirk: The man who made special education special. *Learning Disabilities Research and Practice, 13*(1), 15–21.

## Ogden Lindsley (1922–2004)

*American psychologist who specialized in behavior research, measurement, and performance technology*

Ogden Lindsley was born on August 11, 1922, in Providence, Rhode Island. He received his bachelor's degree in psychology from Brown University in 1948, his master's degree in experimental psychology and histochemistry from Brown in 1950, and his doctoral degree in psychology from Harvard University in 1957.

At Harvard, Lindsley studied under the influential psychologist B. F. Skinner, and together they founded the Behavior Research Laboratory at Harvard Medical School. As co-director of the program, Lindsley was involved in behavioral research with human subjects. In describing his research and results, he coined the term "behavioral therapy." He analyzed schizophrenia patients in what is considered the first human operant laboratory.

After receiving his Ph.D., Lindsley continued to work at Harvard as a research associate in psychiatry and as an associate in psychology. In 1965 Lindsley changed the focus of his work from research to the training of teachers in special education. That year, he moved to the University of Kansas, where he was Director of Educational Research for the school's medical center and a research associate in the Bureau of Child Research.

It was at Kansas that Lindsley developed the theories for which he is best known, Precision Teaching and Celeration Charting. Precision Teaching is a measurement system designed to provide direct measures of a student's performance, resulting in rapid learning and higher retention of material. Lindsley wanted to replace the established measurement model of "percentage correct" in learning with a method that was based instead on frequency of response. The goals of Precision Teaching were retention, endurance, and application of learning. Lindsley used the method successfully on a wide variety of students, from early elementary through post-secondary levels, including those with severe intellectual disabilities.

Lindsley developed the Standard Celeration Chart—a method of graphing used by teachers and students to chart improvement—as a way to measure subtle changes in behavior. His theories proved to be successful among students and in professional organizations. Although they were never widely adopted in public education, they have been used successfully in organizational management, inspiring the creation of such groups as the Standard Celeration Society and International Association for Behavior Analysis.

Lindsley was a prolific writer on a number of topics reflecting his wide-ranging interests and research, including psychiatry, education, geriatrics, advertising, and pharmacology. He served as president of the National Association of Gifted Children, the Association of Behavior Analysis, and the Standard Celeration Society. His honors and awards include the Hofheimer Research Prize from the American Psychiatric Association and the Outstanding Contributor Award from the Northern California Association for Behavior Analysis. Lindsley died on October 10, 2004.

## Further Reading

Lindsley, O. R. (1990, Spring). Precision teaching: By teachers for children. *Teaching Exceptional Children*, 22(3), 10–15.

Lindsley, O. R. (1992). Why aren't effective teaching tools widely adopted? *Journal of Applied Behavior Analysis*, 25(1), 51–57.

# Nicholas Long (1956– )

*American academic specializing in adolescent mental health and parenting education*

Nicholas James Long was born in 1956. He received his bachelor of science degree in psychology from McMaster University in 1978, his master of science degree in psychology from Mississippi State University in 1980, and his doctoral degree from the University of Georgia in 1985. He served as an intern in psychology in the Clinical Child and Pediatric Psychology program at Children's Hospital National Medical Center from 1983 to 1984, and was a post-doctoral fellow in psychology at the University of Georgia from 1985 to 1986.

Long is currently a member of the faculty at the University of Arkansas for Medical Sciences, where he is a Professor of Pediatrics and Director of Pediatric Psychology. He is also on the staff of the Arkansas Children's Hospital. Long serves as the Director and Principal Investigator of the Arkansas State Parental Information and Resource Center Program for Effective Parenting—a program funded by the U.S. Department of Education—where he directs collaborative projects in the area of parent training and education. An earlier study he headed, the "Parents Matter" study funded by the Centers for Disease Control and Prevention, examined the efficacy of early prevention efforts by parents to reduce sexual intentions in teenagers.

Long's special focus in psychology is the mental health and well-being of children and the education of parents. He has written extensively in the area of parenting programs, for professional and non-professional audiences alike, including *Parenting the Strong-Willed Child*. He has also taught classes for educators in crisis intervention for youth, and is the co-author of *Conflict in the Classroom* and of *Life Space Intervention: Talking to Children in Crisis*. These books offer teachers, counselors, special educators, and mental health and juvenile justice staff strategies in dealing with troubled and at-risk youth who engage in destructive or self-defeating behaviors.

Long also continues to give workshops and classes to some 600 parents each year. In addition, he is a member of several national organizations devoted to the health and well-being of parents and children. Long is the recipient of the Educational Research Award for 2007–2008 and the Chancellor's Faculty Teaching Award for 2008 from the College of Medicine at the University of Arkansas for Medical Sciences.

## Further Reading

Long, N. (2005). Child and adolescent mental health care in the primary health-care system: Improving the interface. *Clinical Child Psychology and Psychiatry, 10*(4), 453–455.

Long, N., et al. (2004). Lessons learned from the Parents Matter! Program. *Journal of Child and Family Studies, 13*(1), 101–112.

# O. Ivar Lovaas (1927–2010)

*Norwegian-born American psychologist who developed a method for treating autism*

Ole Ivar Lovaas was born on May 8, 1927, in Lier, Norway. His father was a journalist and his mother was a homemaker, but the entire family worked as forced agricultural laborers during the Nazi occupation of Norway in World War II. After immigrating to the United States, Lovaas attended Luther College in Iowa, receiving his bachelor's degree in music in 1951. He received his doctoral degree in psychology from the University of Washington in 1958, and he joined the faculty of the University of California, Los Angeles in 1961.

Lovaas began his study of autism at UCLA in the 1960s, at a time when the condition was considered to be caused by neurosis, and autistic children were most often institutionalized and treated with psychotherapy. Lovaas took a distinctly different approach: he was the first researcher to suggest that autism was treatable in some children. He developed a method of intense one-on-one treatment based on the principles of applied behavior analysis, or ABA. This program employed early intervention, repetition, and rewards and punishments to modify behavior. Children worked for 30 to 40 hours a week on a simple task that was broken down to its simplest components, practicing each component again and again.

When *Life* magazine produced a profile on Lovaas and his technique, it showed researchers physically punishing children for bad behaviors, including the use of electric shocks. Facing a storm of criticism, Lovaas replaced punishment with positive reinforcement. His treatment method then gained wider acceptance, especially after he published a 1987 article describing his research results, "Behavioral Treatment and Normal Educational and Intellectual Functioning in Young Autistic Children." In the article, he outlined the results of a long-term study, begun in 1970, of a group of low-functioning 2- and 3-year-olds with autism. One group received 40 hours of Lovaas's treatment program each week, and another group received 10 hours of treatment each week. At the end of several years, the children were tested. The results showed that 9 of the 19 children in the intensive therapy group had gained 30 IQ points and were able to attend school in regular classrooms, while those who had received less therapy registered little change.

While some autism researchers questioned Lovaas's results, the impact of his study was enormous. Parents who had been told that autism was untreatable were eager to have their children treated with the new methods. Lovaas launched an institute to train teachers, and today thousands of children with Autism Spectrum Disorder receive treatment using his therapeutic techniques. Lovaas's therapy is useful for some, but not all children with autism, and other researchers have yet to replicate his groundbreaking results. But at the time of his death on August 2, 2010, he was lauded as one of the most important pioneers in the treatment of autism, and some of the behavioral therapies he created have become standard around the world.

## Further Reading

Lovaas, O. I. (1987, February). Behavioral treatment and normal educational and intellectual functioning in young autistic children. *Journal of Consulting and Clinical Psychology, 55*(1), 3–9.

Lovaas, O. I. (2002). *Teaching individuals with developmental delays: Basic intervention techniques.* Austin, TX: Pro-Ed.

# G. Reid Lyon (1949– )

*American psychologist, educator, and administrator*
*who created the "Reading First" program*

G. Reid Lyon was born in 1949. After serving in the army from 1967 to 1970, he earned his bachelor's degree in experimental psychology from

North Carolina Wesleyan College in 1973. He went on to attend the University of New Mexico, earning his master's degree in learning disabilities in 1974 and his doctoral degree in special education and psychology in 1978.

While in graduate school, Lyon taught third grade and special education at a local public school. This experience led him to question how children learn to read, and what happens when they have learning difficulties. He began his academic career at the University of Alabama–Birmingham, where he worked in the department of special education and psychology from 1978 to 1980, then took a position at Northwestern University, where he worked in the department of communication science and disorders from 1980 to 1983. His next position was at the University of Vermont School of Medicine, where he worked until 1991. The focus of Lyon's academic work was in learning disabilities, specifically reading disabilities, studied from multiple points of view, including neurology, educational methods, and cognitive science.

In 1992 Lyon joined the staff of the National Institutes of Health, where he was a research psychologist and the chief of the Child Development and Behavior Branch, part of the National Institute of Child Health and Human Development. He was responsible for the development and management of research programs in developmental psychology, cognitive neuroscience, behavioral pediatrics, reading development, learning disabilities, and early childhood development.

During his years at NIH, Lyon served as an advisor to President George W. Bush and as a member of the President's Commission on Excellence in Special Education. He also worked with the administration, the Department of Education, and the U.S. Congress to develop the Reading First program. This $1 billion federal initiative, part of the No Child Left Behind education reforms, was designed to improve student reading scores, especially in high-poverty, low-performing school districts. Although the program was based on scientific research, it proved to be controversial among some reading education professionals, who questioned Lyon's research methodology and results. Yet his impact on the field, especially his now widely accepted focus on evidence-based practices in reading instruction, make him one of the most influential leaders in reading research.

Lyon left NIH in 2005 and moved to Dallas, Texas, where he became the Vice President for Research and Evaluation at Higher Ed Holdings. In 2008 Lyon founded his own educational services firm, Synergistic Education Solutions, which provides professional development, research, and assessment services to public and private educational institutions and organizations. In addition, he serves as Distinguished Professor of Education Leadership and Policy at Southern Methodist University and as Distinguished Scientist in Brain and Behavior Science at the University of Texas–Dallas. He is the author of more than 130 scientific articles, books, and book chapters in the field of education.

## Further Reading

Dr. G. Reid Lyon: Converging evidence, reading research: What it takes to read. (2010). Retrieved from http://www.childrenofthecode.org/interviews/lyon.htm

Shaughnessy, M. F. (2008, February 4). An on-going conversation with Reid Lyon: About Reading First. *EducationNews*. Retrieved from http://www.ednews.org/articles/an-on-going-conversation-with-reid-lyon–about-reading-first.html

## Donald MacMillan (1940– )

*American academic researcher focusing on classification of children with mild disabilities and at-risk populations*

Donald Lee MacMillan was born on January 1, 1940, in Cleveland, Ohio. His father, Alexander MacRae MacMillan, was an engineer, and his mother, Arline Marnie MacMillan, was a homemaker. MacMillan received his bachelor's degree from Western Reserve University (now Case Western Reserve University) in 1962. He went on to pursue graduate studies at the University of California, Los Angeles, earning his master's degree in education in 1963 and his doctoral degree in education (Ed.D.) in 1967.

In 1968 MacMillan joined the faculty of the University of California, Irvine, where he taught in the Graduate School of Education and continues as Professor Emeritus. His main areas of interest in research include classification and treatment problems in children with mild disabilities, risk factors that relate to disabilities, social and affective characteristics of students with disabilities, and behavior and conduct problems in children and adolescents. He has also addressed the problems facing the public educational system in dealing with the increased population of students with learning disabilities, from the point of view of correct diagnosis, classification, and treatment, especially as they affect the assessment and educational needs of children with mild learning disabilities.

In addition to his academic appointment, MacMillan has served as a research specialist for the California Department of Mental Hygiene, a research educationist for the Pacific-Neuropsychiatric Institute at the University of California, Los Angeles, and as a consultant to the Bureau of the Education of the Handicapped, U.S. Office of Education. He is a member of the American Association on Mental Deficiency, the American Educational Research Association, the Council for Exceptional Children, the Society for Research in Child Development, and the California Association of Professors of Special Education.

MacMillan is the author of numerous books and articles in the field of special education, including *Behavior Modification in Education* and *Hidden Youth: Dropouts From Special Education.* He has been the recipient of many awards, including the 1989 Edgar A. Doll Award from the American Psychological Association, the 1990 Education Award from the American Association on Mental Retardation, the 1995 Humanitarian Award from the American Association on Mental Retardation, the 1998 Research Award from the Council for Exceptional Children, and the 1998 Outstanding Research Award from the Special Education Special Interest Group of the American Educational Research Association.

## Further Reading

MacMillan, D. L. (1991). *Hidden youth: Dropouts from special education.* Reston, VA: Council for Exceptional Children.

MacMillan, D. L. (1998). *Mental retardation in school and society.* Boston: Little, Brown.

## Donald H. Meichenbaum (1946– )

*American founder of cognitive behavior therapy and expert on the psychological impact of violence and trauma*

Donald H. Meichenbaum was born on June 10, 1946, in New York, New York. He received his bachelor's degree from City College of New York in 1962, and his master's and doctoral degrees from the University of Illinois.

Meichenbaum then began a 30-year career as an educator and researcher at the University of Waterloo in Ontario, Canada. The focus of his research includes the impact of trauma on individuals, as well as the effects of anger and violence in the culture. He has researched and written about the effects of anger and violence on various populations, including psychiatric patients, children and adolescents in residential treatment programs, prison inmates, individuals with traumatic brain injury, and those with developmental disabilities.

Meichenbaum is one of the founders of cognitive behavior therapy, a method of behavior modification that he elucidated in textbooks, including *Cognitive Behavior Modification: An Integrative Approach*. In recent years, he has focused on post-traumatic stress disorder (PTSD), especially in the training of therapists and researchers to deal with victims of violence. He has worked with patients who have been victims of domestic violence, as well as with groups of people in the aftermath of violence, including the Oklahoma City bombing and the Balkan wars of the 1990s. He was one of the first researchers to focus on the victims' narrative portrayals of their trauma as a means to defining treatment for victims of violence.

After his retirement from the University of Waterloo in 1998, Meichenbaum helped found the Melissa Institute in Miami, Florida, an organization devoted to the prevention of violence. It was created in the memory of Florida resident Melissa Aptman, who was murdered in St. Louis in 1995, just before her college graduation. The Melissa Institute seeks to reduce violence and to help victims of violence through educational outreach, as well as by connecting researchers, therapists, and policymakers.

Meichenbaum is a prolific author and speaker, and he has served on the editorial boards of key journals in his field. He received the Izaak Killiam Research Fellowship Award, and he is the past president of the Canadian Psychological Association. He now lives in Florida, where, in addition to his duties as Research Director of the Melissa Institute, he serves as a Distinguished Visiting Professor in the School of Education at the University of Miami.

## Further Reading

Meichenbaum, D. M. (1995). *Clinical handbook/treatment for PTSD*. Minneapolis, MN: Institute Press.

Meichenbaum, D. M. (2003). *Treatment of individuals with anger-control problems and aggressive behavior*. New York: Crown.

## Maria Montessori (1870–1952)

*Italian educator and physician who created the
Montessori education method for children*

Maria Montessori was born on August 31, 1870, in Chiaravalle, Italy. Her father, Allessandro, was an army officer, and her mother, Renilde, was a homemaker. Growing up at a time when women were discouraged from pursuing careers of any kind, Montessori defied tradition. After studying engineering, mathematics, and biology as a teenager, she went on to medical school at the University of Rome. In 1894 she became the first Italian woman to receive a medical degree.

In 1900 Montessori was named director of the Orthophrenic School at the University of Rome, where she worked with children with intellectual disabilities. At that time, such children were labeled "deficient and insane" and kept in asylums with adults. Montessori believed that these children could be educated, and she designed a program that was based on her own background in science and on the theories of intellectual development created by Jean-Marc Gaspard Itard and Edouard Seguin. She studied her young patients carefully as she implemented Seguin's concept of breaking down everyday tasks into small steps. Once she inaugurated this approach with the children with intellectual disabilities in her care, many of them learned to perform such tasks as preparing food and cleaning with such ability that they were able to transition into regular schools.

Next, Montessori tested her theories on children without disabilities. Unable to obtain support from the Italian government, she opened a school of her own, Casa dei Bambini (Children's House). It was basically a day-care facility for the children of workers, most of whom were poor, in one of Rome's worst slums. With only one aide, Montessori took on a classroom of 50 preschoolers. The students responded to her educational methods immediately, taking pride in learning everyday tasks, which reinforced the self-respect and independence crucial to her method. They were also eager to learn to read and write and soon were able to do both, and they also learned math, employing Montessori's manipulative materials that she devised to develop concepts and coordination.

Montessori's methods were based on careful observations of children and developed to respond to their spontaneity, as well as their innate need for order and continuity. She built her schools to size for her young pupils, with tables, chairs, sinks, and shelves made specifically to fit them. The result was a tremendously effective method of education that became successful worldwide. It also validated Montessori's deeply held beliefs in equality among people of different economic and social classes, for the children of the poor working class proved to be as able intellectually as those of the wealthier classes.

Maria Montessori died on May 8, 1870, in Noordwijk, the Netherlands. In the early decades of the 20th century, schools embracing the Montessori method were established in Europe and North America. By the 1940s, however, her methods had lost much of their appeal, due in large part to the writings of educator William Kilpatrick, who declared Montessori outdated. But the methods have experienced a resurgence in the last 20 years, and today there are more than 6,000 Montessori schools in the United States, operating as both private and public institutions.

## Further Reading

Kramer, R. (1976). *Maria Montessori: A biography.* New York: Putnam.

Maria Montessori. (2003). In J. W. Guthrie (Ed.), *Encyclopedia of education.* New York: Macmillan.

## Jean Piaget (1896–1980)

*Swiss educator and psychologist who is considered the most influential developmental psychologist of the 20th century*

Jean Piaget was born on August 9, 1896, in Neuchatel, Switzerland. His father, Arthur, was a history professor, and his mother, Rebecca, was a homemaker. He was an avid learner from a young age, and he published his first scientific paper, about a species of sparrow, at 11. Piaget studied natural sciences at the University of Neuchatel, earning his bachelor's degree in 1915 and his Ph.D. in 1918.

Shortly after he finished his doctorate, Piaget moved to France, where he worked on translations of intelligence tests written by an English psychologist. To make sure that his translations were clear, he tested several children using the French version of the test. The results set him on a path to the greatest career in developmental psychology of the modern era. Many of the children answered the questions incorrectly, and they did so in such a way that Piaget knew he had come upon a groundbreaking insight into human development: children constructed their own reality, and their perception of the world reflected a specific stage in the development of the human brain.

This discovery set Piaget on a lifelong quest to understand how the human brain develops, and specifically how children learn. In 1923 Piaget married Valentine Châtenay, and their three children—Jacqueline, Lucienne, and Laurent—became the objects of his continued research into intellectual development. In studying his children, Piaget discerned four stages of mental growth. From birth to age two, children experience the sensory-motor stage, during which they concentrate on concrete objects. From age two to age seven, children experience the pre-operational stage, during which they concentrate on learning symbols in language, fantasy, play, and dreams. The third stage is the concrete operational stage, during which children ages 7 to 11 learn to master classification, including relationships, numbers, and ways of reasoning. The fourth stage, the formal operational stage, begins around the age of 11 and is characterized by children becoming able to master independent thought and abstraction, as well as developing insights into other people's thinking.

Piaget's concepts of child development gained worldwide acceptance and have affected the study of education, psychology, and many of the social sciences. He challenged many existing concepts of human development, including those that stated that intelligence was hereditary and fixed, and those that viewed children as "miniature adults" who perceive the world exactly as adults do. Piaget also influenced traditional pedagogy, arguing that teaching methods must reinforce learning by allowing children to apply their developing intellectual abilities at each stage. "The goal of education is not to increase the amount of knowledge but to create the possibilities for a child to invent and discover, to create men who are capable of doing new things," he declared.

For many decades, Piaget combined his research with teaching appointments at many major universities in Europe. In 1955 he established the International Center for Genetic Epistemology, the name he gave to the field of developmental psychology he had created, and he worked there until his death on September 17, 1980. During his lifetime, the prolific Piaget published more than 50 books and 500 papers, as well as the 37-volume series *Etudes d'Epistémologie Génétique* (Studies in Genetic Epistemology).

## Further Reading

Kitchener, R. (1986). *Piaget's theory of knowledge.* New Haven, CT: Yale University Press.

Smith, L. (1997). Jean Piaget. In N. Sheehy, A. Chapman, & W. Conroy (Eds.), *Biographical dictionary of psychology.* London: Routledge.

# Maynard C. Reynolds (1922– )

*American academic and pioneer of special education*

Maynard Clinton Reynolds was born in 1922 in Doyen, North Dakota. He received his bachelor of science degree in education from Moorhead State University in 1942. After serving in World War II, he attended the University of Minnesota, earning his master's degree in 1947 and his doctoral degree in 1950.

Reynolds taught briefly at the University of Northern Iowa and Long Beach State University before returning to the University of Minnesota, where he became director of the Clinic for Psychoeducation and then chair of the Department of Special Education. Reynolds was professor of educational psychology and special education at Minnesota until his retirement and is now professor emeritus. His research centered on the diagnosis and measurement of children with learning and other disabilities. He also served as president of the Council for Exceptional Children and chair of its policy commission.

Reynolds was an early champion of the effort to include all children in public education. After the passage of P.L. 94-142, the Education for All Handicapped Children Act of 1975, he became involved in the implementation of the landmark bill, helping school districts nationwide create programs in special education for students with disabilities. He was the author of several key texts used in the training of special education teachers, including *Knowledge Base for the Beginning Teacher*, which has been published in many editions, and *Teaching Exceptional Children in All America's Schools*.

In addition to his work at Minnesota, Reynolds was a senior research associate at the Center for Research on Human Development and Education at Temple University. At Temple he worked with Margaret Wang, with whom he wrote the five-volume *Handbook of Special Education*, which is considered a standard text in the field.

Reynolds has been the recipient of many awards, including the J. E. Wallace Wallin Award from the Council for Exceptional Children, the University Outstanding Achievement Award from the University of Minnesota, and the Mildred Thompson Award from the American Association on Mental Deficiencies.

## Further Reading

Reynolds, M. C. (1994, August). Child disabilities: Who's in, who's out. *Journal of School Health, 64*(6), 238–241.

Wang, M. C., Reynolds, M. C., & Wahlberg, J. (Eds.). (1987–1992). *Handbook of special education* (5 vols.). Oxford, UK: Pergamon Press.

# Edouard Seguin (1812–1880)

*French psychiatrist and pioneer in the treatment
and education of people with disabilities*

Edouard Seguin was born on January 20, 1812, in Clamecy, France. He hailed from a family of physicians and received his medical education at the College of Auxerre and the Lycee St. Louis in Paris. After completing his studies, Seguin became a student of the physician and educator Jean-Marc Gaspard Itard, who was a pioneer in the treatment of children with intellectual disabilities. At that time, such children were referred to as "idiots" and were considered incapable of learning.

Using Itard's work as a foundation, Seguin developed his own approach to treating and teaching children with severe intellectual disabilities. Using what he termed a "physiological" approach, Seguin taught the children basic skills in letter and number recognition as well basic life skills. He used methods that developed the children's physical and sensory responses to educational stimuli as well as their mental abilities. His methods included instruction in an established sequence of tasks, reinforced with positive responses and behaviors, with the purpose of developing mental abilities as well as independence and self-reliance. In 1839 Seguin established a hospital for children with severe disabilities in France, where he further refined his methods. He later published a series of books based on his successful methods that proved that children with intellectual disabilities could indeed be educated.

Around 1850 Seguin left France and moved to the United States, where he helped establish institutions for children with intellectual disabilities in New York, including an asylum in Albany. After receiving a medical degree from the Medical Department of the University of the City of New York in 1861, he helped establish a school for people with intellectual disabilities on Randall's Island, off Manhattan. In 1866 Seguin published a book in English on his methods, *Idiocy and Its Treatment by the Physiological Method*, which was widely influential in America. Shortly before his death in 1880, Seguin founded a school for children with disabilities in New York City, which was later moved to East Orange, New Jersey.

Seguin is remembered today for his groundbreaking theories about the mental and physical potential of people with disabilities. His methods proved that people with disabilities are capable of learning, and they were widely influential with future generations of educators, including Maria Montessori.

## Further Reading

Edouard Seguin. (2005). In *Encyclopedia of New York State.* Syracuse, NY: Syracuse University Press.

Wright, D. (2001). Developmental and physical disabilities: The "blind," "deaf and dumb," and "idiot." In P. Stearns (Ed.), *Encyclopedia of European social history.* New York: Scribner.

# Harold Skeels (1901–1970)

*American psychologist and pioneer in the field of child development*

Harold Manville Skeels was born on March 8, 1901, in Denver, Colorado. He grew up in northern Iowa, and he received his bachelor's degree in animal husbandry and his doctoral degree in child development from Iowa State College (now Iowa University) in 1932.

After receiving his Ph.D., Skeels spent the next decade as a researcher with the Child Welfare Research Station and the Iowa Board of Control of State Institutions, where he directed studies that used institutionalized patients as subjects. During the 1930s, he conducted research into how the IQs of young children could be improved and maintained. Skeels's studies of institutionalized children demonstrated that those who were raised in unstimulating environments did not develop normally, and subsequently had lower IQs that continued to decline as they grew. In contrast, children who were either adopted into families or placed in a stimulating environment, such as nursery school, developed normally and were able to increase their IQs substantially. The results made Skeels an outspoken advocate for adoption instead of the institutionalization of infants, a philosophy that gained great popularity across the country.

Yet the findings of Skeels and his colleagues, called the "Iowa group," caused a furor among some child development specialists. At that time, many people believed that intelligence was a fixed characteristic of human personality, based on heredity rather than experience. This conflict has become known as "nature versus nurture" in the common vernacular. Skeels's research in Iowa ended in 1942, when the United States entered World War II and he served in the Army Air Corps. When he returned from military service, Skeels worked for the U.S. Public Health Service and the National Institute of Mental Health, focusing on community mental health development programs.

In 1960 Skeels decided to do a follow-up study of the children he had first investigated in the 1930s. He presented his findings in 1965, at the annual meeting of the American Association on Mental Deficiency. The results of his follow-up study reaffirmed his earlier findings: the children who had been adopted or raised in an enriched, stimulating environment had continued to develop normally and had become normal adults, while those who had been raised in institutions without early intervention had continued to decline. Skeels's results were widely cited when nationwide programs in early childhood learning, including Head Start, were implemented in the 1960s.

Skeels was the recipient of many awards for his research, including the G. Stanley Hall Award from the American Psychological Association Division of Developmental Psychology in 1967, the Joseph P. Kennedy International Award for Research in Mental Retardation in 1968, and the American Association of Mental Deficiency Award for Research Contributions, also in 1968. Skeels retired from the National Institute of Mental Health in 1965 and died on March 28, 1970.

## Further Reading

Cossey, M. S. (1970, July). Harold Manville Skeels. *American Journal of Mental Deficiency, 75*, 1–3.

Skeels, H. M. (1966). Adult status of children with contrasting early life experiences: A follow-up study. *Monographs of the Society for Research in Child Development, 31*(3), 1–65.

# B. F. Skinner (1904–1990)

*American psychologist and proponent of behaviorism*

Burrhus Frederick Skinner was born on March 20, 1904, in Susquehanna, Pennsylvania, to William Skinner, who was an attorney, and Grace Burrhus Skinner. After receiving his bachelor's degree from Hamilton College in 1929, he pursued graduate studies at Harvard University, earning his master's degree in 1930 and his doctoral degree in 1931. He married Yvonne Blue in 1936, and they had two daughters, Julie and Deborah.

Skinner began his academic career at Harvard in 1933, then moved to the University of Minnesota and Indiana University. He returned to Harvard in 1948, where he remained until his retirement in 1974. It was at Harvard in the 1930s that Skinner began his famous laboratory experiments that led him to become the leading exponent of "behaviorism," the theory that both human and animal behavior is predicated on the response to reward and punishment, rather than on independent motivation. Skinner developed his theories based on his experiments with rats and pigeons. He trained the animals to perform tasks and gave them rewards when they did the tasks correctly. This method, which he called "positive reinforcement," became a catchword in everyday parlance when referring to behavior modification in animals or, increasingly, in humans.

Skinner also created a soundproof box, called the "Skinner Box," which he used for his experiments. In 1943 he adapted the concept for children, creating what he called the "Air-Crib," an enclosed bed with a constantly warm temperature that allowed a child to spend time in a crib without restrictive clothing. Skinner's daughter, Deborah, slept in the crib for two years. The Air-Crib was featured in many newspaper and magazine articles, and the reaction was largely negative, with some critics arguing that he had used his own children in unethical experiments. Skinner maintained that he and his crib had been misrepresented and misunderstood.

Despite such criticism, Skinner's theories of behavior modification were widely used in education and psychotherapy, especially in the treatment of people with learning and intellectual disabilities. They influenced the creation of the concept of programmed learning, in which a task such as dressing is broken down to its most basic elements, practiced, and reinforced through positive feedback. It has become a learning technique commonly used in the treatment of children with severe disabilities, including those with autism.

Skinner was the author of several widely influential books based on his theories. In *Verbal Behavior* (1957), he outlined what formed the basis of the "behavior analysis" approach to the study of human behavior that is still practiced by psychologists. Two other well-known books that promulgated his theories include a novel, *Walden Two* (1948), and a nonfiction work, *Beyond Freedom and Dignity* (1971). In these books he argued for a society that implemented his behaviorist theories to control, and ideally end, negative human behavior through positive reinforcement.

B. F. Skinner died in Cambridge, Massachusetts, on August 18, 1990. He received several major awards in his lifetime, including the National Medal of Science in 1968 and American Psychological Association Gold Medal in 1971.

## Further Reading

Bjork, D. W. (1997). *B. F. Skinner: A life.* New York: American Psychological Association.

Skinner, B. F. (1976). *Particulars of my life.* New York: New York University Press.

Skinner, B. F. (1979). *The shaping of a behaviorist.* New York: New York University Press.

Skinner, B. F. (1983). *A matter of consequences.* New York: Knopf.

## Ann P. Turnbull (1947– )

*American academic focusing on issues of family and disability*

Ann Patterson Turnbull was born on October 19, 1947, in Tuscaloosa, Alabama. She received her bachelor's degree in special education and mental retardation from the University of Georgia in 1968, her master's degree in special education and mental retardation from Auburn University in 1971, and her doctoral degree in special education and mental retardation from the University of Alabama in 1972. She is married to Rud Turnbull, with whom she is co-director of the Beach Center on Disability at the University of Kansas. They had three children, Amy, Kate, and Jesse, called Jay. Jay, who died in 2009, was born with multiple disabilities and was the inspiration for the Beach Center.

Ann Turnbull has worked in the field of disability studies as a researcher, teacher, professor, and advocate for almost 40 years. She began her career as an assistant professor in the School of Education at the University of North Carolina at Chapel Hill, where she worked from 1973 to

1980. In 1980 she joined the faculty of the University of Kansas, where she is currently Distinguished Professor in the Department of Special Education, senior scientist at the Schiefelbusch Institute for Life Span Studies, and co-director of the Beach Center on Disability.

The focus of Turnbull's research is the family and disability, including family involvement and advocacy, school and community inclusion, and education policy. She has been principal investigator on over 20 research grants from the federal government and a Public Policy Fellow in Mental Retardation for the Joseph P. Kennedy Jr. Foundation. The author of 14 books, including several key textbooks in the area of special education, Turnbull has also written or contributed more than 200 professional articles and book chapters. She serves on the editorial boards and contributes to several key journals in her field, including *Exceptional Children, Mental Retardation,* and the *Journal of the Association for Persons With Severe Handicaps.*

The Beach Center, founded by the Turnbulls in 1988, is devoted to research, training teachers and graduate students, and providing assistance and information to families and individuals with disabilities. The Center includes six subcenters that focus on families, public policy, school-wide reform, self-determination (including access to curriculum and technology), legal implications of the human genome project, and the education of students with significant support needs, including deaf-blindness.

Turnbull is the recipient of many awards for her research and service, including the Century Award in Mental Retardation, which was presented in 1999 by a consortium of organizations to 36 individuals who made the most significant impact in the fields of developmental disabilities and intellectual disabilities in the 20th century. In addition, Ann and Rud Turnbull share the Marianna and Ross Beach Distinguished Professorship at the University of Kansas.

## Further Reading

Attitudes toward the intellectually disabled [Interview]. (2009, August 11). NPR, Talk of the Nation. Retrieved from http://www.npr.org/templates/story/story.php?storyId=111781649

Dr. Ann Turnbull. Retrieved from http://www.beachcenter.org/staff/staffdetail.aspx?id=24

# Rud Turnbull (1937– )

*American academic and lawyer focusing
on disability law and policy*

H. Rutherford Turnbull III, known as Rud, was born on September 22, 1937, in New York City. He received his bachelor's degree from Johns Hopkins University in 1959, his law degree from the University of Maryland Law School in 1964, and his master of law degree from Harvard Law School in 1969. He is married to Ann Turnbull, with whom he is co-director of the Beach Center on Disability at the University of Kansas. They had three children, Amy, Kate, and Jesse, called Jay. Jay, who died in 2009, was born with multiple disabilities and was the inspiration for the Beach Center.

Although he is now a non-practicing attorney, Turnbull began his professional career as a lawyer, and he worked in private practice from 1968 to 1969. In 1969 he joined the Institute of Government at the University of North Carolina at Chapel Hill as a professor of public law and government, and he was also a faculty member at the Bush Institute on Policy for Families and Children.

In 1980 Turnbull joined the faculty of the University of Kansas, where he is the co-director of the Beach Center on Disability, the Marianna and Ross Beach Distinguished Professor, and senior research scientist at the Life Span Institute. The focus of his research is law and policy in several key areas of disability studies, including special education, mental disability, the ethics of intervention with people with disabilities, and issues regarding families of people with disabilities.

Turnbull has authored or co-authored 28 books, more than 50 monographs, more than 150 professional articles, and more than 75 book chapters. He writes on a wide range of disability policy issues, including the nature of core concepts in disability, the effects of policy on people with disabilities and their families, the development and implementation of disability policy, disability and criminal justice, abuse and neglect of people with disabilities, and long-term care and end-of-life decisions for people with disabilities.

The Beach Center, founded by the Turnbulls in 1988, is devoted to research, training teachers and graduate students, and providing assistance and information to individuals with disabilities and their families. The center includes six subcenters that focus on families, public policy, school-wide reform, self-determination (including access to curriculum and technology), legal implications of the human genome project, and the education of students with significant support needs, including deaf-blindness.

Turnbull has served as president of the American Association on Mental Retardation and as chairman of the American Bar Association Commission on Disability Law, and he has testified before the U.S. Congress on disability law and the rights of people with disabilities. He is the recipient of many awards, including the Century Award in Mental Retardation, given by a consortium of organizations to 36 individuals who made the most significant impact in the fields of developmental disabilities and intellectual disabilities in the 20th century.

## Further Reading

Rud Turnbull. Retrieved from http://www.beachcenter.org/staff/staffdetail .aspx?id=15

Turnbull, A., & Turnbull, R. (2002, Fall). Get a life! A model for enhancing the quality of life for adults with autism and their families. *Newsletter of the Beach Center on Families and Disabilities*. Retrieved from http://www.partoparvt .org/getalife.html

# Hill Walker (1939– )

*American academic focusing on violence*
*and behavior problems in adolescents*

Hill Montague Walker was born on June 21, 1939, in Front Royal, Virginia, to Edward and Matilda Walker. After receiving his bachelor's degree in secondary education in 1962 from Eastern Oregon College, he pursued graduate studies at the University of Oregon, earning his master's degree in counseling psychology in 1964 and his Ph.D. in special education and counseling psychology in 1967.

Walker began his career in education teaching seventh and eighth grade in Eugene, Oregon, while completing his doctorate. He began his academic career at the University of Oregon in 1967, working as a professor of special education and serving as director of the Center at Oregon for Research in the Behavior Education of the Handicapped from 1971 to 1979.

Currently, Walker is professor of special education, co-founder and co-director of the Institute on Violence and Destructive Behavior, and director of the Center on Human Development in the College of Education at the University of Oregon. His primary area of research is the assessment of children with a variety of behavioral disorders, and the development of effective intervention techniques in dealing with such behaviors in the school setting. He has been involved in longitudinal studies of aggression and antisocial behaviors, as well as in the development of assessment tools and early screening policies for identifying at-risk students and preventing the development of behavioral and academic problems.

Walker has directed many federally funded projects in his area of expertise, including the First Steps Program, an early intervention program for at-risk kindergartners that is funded by the U.S. Office of Special Education. He also helped implement the program in Oregon's public schools. From 1979 to 1982, he was the director of a handicapped children's program on mainstreaming, also funded by the U.S. Office of Special Education. In 1982 Walker became the director of the University of Oregon's University Center for Excellence in Developmental Disabilities. More recently, he headed the National Institute of Child Health and Development's Supporting School Readiness in Social and Literacy Domains and the National Institute of Mental Health's Head Start Mental Health Research Consortium.

Walker is also a prolific author, and he has published many professional articles and book chapters. In 1993 he was the recipient of the Research Award from the Council for Exceptional Children in recognition of his 30 years of research investigating school-related behavior disorders. In 2000 he received the University of Oregon Presidential Medal.

## Further Reading

Strain, P. S., Guralnick, M. J., & Walker, H. M. (Eds.). (1986). *Children's social behavior: Development, assessment, and modification.* Orlando, FL: Academic.

Walker, H. M., Colvin, G., & Ramsey, E. (1995). *Antisocial behavior in school: Strategies and best practices.* Pacific Grove, CA: Brooks/Cole.

## Paul Wehman (1948– )

*American academic focusing on the
transition from education to adulthood and
supported employment for people with disabilities*

Paul Wehman was born on September 25, 1948. He received his bachelor's degree in business administration from Western Illinois University in 1970, his master's degree in general and experimental psychology from Illinois

State University in 1972, and his Ph.D. in behavioral disabilities and rehabilitation psychology from the University of Wisconsin–Madison in 1976.

Wehman joined the faculty of Virginia Commonwealth University in 1976, and over the past 35 years, he has pioneered the development of supported employment. He has focused his research on expanding supported employment to people with severe disabilities, including those with intellectual disabilities, traumatic brain injury, spinal cord injury, and autism. He has also written extensively on transition issues for young adults with disabilities, especially in the movement from school to employment.

Currently, Wehman is a professor in the Department of Physical Medicine and Rehabilitation at VCU, with a joint appointment in the Department of Teaching and Learning Rehabilitation Counseling. He is also director of the Rehabilitation Research and Training Center on Workplace Supports and Job Retention, and chair of the Division of Rehabilitation Research. Since joining VCU, he has been the principal investigator for many federally funded research grants, including the U.S. Department of Labor's Training and Technical Assistance Project on Self Employment and VCU's Diversity and Empowerment Project. He is responsible for a $6.25 million annual budget for the Research and Training Center, with fiscal and program oversight for over 20 federal grants and a staff of 65 researchers and staff.

Wehman is a prolific author, co-author, and editor, with more than 200 professional articles, 24 book chapters, and 40 books among his publications. He is also the editor-in-chief of the *Journal of Vocational Rehabilitation.* He is the recipient of many awards, including the Joseph P. Kennedy Jr. Foundation International Award in Mental Retardation, the Distinguished Service Award from the President's Committee on Employment for Persons with Disabilities, and the Mary Switzer Fellowship for the National Rehabilitation Association. In 2000 Wehman was named one of the 50 most influential special educators of the millennium by *Remedial and Special Education.* In 2006 he was elected a Life Long Emeritus Member of APSE: The Employment Network, and in 2007 he received the VCU School of Medicine Research Recognition Award.

## Further Reading

Getzel, E. E., & Wehman, P. (Eds.). (2005). *Going to college: Expanding opportunities for people with disabilities.* Baltimore, MD: Brookes.

Wehman, P., Smith, M. D., & Schall, C. (2009). *Autism and the transition to adulthood: Success beyond the classroom.* Baltimore, MD: Brookes.

# Michael Wehmeyer (1957– )

*American academic focusing on education and self-determination for people with disabilities*

Michael Wehmeyer was born on October 9, 1957, in Wichita, Kansas. He studied special education and mental retardation at the University of Tulsa, receiving his bachelor's degree in 1980 and his master's degree in 1982. He also earned a master's degree in experimental psychology at the University of Sussex in 1988, and he received his doctoral degree in human development and communication sciences from the University of Texas at Dallas in 1989.

Wehmeyer began his career at the Texas Department of Mental Health and Mental Retardation in 1989. From 1990 to 1999, he worked for The Arc of the United States, serving in a number of roles, including director of its Self-Determination Program. He is currently professor of special education at the University of Kansas, where he is also director of the Center on Developmental Disabilities and associate director of the Beach Center on Disability.

The Beach Center, founded by Ann and Rud Turnbull in 1988, is devoted to research, training teachers and graduate students, and providing assistance and information to individuals with disabilities and their families. The center includes six subcenters that focus on families, public policy, school-wide reform, self-determination (including access to curriculum and technology), legal implications of the human genome project, and the education of students with significant support needs, including deaf-blindness.

The focus of Wehmeyer's research is self-determination, transition, and educational issues, including access to the general curriculum for students with significant disabilities and technology use by people with cognitive disabilities. He directs many federally funded research projects in the area of the education of students with intellectual and developmental disabilities.

Wehmeyer has published more than 180 articles or book chapters, and he has also been the author, co-author, or co-editor of 19 books on disability. He is editor-in-chief for the journal *Remedial and Special Education* and also serves as a consulting editor for a number of professional journals, including *Exceptional Children, Intellectual and Developmental Disabilities, Journal of Special Education,* and the *American Journal of Mental Retardation.*

Wehmeyer is currently president of the American Association on Intellectual and Developmental Disabilities and is a past president of the Council for Exceptional Children's Division on Career Development and

Transition. He is the recipient of many awards, including the first Distinguished Early Career Research Award from the Council for Exceptional Children's Division for Research, which he received in 1999. In May 2003 he was honored with the American Association on Mental Retardation's National Education Award.

## Further Reading

Michael Wehmeyer. Retrieved from http://www.beachcenter.org/staff/staff_detail.aspx?id=18&JScript=1

Turnbull, H. R., Turnbull, A., & Wehmeyer, M. (2010). *Exceptional lives: Special education in today's schools* (6th ed.). Upper Saddle River, NJ: Merrill/Prentice Hall.

# Naomi Zigmond (1941– )

*American academic focusing on learning*
*disabilities and issues in special education*

Naomi Zigmond was born in 1941. After receiving her bachelor of science degree from McGill University in Montreal in 1962, she pursued graduate studies at Northwestern University, earning her master's degree in 1963 and her doctoral degree in learning disabilities in 1966. That same year she married Michael J. Zigmond, a neurologist; they have two children, Daniel and Leah.

While completing her Ph.D., Zigmond worked as a clinical teacher at Northwestern's institute for language disorders. After receiving her degree, she taught at Harvard University from 1966 to 1967 and at Boston University from 1968 to 1970. In 1970 she joined the faculty at the University of Pittsburgh, where she is now Distinguished Professor of Special Education in the Department of Instruction and Learning in the School of Education. Her research is focused on several key areas in special education, including assessment—especially alternative assessment of students with disabilities—early intervention programs, reading instruction for students with significant disabilities, and full inclusion of special education students into general school populations.

Zigmond is the author of hundreds of professional articles, as well as book chapters and presentations in her areas of expertise. She also serves on the editorial boards of *Exceptional Children* (where she was editor from

1989 to 1995), *Remedial and Special Education,* and several other journals. She is a member of many professional organizations, including the American Educational Research Association, the Association for Children with Learning Disabilities, and the Council for Exceptional Children, where she serves on the Board of Governors. In addition, Zigmond has been the recipient of many federal and state grants to pursue her research, and she has conducted studies for the National Institute of Mental Health and the U.S. Department of Education. In Pennsylvania, where she has been involved in research projects for over 40 years, she was instrumental in the design of an alternate system of statewide assessment for students with severe disabilities. She has also been involved in the development and evaluation of the Pennsylvania Reading First Initiative and has served on numerous boards on special education and instruction for the state.

In 1997 Zigmond received the Research Award from the Council for Exceptional Children "in recognition of research that has contributed significantly to the body of knowledge about the education of exceptional children and youth."

## Further Reading

Zigmond, N. (1995). An exploration of the meaning and practice of special education in the context of full inclusion of students with learning disabilities: Introduction. *Journal of Special Education, 29*(?), 109–115.

Zigmond, N., Kloo, A., & Volonino, V. (2009). What, where, and how: Special education in the climate of full inclusion. *Exceptionality, 17*(4), 189–204.

# Five

# Annotated Data, Statistics, Tables, and Graphs

Amy C. Stevens Griffith and
Cheryl Hanley-Maxwell

C hapters 1 and 2 discuss trends in disability diagnosis for special education eligibility and the services provided to eligible students under
the Individuals with Disabilities Education Act (IDEA). In this chapter we
will present and consider data relevant to those trends across four areas:
(1) eligibility, (2) proportionality by race, (3) placement, and (4) discipline.
We also present data on in-school student outcomes related to high-stakes
testing, as well as student perceptions, school completion, and post-
secondary school outcomes.

## Eligibility

Table 1 illustrates patterns in the numbers of students identified in each
disability category by school year. The data begin with 1976–1977, the first
school year after P.L. 94-142 (the Individuals with Disabilities Education
Act) was ratified, and end with 2007–2008, the last year for which data are

available. The first part of the table presents the number of students served in each of the federally defined disability categories. Although the total number of students eligible for special education has increased in the 30-year span, the numbers enrolled in special education classes have remained relatively the same for the last decade (the numbers of children served in some individual disability categories have changed more dramatically). For example, from 1976–1977 to 2000, the number of children served in the category of learning disabilities increased 360%, but this number has slightly but steadily decreased over the past decade. However, the number of children identified for services in the category of mental retardation (intellectual disabilities) has decreased since 1976–1977, with the largest drop occurring between 1980 and 1990. Five new categories (multiple disabilities, deaf-blind, autism, traumatic brain injury, and developmental delay) were added after 1976–1977. With the exception of deaf-blindness, all have shown steady increases since their introduction.

The second portion of this table, Percentage Distribution of Children Served, provides the data needed to understand the distribution of students with disabilities across the eligibility categories in each year. This data describe how students gained access to special education across time and identify changes in patterns of disability identification. Notable is the drop in percentage for specific learning disability (SLD) around the time that attention deficit hyperactivity disorder (ADHD) became a more common diagnosis. The percent of children identified as SLD has continued to drop since it reached its largest percentage in 1995–1996. The reasons for the decline are unclear. The data also indicate that the percentage of students who are eligible for special education in the category of mental retardation has undergone a steady decline over time since 1990. This may be due, in part, to the addition of traumatic brain injury (TBI) and Autism Spectrum Disorder (ASD) as eligibility categories. Additionally, there has been a decrease in the percentage of students eligible due to emotional disturbance (ED). Finally, the percentage of children identified as other health impairments (OHI) has steadily increased over time; this is potentially a result of the growing number of children identified with ADHD and their inclusion in this disability category.

The Number Served as a Percent of Total Enrollment (of all school-age students) documents the increased percentage of students educated who qualify for special education due to a documented disability. Note the rise and fall of the percentage of the total number of students who qualify as LD or ED. The gradual decrease in the percent of enrolled students eligible as MR is notable, as is the gradual increase in OHI and ASD.

**Table 1**  Children (3–21 Years Old) Served Under Individuals with Disabilities Education Act, Part B, by Types of Disability

| Type of Disability | 1976–77 | 1980–81 | 1990–91 | 1995–96 | 1997–98 | 1998–99 | 1999–00 | 2000–01 | 2001–02 | 2002–03 | 2003–04 | 2004–05 | 2005–06 | 2006–07 | 2007–08[1] |
|---|---|---|---|---|---|---|---|---|---|---|---|---|---|---|---|
| | | | | | | Number served (in thousands) | | | | | | | | | |
| All disabilities | 3,694 | 4,144 | 4,710 | 5,572 | 5,908 | 6,056 | 6,195 | 6,296 | 6,407 | 6,523 | 6,634 | 6,719 | 6,713 | 6,636 | 6,606 |
| Specific learning disabilities | 796 | 1,462 | 2,129 | 2,578 | 2,727 | 2,790 | 2,834 | 2,868 | 2,861 | 2,848 | 2,831 | 2,798 | 2,735 | 2,665 | 2,573 |
| Speech or language impairments | 1,302 | 1,168 | 985 | 1,022 | 1,060 | 1,068 | 1,080 | 1,409 | 1,391 | 1,412 | 1,441 | 1,463 | 1,468 | 1,475 | 1,456 |
| Mental retardation | 961 | 830 | 534 | 571 | 589 | 597 | 600 | 624 | 616 | 602 | 593 | 578 | 556 | 534 | 500 |
| Emotional disturbance | 283 | 347 | 389 | 437 | 454 | 462 | 469 | 481 | 483 | 485 | 489 | 489 | 477 | 464 | 442 |
| Hearing impairments | 88 | 79 | 58 | 67 | 69 | 70 | 71 | 78 | 78 | 78 | 79 | 79 | 79 | 80 | 79 |
| Orthopedic impairments | 87 | 58 | 49 | 63 | 67 | 69 | 71 | 83 | 83 | 83 | 77 | 73 | 71 | 69 | 67 |
| Other health impairments[2] | 141 | 98 | 55 | 133 | 190 | 220 | 253 | 303 | 350 | 403 | 464 | 521 | 570 | 611 | 641 |
| Visual impairments | 38 | 31 | 23 | 25 | 26 | 26 | 26 | 29 | 28 | 29 | 28 | 29 | 29 | 29 | 29 |

| Type of Disability | 1976-77 | 1980-81 | 1990-91 | 1995-96 | 1997-98 | 1998-99 | 1999-00 | 2000-01 | 2001-02 | 2002-03 | 2003-04 | 2004-05 | 2005-06 | 2006-07 | 2007-08[1] |
|---|---|---|---|---|---|---|---|---|---|---|---|---|---|---|---|
| Multiple disabilities | — | 68 | 96 | 93 | 106 | 105 | 111 | 133 | 136 | 138 | 140 | 140 | 141 | 142 | 138 |
| Deaf-blindness | — | 3 | 1 | 1 | 1 | 2 | 2 | 1 | 2 | 2 | 2 | 2 | 2 | 2 | 2 |
| Autism | — | — | — | 28 | 42 | 53 | 65 | 94 | 114 | 137 | 163 | 191 | 223 | 258 | 296 |
| Traumatic brain injury | — | — | — | 9 | 12 | 13 | 14 | 16 | 22 | 22 | 23 | 24 | 24 | 25 | 25 |
| Developmental delay | — | — | — | — | 2 | 12 | 19 | 178 | 242 | 283 | 305 | 332 | 339 | 333 | 358 |
| Preschool disabled[3] | + | + | 390 | 544 | 565 | 568 | 581 | + | + | + | + | + | + | + | + |
| *Percentage distribution of children served* | | | | | | | | | | | | | | | |
| All disabilities | 100.0 | 100.0 | 100.0 | 100.0 | 100.0 | 100.0 | 100.0 | 100.0 | 100.0 | 100.0 | 100.0 | 100.0 | 100.0 | 100.0 | 100.0 |
| Specific learning disabilities | 21.5 | 35.3 | 45.2 | 46.3 | 46.2 | 46.1 | 45.7 | 45.5 | 44.7 | 43.7 | 42.7 | 41.6 | 40.7 | 39.9 | 39.0 |
| Speech or language impairments | 35.2 | 28.2 | 20.9 | 18.3 | 17.9 | 17.6 | 17.4 | 22.4 | 21.7 | 21.6 | 21.7 | 21.8 | 21.9 | 22.1 | 22.0 |
| Mental retardation | 26.0 | 20.0 | 11.3 | 10.2 | 10.0 | 9.9 | 9.7 | 9.9 | 9.6 | 9.2 | 8.9 | 8.6 | 8.3 | 8.0 | 7.6 |

*(Continued)*

**Table 1** (Continued)

| Type of Disability | 1976–77 | 1980–81 | 1990–91 | 1995–96 | 1997–98 | 1998–99 | 1999–00 | 2000–01 | 2001–02 | 2002–03 | 2003–04 | 2004–05 | 2005–06 | 2006–07 | 2007–08[1] |
|---|---|---|---|---|---|---|---|---|---|---|---|---|---|---|---|
| Emotional disturbance | 7.7 | 8.4 | 8.3 | 7.8 | 7.7 | 7.6 | 7.6 | 7.6 | 7.5 | 7.4 | 7.4 | 7.3 | 7.1 | 6.9 | 6.7 |
| Hearing impairments | 2.4 | 1.9 | 1.2 | 1.2 | 1.2 | 1.2 | 1.1 | 1.2 | 1.2 | 1.2 | 1.2 | 1.2 | 1.2 | 1.2 | 1.2 |
| Orthopedic impairments | 2.4 | 1.4 | 1.0 | 1.1 | 1.1 | 1.1 | 1.1 | 1.3 | 1.3 | 1.3 | 1.2 | 1.1 | 1.1 | 1.0 | 1.0 |
| Other health impairments[2] | 3.8 | 2.4 | 1.2 | 2.4 | 3.2 | 3.6 | 4.1 | 4.8 | 5.5 | 6.2 | 7.0 | 7.7 | 8.5 | 9.1 | 9.7 |
| Visual impairments | 1.0 | 0.7 | 0.5 | 0.4 | 0.4 | 0.4 | 0.4 | 0.5 | 0.4 | 0.4 | 0.4 | 0.4 | 0.4 | 0.4 | 0.4 |
| Multiple disabilities | — | 1.6 | 2.0 | 1.7 | 1.8 | 1.8 | 1.8 | 2.1 | 2.1 | 2.1 | 2.1 | 2.1 | 2.1 | 2.1 | 2.1 |
| Deaf-blindness | — | 0.1 | # | # | # | # | # | # | # | # | # | # | # | # | # |
| Autism | — | — | — | 0.5 | 0.7 | 0.9 | 1.0 | 1.5 | 1.8 | 2.1 | 2.5 | 2.8 | 3.3 | 3.9 | 4.5 |
| Traumatic brain injury | — | — | — | 0.2 | 0.2 | 0.2 | 0.2 | 0.2 | 0.3 | 0.3 | 0.4 | 0.4 | 0.4 | 0.4 | 0.4 |
| Developmental delay | — | — | — | — | 0.0 | 0.2 | 0.3 | 2.8 | 3.8 | 4.3 | 4.6 | 4.9 | 5.1 | 5.0 | 5.4 |
| Preschool disabled[3] | + | + | 8.3 | 9.8 | 9.6 | 9.4 | 9.4 | + | + | + | + | + | + | + | + |

Number served as a percent of total enrollment

| Type of Disability | 1976–77 | 1980–81 | 1990–91 | 1995–96 | 1997–98 | 1998–99 | 1999–00 | 2000–01 | 2001–02 | 2002–03 | 2003–04 | 2004–05 | 2005–06 | 2006–07 | 2007–08[1] |
|---|---|---|---|---|---|---|---|---|---|---|---|---|---|---|---|
| All disabilities | 8.3 | 10.1 | 11.4 | 12.4 | 12.8 | 13.0 | 13.2 | 13.3 | 13.4 | 13.5 | 13.7 | 13.8 | 13.7 | 13.6 | 13.4 |
| Specific learning disabilities | 1.8 | 3.6 | 5.2 | 5.8 | 5.9 | 6.0 | 6.0 | 6.1 | 6.0 | 5.9 | 5.8 | 5.7 | 5.6 | 5.4 | 5.2 |
| Speech or language impairments | 2.9 | 2.9 | 2.4 | 2.3 | 2.3 | 2.3 | 2.3 | 3.0 | 2.9 | 2.9 | 3.0 | 3.0 | 3.0 | 3.0 | 3.0 |
| Mental retardation | 2.2 | 2.0 | 1.3 | 1.3 | 1.3 | 1.3 | 1.3 | 1.3 | 1.3 | 1.2 | 1.2 | 1.2 | 1.1 | 1.1 | 1.0 |
| Emotional disturbance | 0.6 | 0.8 | 0.9 | 1.0 | 1.0 | 1.0 | 1.0 | 1.0 | 1.0 | 1.0 | 1.0 | 1.0 | 1.0 | 0.9 | 0.9 |
| Hearing impairments | 0.2 | 0.2 | 0.1 | 0.1 | 0.1 | 0.2 | 0.2 | 0.2 | 0.2 | 0.2 | C.2 | 0.2 | 0.2 | 0.2 | 0.2 |
| Orthopedic impairments | 0.2 | 0.1 | 0.1 | 0.1 | 0.1 | 0.1 | 0.2 | 0.2 | 0.2 | 0.2 | 0.2 | 0.2 | 0.1 | 0.1 | 0.1 |
| Other health impairments[2] | 0.3 | 0.2 | 0.1 | 0.3 | 0.4 | 0.5 | 0.5 | 0.6 | 0.7 | 0.8 | 1.0 | 1.1 | 1.2 | 1.2 | 1.3 |
| Visual impairments | 0.1 | 0.1 | 0.1 | 0.1 | 0.1 | 0.1 | 0.1 | 0.1 | 0.1 | 0.1 | 0.1 | 0.1 | 0.1 | 0.1 | 0.1 |
| Multiple disabilities | — | 0.2 | 0.2 | 0.2 | 0.2 | 0.2 | 0.2 | 0.3 | 0.3 | 0.3 | 0.3 | 0.3 | 0.3 | 0.3 | 0.3 |

(Continued)

**Table 1** (Continued)

| Type of Disability | 1976–77 | 1980–81 | 1990–91 | 1995–96 | 1997–98 | 1998–99 | 1999–00 | 2000–01 | 2001–02 | 2002–03 | 2003–04 | 2004–05 | 2005–06 | 2006–07 | 2007–08[1] |
|---|---|---|---|---|---|---|---|---|---|---|---|---|---|---|---|
| Deaf-blindness | — | # | # | # | # | # | # | # | # | # | # | # | # | # | # |
| Autism | — | — | — | 0.1 | 0.1 | 0.1 | 0.1 | 0.2 | 0.2 | 0.3 | 0.3 | 0.4 | 0.5 | 0.5 | 0.6 |
| Traumatic brain injury | — | — | — | # | # | # | # | # | # | # | # | # | # | 0.1 | 0.1 |
| Developmental delay | — | — | — | — | # | # | # | 0.4 | 0.5 | 0.6 | 0.6 | 0.7 | 0.7 | 0.7 | 0.7 |
| Preschool disabled[3] | † | † | 0.9 | 1.2 | 1.2 | 1.2 | 1.2 | † | † | † | † | † | † | † | † |

—Not available.

†Not applicable.

#Rounds to zero.

[1]Data do not include Vermont, for which 2007–2008 data were not available. In 2006–2007, the total number of 3- to 21-year-olds served in Vermont was 14,010.

[2]Other health impairments include having limited strength, vitality, or alertness due to chronic or acute health problems such as a heart condition, tuberculosis, rheumatic fever, nephritis, asthma, sickle cell anemia, hemophilia, epilepsy, lead poisoning, leukemia, or diabetes.

[3]Prior to 1990–1991 and after 1999–2000, preschool children are included in the counts by disability condition. For other years, preschool children are not included in the counts by disability condition, but are separately reported.

*Source:* National Center of Education Statistics. (2010, April). *Digest of educational statistics: 2009* (NCES 2010-013), Table 50. Retrieved from http://nces.ed.gov/programs/digest/2009menu_tables.asp

# Proportionality by Race

Absolute numbers of students tell only part of the story of special education eligibility. Who is identified as needing special education is another part of the eligibility story. As described in Chapter 2, identification of educational disability is not an objective process. The process involves cultural assumptions about appropriate behavior and how children learn, and sometimes results in a mismatch between the needs and assets of students and the educational services provided. The extent of this mismatch is seen in the data that document the disproportionate placement of students from minority racial/ethnic groups in special education. Tables 2, 3, and 4 illustrate this trend.

Table 2 documents the racial/ethnic proportions of students served in special education, depicting the disparity between predicted incidence and actual eligibility in all racial/ethnic groups in 2008. Review of the remainder of the table reveals that Black and American Indian/Alaska Native groups are increasingly overrepresented while White and Asian/Pacific Islander groups are consistently underrepresented, as compared to the general population. Tables 3 and 4 depict the numbers and percentage of all children served in special education by age and race/ethnicity from 1998 to 2007 (Table 3) and by age, race/ethnicity, and disability (Table 4). The percentages depicted on both tables reflect the percentage of children with disabilities in the entire United States for the given age and racial/ethnic group. For example, in 1998, 4.9% of all White children ages 3 to 5 were served under IDEA (Table 3). When compared with the percentage of all children served in this age range during 1998, the percentage of White children slightly exceeds what would have been predicted by the total. The table also reveals that, in general, Hispanic and Asian/Pacific Islander 3- to 5-year-olds are underidentified and American Indian/Alaska Native and White 3- to 5-year-olds are over indentified. For students ages 6 to 21, Black and American Indian/Alaska Native children are overidentified while Asian/Pacific Islander children are underidentified. Table 4 provides greater detail about the 2007 data summarized in Table 3, breaking it down by race/ethnicity and disability category. In both age groups, American Indian/Alaskan Natives are overrepresented in nearly all disability categories and Black students, ages 6 to 21, are overrepresented in all categories except visual impairment.

**Table 2**  Racial/Ethnic Distribution of Students Receiving Special Education Services

|  | White (non-Hispanic) | Black (non-Hispanic) | Hispanic | Asian/ Pacific Islander | American Indian/ Alaska Native | Total % Served by IDEA |
|---|---|---|---|---|---|---|
| 2008 total U.S. population | 65.6 | 12.2 | 15.4 | 4.5 | 0.8 | |
| 2008 | 58.7 | 25.0 | 10.0 | 2.8 | 3.6 | 100 |
| 2007 | 57.7 | 20.5 | 18.0 | 2.3 | 1.5 | 100 |
| 2006 | 66.2 | 16.5 | 13.2 | 2.5 | 1.6 | 100 |
| 2005 | 59.0 | 20.7 | 16.7 | 2.1 | 1.5 | 100 |
| 2004 | 59.5 | 20.8 | 16.2 | 2.8 | 1.5 | 100 |

*Totals may not add exactly to 100% due to rounding of data.

*Sources:* National Center for Educational Statistics. (2010). *Status and trends in the education of racial and ethnic minorities* (NCES 2010:015), Table 1b and Table 8.1a. Retrieved from http://nces .ed.gov/pubs2010/2010015/tables/table_1_b.asp   and   http://nces.ed.gov/pubs2010/ 2010015/tables/table_8_1a.asp; Data Accountability Center. *Individuals with Disabilities Education Act (IDEA) data,* Table AB2. Retrieved from http://www.ideadata.org/PartBData.asp

**Table 3**  Percentage of Children (Ages 3–5 and 6–21) Served Under the Individuals with Disabilities Education Act (IDEA), by Race/Ethnicity

| Age Group and Year | Total | White | Black | Hispanic | Asian/ Pacific Islander | American Indian/ Alaska Native |
|---|---|---|---|---|---|---|
| 3 to 5 years | | | | | | |
| 1998 | 4.8 | 4.9 | 4.4 | 3.0 | 2.3 | 5.7 |
| 1999 | 5.0 | 5.5 | 5.0 | 3.5 | 2.5 | 5.8 |

| Age Group and Year | Total | White | Black | Hispanic | Asian/ Pacific Islander | American Indian/ Alaska Native |
|---|---|---|---|---|---|---|
| **3 to 5 years** | | | | | | |
| 2000 | 5.1 | 5.6 | 5.3 | 3.5 | 2.8 | 6.6 |
| 2001 | 5.3 | 5.8 | 5.5 | 3.8 | 3.0 | 7.1 |
| 2002 | 5.6 | 6.1 | 5.8 | 4.0 | 3.2 | 7.7 |
| 2003 | 5.8 | 6.4 | 5.9 | 4.3 | 3.6 | 8.3 |
| 2004 | 5.9 | 6.5 | 5.9 | 4.4 | 3.8 | 8.6 |
| 2005 | 5.8 | 6.5 | 5.7 | 4.4 | 4.0 | 8.8 |
| 2006 | 5.8 | 6.4 | 5.7 | 4.5 | 4.0 | 9.0 |
| 2007 | 5.7 | 6.3 | 5.6 | 4.5 | 4.2 | 8.6 |
| **6 to 21 years** | | | | | | |
| 1998 | 8.6 | 8.5 | 11.4 | 7.5 | 3.8 | 10.2 |
| 1999 | 8.7 | 8.3 | 11.2 | 7.4 | 3.9 | 11.9 |
| 2000 | 8.7 | 8.5 | 11.8 | 7.5 | 4.2 | 12.4 |
| 2001 | 8.8 | 8.6 | 12.0 | 7.7 | 4.2 | 12.9 |
| 2002 | 8.9 | 8.6 | 12.2 | 8.0 | 4.4 | 13.2 |
| 2003 | 9.1 | 8.7 | 12.4 | 8.2 | 4.5 | 13.8 |
| 2004 | 9.2 | 8.8 | 12.6 | 8.4 | 4.7 | 14.1 |
| 2005 | 9.2 | 8.7 | 12.5 | 8.5 | 4.8 | 14.3 |
| 2006 | 9.1 | 8.7 | 12.4 | 8.5 | 4.8 | 14.3 |
| 2007 | 9.0 | 8.5 | 12.2 | 8.5 | 4.8 | 14.4 |

*Note:* Race categories exclude persons of Hispanic ethnicity.

*Source:* Status and Trends in the Education of Racial and Ethnic Minorities (NCES 2010-015), Table 8.1a, July 2010. Retrieved from http://nces.ed.gov/pubs2010/2010015/tables/table_8_1a.asp

**Table 4**    Number and Percentage of Children (Ages 3–5 and 6–21) Served Under the Individuals with Disabilities Education Act (IDEA), by Race/Ethnicity and Type of Disability in 2007

| Age Group and Type of Disability | Total | White | Black | Hispanic | Asian/ Pacific Islander | American Indian/Alaska Native |
|---|---|---|---|---|---|---|
| *3 to 5 years* | | | | | | |
| | *Number* | | | | | |
| Any disability[1] | 700,166 | 439,421 | 100,133 | 124,796 | 23,649 | 9,377 |
| Specific learning disability | 11,922 | 6,875 | 1,502 | 3,131 | 313 | 101 |
| Speech or language impairment | 318,937 | 207,627 | 39,230 | 59,320 | 8,939 | 3,821 |
| Mental retardation | 12,380 | 5,428 | 2,308 | 3,970 | 585 | 89 |
| Emotional disturbance | 3,416 | 2,143 | 742 | 425 | 58 | 48 |
| Autism | 39,041 | 23,602 | 4,834 | 7,251 | 3,112 | 242 |
| Hearing impairment | 7,678 | 4,373 | 899 | 1,850 | 469 | 87 |
| Visual impairment | 3,200 | 1,875 | 399 | 732 | 138 | 56 |
| | *Percent* | | | | | |
| Any disability[1] | 5.74 | 6.31 | 5.58 | 4.50 | 4.19 | 8.62 |
| Specific learning disability | 0.10 | 0.10 | 0.08 | 0.11 | 0.06 | 0.09 |
| Speech or language impairment | 2.61 | 2.98 | 2.19 | 2.14 | 1.58 | 3.51 |
| Mental retardation | 0.10 | 0.08 | 0.13 | 0.14 | 0.10 | 0.08 |
| Emotional disturbance | 0.03 | 0.03 | 0.04 | 0.02 | 0.01 | 0.04 |

| Age Group and Type of Disability | Total | White | Black | Hispanic | Asian/ Pacific Islander | American Indian/Alaska Native |
|---|---|---|---|---|---|---|
| *3 to 5 years* | | | | | | |
| Autism | 0.32 | 0.34 | 0.27 | 0.26 | 0.55 | 0.22 |
| Hearing impairment | 0.06 | 0.06 | 0.05 | 0.07 | 0.08 | 0.08 |
| Visual impairment | 0.03 | 0.03 | 0.02 | 0.03 | 0.02 | 0.05 |
| *6 to 21 years* | | | | | | |
| | *Number* | | | | | |
| Any disability[1] | 5,912,586 | 3,399,744 | 1,208,195 | 1,060,112 | 135,098 | 90,741 |
| Specific learning disability | 2,563,665 | 1,372,432 | 552,552 | 558,082 | 46,542 | 47,703 |
| Speech or language impairment | 1,085,497 | 698,670 | 174,920 | 207,919 | 37,360 | 15,696 |
| Mental retardation | 487,854 | 240,576 | 155,151 | 73,136 | 10,734 | 6,402 |
| Emotional disturbance | 438,867 | 248,041 | 126,384 | 50,523 | 5,044 | 7,029 |
| Autism | 79,085 | 172,020 | 36,264 | 31,707 | 14,095 | 1,889 |
| Hearing impairment | 71,332 | 38,362 | 11,514 | 16,678 | 3,741 | 860 |
| Visual impairment | 25,855 | 15,176 | 4,404 | 4,796 | 1,066 | 334 |
| | *Percent* | | | | | |
| Any disability[1] | 8.96 | 8.47 | 12.15 | 8.51 | 4.85 | 14.38 |
| Specific learning disability | 3.89 | 3.42 | 5.32 | 4.55 | 1.60 | 7.09 |
| Speech or language impairment | 1.65 | 1.74 | 1.76 | 1.67 | 1.34 | 2.49 |

*(Continued)*

**Table 4** (Continued)

| Age Group and Type of Disability | Total | White | Black | Hispanic | Asian/ Pacific Islander | American Indian/Alaska Native |
|---|---|---|---|---|---|---|
| 6 to 21 years | | | | | | |
| Mental retardation | 0.74 | 0.60 | 1.56 | 0.59 | 0.39 | 1.01 |
| Emotional disturbance | 0.67 | 0.62 | 1.27 | 0.41 | 0.18 | 1.11 |
| Autism | 0.12 | 0.43 | 0.36 | 0.25 | 0.51 | 0.30 |
| Hearing impairment | 0.11 | 0.10 | 0.12 | 0.13 | 0.13 | 0.14 |
| Visual impairment | 0.04 | 0.04 | 0.04 | 0.04 | 0.04 | 0.05 |

[1]Total includes other disabilities not separately shown.

*Note:* Race categories exclude persons of Hispanic ethnicity.

*Source:* National Center for Educational Statistics. (2010, July). *Status and trends in the education of racial and ethnic minorities* (NCES 2010-015), Table 8.1b. Retrieved from http://nces.ed.gov/pubs2010/2010015/tables/table_8_1b.asp

# Placement

Once found eligible for special education, students may be served in a variety of environments. These environments for students receiving special education services have changed, with each revision of IDEA calling for greater inclusion in general education. Table 5 depicts schools' responses to this emphasis, which have been to include more students with disabilities in general education environments for greater length of time during the school day, with parallel reductions in segregated settings. As Table 5 indicates, the percentage of students who spend less than 20% of educational time in a special education environment has increased steadily over time, while the percentage of students who spend more than 20% of educational time in special education environments has decreased steadily. Placement in separate residential facilities, the most restrictive educational environments, also shows a steady decline. Table 6 documents the increase in less restrictive educational settings for students from all eligibility categories. It shows, by disability area, the percentage of students in each eligibility category who spend more than 20% of their educational time in the general education environments for selected years from 1990 to 2007.

**Table 5** Percentage of Students (6–21 Years Old) Served Under Individuals with Disabilities Education Act, Part B, by Educational Environment

| | | 1989 | 1990 | 1994 | 1996 | 1998 | 2000 | 2002 | 2004 | 2005 | 2006 | 2007 |
|---|---|---|---|---|---|---|---|---|---|---|---|---|
| Percent regular school time in general education | >80 | 31.7 | 33.1 | 44.3 | 46.1 | 46.0 | 46.5 | 48.2 | 51.9 | 54.2 | 53.7 | 56.8 |
| | 40–80 | 37.5 | 36.4 | 28.5 | 28.3 | 29.9 | 29.8 | 28.7 | 26.5 | 25.1 | 23.7 | 22.4 |
| | <40 | 24.9 | 25.0 | 22.4 | 21.4 | 20.0 | 19.5 | 19.0 | 17.6 | 16.7 | 17.6 | 15.4 |
| Separate school for students with disabilities | | 4.5 | 4.2 | 3.0 | 3.0 | 3.0 | 3.0 | 2.9 | 3.0 | 3.0 | 2.9 | 3.0 |
| Separate residential facilities | | 1.0 | 0.9 | 0.8 | 0.7 | 0.7 | 0.7 | 0.4 | 0.3 | 0.6 | 0.4 | 0.4 |
| Home-bound/hospital | | 0.6 | 0.5 | 0.6 | 0.5 | 0.5 | 0.5 | 0.5 | 0.4 | 0.5 | 0.4 | 0.4 |
| Correctional facilities* | | | | | | | | | | | 0.4 | 0.4 |

*Data unavailable until 2006.

*Note:* Percentages represent children/youth in 50 states, District of Columbia, and Bureau of Indian Education. Vermont is excluded from 2006–2007 data (total special education eligible 14,010).

*Source:* U.S. Department of Education, Office of Special Education Programs. *Individuals with Disabilities Education Act (IDEA) database.* Retrieved from https://www.ideadata.org

**Table 6**   Students With Disabilities (6–21 Years Old) Spending More Than 80% of Educational Time in General Education

|  | 1990* | 1995* | 2000[†] | 2005[‡] | 2006[‡] | 2007[‡] |
|---|---|---|---|---|---|---|
| All students with disabilities | 32.8 | 45.4 | 46.5 | 54.2 | 53.7 | 56.8 |
| Specific learning disabilities | 22.5 | 42.4 | 44.3 | 54.5 | 54.8 | 59.0 |
| Speech or language impairments | 78.9 | 88.6 | 85.6 | 88.7 | 84.2 | 86.7 |
| Mental retardation | 7.4 | 10.3 | 13.2 | 14.1 | 16.0 | 15.8 |
| Emotional disturbance | 16.8 | 23.5 | 26.7 | 34.7 | 35.1 | 37.3 |
| Multiple disabilities | 6.6 | 9.5 | 12.1 | 13.3 | 13.4 | 12.9 |
| Hearing impairment | 26.9 | 36.2 | 42.3 | 48.8 | 48.8 | 51.9 |
| Orthopedic impairments | 29.6 | 40.9 | 46.3 | 49.5 | 47.0 | 50.0 |
| Other health impairments | 30.2 | 43.2 | 45.1 | 56.0 | 54.8 | 59.0 |
| Visual impairments | 42.1 | 47.7 | 50.5 | 58.2 | 57.2 | 60.1 |
| Autism | 4.7 | 12.0 | 24.31 | 31.4 | 32.3 | 34.6 |
| Deaf-blindness | 10.5 | 10.8 | 18.0 | 22.8 | 21.0 | 20.8 |
| Traumatic brain injury | 8.0 | 28.5 | 32.3 | 40.0 | 41.7 | 43.9 |

*Sources:* *U.S. Department of Education. (2002). *Twenty-fourth annual report to Congress on the implementation of the Individuals with Disabilities Education Act,* Table AB7 (pp. A219–A221). Washington, DC: Author. Retrieved from http://www.pluk.org/Pubs/Fed/IDEAreport_2002_4.8M.pdf; †Data Accountability Center. *Individuals with Disabilities Education Act (IDEA) data,* Table AB2. Retrieved from http://www.ideadata.org/tables25th%5Car_ab2.htm; ‡U.S. Department of Education, Institute of Education Sciences, National Center of Education Statistics. (2010, April). *Digest of educational statistics: 2009* (NCES 2010-013), Table 51. Retrieved from http://nces.ed.gov/programs/digest/d09/tables/dt09_051.asp

# Discipline

Students with disabilities can be excluded from general education environments through disciplinary actions such as frequent and/or long-term suspension, expulsion, or placement in alternative environments. Because suspension and expulsion can result in denial of the student's right to an education and needed special education services, court cases and IDEA amendments have stressed the importance of limiting their use to situations in which the offending behaviors are not manifestations of the student's disability or pose safety risks to the student or others (including drug- and weapons-related issues). Furthermore, as of the 1997 IDEA amendments, students with disabilities cannot be suspended for more than 10 consecutive days without the provision of special education services starting after the 10th day. Finally, the 2004 IDEA amendments are even more explicit, stating that students with disabilities cannot be expelled or suspended for more than 10 days when their behavior is related to their disabilities. Alternative settings may be used when the offending behaviors are not disability related.

As shown in Table 7, discipline data for three of the most recent data years demonstrate that unilateral removal of students with disabilities to alternative educational settings has decreased slightly, while suspensions/ expulsion increased by the same percentage. Table 8 documents, by disability category, the percentage of students who were removed and placed in alternative settings or expelled or suspended for more than 10 days during the 2003–2004 school year. According to this data, while the total percentage of students with any disability removed, expelled, or suspended equals 2.23%, the percentage varies across the disability categories. Students with emotional disturbance (ED) were removed or suspended/expelled in the largest proportions (7.83%), followed by students with other health impairments, including ADHD (2.98%), learning disabilities (2.59%), and mental retardation (2.43%). Less than 1% of students in eight of the ten remaining disability categories were removed or expelled/suspended for more than 10 days. By definition of their disabilities, students with emotional disturbance are the most likely group of students to exhibit the inappropriate behaviors that lead to removal, suspension, or expulsion. Even factoring out drugs, weapons, and safety-related disciplinary actions, school districts expelled or suspended for more than 10 days over 7% of these students during the 2003–2004 school year. As a result, the data raise questions about the rate at which school districts expel and suspend students with emotional disabilities for behaviors that supposedly are not related to their disabilities.

**Table 7**   Number and Percent of Students With Disabilities Removed, Suspended, or Expelled From School

| | Removals to Interim Alternative Education Setting | | | | Suspensions/Expulsions | | | |
| | By School Personnel for Drugs/Weapons | | By Hearing Officer for Likely Injury | | >10 Days/Year | | Multiple Days Summed to >10 | |
| | n | % | n | % | n | % | n | % |
|---|---|---|---|---|---|---|---|---|
| 2003–2004 | 15,252 | .23 | 1,118 | .02 | 71,955 | 1.09 | 59,264 | .89 |
| 2004–2005 | 13,059 | .19 | 1,222 | .02 | 67,966 | 1.00 | 56,595 | .83 |
| 2005–2006 | 12,963 | .19 | 1,580 | .02 | 76,036 | 1.13 | 63,073 | .95 |

*Source:* Data Accountability Center. *Individuals with Disabilities Education Act (IDEA) data,* Table AB2. Retrieved from http://www.ideadata.org

# High-Stakes Testing

With increased accountability at state and federal levels, more students with disabilities are included in statewide assessment systems. This section presents testing data results, generally focused on the high-stakes areas of reading and math. It also includes data on alternate assessment (for students who are unable to participate in regular education assessments).

## Regular Assessment

The following six figures (Figures 1–6) document the percentage of students who score proficient or higher on statewide assessments for the majority of states in the United States. Each figure presents the results for elementary, middle, or high school reading or math performance for the 2006–2007 school year. For some of the general education results, special education students might be included in the general education proficiency rates due to idiosyncrasies in state reporting procedures. Comparison across states is discouraged because each state determines the content of the statewide exam used, and some states provide a total of all students taking the exam—rather than just the non-disabled student population—for the "regular student" percentage. Despite these cautions, it is clear that fewer students with disabilities reach the proficient or higher level in reading or math in elementary, middle, and high school, illustrating the continuing achievement gap between students with and without disabilities.

**Table 8**  Students With Disabilities (Ages 3–21) Unilaterally Removed During the 2003–2004 School Year

| | Removals to Interim Alternative Education Setting | | | | Suspensions/Expulsions | | | |
| | By School Personnel for Drugs/Weapons | | By Hearing Officer for Likely Injury | | >10 Days/Year | | Multiple Days Summed to >10 | |
| | n | % | n | % | n | % | n | % |
|---|---|---|---|---|---|---|---|---|
| Total students with disabilities | 15,252 | .23 | 1,118 | .02 | 71,955 | 1.09 | 59,264 | .89 |
| Significant learning disabilities | 9,196 | .32 | 571 | .02 | 35,365 | 1.25 | 28,308 | 1.00 |
| Speech & language impairments | 385 | .03 | 23 | .00 | 2,161 | .15 | 1,709 | .12 |
| Mental retardation | 1,041 | .18 | 142 | .02 | 7,131 | 1.20 | 6,110 | 1.03 |
| Emotional disturbance | 2,851 | .59 | 269 | .06 | 18,764 | 3.85 | 16,201 | 3.33 |
| Multiple disabilities | 115 | .08 | 4 | .00 | 624 | .45 | 549 | .39 |
| Hearing impairment | 93 | .12 | 4 | .01 | 246 | .31 | 176 | .22 |
| Orthopedic impairments | 50 | .07 | 4 | .01 | 348 | .45 | 276 | .36 |

(Continued)

**Table 8** (Continued)

| | Removals to Interim Alternative Education Setting | | | | Suspensions/Expulsions | | | |
| | By School Personnel for Drugs/Weapons | | By Hearing Officer for Likely Injury | | >10 Days/Year | | Multiple Days Summed to >10 | |
| | n | % | n | % | n | % | n | % |
|---|---|---|---|---|---|---|---|---|
| Other health impairments | 1,400 | .30 | 94 | .02 | 6,796 | 1.47 | 5,535 | 1.19 |
| Visual impairments | 17 | .06 | 0 | .00 | 89 | .31 | 75 | .26 |
| Autism | 30 | .02 | 6 | .00 | 139 | .09 | 103 | .06 |
| Deaf-blindness | 7 | .38 | 0 | .00 | 8 | .44 | 7 | .38 |
| Traumatic brain injury | 45 | .19 | 1 | .00 | 156 | .67 | 127 | .54 |
| Developmental disabilities | 22 | .01 | 0 | .00 | 128 | .04 | 88 | .03 |

*Source:* U.S. Department of Education, Office of Special Education and Rehabilitative Services, Office of Special Education Programs. (2009). *28th annual report to Congress on the implementation of the Individuals with Disabilities Education Act, 2006* (vol. 2), Tables 5.1, 5.2, E.1. Washington, DC: Author. Retrieved from http://www2.ed.gov/about/reports/annual/osep/2006/parts-b-c/28th-vol-2.pdf

**Figure 1** Elementary School Reading Performance on the Regular Assessment for 2006–2007

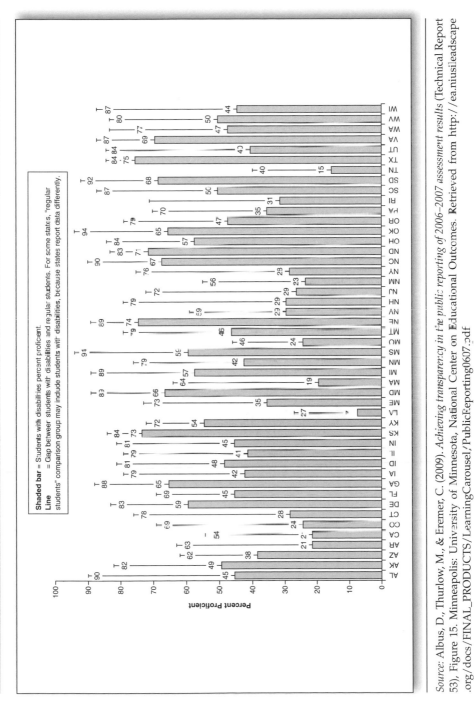

*Source:* Albus, D., Thurlow, M., & Eremer, C. (2009). *Achieving transparency in the public reporting of 2006–2007 assessment results* (Technical Report 53). Figure 15. Minneapolis: University of Minnesota, National Center on Educational Outcomes. Retrieved from http://ea.niusileadscape .org/docs/FINAL_PRODUCTS/LearningCarousel/PublicReporting0607.pdf

221

**Figure 2**  Middle School Reading Performance on the Regular Assessment for 2006–2007

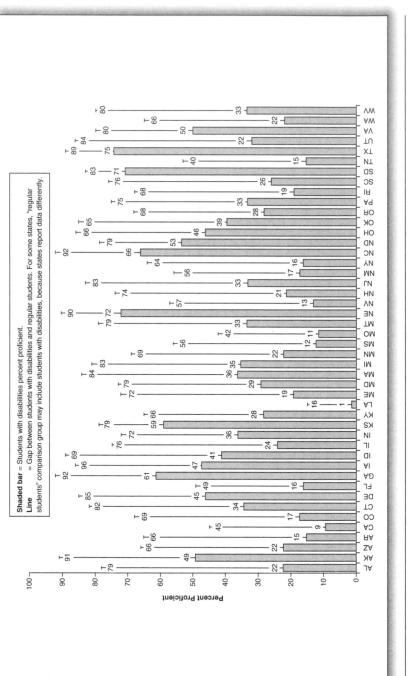

*Source:* Albus, D., Thurlow, M., & Bremer, C. (2009). *Achieving transparency in the public reporting of 2006–2007 assessment results* (Technical Report 53). Figure 16. Minneapolis: University of Minnesota, National Center on Educational Outcomes. Retrieved from http://ea.niusileadscape .org/docs/FINAL_PRODUCTS/LearningCarousel/PublicReporting0607.pdf

**Figure 3**   High School Reading Performance on the Regular Assessment for 2006–2007

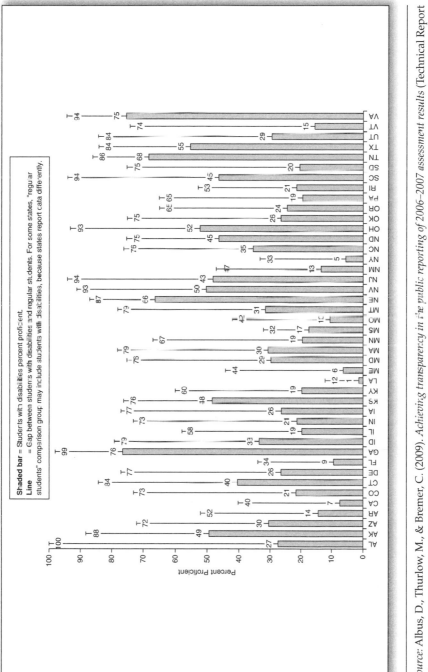

*Source:* Albus, D., Thurlow, M., & Bremer, C. (2009). *Achieving transparency in the public reporting of 2006–2007 assessment results* (Technical Report 53), Figure 17. Minneapolis: University of Minnesota, National Center on Educational Outcomes. Retrieved from http://ea.niusileadscape .org/docs/FINAL_PRODUCTS/LearningCarousel/PublicReporting0607.pdf

223

**Figure 4** Elementary Mathematics Performance on the Regular Assessment for 2006–2007

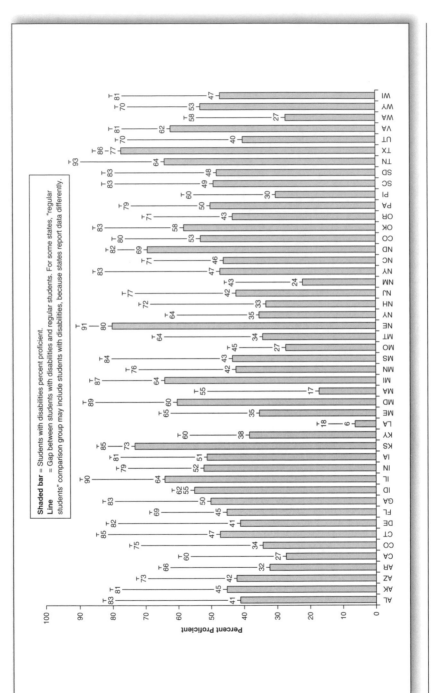

*Source:* Albus, D., Thurlow, M., & Bremer, C. (2009). *Achieving transparency in the public reporting of 2006–2007 assessment results* (Technical Report 53). Figure 18. Minneapolis: University of Minnesota, National Center on Educational Outcomes. Retrieved from http://ea.niusileadscape.org/docs/FINAL_PRODUCTS/LearningCarousel/PublicReporting0607.pdf

**Figure 5** Middle School Mathematics Performance on the Regular Assessment for 2006–2007

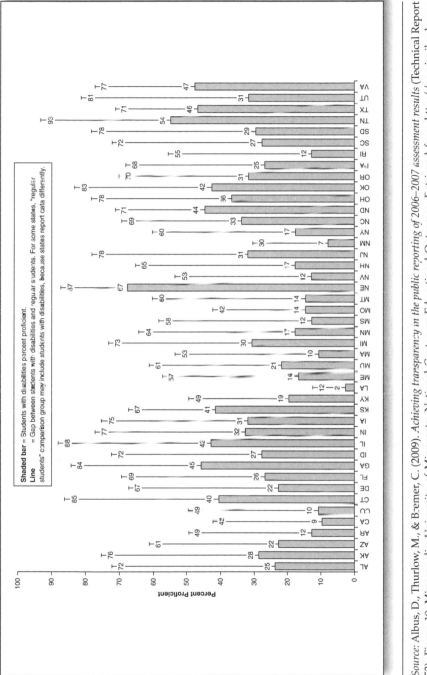

Shaded bar = Students with disabilities percent proficient.
Line = Gap between students with disabilities and regular students. For some states, "regular students" comparison group may include students with disabilities, because states report data differently.

*Source:* Albus, D., Thurlow, M., & Bremer, C. (2009). *Achieving transparency in the public reporting of 2006–2007 assessment results* (Technical Report 53). Figure 19. Minneapolis: University of Minnesota, National Center on Educational Outcomes. Retrieved from http://ea.niusileadscape .org/docs/FINAL_PRODUCTS/LearningCarousel/PublicReporting6607.pdf

**Figure 6** High School Mathematics Performance on the Regular Assessment for 2006–2007

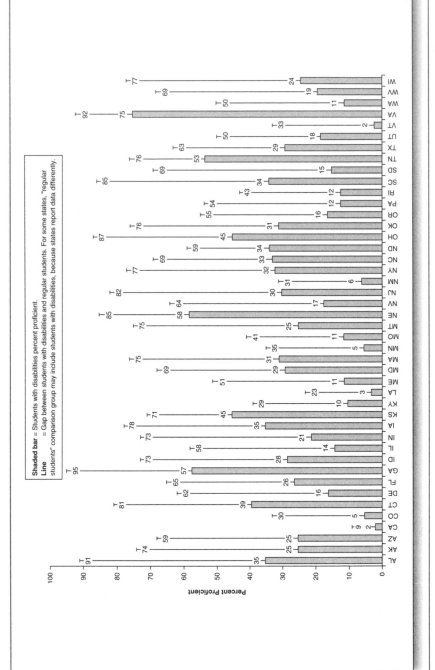

Shaded bar = Students with disabilities percent proficient.
Line = Gap between students with disabilities and regular students. For some states, "regular students" comparison group may include students with disabilities, because states report data differently.

*Source:* Albus, D., Thurlow, M., & Bremer, C. (2009). *Achieving transparency in the public reporting of 2006–2007 assessment results* (Technical Report 53), Figure 20. Minneapolis: University of Minnesota, National Center on Educational Outcomes. Retrieved from http://ea.niusileadscape.org/docs/FINAL_PRODUCTS/LearningCarousel/PublicReporting0607.pdf

## Alternate Assessment

The National Study of Alternate Assessments (NSAA) Teacher Survey (2009) examined feedback from teachers of students with significant cognitive disabilities (Cameto et al., 2010). Figure 7 indicates that a very small number of students on each teacher's caseload take alternative assessments. Figures 8–13 describe the students who take alternative assessments. Figure 14 depicts teacher responses to questions about alternative assessments, standards, and academic instruction. In general, the teachers are evenly split over the benefit and effectiveness of alternative assessments and alternative state standards. Approximately 70% of the teachers believe the assessments do not reflect the achievement or progress of the students. However, more than 90% believe it is important to provide academic instruction to students with significant cognitive disabilities.

**Figure 7**   Number of Students in a Teacher's Classroom or on Caseload Who Took the Alternative Assessment in 2008–2009

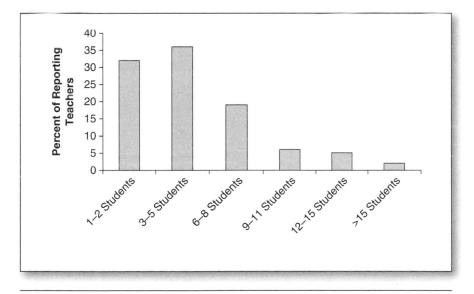

*Source:* Cameto, R., Bergland, F., Knokey, A.-M., Nagle, K. M., Sanford, C., Kalb, S. C., Blackorby, J., Sinclair, B., Riley, D. L., & Ortega, M. (2010). *Teacher perspectives of school-level implementation of alternate assessments for students with significant cognitive disabilities. A report from the National Study on Alternate Assessments* (NCSER 2010-3007). Menlo Park, CA: SRI International. Retrieved from ERIC database.

**Figure 8**    Number of Years Below Grade Level at Which Target
Students Performed in 2008–2009

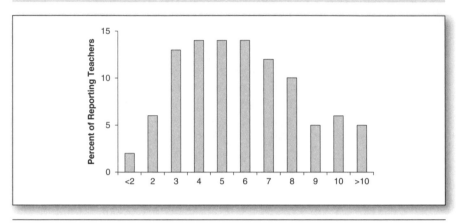

*Source:* Cameto, R., Bergland, F., Knokey, A.-M., Nagle, K. M., Sanford, C., Kalb, S. C., Black-
orby, J., Sinclair, B., Riley, D. L., & Ortega, M. (2010). *Teacher perspectives of school-level implementation of alternate assessments for students with significant cognitive disabilities. A report from the
National Study on Alternate Assessments* (NCSER 2010-3007). Menlo Park, CA: SRI International.
Retrieved from ERIC database.

**Figure 9**    Percent of Target Students Taking Alternative Assessment
Who Are English Language Learners, 2008–2009

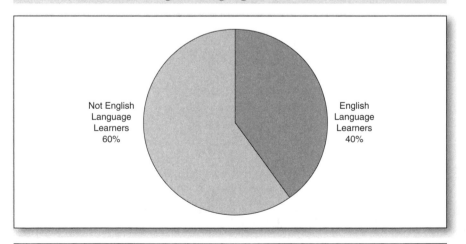

*Source:* Cameto, R., Bergland, F., Knokey, A.-M., Nagle, K. M., Sanford, C., Kalb, S. C., Black-
orby, J., Sinclair, B., Riley, D. L., & Ortega, M. (2010). *Teacher perspectives of school-level implementation of alternate assessments for students with significant cognitive disabilities. A report from the
National Study on Alternate Assessments* (NCSER 2010-3007). Menlo Park, CA: SRI International.
Retrieved from ERIC database.

**Figure 10**    Communication Level of Target Students Taking
Alternative Assessments, 2008–2009

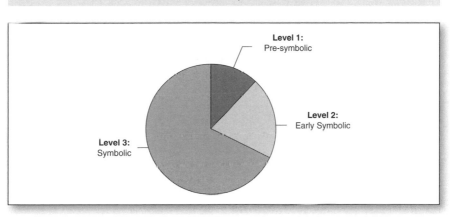

*Source:* Cameto, R., Bergland, F., Knokey, A.-M., Nagle, K. M., Sanford, C., Kalb, S. C., Black-orby, J., Sinclair, B., Riley, D. L., & Ortega, M. (2010). *Teacher perspectives of school-level imple-mentation of alternate assessments for students with significant cognitive disabilities. A report from the National Study on Alternate Assessments* (NCSER 2010-3007). Menlo Park, CA: SRI Interna-tional. Retrieved from ERIC database.

**Figure 11**    Level of Engagement of Target Students Taking
Alternative Assessments, 2008–2009

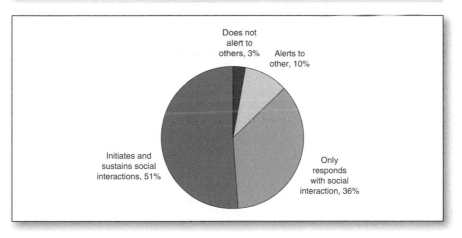

*Source:* Cameto, R., Bergland, F., Knokey, A.-M., Nagle, K. M., Sanford, C., Kalb, S. C., Black-orby, J., Sinclair, B., Riley, D. L., & Ortega, M. (2010). *Teacher perspectives of school-level imple-mentation of alternate assessments for students with significant cognitive disabilities. A report from the National Study on Alternate Assessments* (NCSER 2010-3007). Menlo Park, CA: SRI Interna-tional. Retrieved from ERIC database.

**Figure 12**    Reading Ability of Target Students Taking Alternative Assessments, 2008–2009

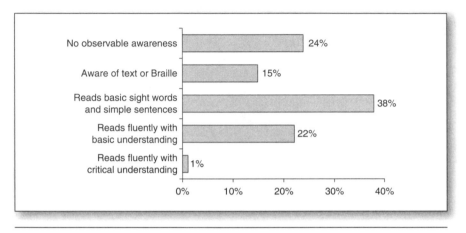

*Source:* Cameto, R., Bergland, F., Knokey, A.-M., Nagle, K. M., Sanford, C., Kalb, S. C., Blackorby, J., Sinclair, B., Riley, D. L., & Ortega, M. (2010). *Teacher perspectives of school-level implementation of alternate assessments for students with significant cognitive disabilities. A report from the National Study on Alternate Assessments* (NCSER 2010-3007). Menlo Park, CA: SRI International. Retrieved from ERIC database.

**Figure 13**    Mathematics Ability of Target Students Taking Alternative Assessment, 2008–2009

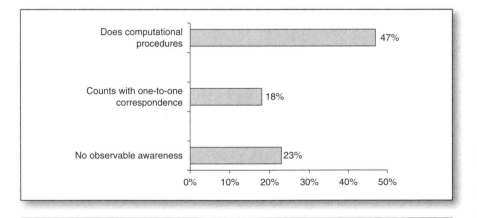

*Source:* Cameto, R., Bergland, F., Knokey, A.-M., Nagle, K. M., Sanford, C., Kalb, S. C., Blackorby, J., Sinclair, B., Riley, D. L., & Ortega, M. (2010). *Teacher perspectives of school-level implementation of alternate assessments for students with significant cognitive disabilities. A report from the National Study on Alternate Assessments* (NCSER 2010-3007). Menlo Park, CA: SRI International. Retrieved from ERIC database.

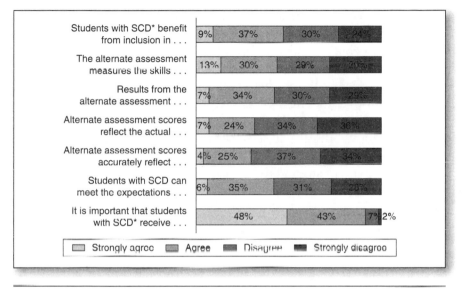

**Figure 14**   Benefits, Results, and Expectations of the Alternate Assessment System by Percent of Teachers in Agreement, 2008–2009

\* Significant cognitive disabilities.

*Note:* Strongly disagree percentage was left off the original chart.

*Source:* Cameto, R., Bergland, F., Knokey, A.-M., Nagle, K. M., Sanford, C., Kalb, S. C., Blackorby, J., Sinclair, B., Riley, D. L., & Ortega, M. (2010). *Teacher perspectives of school-level implementation of alternate assessments for students with significant cognitive disabilities. A report from the National Study on Alternate Assessments* (NCSER 2010-3007). Menlo Park, CA: SRI International. Retrieved from ERIC database.

# Student Perceptions

This set of tables and figures, taken from the National Center for Special Education Research study *Perceptions and Expectations of Youth with Disabilities NLTS2* (2007), presents information about the education of students with disabilities from the perspective of the students themselves. Both the tables and figures represent the perceptions of students with disabilities in relation to the difficulty of school, homework completion, and attention. The tables provide this data by disability category, while the figures describe students' responses as a whole group. The figures also include student perceptions related to self-advocacy and feelings of belonging. Data related to student perceptions of interpersonal challenges, perceived safety, and enjoyment of school is presented in the final three tables in this section. This data is reported as means with standard deviations in parentheses.

Table 9 illustrates that students with disabilities feel secure about school personnel listening to their needs. They also believe that they know how to obtain needed information. However, a large percentage of these students frequently withhold their opinions about the services they receive. Figure 15 indicates that more than half of students with disabilities feel confident that they can advocate for themselves. Furthermore, Figure 16 reveals that approximately two out of three students with disabilities feel at least somewhat connected to their school environment.

Table 10 depicts students with disabilities' perceptions about the challenge of academic tasks, attention to tasks, and homework completion. This data suggest that students with disabilities frequently feel unchallenged by their academic coursework. The second section of the table documents the frequency with which students with disabilities have difficulty paying attention in school. More than half the students in the autism category and approximately 30%–40% of students in all remaining categories except visual impairment, orthopedic impairment, and deaf-blindness report daily to weekly difficulties. Perceptions about the difficulty of homework completion are summarized in the final section of the table. Figures 17 and 18 provide broad overviews of the patterns described above. More than half of the surveyed students believe school is unchallenging (Figure 17), and about one-third of them report some difficulty paying attention and completing homework (Figure 18).

Tables 11–13 describe the students' perceptions of their interpersonal challenges, safety, and level of enjoyment of school. With only modest variations across all disability categories, most students report very little difficulty in getting along with their teachers and other students, and most indicate that they have an adult at school who cares about them (Table 11). As described in Table 12, very few students report not feeling safe at school. Table 13, meanwhile, surveys the level of enjoyment with school experienced by students with disabilities. It indicates that a majority of students in all disability categories enjoy school to varying degrees.

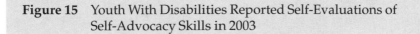

**Figure 15    Youth With Disabilities Reported Self-Evaluations of Self-Advocacy Skills in 2003**

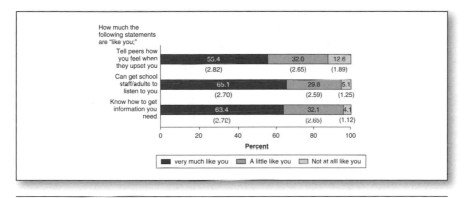

*Note:* Standard errors are in parentheses.

*Source:* U.S. Department of Education, Institute of Education Sciences, National Center for Special Education Research. (2003). *Perceptions and expectations of youth with disabilities,* National Longitudinal Transition Study-2 (NLTS2), Wave 2 youth telephone interview/mail survey (NCES 2007-3006). Retrieved from http://ies.ed.gov/ncser/pubs/20073006/figures/fig7.asp

**Figure 16    Youth With Disabilities Reported Feelings About Being Part of Their School in 2003**

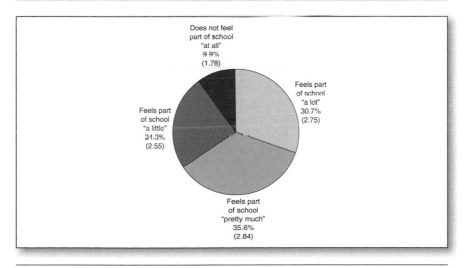

*Note:* Standard errors are in parentheses.

*Source:* U.S. Department of Education, Institute of Education Sciences, National Center for Special Education Research. (2003). *Perceptions and expectations of youth with disabilities,* National Longitudinal Transition Study-2 (NLTS2), Wave 2 youth telephone interview/mail survey (NCES 2007-3006). Retrieved from http://ies.ed.gov/ncser/pubs/20073006/figures/fig12.asp

**Table 9** Youth With Disabilities' Feelings of Competence, by Disability Category*

| | Learning Disability | Speech/ Language Impairment | Mental Retardation | Emotional Disturbance | Hearing Impairment | Visual Impairment | Orthopedic Impairment | Other Health Impairments | Autism | Traumatic Brain Injury | Multiple Disabilities | Deaf-Blindness |
|---|---|---|---|---|---|---|---|---|---|---|---|---|
| *Can get school staff and adults to listen to you* | | | | | | | | | | | | |
| Very much like you | 66.7 (4.01) | 57.5 (4.40) | 61.6 (5.68) | 65.5 (4.40) | 60.4 (6.02) | 70.3 (5.77) | 67.7 (5.38) | 60.3 (4.59) | 56.1 (7.31) | 69.1 (8.32) | 63.6 (7.10) | 73.1 (8.00) |
| A little like you | 29.3 (3.88) | 36.3 (4.28) | 30.9 (5.39) | 27.7 (4.14) | 30.9 (5.69) | 25.7 (5.52) | 29.5 (5.25) | 34.5 (4.46) | 36.4 (7.09) | 26.5 (7.95) | 26.7 (6.53) | 18.6 (7.02) |
| Not at all like you | 4.1 (1.69) | 6.2 (2.15) | 7.5 (3.07) | 6.8 (2.33) | 8.7 (3.47) | 3.9 (2.44) | 2.8 (1.90) | 5.3 (2.10) | 7.5 (3.88) | 4.4 (3.69) | 9.7 (4.37) | 8.3 (4.98) |
| *Know how to get information you need* | | | | | | | | | | | | |
| Very much like you | 63.5 (4.09) | 61.6 (4.33) | 57.4 (5.76) | 74.3 (4.05) | 63.6 (5.91) | 77.4 (5.32) | 60.0 (5.63) | 61.2 (4.58) | 63.2 (7.11) | 66.6 (8.49) | 60.7 (7.34) | 66.7 (8.51) |
| A little like you | 33.4 (4.01) | 33.6 (4.20) | 32.9 (5.48) | 22.5 (3.87) | 33.3 (5.79) | 21.6 (5.23) | 36.3 (5.52) | 34.8 (4.48) | 32.2 (6.89) | 27.5 (8.04) | 31.1 (6.96) | 33.3 (8.51) |
| Not at all like you | 3.1 (1.47) | 4.8 (1.90) | 9.7 (3.45) | 3.1 (1.61) | 3.1 (2.13) | 1.0 (1.27) | 3.7 (2.17) | 4.0 (1.84) | 4.6 (3.09) | 5.9 (4.24) | 8.1 (4.10) | + |

| | Learning Disability | Speech/Language Impairment | Mental Retardation | Emotional Disturbance | Hearing Impairment | Visual Impairment | Orthopedic Impairment | Other Health Impairments | Autism | Traumatic Brain Injury | Multiple Disabilities | Deaf-Blindness |
|---|---|---|---|---|---|---|---|---|---|---|---|---|
| | Tell professionals their opinions or services provided | | | | | | | | | | | |
| Often | 33.3 (9.83) | 23.0 (9.85) | 48.6 (16.42) | 31.5 (10.22) | 25.7 (8.90) | 23.6 (8.03) | 23.0 (7.92) | 30.7 (8.14) | 23.2 (9.41) | 35.7 (15.28) | 18.5 (9.45) | ‡ |
| Sometimes | 33.0 (9.81) | 45.2 (11.65) | 29.0 (14.91) | 33.3 (10.37) | 47.7 (10.18) | 50.6 (9.46) | 47.9 (9.40) | 38.9 (8.61) | 34.8 (10.62) | 33.2 (15.02) | 54.6 (12.12) | ‡ |
| Hardly ever | 33.7 (9.86) | 31.9 (10.91) | 22.4 (13.70) | 35.1 (10.50) | 26.5 (9.01) | 25.9 (8.29) | 29.1 (8.55) | 30.4 (8.12) | 42.1 (11.01) | 31.1 (14.77) | 26.8 (10.78) | ‡ |

*Data in percent (standard error).

† Rounds to zero.

‡ Responses for items with fewer than 30 respondents are not reported.

Source: U.S. Department of Education, Institute of Education Sciences, National Center for Special Education Research. (2003). *Perceptions and expectations of youth with disabilities*, National Longitudinal Transition Study-2 (NLTS2), Wave 2 youth telephone interview/mail survey (NCES 2007-3006). Retrieved from http://ies.ed.gov/ncser/pubs/20073006/tables/table_06.asp

**Table 10** Youth's Reported Perceptions of Academic Challenges, by Disability Category in 2003*

| | Learning Disability | Speech/Language Impairment | Mental Retardation | Emotional Disturbance | Hearing Impairment | Visual Impairment | Orthopedic Impairment | Other Health Impairments | Autism | Traumatic Brain Injury | Multiple Disabilities | Deaf-Blindness |
|---|---|---|---|---|---|---|---|---|---|---|---|---|
| *Percentage reporting school is:* | | | | | | | | | | | | |
| Not hard at all | 9.6 (2.67) | 16.0 (3.45) | 22.4 (4.96) | 26.8 (4.64) | 16.7 (4.83) | 12.9 (4.20) | 12.8 (4.04) | 14.3 (3.61) | 14.0 (5.33) | 14.4 (6.62) | 23.6 (6.54) | 11.2 (5.95) |
| Not very hard | 49.4 (4.54) | 42.5 (4.65) | 34.1 (5.64) | 34.7 (4.99) | 40.1 (6.48) | 40.4 (6.27) | 43.0 (5.99) | 41.8 (5.09) | 39.4 (7.50) | 43.3 (9.35) | 37.5 (7.45) | 34.1 (8.94) |
| Pretty hard | 36.3 (4.36) | 37.5 (4.56) | 36.6 (5.73) | 31.7 (4.88) | 27.9 (5.81) | 31.2 (5.81) | 35.0 (5.77) | 37.6 (5.00) | 39.4 (7.50) | 35.5 (9.03) | 30.9 (7.11) | 48.0 (9.42) |
| Very hard | 4.7 (1.92) | 3.9 (1.82) | 6.9 (3.02) | 6.9 (2.66) | 4.3 (2.90) | 4.5 (2.86) | 9.2 (3.50) | 6.3 (2.51) | 7.2 (3.97) | 6.7 (4.72) | 8.0 (4.18) | 6.7 (4.71) |
| *Percentage reporting having trouble:* | | | | | | | | | | | | |
| **Paying attention at school** | | | | | | | | | | | | |
| Never | 23.5 (3.84) | 18.0 (3.61) | 34.9 (5.72) | 20.1 (4.20) | 31.0 (6.03) | 33.5 (5.90) | 30.5 (5.44) | 14.2 (3.59) | 20.7 (6.23) | 14.6 (6.55) | 30.0 (7.04) | 38.8 (9.19) |
| Just a few times | 40.3 (4.44) | 53.4 (4.69) | 33.8 (5.67) | 36.9 (5.05) | 33.3 (6.14) | 42.5 (6.18) | 43.4 (5.86) | 44.9 (5.12) | 28.5 (6.94) | 54.1 (9.24) | 37.6 (7.44) | 38.4 (9.17) |
| At least weekly but not daily | 29.5 (4.13) | 19.7 (3.74) | 15.9 (4.39) | 32.0 (4.89) | 24.5 (5.60) | 19.2 (4.92) | 19.3 (4.66) | 36.1 (4.94) | 42.5 (7.60) | 23.5 (7.86) | 18.3 (5.94) | 20.6 (7.62) |
| Daily | 6.7 (2.26) | 8.9 (2.68) | 15.5 (4.34) | 11.0 (3.28) | 11.2 (4.11) | 4.8 (2.67) | 6.8 (2.97) | 4.8 (2.20) | 8.3 (4.24) | 7.8 (4.97) | 14.1 (5.35) | 2.2 (2.77) |

236

| Finishing homework | Learning Disability | Speech/ Language Impairment | Mental Retardation | Emotional Disturbance | Hearing Impairment | Visual Impairment | Orthopedic Impairment | Other Health Impairments | Autism | Traumatic Brain Injury | Multiple Disabilities | Deaf-Blindness |
|---|---|---|---|---|---|---|---|---|---|---|---|---|
| Never | 24.7 (3.95) | 25.7 (4.12) | 37.9 (5.83) | 27.1 (4.77) | 30.4 (6.01) | 44.3 (6.31) | 36.5 (5.78) | 30.7 (4.84) | 26.4 (6.83) | 38.4 (9.01) | 42.1 (7.81) | 41.0 (9.27) |
| Just a few times | 44.0 (4.54) | 44.9 (4.69) | 29.6 (5.49) | 31.4 (4.98) | 35.0 (6.23) | 32.5 (5.95) | 37.6 (5.81) | 30.3 (4.32) | 34.7 (7.37) | 29.8 (8.47) | 29.8 (7.23) | 29.3 (8.58) |
| At least weekly but not daily | 23.4 (3.87) | 18.6 (3.67) | 15.1 (4.30) | 25.7 (4.69) | 17.6 (4.97) | 18.0 (4.88) | 17.5 (4.56) | 30.6 (4.84) | 27.8 (6.94) | 23.2 (7.82) | 10.7 (4.89) | 18.2 (7.27) |
| Daily | 8.0 (2.48) | 10.8 (2.93) | 17.4 (4.56) | 15.8 (3.91) | 17.0 (4.90) | 4.2 (2.82) | 8.5 (3.35) | 8.4 (2.91) | 11.0 (4.85) | 8.6 (5.19) | 17.4 (6.00) | 11.5 (6.01) |

*Data in percent (standard error).

*Source*: U.S. Department of Education, Institute of Education Sciences, National Center for Special Education Research. (2003). *Perceptions and expectations of youth with disabilities*, National Longitudinal Transition Study-2 (NLTS2), Wave 2 youth telephone interview/mail survey (NCES 2007-3006). Retrieved from http://ies.ed.gov/ncser/pubs/20073006/tables/table_08.asp

**Table 11** Youth With Disabilities' Perceptions of Interpersonal Challenges at School in 2003

| | Learning Disability | Speech/Language Impairment | Mental Retardation | Emotional Disturbance | Hearing Impairment | Visual Impairment | Orthopedic Impairment | Other Health Impairments | Autism | Traumatic Brain Injury | Multiple Disabilities | Deaf-Blindness |
|---|---|---|---|---|---|---|---|---|---|---|---|---|
| | | | | | *Percent reporting trouble* | | | | | | | |
| **Getting along with teachers** | | | | | | | | | | | | |
| Never | 44.6 (4.51) | 41.6 (4.63) | 41.8 (5.87) | 30.4 (4.83) | 47.1 (6.51) | 42.1 (6.20) | 59.1 (5.93) | 43.4 (5.10) | 50.4 (7.77) | 52.5 (9.25) | 45.3 (7.67) | 54.5 (9.39) |
| Just a few times | 36.9 (4.38) | 39.0 (4.58) | 31.0 (5.50) | 44.1 (5.22) | 32.0 (6.08) | 46.2 (6.26) | 28.9 (5.47) | 34.1 (4.87) | 25.0 (6.73) | 27.8 (8.30) | 29.6 (7.04) | 29.5 (8.60) |
| At least weekly but not daily | 14.2 (3.39) | 12.2 (3.05) | 14.9 (4.35) | 16.1 (3.99) | 10.1 (4.03) | 7.3 (3.40) | 6.9 (2.79) | 17.3 (4.22) | 19.5 (6.04) | 15.3 (7.36) | 13.8 (5.12) | 13.6 (7.41) |
| Daily | 4.4 (1.86) | 7.3 (2.44) | 12.3 (3.91) | 9.3 (3.05) | 10.8 (4.04) | 4.4 (2.57) | 5.1 (2.65) | 5.2 (2.28) | 5.2 (3.45) | 4.4 (3.80) | 11.4 (4.90) | 2.4 (2.89) |
| **Getting along with others** | | | | | | | | | | | | |
| Never | 40.4 (4.47) | 43.2 (4.68) | 38.8 (5.84) | 29.0 (4.76) | 46.9 (6.49) | 56.0 (6.23) | 53.9 (6.09) | 40.6 (5.08) | 29.8 (7.02) | 49.1 (9.41) | 43.2 (7.71) | 36.2 (9.06) |
| Just a few times | 38.6 (4.44) | 35.6 (4.53) | 31.2 (5.55) | 36.2 (5.05) | 19.7 (5.17) | 26.2 (5.52) | 27.0 (5.42) | 34.9 (4.93) | 37.8 (7.44) | 28.5 (8.49) | 22.9 (6.54) | 34.1 (8.94) |

| | Learning Disability | Speech/Language Impairment | Mental Retardation | Emotional Disturbance | Hearing Impairment | Visual Impairment | Orthopedic Impairment | Other Health Impairments | Autism | Traumatic Brain Injury | Multiple Disabilities | Deaf-Blindness |
|---|---|---|---|---|---|---|---|---|---|---|---|---|
| At least weekly but not daily | 12.6 (2.99) | 12.7 (3.05) | 13.6 (4.28) | 19.6 (4.04) | 20.5 (5.26) | 12.7 (4.12) | 11.6 (3.66) | 15.2 (3.89) | 19.5 (6.14) | 14.1 (6.78) | 10.8 (4.89) | 22.8 (7.89) |
| Daily | 8.4 (2.53) | 8.6 (2.65) | 16.4 (4.44) | 15.2 (3.77) | 12.9 (4.36) | 5.1 (2.76) | 7.4 (3.20) | 9.3 (3.00) | 12.9 (5.14) | 8.3 (5.19) | 23.1 (6.56) | 6.9 (4.78) |
| *Percent agreement that "there is an adult at school who you feel close to and who cares about you"* | | | | | | | | | | | | |
| Agree a lot | 54.6 (4.54) | 48.2 (4.75) | 12.3 (3.94) | 57.4 (5.20) | 60.5 (6.37) | 63.5 (6.03) | 65.5 (5.66) | 58.1 (5.10) | 58.2 (7.63) | 49.7 (9.36) | 66.6 (7.32) | 66.2 (8.92) |
| Agree a little | 30.4 (4.19) | 30.2 (4.37) | 71.9 (5.40) | 26.8 (4.66) | 25.5 (5.68) | 23.8 (5.33) | 26.5 (5.25) | 29.2 (4.70) | 29.1 (7.02) | 36.3 (9.01) | 19.0 (6.08) | 29.3 (8.58) |
| Disagree a little | 11.0 (2.85) | 12.7 (3.17) | 15.4 (4.33) | 8.5 (2.93) | 7.5 (3.43) | 7.7 (3.34) | 5.1 (2.62) | 8.0 (2.81) | 8.5 (4.31) | 9.3 (5.44) | 8.1 (4.23) | 4.5 (3.91) |
| Disagree a lot | 3.9 (1.76) | 8.9 (2.71) | 0.4 (0.76) | 7.4 (2.75) | 6.6 (3.24) | 5.0 (2.73) | 2.9 (2.00) | 4.7 (2.19) | 4.3 (3.14) | 4.7 (3.96) | 6.3 (3.77) | † |

*Note:* Standard errors appear in parentheses.

†Rounds to zero.

*Source:* U.S. Department of Education, Institute of Education Sciences, National Center for Special Education Research. (2003). *Perceptions and expectations of youth with disabilities,* National Longitudinal Transition Study-2 (NLTS2), Wave 2 youth telephone interview/mail survey (NCES 2007-3006). Retrieved from http://ies.ed.gov/ncser/pubs/2007306/tables/table_09.asp

**Table 12** Youth With Disabilities' Reported Perceptions of School Safety in 2003

| | Learning Disability | Speech/ Language Impairment | Mental Retardation | Emotional Disturbance | Hearing Impairment | Visual Impairment | Orthopedic Impairment | Other Health Impairments | Autism | Traumatic Brain Injury | Multiple Disabilities | Deaf-Blindness |
|---|---|---|---|---|---|---|---|---|---|---|---|---|
| | *Percentage reporting at school they feel:* | | | | | | | | | | | |
| Very safe | 35.5 (4.35) | 37.1 (4.55) | 43.9 (5.91) | 45.3 (5.25) | 46.8 (6.49) | 52.0 (6.26) | 39.4 (5.91) | 37.7 (5.02) | 52.6 (7.73) | 47.3 (9.47) | 45.7 (7.72) | 48.3 (9.42) |
| Pretty safe | 56.5 (4.51) | 55.5 (4.68) | 51.5 (5.96) | 41.6 (5.20) | 44.8 (6.47) | 45.7 (6.24) | 55.3 (6.01) | 55.3 (5.15) | 43.4 (7.67) | 47.4 (9.47) | 42.7 (7.66) | 47.2 (9.41) |
| Not very or not at all safe | 7.9 (2.45) | 7.4 (2.46) | 4.6 (2.50) | 13.1 (3.56) | 8.4 (3.61) | 2.3 (1.88) | 5.3 (2.71) | 7.1 (2.66) | 4.0 (3.03) | 5.2 (4.21) | 11.6 (4.96) | 4.5 (3.91) |

*Note:* Standard errors appear in parentheses.

*Source:* U.S. Department of Education, Institute of Education Sciences, National Center for Special Education Research. (2003). *Perceptions and expectations of youth with disabilities,* National Longitudinal Transition Study-2 (NLTS2), Wave 2 youth telephone interview/mail survey (NCES 2007-3006). Retrieved from http://ies.ed.gov/ncser/pubs/20073006/tables/table_09.asp

**Table 13  Youth With Disabilities' Reported Enjoyment of School in 2003**

| | Learning Disability | Speech/Language Impairment | Mental Retardation | Emotional Disturbance | Hearing Impairment | Visual Impairment | Orthopedic Impairment | Other Health Impairments | Autism | Traumatic Brain Injury | Multiple Disabilities | Deaf-Blindness |
|---|---|---|---|---|---|---|---|---|---|---|---|---|
| | *Percentage reporting they enjoy school* | | | | | | | | | | | |
| A lot | 25.3 (3.93) | 27.0 (4.17) | 52.3 (5.94) | 22.8 (4.38) | 29.3 (5.89) | 37.2 (6.03) | 34.0 (5.72) | 20.9 (4.18) | 31.4 (7.11) | 25.7 (8.09) | 50.4 (7.75) | 43.4 (9.34) |
| Pretty much | 43.2 (4.48) | 46.0 (4.68) | 21.4 (4.88) | 29.5 (4.77) | 37.6 (6.27) | 38.5 (6.07) | 42.6 (5.98) | 41.0 (5.06) | 40.2 (7.51) | 42.2 (9.15) | 21.9 (6.41) | 40.8 (9.27) |
| A little | 19.5 (3.58) | 20.0 (3.75) | 19.5 (4.71) | 31.0 (4.83) | 23.5 (5.50) | 16.9 (4.67) | 16.6 (4.50) | 26.5 (4.54) | 20.7 (6.20) | 28.5 (8.36) | 18.6 (6.03) | 11.3 (5.97) |
| Not at all | 12.0 (2.94) | 7.0 (2.39) | 6.8 (2.99) | 16.6 (3.39) | 9.5 (3.80) | 7.4 (3.26) | 6.9 (3.06) | 11.7 (3.30) | 7.7 (4.08) | 3.5 (3.40) | 9.2 (4.48) | 4.5 (3.91) |

*Note:* Standard errors appear in parentheses.

*Source:* U.S. Department of Education, Institute of Education Sciences, National Center for Special Education Research. (2003). *Perceptions and expectations of youth with disabilities, National Longitudinal Transition Study–2 (NLTS2), Wave 2 youth telephone interview/mail survey* (NCES 2007-3006). Retrieved from http://ies.ed.gov/ncser/pubs/20073006/tables/table_09.asp

**Figure 17** Youth With Disabilities' Reported Perceptions of School Being "Hard" in 2003

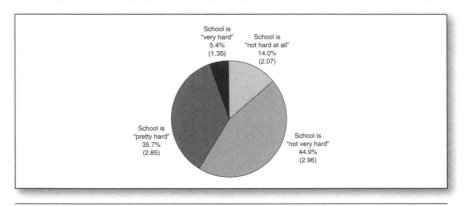

*Note*: Standard errors are in parentheses.

*Source:* U.S. Department of Education, Institute of Education Sciences, National Center for Special Education Research. (2003). *Perceptions and expectations of youth with disabilities,* National Longitudinal Transition Study-2 (NLTS2), Wave 2 youth telephone interview/mail survey (NCES 2007-3006). Retrieved from http://ies.ed.gov/ncser/pubs/20073006/figures/fig9.asp

**Figure 18** Youth With Disabilities' Reported Academic Challenges in 2003

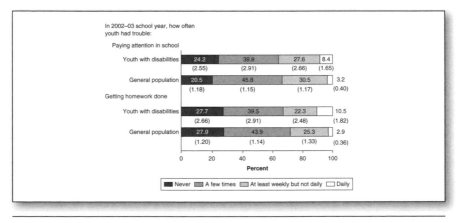

*Note*: Standard errors are in parentheses.

*Sources:* U.S. Department of Education, Institute of Education Sciences, National Center for Special Education Research. (2003). *Perceptions and expectations of youth with disabilities,* National Longitudinal Transition Study-2 (NLTS2), Wave 2 youth telephone interview/mail survey (NCES 2007-3006). Retrieved from http://ies.ed.gov/ncser/pubs/20073006/figures/fig9.asp; National Institute of Child Health and Human Development. (1996). *The National Longitudinal Study of Adolescent Health* (Add Health), Wave 2 youth interviews.

# School Completion

In recent years, special education programs have been more successful in graduating high school students with disabilities with a standard diploma and reducing the number dropping out of school prior to graduation. Table 14 documents these trends. Percentages represented on the table are based on the total number of students with disabilities age 14 and older who leave school for any reason (graduation, completion, maximum age for special education services, death, or dropped out). The individual cells isolate the percentage of those students in each individual disability category who graduated with a diploma or dropped out in each of the given school years.

In general, graduation rates have remained relatively constant when considering all students with disabilities as a group. Although there have been some fluctuations in all categories, the percentage of students with speech and language impairments, emotional disturbance, deaf-blindness, and autism who graduate with a standard diploma has increased, while all other eligibility categories have maintained relatively consistent or slightly decreased. Data for two groups—students with speech and language impairment or emotional disturbance—depict a greater than 10% reduction in dropout rates from 1995–1996 to 2006–2007. Although the reasons for the decline in dropout rates are unknown, it is interesting to note that during this same time several changes occurred in special education. First, students with disabilities increasingly were included in general education classrooms, gaining greater access to challenging curricula and being held to the higher learning expectations associated with general education curricula. Research has suggested that both of these conditions result in greater student engagement in school. Second, the use of functional behavioral assessment and associated behavioral intervention plans for problematic behavior were mandated, probably resulting in direct and more focused intervention targeting those behaviors. Effective interventions could be providing physically and emotionally safer and more productive environments for all students, including those with disabilities.

# Post-Secondary School Outcomes

In this section, we present data about outcomes and expectations for life after secondary school. The first table (Table 15) depicts how many students with disabilities report attending and completing post-secondary education, living independently, and working competitively, along with the mean competitive wage earned. The second table (Table 16) and the

**Table 14** Percentages of Students With Disabilities Ages 14 and Older Who Leave School Due to Standard Graduation or Dropping Out

| | Graduated With a Diploma | | | Dropped Out | | |
|---|---|---|---|---|---|---|
| | 1995–1996 | 1999–2000 | 2006–2007 | 1995–1996 | 1999–2000 | 2006–2007 |
| All students with disabilities | 52.6 | 56.2 | 56.1 | 34.1 | 29.4 | 25.5 |
| Specific learning disability | 58.6 | 62.1 | 60.7 | 32.4 | 27.6 | 24.4 |
| Speech or language impairments | 58.2 | 66.1 | 66.6 | 31.5 | 24.6 | 20.5 |
| Mental retardation | 39.7 | 39.5 | 37.5 | 27.7 | 26.0 | 22.2 |
| Emotional disturbance | 35.7 | 40.1 | 42.9 | 57.1 | 51.4 | 44.5 |
| Other health impairments | 64.0 | 67.7 | 62.9 | 23.8 | 22.4 | 23.0 |
| Multiple disabilities | 40.6 | 48.0 | 45.4 | 16.4 | 16.1 | 19.1 |
| Hearing impairments | 68.2 | 68.4 | 66.6 | 16.7 | 14.4 | 12.8 |
| Orthopedic impairments | 62.2 | 62.5 | 59.6 | 17.5 | 15.4 | 13.4 |
| Visual impairments | 72.6 | 73.4 | 71.4 | 13.2 | 11.9 | 10.7 |
| Autism | 42.2 | 47.3 | 59.3 | 11.8 | 11.1 | 7.1 |
| Deaf-blindness | 43.6 | 48.5 | 75.1 | 3.3 | 10.3 | 7.7 |
| Traumatic brain injury | 64.0 | 65.3 | 63.5 | 17.9 | 18.1 | 15.1 |

*Sources:* U.S. Department of Education. (2002). *24th annual report to Congress on the implementation of the Individuals with Disabilities Education Act, Table AB7* (pp. A219–A221). Retrieved from http://www.pluk.org/Pubs/Fed/IDEAreport_2002_4.8M.pdf; U.S. Department of Education, Office of Special Education Programs. *Individuals with Disabilities Education Act (IDEA) database.* Retrieved from http://www.ideadata.org/PartBData.asp

**Table 15** Percentage of Special Education Students Out of High School Up to 6 Years Attending and Completing Post-Secondary Education, Living Independently, and Working Competitively, 2007

| | All Disabilities[1] | Specific Learning Disabilities | Speech or Language Impairments | Mental Retardation | Emotional Disturbance | Hearing Impairments | Orthopedic Impairments | Other Health Impairments[2] | Visual Impairments | Multiple Disabilities | Deaf-Blindness | Autism | Traumatic Brain Injury |
|---|---|---|---|---|---|---|---|---|---|---|---|---|---|
| | | | | | | *Percent of students ever attended* | | | | | | | |
| Any post-secondary | 57.0 (3.60) | 61.3 (5.28) | 68.5 (5.07) | 35.9 (5.95) | 42.2 (6.01) | 82.9 (7.06) | 66.3 (5.95) | 60.2 (5.39) | 79.0 (5.84) | 36.7 (10.72) | 72.5 (10.11) | 57.7 (8.05) | 66.1 (10.18) |
| 4-year | 15.9 (2.66) | 15.9 (3.96) | 36.3 (4.25) | 8.8! (3.52) | 8.3! (3.37) | 36.6 (9.02) | 28.1 (5.56) | 18.2 (4.25) | 49.7 (7.18) | 12.7! (7.39) | 32.9! (10.64) | 26.1 (7.15) | 16.2! (7.93) |
| 2-year | 41.3 (3.58) | 44.4 (5.38) | 44.4 (5.43) | 26.6 (5.48) | 31.4 (5.65) | 52.8 (9.35) | 52.4 (6.29) | 47.1 (5.49) | 53.5 (7.16) | 22.1! (9.23) | 46.1 (11.29) | 43.4 (8.07) | 48.0 (10.75) |

(Continued)

245

**Table 15** (Continued)

| | All Disabilities[1] | Specific Learning Disabilities | Speech or Language Impairments | Mental Retardation | Emotional Disturbance | Hearing Impairments | Orthopedic Impairments | Other Health Impairments[2] | Visual Impairments | Multiple Disabilities | Deaf-Blindness | Autism | Traumatic Brain Injury |
|---|---|---|---|---|---|---|---|---|---|---|---|---|---|
| Vocational/ technical | 27.9 (3.26) | 29.2 (4.93) | 22.8 (4.58) | 20.9 (5.05) | 24.8 (5.25) | 52.8 (9.35) | 26.7 (5.57) | 33.2 (5.18) | 22.3 (5.98) | 16.8! (8.30) | 20.6! (9.16) | 29.7 (7.44) | 33.4! (10.15) |
| *Percent of students currently attending institution* | | | | | | | | | | | | | |
| Any post-secondary | 20.7 (2.95) | 23.5 (4.59) | 35.8 (5.27) | 6.0! (2.96) | 10.1! (3.68) | 37.2 (9.13) | 28.8 (5.70) | 17.6 (4.20) | 37.0 (6.93) | 19.8! (8.87) | 53.4 (11.48) | 21.7! (6.74) | 20.8! (8.73) |
| 4-year | 9.1 (2.10) | 10.1! (3.27) | 20.6 (4.43) | 1.6! (1.57) | 3.5! (2.23) | 28.9 (8.50) | 10.3! (3.83) | 7.4! (2.88) | 28.7 (6.51) | 10.6! (6.85) | 25.5! (9.87) | 10.3! (4.99) | 8.6! (6.04) |
| 2-year | 12.7 (2.44) | 15.0 (3.89) | 16.1 (4.04) | 4.5! (2.58) | 6.5! (3.00) | 7.8! (5.05) | 22.9 (5.30) | 9.7! (3.27) | 14.6! (5.10) | 9.6! (6.61) | 27.1! (10.24) | 12.3! (5.32) | 14.7! (7.73) |
| Vocational/ technical | 1.8! (0.97) | 1.5! (1.33) | 0.8! (0.99) | 1.2! (1.37) | 3.7! (2.32) | 1.5! (2.32) | 2.3! (1.87) | 3.1! (1.93) | 0.4! (0.94) | 1.9! (3.04) | * (†) | 2.9! (2.77) | 1.3! (2.47) |
| *Percent of students graduated from institution[3]* | | | | | | | | | | | | | |
| Any post-secondary | 24.3 (4.53) | 22.0 (6.12) | 34.2 (6.56) | 23.4! (11.68) | 32.2 (8.70) | 30.7! (10.23) | 27.7 (6.72) | 28.8 (6.26) | 38.5 (8.26) | 21.5! (12.83) | ‡ (†) | 28.0! (9.39) | 26.3! (11.16) |
| 4-year | 10.1! (6.06) | ‡ (†) | 16.0! (7.42) | ‡ (†) | ‡ (†) | 16.4! (9.66) | 13.4! (9.70) | 14.7! (8.79) | 36.3 (10.63) | ‡ (†) | ‡ (†) | 36.1! (15.02) | ‡ (†) |

| | All Disabilities[1] | Specific Learning Disabilities | Speech or Language Impairments | Mental Retardation | Emotional Disturbance | Hearing Impairments | Orthopedic Impairments | Other Health Impairments[2] | Visual Impairments | Multiple Disabilities | Deaf-Blindness | Autism | Traumatic Brain Injury |
|---|---|---|---|---|---|---|---|---|---|---|---|---|---|
| 2-year | 18.9 (4.87) | 16.0! (6.28) | 34.8 (8.50) | ‡ (†) | 30.4! (10.53) | 24.7! (14.33) | 19.5! (7.30) | 26.7 (7.03) | 26.7! (9.98) | ‡ (†) | ‡ (†) | 29.1! (12.22) | ‡ (†) |
| Vocational/technical | 50.1 (9.20) | 54.8 (13.19) | 56.3 (13.12) | 34.7! (21.84) | 41.2! (13.38) | 32.0! (19.45) | 35.5! (12.45) | 38.8! (11.77) | 32.5! (18.76) | 48.0! (19.23) | ‡ (†) | 23.8! (13.73) | 5.6! (11.58) |
| Living independently[4] | 35.6 (3.48) | 39.4 (5.30) | 35.1 (5.25) | 23.5 (5.26) | 32.2 (5.69) | 25.5! (8.17) | 17.8 (4.82) | 33.0 (5.18) | 38.5 (6.99) | 7.5! (5.84) | 16.9! (8.49) | 19.9! (6.50) | 22.5! (8.99) |
| *Percent of students competitively employed[5]* | | | | | | | | | | | | | |
| Currently | 63.2 (3.75) | 70.6 (5.26) | 62.1 (5.49) | 33.6 (6.23) | 59.0 (6.64) | 50.9 (9.94) | 24.7 (5.48) | 62.8 (5.64) | 37.3 (7.27) | 41.8 (12.15) | 18.1! (8.71) | 46.7 (8.96) | 37.1 (10.74) |
| In the past 2 years | 82.8 (2.82) | 88.9 (3.51) | 82.8 (4.15) | 54.0 (6.38) | 85.6 (4.50) | 71.4 (8.73) | 42.6 (6.11) | 83.2 (4.20) | 63.1 (7.15) | 51.0 (11.68) | 28.4! (10.21) | 60.1 (8.36) | 54.9 (10.83) |
| Mean hourly wage at current competitive job | $9.93 (0.45) | $9.98 (0.57) | $9.42 (0.39) | $8.37 (0.52) | $10.79 (1.12) | $9.99 (0.64) | $9.54 (0.95) | $9.29 (0.59) | $11.50 (1.84) | $13.05 (2.22) | ‡ (†) | $8.96 (1.01) | $8.41 (0.66) |

*Note:* Data based on students who had been out of high school up to 6 years and had attended special or regular schools in the 1999–2000 or 2000–2001 school year. Standard errors appear in parentheses.

†Rounds to zero.

*(Continued)*

**Table 15** (Continued)

†Not applicable.

‡Reporting standards not met.

ǃInterpret data with caution.

¹Includes disability categories not shown separately.

²Other health impairments include having limited strength, vitality, or alertness due to chronic or acute health problems (such as a heart condition, rheumatic fever, asthma, hemophilia, and leukemia) and that adversely affects educational performance.

³Among students who had ever attended the type of institution specified, the percentage who received a diploma, certificate, or license.

⁴Living independently includes living alone, with a spouse or roommate, in a college dormitory, in Job Corps housing, or in military housing as a service member.

⁵Competitively employed refers to those receiving more than minimum wage and working in an environment where the majority of workers are not disabled.

*Source:* National Center for Educational Statistics. (2010). *Digest of educational statistics: 2009* (NCES Pub. No. 2010-013), Table 390. Retrieved from http://nces.ed.gov/programs/digest/d09/tables/dt09_390.asp

**Table 16** Youth With Disabilities' Reported Expectations of Future Educational Attainment in 2003

| Expectations* | Learning Disability | Speech/Language Impairment | Mental Retardation | Emotional Disturbance | Hearing Impairment | Visual Impairment | Orthopedic Impairment | Other health Impairments | Autism | Traumatic Brain Injury | Multiple Disabilities | Deaf-Blindness |
|---|---|---|---|---|---|---|---|---|---|---|---|---|
| *Percentage expected to graduate from high school with a regular diploma* | | | | | | | | | | | | |
| Definitely will | 87.9 (3.50) | 77.0 (4.92) | 73.7 (7.10) | 83.7 (4.47) | 85.9 (7.59) | 90.9 (4.67) | 81.5 (5.75) | 79.9 (4.78) | 77.0 (8.23) | 93.1 (5.84) | 70.4 (9.64) | + |
| Probably will | 9.0 (3.07) | 21.1 (4.77) | 22.5 (6.73) | 13.3 (3.68) | 10.7 (6.83) | 8.0 (4.41) | 17.1 (5.58) | 15.1 (4.27) | 21.4 (8.02) | 6.8 (5.80) | 24.1 (9.03) | + |
| Definitely or probably won't | 3.0 (1.83) | 2.0 (1.64) | 3.7 (3.04) | 6.0 (2.87) | 3.4 (4.00) | 1.1 (1.69) | 1.4 (1.74) | 5.1 (2.62) | 1.6 (2.45) | 0.1 (0.73) | 5.5 (4.82) | + |
| *Percentage expected to get any post-secondary education* | | | | | | | | | | | | |
| Definitely will | 53.3 (4.34) | 58.8 (4.60) | 37.7 (6.25) | 56.2 (4.71) | 79.9 (6.36) | 69.9 (5.86) | 62.2 (5.86) | 49.6 (4.87) | 47.2 (8.44) | 66.9 (9.06) | 47.1 (8.42) | 55.4 (11.17) |
| Probably will | 34.0 (4.30) | 30.6 (6.35) | 41.6 (4.35) | 30.1 (5.72) | 15.4 (5.46) | 24.1 (5.16) | 24.0 (4.67) | 35.8 (8.17) | 37.2 (8.26) | 24.3 (8.18) | 37.8 (4.30) | + |
| Definitely or probably won't | 12.7 (2.90) | 10.6 (2.88) | 20.7 (5.22) | 13.7 (3.26) | 4.7 (3.36) | 6.0 (3.03) | 13.7 (4.15) | 14.6 (3.44) | 15.6 (6.13) | 8.8 (5.45) | 15.1 (6.04) | 19.1 (8.83) |

(Continued)

**Table 16** (Continued)

| Expectations* | Learning Disability | Speech/Language Impairment | Mental Retardation | Emotional Disturbance | Hearing Impairment | Visual Impairment | Orthopedic Impairment | Other Health Impairment | Autism | Traumatic Brain Injury | Multiple Disabilities | Deaf-Blindness |
|---|---|---|---|---|---|---|---|---|---|---|---|---|
| | *Percentage expected to complete post-secondary vocational, technical, or trade school* | | | | | | | | | | | |
| Definitely will | 26.9 (4.97) | 22.4 (5.03) | 22.1 (6.68) | 29.3 (5.65) | 22.5 (9.27) | 17.4 (6.71) | 20.2 (6.32) | 20.0 (5.01) | 13.3 (6.88) | 35.0 (11.43) | 17.8 (8.06) | + |
| Probably will | 34.5 (5.33) | 42.1 (5.96) | 24.6 (6.93) | 35.5 (5.94) | 40.4 (10.90) | 45.3 (8.81) | 34.5 (7.49) | 33.2 (5.89) | 40.2 (9.93) | 31.0 (11.08) | 40.5 (10.35) | + |
| Definitely or probably won't | 38.6 (5.46) | 35.5 (5.77) | 53.3 (8.03) | 35.2 (5.93) | 37.1 (10.73) | 37.3 (8.56) | 45.3 (7.84) | 46.8 (6.25) | 46.5 (10.11) | 34.0 (11.35) | 41.7 (10.39) | + |
| | *Percentage expected to complete 2-year college* | | | | | | | | | | | |
| Definitely will | 36.6 (4.16) | 31.9 (4.18) | 22.5 (5.18) | 32.3 (4.42) | 42.4 (6.31) | 34.6 (6.05) | 32.5 (5.56) | 29.9 (4.38) | 24.5 (6.69) | 52.6 (9.55) | 25.5 (6.69) | 34.1 (8.94) |
| Probably will | 39.0 (4.21) | 37.0 (4.33) | 39.0 (6.06) | 39.7 (4.62) | 28.0 (5.73) | 34.3 (6.04) | 39.0 (5.79) | 37.5 (4.63) | 37.2 (7.52) | 31.0 (8.85) | 35.2 (7.33) | + |
| Definitely or probably won't | 24.4 (3.71) | 31.1 (4.15) | 38.5 (6.04) | 28.0 (4.24) | 29.6 (5.83) | 31.1 (5.89) | 28.5 (5.35) | 32.6 (4.48) | 38.3 (7.56) | 16.4 (7.08) | 39.4 (7.50) | 34.0 (8.93) |

| Expectations* | Learning Disability | Speech/ Language Impairment | Mental Retardation | Emotional Disturbance | Hearing Impairment | Visual Impairment | Orthopedic Impairment | Other Health Impairments | Autism | Traumatic Brain Injury | Multiple Disabilities | Deaf-Blindness |
|---|---|---|---|---|---|---|---|---|---|---|---|---|
| | Percentage expected to complete 4-year college | | | | | | | | | | | |
| Definitely will | 25.2 (3.75) | 35.2 (4.30) | 16.1 (4.53) | 26.8 (4.18) | 47.2 (6.33) | 39.0 (6.23) | 38.7 (5.60) | 22.6 (3.98) | 20.6 (6.16) | 42.9 (9.36) | 24.8 (6.67) | 41.8 (9.41) |
| Probably will | 38.0 (4.19) | 34.7 (4.29) | 35.9 (5.91) | 28.0 (4.24) | 32.3 (5.93) | 42.2 (5.31) | 27.8 (5.15) | 30.3 (4.37) | 33.6 (7.19) | 31.9 (8.82) | 21.1 (6.30) | † |
| Definitely or probably won't | 36.8 (4.16) | 30.1 (4.13) | 48.0 (6.16) | 45.3 (4.70) | 20.5 (5.12) | 18.8 (4.99) | 33.6 (5.43) | 47.1 (4.75) | 45.8 (7.59) | 25.2 (8.21) | 54.1 (7.70) | 30.1 (8.75) |

*Note:* Standard errors appear in parentheses.

*Youth who have attained the outcome are included as "definitely will."

†Responses for items with fewer than 30 respondents are not reported.

*Source:* U.S. Department of Education, Institute of Education Sciences, National Center for Special Education Research. (2003). *Perceptions and expectations of youth with disabilities,* National Longitudinal Transition Study-2 (NLTS2), Wave 2 youth telephone interview/mail survey (NCES 2007-3006), Table 18. Retrieved from http://ies.ed.gov/ncser/pubs/20073006/tables/table_18.asp

following figure (Figure 19) present the expectations of students with disabilities for their future educational attainment. In both tables, standard deviations are in parentheses.

**Figure 19**  Youth With Disabilities' Reported Expectations in 2003 for Their Future Post-Secondary School Completion

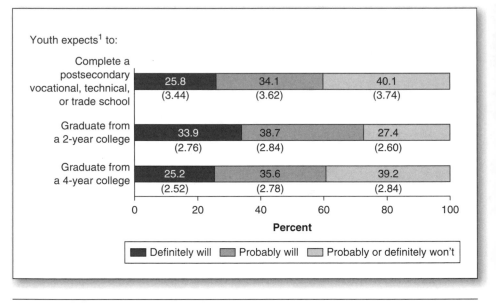

*Note:* Standard errors are in parentheses.

[1]Youth who have attained the outcome are included as "definitely will."

*Source:* U.S. Department of Education, Institute of Education Sciences, National Center for Special Education Research. (2003). *Perceptions and expectations of youth with disabilities,* National Longitudinal Transition Study-2 (NLTS2), Wave 2 youth telephone interview/mail survey (NCES 2007-3006), Figure 20. Retrieved from http://ies.ed.gov/ncser/pubs/20073006/figures/fig20.asp

# *Six*

# Annotated List of Organizations and Associations

## Michelle Raasch, Minyoung Kim, Lana Collet-Klingenberg, and Cheryl Hanley-Maxwell

This chapter provides an annotated list of organizations and associations affiliated with education for individuals with disabilities. This list spans infancy through adulthood and is organized into five major sections. The first four sections (assistive technology, transition, government agencies, and national disability organizations) cut across disability categories. The fifth section focuses on organizations associated with Individuals with Disabilities Education Act (IDEA) disability categories. This list is not and could never be complete because new organizations and associations continue to be created. Throughout the chapter, major special education journals are identified within the descriptions of their parent organizations.

# 1. Assistive Technology

**AAC Institute**
1000 Killarney Dr.
Pittsburgh, PA 15234
Telephone: (412) 523-6424
Fax: (330) 263-4829
E-mail: khill@aacinstitute.org
Web site: http://www.aacinstitute.org
*The AAC Institute provides professionals, consumers, and family members with information about alternative and augmentative communication (AAC) and evidenced-based practices related to AAC. The Institute also supports research, provides education, and other services focusing on AAC.*

**AbilityHub**
P.O. Box 6356
c/o The Gilman Group, LLC
Rutland, VT 05702-6356
Telephone: (802) 775-1993
Fax: (802) 773-1604
E-mail: info@abilityhub.com
Web site: http://www.abilityhub.com
*The mission of AbilityHub is to assist individuals in finding information on adaptive equipment and other assistive technology specific to computers.*

**AbleData**
8630 Fenton St., Suite 930
Silver Spring, MD 20910
Telephone: (301) 608-8998 (V); (800) 227-0216 (V); (301) 608-8912 (TTY)
Fax: (301) 608-8958
E-mail: abledata@macrointernational.com
Web site: http://www.abledata.com/abledata.cfm
*AbleData is an online resource that supplies information regarding "assistive technology products and rehabilitation equipment" utilized by those individuals with disabilities or rehabilitation needs.*

**Alliance for Technology Access**
1304 Southpoint Blvd., Suite 240
Petaluma, CA 94954
Telephone: (707) 778-3011 (V); (707) 778-3015 (TTY)

Fax: (707) 765-2080

E-mail: ATAinfo@ATAccess.org

Web site: http://www.icdri.org/community/ata.htm

*The Alliance for Technology Access supports the ability of individuals with disabilities "to participate more fully in their communities" by providing access to information regarding technology.*

## American Printing House for the Blind (APH)

1839 Frankfort Ave.

P.O. Box 6085

Louisville, KY 40206-0085

Telephone: (502) 895-2405; (800) 223-1839

Fax: (502) 899-2274

E-mail: info@aph.org

Web site: http://www.aph.org

*Created to enhance the "independence of blind and visually impaired persons," the American Printing House for the Blind (APH) also provides options for persons who have multiple handicaps or learning disabilities. APH creates, tests, and provides accessible educational and daily living products. APH also provides training related to its products.*

## Center for Applied Special Technology (CAST)

40 Harvard Mills Square, Suite 3

Wakefield, MA 01880-3233

Telephone: (781) 245-2212 (V); (781) 245-9320 (TTY)

Fax: (781) 245-5212

E-mail: cast@cast.org

Web site: http://www.cast.org/index.html

*The Center for Applied Special Technology (CAST) conducts research and development that expands and improves "learning opportunities for all individuals" through Universal Design for Learning. CAST disseminates information about its research, UDL, and learning tools via its Web site and through professional development activities.*

## Disabilities, Opportunities, Internetworking & Technology (DO-IT)

University of Washington

P.O. Box 354842

Seattle, WA 98195-4842

Telephone: (206) 685-3648 (V); (888) 972-3648 (V/TTY); (509) 328-9331 (Spokane V/TTY)

Fax: (206) 221-4171

E-mail: doit@u.washington.edu
Web site: http://www.washington.edu/doit
*The goal of Disabilities, Opportunities, Internetworking, and Technology (DO-IT) is "to increase the participation of individuals with disabilities in challenging academic programs and careers" through universal design. DO-IT provides information and "resources for students with disabilities, K–12 educators, post-secondary faculty and administrators, librarians, employers, and parents and mentors."*

**Family Center on Technology and Disability (FCTD)**
Academy for Educational Development
1825 Connecticut Ave., NW
Washington, DC 20009
Telephone: (202) 884-8068
Fax: (202) 884-8441
E-mail: fctd@aed.org
Web site: http://www.fctd.info
*The Family Center on Technology and Disability (FCTD) is a resource for agencies and organizations supporting youth with disabilities. The Family Center connects people to online databases of books, research, and disability organizations as well as online conferences and discussions related to assistive technology.*

**Recording for the Blind & Dyslexic (RFB&D)**
20 Roszel Rd.
Princeton, NJ 08540
Telephone: (800) 221-4792
E-mail: custserv@rfbd.org
Web site: http://www.rfbd.org
*Recording for the Blind & Dyslexic (RFB&D) provides audio textbooks and playback equipment to individuals "who cannot read standard print" and their families. It also provides these resources, technical assistance, and support to member schools and agencies.*

**Rehabilitation Engineering and Assistive Technology Society of North America (RESNA)**
1700 N. Moore St., Suite 1540
Arlington, VA 22209-1903
Telephone: (703) 524-6686 (V); (703) 524-6639 (TTY)
Fax: (703) 524-6630
E-mail: resnata@resna.org
Web site: http://www.resna.org
*The Rehabilitation Engineering and Assistive Technology Society of North America (RESNA) seeks to "improve the potential of people with disabilities to achieve their goals*

*through the use of technology." RESNA promotes research and development, advocates, educates, disseminates information, maintains a searchable database of resources, and provides professional development.*

### Technology and Media Division (TAM)—CEC
1110 N. Glebe Rd.
Arlington, VA 22201-5704
Web site: http://www.tamcec.org
*A division of the Council for Exceptional Children, the Technology and Media Division (TAM) has a mission to support the education of individuals with disabilities by "monitoring and disseminating" information regarding technology and media. TAM provides information regarding current research, technical standards, "technical assistance, and inservice and preservice education on the uses of technology." TAM also publishes the* Journal of Special Education Technology.

### Trace Research and Development Center (Trace Center)
University of Wisconsin
1550 Engineering Dr.
2107 Engineering Centers Bldg.
Madison, WI 53706
Telephone: (608) 262-6966 (V); (608) 263-5408 (TTY)
Fax: (608) 262-8848
E-mail: info@trace.wisc.edu
Web site: http://trace.wisc.edu
*The Trace Research and Development Center (Trace Center) uses "emerging information and telecommunication technologies . . . to create a world that is as accessible and usable as possible for as many people as possible." In addition to adapting commercially/ publically available technologies, the Trace Center focuses on enhancing access through industry and university training activities and providing resources to consumers, advocates, industry, educators, and developers.*

# 2. Transition

### Division on Career Development & Transition (DCDT)
P.O. Box 79026
Baltimore, MD 21279-0026
E-mail: jrazeghi@gmu.edu
Web site: http://www.cms4schools.com/dcdt
*A division of the Council for Exceptional Children, the Division on Career Development & Transition (DCDT) promotes the participation of students with disabilities in transition planning services as well as career and vocational education and training. DCDI publishes* Career Development for Exceptional Individuals.

**HEATH Resource Center**
George Washington University
2134 G St. NW
Washington, DC 20052-0001
E-mail: AskHEATH@gwu.edu
Web site: http://www.heath.gwu.edu
*Located within the Graduate School of Education and Human Development at George Washington University, the HEATH Resource Center provides an "online clearinghouse" for the exchange of information and resources regarding a variety of issues related to post-secondary education for people with disabilities.*

**National Center on Secondary Education and Transition (NCSET)**
University of Minnesota
6 Pattee Hall
150 Pillsbury Drive, SE
Minneapolis, MN 55455
Telephone: (612) 624-2097
Fax: (612) 624-9344
E-mail: ncset@umn.edu
Web site: http://www.ncset.org
*In an effort to "create opportunities for youth with disabilities to achieve successful futures," the National Center on Secondary Education and Transition (NCSET) organizes and distributes information relevant to post-secondary education and transition. NCSET helps students with disabilities prepare for post-secondary education as well as other experiences related to transition including employment and independent living.*

**National Collaborative on Workforce and Disability (NCWD/Youth)**
4455 Connecticut Avenue NW, Suite 310
Washington, DC 20008
Telephone: (877) 871-0744 (V); (877) 871-0665 (TTY)
Web site: http://www.ncwd-youth.info
*The National Collaborative on Workforce and Disability (NCWD/Youth) provides resources, education, and training to professionals and organizations supporting youth in transition. NCWD/Youth ensures "full access to high quality services" for individuals with disabilities working toward employment, further education, and/or living independently.*

**National Secondary Transition Technical Assistance Center (NSTTAC)**
Department of Special Education & Child Development
9201 University City Blvd.
University of North Carolina–Charlotte

Charlotte, NC 28223
Telephone: (704) 687-8853
Fax: (704) 687-2916
E-mail: dwtest@uncc.edu
Web site: http://www.nsttac.org
*National Secondary Transition Technical Assistance Center (NSTTAC) assists state education agencies with IDEA data collection, creates and disseminates information about effective transition practices and the improvement of post-school outcomes, and assists state and local education agencies in providing effective transition services.*

# 3. Government Agencies

## Disability.gov
U.S. Department of Labor's Office of Disability Employment Policy (ODEP)
Frances Perkins Building
200 Constitution Ave., NW
Washington, DC 2021
E-mail: disability@dol.gov
Web site: http://www.disability.gov
*Disability.gov is an online resource that provides information and resource links related to disability programs and services to "help people with disabilities lead full, independent lives." Disability.gov supplies links to state resources and information on a multitude of topics, including but not limited to education, employment, transportation, and technology.*

## National Institute on Disability and Rehabilitation Research (NIDRR)
U.S. Department of Education
400 Maryland Ave., SW
Mailstop PCP-6038
Washington, DC 20202
Telephone: (202) 245-7640 (V/TTY)
Fax: (202) 245-7323
Web site: http://www2.ed.gov/about/offices/list/osers/nidrr/index.html
*The National Institute on Disability and Rehabilitation Research (NIDRR) is one of three organizational components within the Office of Special Education and Rehabilitative Services (OSERS). Through research and related activities, NIDRR generates "new knowledge" to assist people with disabilities in engaging in their communities and "to expand society's capacity to provide full opportunities and accommodations for its citizens with disabilities." NIDRR focuses on "full inclusion, social integration, employment and independent living."*

**National Library Service for the Blind and Physically Handicapped (NLS)**
Library of Congress
Washington, DC 20542
Telephone: (888) 657-7323; (202) 707-5100 (V); (202) 707-0744 (TDD)
Fax: (202) 707-0712
E-mail: nls@loc.gov
Web site: http://www.loc.gov/nls
*The National Library Service for the Blind and Physically Handicapped (NLS) is a network of cooperating libraries that circulates free Braille and audio materials "to eligible borrowers in the United States by postage-free mail."*

**Office of Special Education and Rehabilitative Services (OSERS)**
U.S. Department of Education
400 Maryland Ave., SW
Washington, DC 20202-7100
Telephone: (202) 245-7468
Web site: http://www2.ed.gov/about/offices/list/osers/index.html
*The Office of Special Education and Rehabilitative Services (OSERS) is composed of the National Institute on Disability and Rehabilitation Research (NIDRR), the Office of Special Education Programs (OSEP), the Rehabilitation Services Administration (RSA), and the Office of the Assistant Secretary. The mission of OSERS is to ensure that people with disabilities have "equal opportunity and access to, and excellence in, education, employment, and community living." In addition to its components, OSERS administers the American Printing House for the Blind, the National Technical Institute for the Deaf, and Gallaudet University. The work of OSERS informs the development of policy intended to improve "outcomes for persons with disabilities in the United States and throughout the world."*

**Office of Special Education Programs (OSEP)**
U.S. Department of Education
400 Maryland Ave., SW
Washington, DC 20202-7100
Telephone: (202) 245-7459
Web site: http://www2.ed.gov/about/offices/list/osers/osep/index .html?src=mr
*The second component of OSERS, the Office of Special Education Programs (OSEP), is a federal agency that offers support to state and local districts by "developing, communicating, and disseminating federal policy and information." OSEP educates and promotes and supports training of state and local district school-related personnel.*

**Rehabilitation Services Administration (RSA)**
U.S. Department of Education
400 Maryland Ave., SW
Washington, DC 20202-2800
Telephone: (202) 245-7488
Web site: http://www2.ed.gov/about/offices/list/osers/rsa/index.html
*The Rehabilitation Services Administration (RSA), the third component of OSERS, over-sees the implementation of the Rehabilitation Act of 1973. RSA monitors the development and implementation of rehabilitation services for vocational training, employment and transition assistance, and independent living, and supports research and training related to these services.*

**Substance Abuse and Mental Health Services Administration (SAMHSA)**
SAMHSA's Health Information Network
P.O. Box 2345
Rockville, MD 20847-2345
Telephone: (877) 726-4727 (V); (800)-487-4889 (TTY)
Fax: (240) 221-4292
E-mail: SHIN@samhsa.hhs.gov
Web site: http://www.samhsa.gov/shin
*The mission of the Substance Abuse and Mental Health Services Administration (SAM HSA) is to diminish the effects that substance abuse and mental illnesses have on communities. SAMSHA is composed of four centers (Mental Health Services, Substance Abuse Prevention, the Center for Substance Abuse Treatment, and the Office of Applied Studies). It has eight major grant programs, including Children's Mental Health Services, Substance Abuse Prevention and Treatment Block Grant, and Access to Recovery. Through the programs and centers, SAMSHA supports research, public education, interventions, and other activities.*

# 4. National Disability Organizations

**American Academy of Special Education Professionals (AASEP)**
Metro Center
700 12th St. NW
Suite 700
Washington, DC 20005
Telephone: (800) 754-4421, ext. 106
Fax: (800) 424-0371

E-mail: info@aasep.org
Web site: http://aasep.org

*The mission of the American Academy of Special Education Professionals (AASEP) "is to attain optimal academic, psychological, physical, and social success" for children (infants to young adults). AASEP employs networking, research, and publications to develop a continually learning, collaborative community of professionals. AASEP publishes the* Journal of the American Academy of Special Education Professionals.

## American Council on Rural Special Education (ACRES)

Montana Center on Disabilities
Montana State University-Billings
1500 University Dr.
Billings, MT 59101
Telephone: (406) 657-2312 (V); (888) 866-3822 (V/TDD)
Fax: (406) 657-2313
E-mail: inquiries@acres-sped.org
Web site: http://www.acres-sped.org

*The American Council on Rural Special Education (ACRES) works to support and enhance services for students with disabilities in rural communities, their families, and the professionals who work with them. ACRES publishes* Rural Special Education Quarterly.

## American Counseling Association (ACA)

5999 Stevenson Ave.
Alexandria, VA 22304
Telephone: (800) 347-6647
Fax: (800) 473-2329
Web site: http://www.counseling.org

*The American Counseling Association (ACA) is a "professional and educational organization" that is responsible for the development of "leadership training, publications, continuing education opportunities and advocacy services" for professional counselors from a variety of disciplines. ACA publishes ten journals.*

## American Psychological Association (APA)

750 First St. NE
Washington, DC 20002-4242
Telephone: (800) 374-2721 (V); (202) 336-6123 (TTY)
Web site: http://www.apa.org

*The mission of the American Psychological Association (APA) is to promote innovation and advancements in the field of psychology for "psychological scientists, practitioners, and educators." APA is a scientific and professional resource for psychologists from around the world. The APA publishes 61 journals and many other publications.*

## American Rehabilitation Counseling Association (ARCA)
5999 Stevenson Ave.

Alexandria, VA 22304

Telephone: (800) 347-6647

Fax: (800) 473-2329

Web site: http://www.arcaweb.org

*A division of the American Counseling Association, The American Rehabilitation Counseling Association's (ARCA) mission is "to enhance the development of people with disabilities throughout the life span" and to continually improve the rehabilitation counseling profession. Among other publications, ARCA publishes the* Rehabilitation Counseling Bulletin.

## Association on Higher Education and Disability (AHEAD)
107 Commerce Center Drive, Suite 204

Huntersville, NC 28078

Telephone: (704) 947-7779

Fax: (704) 948-7779

Web site: http://www.ahead.org

*The Association on Higher Education and Disability (AHEAD) is a professional organization focused on advocacy and the provision of services to higher education students with disabilities. AHEAD's goal is to create "educational and societal environments that value disability and embody equality of opportunity."*

## Council for Educational Diagnostic Services (CEDS)–CEC
1110 N. Glebe Road

Arlington, VA 22201

Web site: http://www.ceds.us

*The Council for Educational Diagnostic Services (CEDS) of the Council for Exceptional Children (CEC) focuses on enhancing "quality diagnostic and prescriptive procedures involved in the education of individuals with disabilities and/or who are gifted." CEDS publishes* Assessment for Effective Intervention.

## Council for Exceptional Children (CEC)
1110 North Glebe Road, Suite 300

Arlington, VA 22201

Telephone: (703) 620-3660 (V); (888) 232-7733 (V); (866) 915-5000 (TTY)

Fax: (703) 264-9494

E-mail: service@cec.sped.org

Web site: http://www.cec.sped.org

*The Council for Exceptional Children (CEC) is a resource for educational professionals, families, and students involved in special education. In an effort to meet the educational needs of children and youth with disabilities, CEC "advocates for appropriate governmental policies, sets professional standards, provides professional development, advocates for individuals with exceptionalities, and helps professionals obtain conditions and resources necessary for effective professional practice." CEC publishes CEC SmartBriefs (an e-mail news service),* Exceptional Children, *and* Teaching Exceptional Children.

## Council of Administrators of Special Education (CASE)–CEC
Osigian Office Center
101 Katelyn Circle, Suite E
Warner Robins, GA 31088
Telephone: (478) 333-6892
Fax: (478) 333-2453
E-mail: lpurcell@casecec.org
Web site: http://www.casecec.org
*A division of the Council for Exceptional Children, the Council of Administrators of Special Education (CASE) states its objective as providing "leadership and support" to local administrators in special education. CASE publishes the* Journal of Special Education Leadership.

## Disability Rights Education and Defense Fund (DREDF)
3075 Adeline St., Suite 210
Berkeley, CA 94703
Telephone: (510) 644-2555 (V/TTY); (800) 348-4232 (V/TTY)
Fax: (510) 841-8645
E-mail: info@dredf.org
Web site: http://www.dredf.org
*The Disability Rights Education and Defense Fund (DREDF) is "a leading national civil rights law and policy center." The purpose of DREDF is to provide education and awareness to individuals with disabilities as well as professionals in the legal and educational fields.*

## Division for Culturally and Linguistically Diverse Exceptional Learners (DDEL)–CEC
1110 North Glebe Road, Suite 300
Arlington, VA 22201
Telephone: (888) 232-7733 (V); (866) 915-5000
Fax: (703) 264-9494
Web site: http://www.cec.sped.org/Content/NavigationMenu/AboutCEC/
    Communities/Divisions/Division_for_Culturally_and_Linguistically_
    Diverse_Exceptional_Learners__DDEL_.htm
*The Division for Culturally and Linguistically Diverse Exceptional Learners (DDEL) is a division of the Council for Exceptional Children that seeks to improve the "educational*

*opportunities for culturally and linguistically diverse learners with disabilities and/or who are gifted, their families, and the professionals who serve them."* DDEL publishes Multiple Voices for Ethnically Diverse Exceptional Learners.

### Division for Early Childhood (DEC)–CEC
27 Fort Missoula Rd., Suite 2
Missoula, MT 59804
Telephone: (406) 543-0872
Fax: (406) 543-0887
E-mail: dec@dec-sped.org
Web site: http://www.dec-sped.org
*The Council for Exceptional Children's Division for Early Childhood (DEC) is designed to meet the needs of "individuals who work with or on behalf of children with special needs, birth through age 8, and their families." DEC publishes the* Journal of Early Intervention *and* Young Exceptional Children.

### Division for Research–CEC (CEC-DR)
Web site: http://www.cecdr.org
*A division of the Council for Exceptional Children, the Division for Research (CEC-DR) focuses on working in concert with research practitioners in disseminating research in special education. CEC DR publishes* Current Practice Alerts *and the* Journal of Special Education.

### Division of International Special Education and Services (DISES)–CEC
2900 Crystal Drive, Suite 1000
Arlington, VA 22202-3557
Telephone: (888) 232-7733 (V), (866) 915-5000 (TTY)
Fax: (703) 264-9494
Web site: http://www.cec.sped.org/Content/NavigationMenu/AboutCEC/
    International/DISES
*The Division of International Special Education and Services (DISES) spotlights "special education programs and services around the world." DISES publishes the* Journal of International Special Needs Education.

### Easter Seals
233 South Wacker Dr., Suite 2400
Chicago, IL 60606
Telephone: (312) 726-6200 (V); (800) 221-6827 (V); (312) 726-4258 (TTY)
Fax: (312) 726-1494
Web site: http://www.easterseals.com/site/PageServer
*Easter Seals assists individuals with disabilities by providing a variety of programs for individuals across the life span, from infant to senior citizen. Easter Seals programs include*

*but are not limited to (1) education; (2) medical rehabilitation; (3) advocacy; (4) employment and training; and (5) camping and recreation services.*

**Family Village**
Waisman Center
University of Wisconsin–Madison
1500 Highland Ave.
Madison, WI 53705
E-mail: familyvillage@waisman.wisc.edu
Web site: http://www.familyvillage.wisc.edu
*The Family Village is a "global community" with resources on a variety of diagnoses/disabilities, adaptive products, technology, and activities, as well as a network of services and support.*

**Federation for Children With Special Needs (FCSN)**
1135 Tremont St., Suite 420
Boston, MA 02120
Telephone: (617) 236-7210; (800) 331-0688 (in MA)
Fax: (617) 572-2094
E-mail: fcsninfo@fcsn.org
Web site: http://fcsn.org/index.php
*The Federation for Children with Special Needs (FCSN) is a parent organization committed to providing "information, support, and assistance to parents of children with disabilities, their professional partners, and their communities."*

**International Center for Disability Resources on the Internet (ICDRI)**
5212 Covington Bend Dr.
Raleigh, NC 27613
Telephone: (919) 349-6661
E-mail: icdri@icdri.org
Web site: http://www.icdri.org
*The mission of ICDRI is to provide a comprehensive online database of "quality disability resources and best practices and to provide education, outreach, and training based on these core resources."*

**National Association of School Psychologists (NASP)**
4340 East West Hwy., Suite 402
Bethesda, MD 20814
Telephone: (866) 331-6277 (V); (301) 657-4155 (TTY)

Fax: (301) 657-0275

Web site: http://www.nasponline.org

*The National Association of School Psychologists (NASP) is a division of the American Psychological Association. NASP provides professional resources for school psychologists working "to meet the learning and mental health needs of all children and youth." NASP publishes the* School Psychology Review.

## National Association of Special Education Teachers (NASET)

1250 Connecticut Avenue, NW, Suite 200

Washington, DC 20036

Telephone and Fax: (800) 754-4421

E-mail: contactus@naset.org

Web site: http://www.naset.org

*The mission of the National Association of Special Education Teachers (NASET) is to support and prepare teachers either entering or currently working in the field of special education by providing information regarding current special education "research, practice, and policy."*

## National Association of State Directors of Special Education (NASDSE)

1800 Diagonal Rd., Suite 320

Alexandria, VA 22314

Telephone: (703) 519-3800

Fax: (703) 519-3808

Web site: http://www.nasdse.org

*The National Association of State Directors of Special Education (NASDSE) is a resource for special education professionals and related service providers. The purpose of NASDSE is to provide information and "services to state agencies to facilitate their efforts to maximize educational outcomes for individuals with disabilities."*

## National Center for Educational Outcomes (NCEO)

University of Minnesota

207 Pattee Hall

150 Pillsbury Dr., SE

Minneapolis, MN 55455

Telephone: (612) 626-1530

Fax: (612) 624-0879

E-mail: nceo@umn.edu

Web site: http://www.cehd.umn.edu/nceo

*In collaboration with state and federal organizations, the National Center on Educational Outcomes (NCEO) endeavors to create a system of "educational assessments and accountability" for "all students, including students with disabilities and English Language Learners."*

## National Center on Birth Defects and Developmental Disabilities (NCBDDD)

Centers for Disease Control and Prevention
1600 Clifton Rd.
Atlanta, GA 30333
Telephone: (800) 232-4636; (888) 232-6348 (TTY)
E-mail: cdcinfo@cdc.gov
Web site: http://www.cdc.gov/ncbddd

*Founded by the Center for Disease Control (CDC), the mission of the National Center on Birth Defects and Developmental Disabilities (NCBDDD) is to promote health throughout the life span and to "enhance the potential for full, productive living." This organization utilizes research, education, and partnerships with other organizations to identify causes of birth defects and developmental disabilities and promote the health and wellness of people with disabilities of all ages.*

## National Clearinghouse for Professions in Special Education (NCPSE)

1920 Association Dr.
Reston, VA 20191-9476
Telephone: (800) 641-7824
Fax: (703) 264-1637
E-mail: ncpse@cec.sped.org
Web site: http://www.cec.sped.org/ncpse.htm

*The National Clearinghouse for Professions in Special Education (NCPSE) is "an information resource" for those individuals working in the field of special education or preservice teachers preparing to begin careers in special education. NCPSE maintains data on "recruitment, pre-service preparation, employment opportunities, and attrition and retention issues."*

## National Disability Rights Network (NDRN)

900 Second St. NE, Suite 211
Washington, DC 20002
Telephone: (202) 408-9514 (V); (202) 408-9521 (TTY)
Fax: (202) 408-9520
E-mail: info@ndrn.org
Web site: http://www.napas.org

*The National Disability Rights Network (NDRN) provides "legally based advocacy services to people with disabilities in the United States" through education, training, and support.*

## National Dissemination Center for Children with Disabilities (NICHCY)

1825 Connecticut Ave. NW, Suite 700

Washington, DC 20009

Telephone: (202) 884-8200 (V/TTY); (800) 695-0285 (V/TTY)

Fax: (202) 884-8441

E-mail: nichcy@aed.org

Web site: http://www.nichcy.org

*The National Dissemination Center for Children with Disabilities (NICHCY) is an informational resource on a multitude of topics related to individuals with disabilities and special education.*

## Parent Advocacy Coalition for Educational Rights (PACER) Center

8161 Normandale Blvd.

Bloomington, MN 55437

Telephone: (800) 537-2237 (V); (952) 838-0190 (TTY)

Fax: (952) 838-0199

Web site: http://www.pacer.org

*"Based on the concept of parents helping parents," the Parent Advocacy Coalition for Educational Rights (PACER) Center provides numerous resources to families of children and youth with disabilities. The PACER Center offers access to workshops, assistance programs, and information.*

## Society for Disability Studies (SDS)

Executive Offices

107 Commerce Centre Dr., Suite 204

Huntersville, NC 28078

Telephone: (704) 274-9240

Fax: (704) 948-7779

E-mail: info@disstudies.org

Web site: http://www.disstudies.org

*The Society for Disability Studies (SDS) "is a scholarly organization that is dedicated to the cause of promoting disability studies as an academic discipline." SDS members advocate for social change, work to increase awareness of the historical and cultural understandings of disability, and promote awareness of the lives of people with disabilities through research, the arts, education, and social and political action. SDS publishes* Disability Studies Quarterly.

## Specialized Training of Military Parents (STOMP)

6316 S. 12th St.

Tacoma, WA 98465

Telephone: (800) 572-7368; (253) 565-2266

Fax: (253) 566-8052

E-mail: stomp@washingtonpave.com

Web site: http://www.stompproject.org

*Military parents stationed in the United States and overseas can get "individual assistance and information" related to special education from Specialized Training of Military Parents (STOMP). STOMP informs these parents of their "rights/responsibilities in special education" for their children who are located in the United States or overseas.*

## TASH

1025 Vermont Ave. NW, Suite 300

Washington, DC 20005

Telephone: (202) 540-9020

Fax: (202) 540-9019

E-mail: Operations@TASH.org

Web site: http://www.tash.org

*TASH (formerly The Association for Persons with Severe Handicaps) is "an international association of people with disabilities, their family members, other advocates, and professionals." It provides resources and information regarding research, advocacy, legislation, and litigation. TASH publishes* Research and Practice for Persons with Severe Disabilities *(formerly* JASH*).*

## Teacher Education Division (TED)–CEC

E-mail: rfgreen@uncc.edu

Web site: http://www.tedcec.org

*A division of the Council for Exceptional Children, the Teacher Education Division (TED) is "a diverse community of professionals" collaborating with one another in an effort to meet the needs of students with disabilities and their families. TED provides information regarding research, effective policies and practices, and professional development. TED publishes* Teacher Education and Special Education.

## VSA arts

818 Connecticut Ave. NW, Suite 600

Washington, D.C. 20006

Telephone: (202) 628-2800 (V); (800) 933-8721 (V); (202) 737-0645 (TDD)

Fax: (202) 429-0868

E-mail: Info@vsarts.org

Web site: http://www.vsarts.org/x11.xml

*VSA arts was designed to "create a society where people with disabilities learn through, participate in, and enjoy the arts." Educators, parents, and artists support arts programming through VSA arts resources and the tools. VSA arts acknowledges "the artistic achievements of young adults with disabilities" through numerous awards and events.*

**Wrightslaw**
Web site: http://www.wrightslaw.com
*Wrightslaw is an online resource that provides families and professionals access to current information regarding both education law and special education law in order to ensure the rights of children with disabilities.*

# 5. Organizations Associated With IDEA Disability Categories

## Autism

### Asperger Syndrome Education Network (ASPEN)
9 Aspen Circle
Edison, NJ 08820
Telephone: (732) 321-0880
E-mail: info@aspennj.org
Web site: http://www.aspennj.org
*Asperger Syndrome Education Network (ASPEN) provides education, support, and advocacy services to individuals who have autism spectrum disorders and their families. ASPEN provides information about autism spectrum disorders issues, educational programs, research findings, and adult issues. It also promotes "public awareness and understanding" of Asperger's.*

### Autism Society of America (ASAF)
4340 East-West Hwy., Suite 350
Bethesda, MD 20814
Telephone: (301) 657-0881; (800) 3AUTISM (800-328-8476)
Web site: http://www.autism-society.org
*The mission of the Autism Society of America (ASAF) is to provide information to the autism community in an effort to promote "meaningful participation and self-determination in all aspects of life for individuals on the autism spectrum and their families." ASAF makes available information on treatment options, current research, and education.*

### Autism Speaks
2 Park Ave., 11th Floor
New York, NY 10016
Telephone: (212) 252-8584
Fax: (212) 252-8676

E-mail: contactus@autismspeaks.org

Web site: http://www.autismspeaks.org

*The mission of Autism Speaks "is to change the future for all who struggle with autism spectrum disorders" by helping obtain funding for biomedical research that will lead to a better understanding of the causes, treatments, and potential cures for autism. In addition, the goal of Autism Speaks is to help promote awareness and understanding of individuals with autism spectrum disorders.*

### Division on Autism and Developmental Disabilities (DADD)–CEC

Web site: http://www.daddcec.org

*A division of the Council for Exceptional Children, the Division on Autism and Developmental Disabilities (DADD) focuses on advancing the "knowledge base of the field" by working to "enhance the competence of persons who work with individuals with cognitive disabilities/mental retardation, autism, and related disabilities." DADD publishes* Education and Training in Autism and Developmental Disabilities *and* Focus on Autism and Other Developmental Disabilities.

### Ohio Center on Autism and Low Incidence (OCALI)

470 Glenmont Ave.

Columbus, OH 43214

Telephone: (614) 410-0321(V); (866) 886-2254 (V)

Fax: (614) 262-1070

Web site: http://www.ocali.org

*The mission of the Ohio Center on Autism and Low Incidence (OCALI) is "to build state- and system-wide capacity" in order to equip families and professionals with the knowledge, skills, and resources they need to better assist students with autism and low incidence disabilities. These resources include "leadership, training and professional development, technical assistance, collaboration, and technology."*

### Treatment and Education of Autistic and Related Communication-Handicapped Children (TEACCH)

100 Renee Lynne Ct.

Carrboro, NC 27510

Telephone: (919) 966-2174

Fax: (919) 966-4127

E-mail: TEACCH@unc.edu

Web site: http://www.teacch.com

*The mission of Treatment and Education of Autistic and Related Communication-Handicapped Children (TEACCH) is to "enable individuals with autism to function as meaningfully and as independently as possible in the community" by providing "exemplary services" in the areas of intervention services, supported employment, and vocational training. TEACCH also provides professional development workshops and skills training for professionals who work with individuals with autism.*

# Deaf-Blindness

### American Association of the Deaf-Blind (AABD)
8630 Fenton St., Suite 121
Silver Spring, MD 20910
Telephone: (301) 495-4403 (V); (301) 495-4402 (TTY)
Fax: (301) 495-4404
E-mail: aadb-info@aadb.org
Web site: http://www.aadb.org
*The American Association of the Deaf-Blind (AADB) is an organization that assists people with deaf-blindness to "achieve their maximum potential" by promoting "independence, productivity, and integration into the community."*

### National Consortium on Deaf-Blindness (NCDB)
345 N. Monmouth Ave.
Monmouth, OR 97361
Telephone: (800) 438-9376 (V); (800) 854-7013 (TTY)
Fax: 503-838-8150
E-mail: info@nationaldb.org
Web site: http://www.nationaldb.org
*The National Consortium on Deaf-Blindness (NCDB) is a resource for children and youth who are deaf and blind as well as the professionals who assist them. NCDB provides information and supports to promote academic success, including early intervention supports, transition education, and technological assistance; evidence-based practices; and research results. The organization also offers professional development services.*

### National Family Association for Deaf-Blind (NFADB)
111 Middle Neck Rd.
Sands Point, NY 11050-1129
Telephone: (800) 255-0411, ext. 275
E-mail: NFADB@aol.com
Web site: http://www.nfadb.org
*National Family Association for Deaf-Blind (NFADB) advocates for people who are deaf-blind and their families. NFADB trains and supports families to become effective advocates; advises researchers, educators, and service providers; and collaborates with other professional organizations "to strengthen consumer and family representation at the national level."*

# Deafness

**American Society for Deaf Children (ASDC)**
800 Florida Ave. NE, #2047
Washington, DC 20002-3695
Telephone: (717) 703-0073
Fax: (717) 909-5599
E-mail: asdc@deafchildren.org
Web site: http://www.deafchildren.org
*The American Society for Deaf Children (ASDC) provides information for families and professionals regarding programs and services that promote "the optimal intellectual, social, and emotional development" of children who are deaf and hard of hearing.*

**Division for Communicative Disabilities and Deafness (DCDD)–CEC**
Web site: http://www.dcdd.us
*A division of the Council for Exceptional Children, the Division for Communicative Disabilities and Deafness (DCDD) is a source of information for educational professionals and family members of children with communicative disorders, children who are deaf, and children who are hard of hearing. DCDD provides access to current research, advocacy work, and professional development activities. DCDD publishes* Communication Disorders Quarterly.

**National Association of the Deaf (NAD)**
8630 Fenton St., Suite 820
Silver Spring, MD 20910
Telephone: (301) 587-1788 (V); (301) 587-1789 (TTY)
Fax: (301) 587-1791
Web site: http://www.nad.org
*The mission of the National Association of the Deaf (NAD) is "to promote, protect, and preserve the civil, human and linguistic rights" of people who are deaf and hard of hearing.*

# Emotional Disturbance

**American Academy of Child and Adolescent Psychiatry (AACAP)**
3615 Wisconsin Ave., NW
Washington, DC 20016-3007
Telephone: (202) 966-7300
Fax: (202) 966-2891
Web site: http://www.aacap.org
*The American Academy of Child and Adolescent Psychiatry (AACAP) serves its members and the parents and families of children with developmental, behavioral, and mental disorders. AACAP uses research, training, advocacy, prevention, assessment, treatment and support to*

*promote "mentally healthy children, adolescents and families." AACAP provides information on child and adolescent psychiatry, fact sheets for parents and caregivers, medications, legislation, current research, practice guidelines, managed care information, and a variety of information specific to professionals and AACAP members.*

### Council for Children With Behavioral Disorders (CCBD)–CEC
Web site: http://www.ccbd.net
*A division of the Council for Exceptional Children, Council for Children With Behavioral Disorders (CCBD) is "an international community of educators" supporting and collaborating with one another in their efforts to teach children and youth with emotional and behavioral disorders. The CCBD provides a way for individuals (1) to share information regarding current research, (2) to engage in opportunities to grow professionally, and (3) to promote public awareness and understanding of emotional and behavioral disorders. CCBD publishes* Behavioral Disorders *and* Beyond Behavior.

### National Alliance on Mental Illness (NAMI)
3803 N. Fairfax Dr., Ste. 100
Arlington, VA 22203
Telephone: (703) 524-7600
Fax: (703) 524-9094
Web site: http://www.nami.org
*The National Alliance on Mental Illness (NAMI) provides access to education, advocacy, and volunteer opportunities for those involved with individuals and families affected by mental illness.*

### National Federation of Families for Children's Mental Health
9605 Medical Center Dr.
Rockville, MD 20850
Telephone: (240) 403-1901
Fax: (240) 403-1909.
E-mail: ffcmh@ffcmh.com
Web site: http://www.ffcmh.org
*The National Federation of Families for Children's Mental Health was created to help "children and youth with emotional, behavioral and mental health challenges and their families obtain needed supports and services." The National Federation provides national advocacy, and extends leadership, training, and technical assistance to a nationwide network of chapters.*

### Research and Training Center on Family Support
P.O. Box 751
Portland, OR 97207-0751

Telephone: (503) 725-4040
Fax: (503) 725-4180
E-mail: janetw@pdx.edu
Web site: http://www.rtc.pdx.edu/index.php
*The Research and Training Center on Family Support conducts collaborative "multi-level research and capacity building" activities that are designed to transform mental health care by promoting "effective community-based, culturally competent, family-centered services for families and their children."*

## Hearing Impairment

### Alexander Graham Bell Association for the Deaf and Hard of Hearing (AG Bell)

3417 Volta Place, NW
Washington, DC 20007
Telephone: (202) 337-5220 (V); (202) 337-5221 (TTY)
Fax: (202) 337-8314
E-mail: info@agbell.org
Web site: http://www.agbell.org
*By "advocating independence through listening and talking," the Alexander Graham Bell Association for the Deaf and Hard of Hearing (AG Bell) is an organization that provides information regarding education, research, and funding to individuals who are deaf and hard of hearing and the family members and professionals who support them.*

### Hearing Loss Association of America (HLAA)

7910 Woodmont Ave., Suite 1200
Bethesda, MD 20814
Telephone: (301) 657-2248
Fax: (301) 913-9413
Web site: http://www.hearingloss.org
*The Hearing Loss Association of America (HLAA) supports individuals with hearing loss by providing a forum for people to access research, publications, newsletters, chat rooms, message boards, conventions, and service providers.*

## Intellectual Disabilities

### American Association on Intellectual and Developmental Disabilities (AAIDD)

501 3rd St. NW, Suite 200
Washington, DC 20001
Telephone: (800) 424-3688

Fax: (202) 387-2193
E-mail: anam@aaidd.org
Web site: http://www.aamr.org/
*The mission of American Association on Intellectual and Developmental Disabilities (AAIDD) is to support people with intellectual and developmental disabilities by advancing "progressive policies, sound research, and effective practices." AAIDD publishes the* American Journal on Intellectual and Developmental Disabilities.

### Arc of the United States (The Arc)

1660 L St. NW, Suite 301
Washington, DC 20036
Telephone: (202) 534-3700; (800) 433-5255
Fax: (202) 534-3731
E-mail: info@thearc.org
Web site: http://www.thearc.org
*"The world's largest community-based organization of and for people with intellectual and developmental disabilities," The Arc of the United States (The Arc) is committed to helping its members access supports and services in their local communities. Chapters of The Arc can be found in local communities throughout the United States.*

### Division on Autism and Developmental Disabilities (DADD)–CEC

Web site: http://www.daddcec.org
*A division of the Council for Exceptional Children, the Division on Autism and Developmental Disabilities (DADD) focuses on advancing the knowledge base of the field by working to "enhance the competence of persons who work with individuals with cognitive disabilities/mental retardation, autism, and related disabilities." DADD publishes* Education and Training in Autism and Developmental Disabilities *and* Focus on Autism and Other Developmental Disabilities.

### National Association of Councils on Developmental Disabilities (NACDD)

1660 L St. NW, Suite 700
Washington, DC 20036
Telephone: (202) 506-5813
Fax: (202) 506-5846
E-mail: info@nacdd.org
Web site: http://www.nacdd.org
*The National Association of Councils on Developmental Disabilities (NACDD) is an organization that represents "55 state and territorial Councils on Developmental Disabilities." The purpose of NACDD is to encourage and support the local councils in promoting the self-determination, inclusion, and integration of individuals with developmental disabilities.*

**National Down Syndrome Society (NDSS)**
666 Broadway
New York, NY 10012
Telephone: (800) 221-4602
Fax: (212) 979-2873
E-mail: info@ndss.org
Web site: http://www.ndss.org
*The mission of the National Down Syndrome Society (NDSS) is to "be the national advocate for the value, acceptance and inclusion of people with Down syndrome." NDSS contributes to the funding of Down syndrome research in the United States, helps shape public policy and public awareness of Down syndrome, and assists in developing educational programs for individuals with Down syndrome.*

## Orthopedic Impairment

**American Occupational Therapy Association, Inc. (AOTA)**
4720 Montgomery Lane
P.O. Box 31220
Bethesda, MD 20824-1220
Telephone: (301) 652-2682 (V); (800) 377-8555 (TTY)
Fax: (301) 652-7711
Web site: http://www.aota.org
*The American Occupational Therapy Association (AOTA) is a national organization that represents occupational therapists currently practicing as well as students in occupational therapy training programs. AOTA supports the occupational therapy profession "through standard-setting, advocacy, education, and research on behalf of its members and the public." AOTA publishes the* American Journal of Occupational Therapy.

**American Physical Therapy Association (APTA)**
1111 North Fairfax St.
Alexandria, VA 22314-1488
Telephone: (800) 999-2782 (V); (703) 683-6748 (TTY)
Fax: (703) 684-734
Web site: http://www.apta.org
*The American Physical Therapy Association (APTA) is a national organization that "promotes the profession of physical therapy." The mission of APTA is to provide information and professional development opportunities to physical therapists in the areas of research, education and training, and best practices in treatment. APTA publishes the journal* Physical Therapy.

**Division for Physical, Health, and Multiple Disabilities (DPHMD)–CEC**
Web site: http://web.utk.edu/~dphmd
*A division of the Council for Exceptional Children, the Division for Physical, Health, and Multiple Disabilities (DPHMD) is working for "quality education for all individuals with physical disabilities, multiple disabilities, and special health care needs served in schools, hospitals, or home settings."* DPHMD publishes Physical Disabilities: Education and Related Services.

**Muscular Dystrophy Association (MDA)**
USA National Headquarters
3300 E. Sunrise Dr.
Tucson, AZ 85718
Telephone: (800) 572-1717
E-mail: mda@mdausa.org
Web site: http://www.mdausa.org
*The Muscular Dystrophy Association (MDA) is dedicated to combating and curing muscular dystrophy. To accomplish this, MDA funds research, provides services, and provides professional and public health education. Its services include "diagnostic and follow-up medical consultations, flu shots, support groups, MDA summer camps for children, a medical equipment loan program, assistance with medical equipment repairs, and resource referral."*

**National Spinal Cord Injury Association (NSCIA)**
1 Church St. #600
Rockville, MD 20850
Telephone: (800) 962-9629
Fax: (866) 387-2196
E-mail: infor@spinalcord.org
Web site: http://www.spinalcord.org
*The mission of the National Spinal Cord Injury Association (NSCIA) is to "educate and empower people with spinal cord injury and disease (SCI/D)." NSCIA advocates for effective practices and policies. It also maintains a National Peer Support Network and a resource center that allows users to access information and referral services.*

**United Cerebral Palsy (UCP)**
1660 L St. NW, Suite 700
Washington, DC 20036
Telephone: (800) 872-5827
Fax: (202) 776-0414

E-mail: infor@ucp.org
Web site: http://www.ucp.org
*United Cerebral Palsy (UCP) is a national organization with local community associations whose mission is to advance "the independence, productivity, and full citizenship of people with disabilities." UCP provides a multitude of services including early intervention services, housing and independent living assistance, transition and employment education, therapeutic services, and assistive technology services.*

## Other Health Impairments

**American Epilepsy Society (AES)**
342 North Main St.
West Hartford, CT 06117-25-7
Telephone: (860) 586-7505
Web site: http://www.aesnet.org
*The American Epilepsy Society (AES) seeks to connect professionals in the epilepsy community with one another in an effort to promote the exchange of information and research between professionals from a variety of disciplines.*

**Asthma and Allergy Foundation of America (AAFA)**
8201 Corporate Dr., Suite 1000
Landover, MD 20785
Telephone: (800) 727-8462
E-mail: Info@aafa.org
Web site: http://www.aafa.org
*Asthma and Allergy Foundation of America (AAFA) provides advocacy, information, services, and support to those affected by asthma and/or allergies. The organization also funds research for treatments and cures.*

**Attention Deficit Disorder Association (ADDA)**
P.O. Box 7557
Wilmington, DE 19803-9997
Telephone: (800) 939-1019
Fax: (800) 939-1019
E-mail: info@add.org
Web site: http://www.add.org
*The Attention Deficit Disorder Association (ADDA) provides adults with attention deficit/hyperactivity disorder (ADHD) access to information and resources. In addition, ADDA helps people with ADHD connect and network with one another.*

## Candlelighters Childhood Cancer Foundation (CCCF)
10400 Connecticut Ave., Suite 205
Kensington, MD 20895
Telephone: (800) 366-2223
Fax: (301) 962-3521
E-mail: staff@candlelighters.org
Web site: http://www.candlelighters.org
*The mission of Candlelighters Childhood Cancer Foundation (CCCF) is "to provide infor-*
*mation and awareness for children and adolescents with cancer and their families, to advo-*
*cate for their needs, and to support research so every child survives and leads a long and*
*healthy life."*

## Children and Adults With Attention Deficit/Hyperactivity Disorder (CHADD)
8181 Professional Pl., Suite 150
Landover, MD 20785
Telephone: (301) 306-7070
Fax: (301) 306-7090
Web site: http://www.chadd.org
*Children and Adults With Attention Deficit/ Hyperactivity Disorder (CHADD) is a*
*national organization with local chapters throughout the United States. The goal of*
*CHADD is to assist individuals with ADHD and their families in accessing information*
*regarding evidence-based practices, current research, education, and advocacy.*

## Cystic Fibrosis Foundation (CFF)
6931 Arlington Rd., 2nd Fl.
Bethesda, MD 20814
Telephone: (800) 344-4823
Fax: (301) 951-6378
E-mail: info@cff.org
Web site: http://www.cff.org
*The Cystic Fibrosis Foundation (CFF) is devoted to improving the quality of life for those*
*who have cystic fibrosis and to promoting research regarding cure and treatment for the*
*disease.*

## Epilepsy Foundation of America
8301 Professional Pl.
Landover, MD 20785

Telephone: (800) 332-1000

Web site: http://www.epilepsyfoundation.org

*The Epilepsy Foundation is dedicated to improving the lives of people with epilepsy by ensuring their full participation in life. The organization "provides services, education, advocacy, and research" that focus on the prevention of epilepsy, control of seizures and other symptoms, and finding a cure.*

### Juvenile Diabetes Research Foundation International (JDRF)

26 Broadway

New York, NY 10004

Telephone: (800) 533-CURE (2873)

Fax: (212) 785-9595

E-mail: info@jdrf.org

Web site: http://www.jdrf.org

*The Juvenile Diabetes Research Foundation International (JDRF) touts itself as the world's largest charitable funder and advocate of research to cure Type 1 diabetes. It also provides advocacy resources for families.*

### Osteogenesis Imperfecta (OI) Foundation

804 W. Diamond Ave, Suite 210

Gaithersburg, MD 20878

Telephone: (301) 947-0083, (800) 981-2663

Fax: (301) 947-0456

E-mail: bonelink@aol.com

Web site: http://www.oif.org

*The mission of the Osteogenesis Imperfecta (OI) Foundation is to (1) support research; (2) provide up-to-date information related to OI; (3) increase public awareness of OI; and (4) provide mutual support to persons touched by OI. The OI Foundation funds research and research fellows, connects researchers and participants, provides OI-related information and resources, and facilitates mutual support through support groups and electronic social networking systems.*

## Specific Learning Disabilities

### Council for Learning Disabilities (CLD)

11184 Antioch Rd.

Box 405

Overland Park, KS 66210

Telephone: (913) 491-1011

Fax: (913) 491-1012

E-mail: CLDInfo@ie-events.com

Web site: http://www.cldinternational.org

*The Council for Learning Disabilities (CLD) is a multidisciplinary professional organization that promotes "evidence-based teaching, collaboration, research, leadership, and advocacy."* CLD publishes Learning Disabilities Quarterly.

## Division for Learning Disabilities (DLD)–CEC

Web site: http://www.teachingld.org

*A division of the Council for Exceptional Children, the Division for Learning Disabilities (DLD) includes the program TeachingLD. The mission of TeachingLD is to provide information regarding current policies and practices related to learning disabilities. TeachingLD offers information on assessment measures, teacher instructional methods and strategies, and current issues affecting students with learning disabilities and the families and professionals supporting them. DLD publishes* Learning Disabilities Research and Practice *and* Current Practice Alerts.

## International Dyslexia Association (IDA)

40 York Rd., 4th Fl.

Baltimore, MD 21204

Telephone: (410) 296-0232

Fax: (410) 321-5069

Web site: http://www.interdys.org

*The International Dyslexia Association (IDA) provides scientific and educational information on dyslexia in four areas: (1) information and referral services; (2) research; (3) advocacy and public policy; and (4) professional development.*

## Learning Disabilities Association of America (LDA)

4156 Library Rd.

Pittsburgh, PA 15234-1349

Telephone: (412) 341-1515

Fax: (412) 344-0224

Web site: http://www.ldanatl.org

*The Learning Disabilities Association of America (LDA) of America is a national organization with local community affiliates throughout the United States. The mission of LDA "is to create opportunities for success for all individuals affected by learning disabilities" by supplying information on services that support individuals with learning disabilities. In addition, LDA provides opportunities for individuals with learning disabilities, family members, and professionals to engage and collaborate with one another through an assortment of committees and coalitions. LDA publishes the* Journal of Learning Disabilities.

### National Center for Learning Disabilities (NCLD)
381 Park Avenue South, Suite 1401
New York, NY 10016
Telephone: (888) 575-7373
Fax: (212) 545-9665
E-mail: ncld@ncld.org
Web site: http://www.ncld.org
*The mission of the National Center for Learning Disabilities (NCLD) is to help children, adolescents, and adults with learning disabilities "succeed in school, work, and life." NCLD provides up-to-date information regarding learning disability research, assessment and evaluation procedures, and teaching methods. NCLD also advocates in the development of federal legislation and public policy affecting individuals with learning disabilities.*

### Nonverbal Learning Disorders Association (NLDA)
507 Hopmeadow St.
Simsbury, CT 06070
Telephone: (860) 658-5522
Fax: (860) 658-6688
E-mail: Info@NLDA.org
Web site: http://www.nlda.org
*The mission of the Nonverbal Learning Disorders Association (NLDA) is to facilitate "education, research and advocacy for children and adults who manifest disabilities associated with the syndrome of nonverbal learning disorders." Through its Web site, discussion forums, conferences, workshops, and other events, NLDA disseminates information and provides support to individuals with nonverbal learning disorders and their families.*

## Speech or Language Impairment

### American Speech-Language-Hearing Association (ASHA)
2220 Research Blvd.
Rockville, MD 20850-3280
Telephone: (800) 638-8255 (V); (301) 296-565 (TTY)
E-mail: actioncenter@asha.org
Web site: http://www.asha.org
*The American Speech-Language-Hearing Association (ASHA) is a professional resource for therapists and scientists who work with people with communication and related disorders. The mission of the ASHA is to ensure "effective communication, a human right, accessible and achievable for all." ASHA publishes five journals.*

**Childhood Apraxia of Speech Association of North America (CASANA)**
1151 Freeport Rd., #243
Pittsburgh, PA 15238
Telephone: (412) 343-7102
Web site: http://www.apraxia-kids.org
*The Childhood Apraxia of Speech Association of North America (CASANA) is a nonprofit organization with a mission to "strengthen the support systems in the lives of children with apraxia so that each child is afforded their best opportunity to develop speech." The goals of the organization include funding research, providing information and networking to the public to raise awareness and facilitate public policy, and providing training and education on apraxia*

**Division for Communicative Disabilities and Deafness (DCDD)–CEC**
Web site: http://www.dcdd.us
*A division of the Council for Exceptional Children, the Division for Communicative Disabilities and Deafness (DCDD) is a source of information for educational professionals and family members of children with communicative disorders, children who are deaf, and children who are hard of hearing. DCDD provides access to current research, advocacy work, and professional development activities. DCDD publishes* Communication Disorders Quarterly.

**National Stuttering Association (NSA)**
119 W. 40th St., 14th Fl.
New York, NY 10018
Telephone: (800) 937-8888
Fax: (212) 944-8244
E-mail: infor@WeStutter.org
Web site: http://www.nsastutter.org
*The National Stuttering Association (NSA) supports individuals who stutter, their families, and educational professionals and speech therapists by providing access to education and training workshops, information regarding effective therapeutic techniques and strategies, current research, and advocacy, and increased public understanding of stuttering.*

## Traumatic Brain Injury

**Brain Injury Association of America (BIAA)**
1608 Spring Hill Rd., Suite 110
Vienna, VA 22182

Telephone: (703) 761-0750
Fax: (703) 761-0755
E-mail: info@biusa.org
Web site: http://www.biausa.org
*The mission of the Brain Injury Association of American (BIAA) is "creating a better future through brain injury prevention, research, education, and advocacy." BIAA provides education, information, and support through the national association, 40 state affiliates, and local chapters and support groups.*

## Visual Impairment Including Blindness

### American Council of the Blind (ACB)
2200 Wilson Blvd., Suite 650
Arlington, VA 22201
Telephone: (202) 467-5081; (800) 424-8666
Fax: (703) 465-5085
Web site: http://www.acb.org/index.html
*"The American Council of the Blind (ACB) works in cooperation with local and state institutions and organizations to ensure individuals who are blind or visually impaired (1) receive appropriate services, (2) are served in adequate educational and rehabilitation facilities, and (3) possess important information regarding consumer advocacy and legal rights."*

### American Foundation for the Blind (AFB)
2 Penn Plaza, Suite 1102
New York, NY 10121
Telephone: (212) 502-7600
Fax: (212) 502-7777
E-mail: afbinfo@atb.net
Web site: http://www.afb.org
*The American Foundation for the Blind (AFB) connects "people to resources" by providing access to information, technology, and education and skill training to people with vision loss, their families, and the professionals who work with them. AFB publishes the* Journal of Visual Impairment and Blindness.

### Association for Education and Rehabilitation of the Blind and Visually Impaired (AER)
1703 N. Beauregard St., Suite 440
Alexandria, VA 22311
Telephone: (877) 492-2708
Fax: (703) 671-6391
Web site: http://www.aerbvi.org

*The Association for Education and Rehabilitation of the Blind and Visually Impaired (AER) supports "professionals who provide education and rehabilitation services to people with visual impairments." AER accomplishes this mission by providing professionals and specialists with opportunities to obtain additional training and education as well as access to current research literature and professional publications. AER publishes* Research and Practice in Blindness and Visual Impairment.

## Division on Visual Impairments (DVI)–CEC
Web site: http://www.cecdvi.org
*A division of the Council for Exceptional Children, the Division on Visual Impairments (DVI) focuses on "advocating for effective policies, practices, and services addressing the unique educational needs of children and youth who have visual impairments, including those with additional exceptionalities." DVI publishes a quarterly newsletter.*

## Lighthouse International
111 East 59th St.
New York, NY 10022
Telephone: (800) 829-0500 (V); (212) 821-9713 (TTY)
Fax: (212) 821-9707
E-mail: info@lighthouse.org
Web site: http://www.lighthouse.org
*Lighthouse International is dedicated to "fighting vision loss through prevention, treatment, and empowerment." Lighthouse International meets the needs of people with vision loss by providing access to and information regarding rehabilitation and medical services. Lighthouse International also provides a variety of educational opportunities and services for people with vision loss through its Child Development Center and the Greenberg Music School. Lighthouse International supports professional development through the Center for Education.*

## National Federation of the Blind (NFB)
1800 Johnson St.
Baltimore, MD 21230
Telephone: (410) 659-9314
Fax: (410) 685-5653
E-mail: nfb@nfb.org
Web site: http://www.nfb.org
*National Federation of the Blind (NFB) "provides information and referral services, scholarships, literature and publications about blindness, aids and appliances, and other adaptive equipment for the blind." The organization also engages in civil rights advocacy work, provides "employment assistance and support services, and develops and evaluates technology for the blind." In addition to educating the public, NFB seeks to enhance the self-confidence and self-respect of persons who are blind.*

# Seven

# Selected Print and Electronic Resources

## Sharon M. Kolb and Lana Collet-Klingenberg

This chapter consists of suggested resources to assist reader inquiry of topics in areas of special education. Pre-service and in-service educators may use these resources as a launching point for further research. Parents, families, advocates, and other professionals may also use these resources to gain knowledge about identified themes. Resources are presented in three sections: (1) print resources; (2) electronic resources; and (3) professional journals (some available in print, others electronically, and many in both print and electronic formats) that provide information related to education of children and youth with disabilities. Each of the first two sections is annotated and includes general resources related to special education as well as resources specifically pertaining to the 13 disability categories covered by the Individuals with Disabilities Education Act of 2004 (IDEA).

# 1. Print Resources

## General Resources in Special Education

### Assessment

Overton, T. (2008). *Assessing learners with special needs: An applied approach* (6th ed.). Upper Saddle River, NJ: Prentice Hall.
*Designed to teach future special educators how to assess students with mild to moderate disabilities, this book features a step-by-step approach that provides hands-on learning activities.*

Rhodes, R. L., Ochoa, S. H., & Ortiz, S. O. (2005). *Assessing culturally and linguistically diverse students: A practical guide.* New York: Guilford Press.
*This book presents practical, research-based, hands-on tools and techniques for assessing English-language learners and culturally diverse students in schools. Included resources are reproducible worksheets, and checklists and questionnaires.*

Salvia, J., Ysseldyke, J., & Bolt, S. (2009). *Assessment: In special and inclusive education* (11th ed.). Florence, KY: Wadsworth.
*This book provides pre-service and in-service educators with basic information on how to correctly select, administer, and evaluate results of assessments to create learning goals and lessons for students with disabilities.*

### History

Blatt, B., & Kaplan, F. M. (1966). *Christmas in purgatory: A photographic essay on mental retardation.* Boston: Allyn & Bacon.
*In this book, Kaplan and Blatt present images that fueled the deinstitutionalization movement in the 1960s and contributed to the creation of community-based programs for children and adults with disabilities.*

Osgood, R. L. (2008). The history of special education: A struggle for equality in American public schools. In P. F. Clement (Series Ed.), *Growing up: History of children and youth.* Westport, CT: Praeger.
*The author provides a comprehensive look at the history of special education in the United States, describing the shaping forces and processes and how its features and functions have changed over time.*

Winzer, M. A. (1993). *The history of special education: From isolation to integration.* Washington, DC: Gallaudet University Press.
*In this free online book available from Google Books, Winzer provides the historical background for the creation of special education. She traces the beliefs, events, and movements in 16th century Western cultures that have led to inclusive education in today's public schools.*

Wolfensberger, W. (1972). *Normalization: The principle of normalization in human services.* Toronto, ON: National Institute on Mental Retardation.
*This foundational text presents the theories and beliefs that undergirded the creation of services and special education in the United States, particularly for individuals with developmental disabilities.*

## Inclusion

Friend, M., & Bursuck, W. D. (2008). *Including students with special needs: A practical guide for classroom teachers* (5th ed.). Upper Saddle River, NJ: Allyn & Bacon.
*Using a non-categorical approach for students with low- to high-incidence disabilities, the authors provide strategies that promote inclusion for all students.*

Schwarz, P., & Kluth, P. (2007). *You're welcome: 30 innovative ideas for the inclusive classroom.* Portsmouth, NH: Heinemann.
*This book provides classroom teachers with ideas to address peer collaboration, designing classroom centers, integrating the Individualized Education Programs (IEPs), and differentiated instruction.*

## Individualized Education Program Planning

Bateman, B. D., & Herr, C. (2006). *Writing measurable IEP goals and objectives.* Verona, WI: Attainment Company.
*This guide helps educators in generating Present Levels of Performance (PLOPs), objectives, and goals that comply with IDEA laws. It includes examples and tips for writing measureable IEP goals.*

Courtade-Little, G., & Browder, D. (2005). *Aligning IEPs to academic standards for students with moderate and severe disabilities.* Arlington, VA: Council for Exceptional Children.
*Intended to assist educators of students with moderate to severe disabilities in designing educational plans, this book describes how to create parallel activities which are connected to the general curriculum and align the student's IEP to state standards.*

Siegel, L. M. (2009). *The complete IEP guide: How to advocate for your special ed child.* Berkeley, CA: NOLO.
*The author provides families with information to guide them through the IEP process, including assessment, legal implications, and strategies.*

## Legal Resources and Advocacy

Hayden, D., Takemoto, C., Anderson, W., & Chitwood, S. (2008). *Negotiating the special education maze: A guide for parents and teachers.* Bethesda, MD: Woodbine House. *Using clear language, this book provides teachers and parents with information about specific disability categories identified by IDEA and practical strategies to provide students with accommodations and adaptations.*

Reynolds, C. R., & Fletcher-Janzen, E. (2007). *Encyclopedia of special education: A reference for the education of children, adolescents, and adults with disabilities and other exceptional individuals* ( 3rd ed., Vol. 1). Indianapolis, IN: Wiley. *This book is a resource for persons wanting an in-depth view of the field of special education. The authors provide a comprehensive approach to address theory and its impact on practice.*

Weinfeld, R., & Davis, M. (2008). *Special needs advocacy resource book: What you can do now to advocate for your exceptional child's education.* Waco, TX: Prufrock Press. *The authors address IEPs, IDEA, NCLB, and 504 plans in plain language to assist parents, educators, and advocates in effective educational planning, assessment, and accommodations related to special and gifted education.*

Wilmshurst, L., & Brue, A. W. (2005). *A parent's guide to special education: Insider advice on how to navigate the system and help your child succeed.* New York: AMACOM. *This book provides strategies (1) to assist parents in understanding the special education process, supports for their children, and their legal rights and (2) to improve parent-teacher communication and advocacy.*

Wright, P. W. D., & Wright, P. D. (2007). *Wrightslaw: Special education law* (2nd ed.). Hartfield, VA: Harbor House Law Press. *The authors provide insight for educators, advocates, attorneys, and parents/guardians about special education legislation and how to apply this information to gain enhanced services for students with disabilities.*

Yell, M. (1998). *The law and special education.* Upper Saddle River, NJ: Prentice-Hall. *This book describes the history and application of laws related to special education, including how those laws have been applied in public education.*

## Research

Fichtman-Dana, N., & Yendol-Hoppey, D. (2008). *The reflective educator's guide to classroom research: Learning to teach and teaching to learn through practitioner inquiry.* Thousand Oaks, CA: Corwin. *Action research in the classroom is presented in a clear, step-by-step format to assist the practitioner in exploring classroom-based research from a teacher inquiry perspective.*

Mills, G. E. (2010). *Action research: A guide for the teacher researcher* (4th ed.). Upper Saddle River, NJ: Prentice Hall.
*Written for teachers and administrators, this book guides development of classroom inquiry, data collection, and analysis. It also describes how to evaluate research results.*

### Transition

Bakken, J. P., & Obiakor, F. E. (2008). *Transition planning for students with disabilities: What educators and service providers can do.* Springfield, IL: Charles C Thomas.
*This book provides useful content for service providers, educators, and researchers related to models and applications of career development and transition, assistive technology options, work development, cultural and ethnically diverse background perspectives, and collaboration with families.*

O'Brien, J., Pearpoint, J., & Kahn, L. (2010). *The PATH & MAPS handbook: Person-centered ways to build community.* Toronto, ON: Inclusion Press.
*This handbook is a comprehensive resource on person-centered planning for individuals with disabilities and their families. It describes what person-centered planning is and includes step-by-step models to facilitate collaborative planning with all team members.*

Sitlington, P. L., Neubert, D. A., & Clark, G. M. (2009). *Transition education and services for students with disabilities* (5th ed.). Upper Saddle River, NJ: Prentice Hall.
*This book provides pre-service and in-service educators with information about transition education and transition services for students with disabilities, from school-aged through adulthood.*

Wehman, P., & Kregel, J. (in press). *Functional curriculum for elementary, middle, and secondary age students with special needs* (3rd ed.). Austin, TX: Pro-Ed.
*Providing case studies and examples of IEP goals, this book offers educators the foundations of functional curriculum within a longitudinal framework for learners with disabilities.*

## IDEA Categories

### Autism

Anderson, S., Jablonski, A. L., Knapp, V. M., & Thomeer, M. L. (2007). *Self-help skills for people with autism: A systematic teaching approach.* Bethesda, MD: Woodbine House.
*This book is designed to provide parents and educators with strategies and techniques to teach basic self-help skills to individuals with autism.*

Kranowitz, C. S. (2005). *The out-of-sync child: Recognizing and coping with sensory processing disorder.* New York: Berkley.
*The author provides a clear definition of sensory processing disorder along with assessment techniques to identify specific problems related to tactile, vestibular, and proprioceptive*

*dysfunction. This is a practical resource for teachers, parents, and therapists containing advice through case studies related to sensory integration.*

Notbohm, E. (2005). *Ten things every child with autism wishes you knew.* Arlington, TX: Future Horizons.
*This book is written to help the reader understand the disorder by examining it through the eyes of a child with autism. It includes practical discussions of behaviors, characteristics, and insights shared by children with autism.*

Sicile-Kira, C. (2006). *Autism spectrum disorders: The complete guide to understanding autism, Asperger's, pervasive developmental disorders and other ASDs.* New York: Berkley.
*Written from the perspective of a parent, this book offers information related to diagnoses, family life, community experiences, and educational prospects. The forward to the book is written by Temple Grandin.*

### Deaf-Blindness

Jones, C. J. (2001). *Evaluation and educational programming of students with deaf-blindness and severe disabilities: Sensorimotor stage* (2nd ed.). Springfield, IL: Charles C Thomas.
*In this book, specific to students who are deaf-blind, readers will find information on theoretical background, diagnostic, medical, and best practice instructional techniques, program and IEP development, and classroom design to promote sensory stimulation.*

### Deafness. See Hearing Impairment (including deafness)

### Emotional Disturbance

Algozzine, R. F., & Ysseldyke, J. (2006). *Teaching students with emotional disturbance: A practical guide for every teacher.* Thousand Oaks, CA: Corwin.
*Written for teachers who want to gain a deeper understanding of emotional disabilities, as well as practical information on emotional, social, behavioral, and academic needs of students identified with emotional disturbance, this book also includes information on Functional Behavioral Assessments.*

Marsh, D. T., & Fristad, M. A. (2002). *Handbook of serious emotional disorders in children and adolescents.* Hoboken, NJ: Wiley.
*A comprehensive handbook on diagnosing and treating children and adolescents with serious emotional disorders (SED), this resource features information on numerous topics, including anxiety disorders, mood disorders, ADHD, obsessive-compulsive and tic disorders, working with families, the juvenile justice system, and home- and school-based treatment options.*

Papolos, D., & Papolis, J. (2006). *The bipolar child: The definitive and reassuring guide to childhood's most misunderstood disorder* (3rd ed.). New York: Broadway Books.
*This text provides information on the disorder itself, how to get treatment, the impact of the illness on the family, advocacy, and ways to help children with bipolar feel more comfortable in the classroom.*

### Hearing Impairment (including deafness)

Marschark, M. (2007). *Raising and educating a deaf child: A comprehensive guide to the choices, controversies, and decisions faced by parents and educators* (2nd ed.). New York: Oxford University Press.
*A comprehensive guide to assist parents and educators with gaining insight into deaf culture, this book also includes information on technological aids and communication.*

### Mental Retardation

Couwenhoven, T. (2007). *Teaching children with Down syndrome about their bodies, boundaries, and sexuality: A guide for parents and professionals.* Bethesda, MD: Woodbine House.
*This book covers relevant topics of self-care and hygiene, understanding appropriate boundaries in relationships, identifying emotions, and sexuality.*

Ysseldyke, J., & Algozzine, R. F. (2006). *Teaching students with mental retardation: A practical guide for every teacher.* Thousand Oaks, CA: Sage.
*This resource is designed to help special and general educators to support students with intellectual disabilities in the academic, social, and work aspects of their lives. Best practice methods and instructional approaches are provided as ways to enhance learning in inclusive settings.*

### Multiple Disabilities

Batshaw, M. L. (2001). *When your child has a disability: The complete sourcebook of daily and medical care.* Baltimore, MD: Brookes.
*This book provides comprehensive information for parents and caregivers of children with multiple disabilities. Numerous care and disability-specific topics ranging from birth through adulthood are addressed.*

Heller, K. W., Forney, P. E., Alberto, P. A., Best, S. J., & Schwartzman, M. N. (2008). *Understanding physical, health and multiple disabilities* (2nd ed.). Upper Saddle River, NJ: Prentice Hall.
*Content is provided on a wide range of physical, health, and multiple disabilities to help the future teacher work effectively in meeting the safety, health, physical, and academic needs of students with multiple disabilities.*

## Orthopedic Impairment

Batshaw, M. L., Pellegrino, L., & Roizen, N. J. (2007). *Children with disabilities* (6th ed.). Baltimore, MD: Brookes.
*This comprehensive text focuses on orthopedic impairments and other disabilities, with specific content on cerebral palsy, epilepsy, autism spectrum disorders, intellectual disability, Down syndrome, movement disorders, and child development.*

Martin, S. (2006). *Teaching motor skills to children with cerebral palsy and similar move ment disorders.* Bethesda, MD: Woodbine House.
*Written by a physical therapist, this book provides readers with photographs, plain-language strategies, and exercises to strengthen, build, and reinforce motor skill development in children with orthopedic impairments.*

## Other Health Impairments

Clay, D. L. (2004). *Helping school children with chronic health conditions: A practical guide.* New York: Guilford Press.
*This book is a resource for school-based professionals who support students with health problems. Features include reproducible materials for assessments, parent handouts, and student worksheets, along with guidelines for IEP and 504 planning with an emphasis on parent and teacher collaboration.*

Rief, S. F. (2003). *The ADHD book of lists: A practical guide for helping children and teens with attention deficit disorders.* Indianapolis, IN: Wiley.
*This book offers strategies, reproducible checklists, and resources for parents, teachers, and other professionals who are looking for effective supports and interventions for children and adolescents with ADHD.*

## Specific Learning Disability

Bender, W. N. (2008). *Differentiating instruction for students with learning disabilities: Best teaching practices for general and special educators* (2nd ed.). Thousand Oaks, CA: Corwin.
*Presenting step-by-step instructional techniques that focus on strategy instruction, instructional and peer-assisted grouping, performance monitoring, and direct instruction, this book is geared toward educators working with learners in inclusive settings.*

Harwell, J. M. (2001). *Complete learning disabilities handbook: Ready-to-use strategies & activities for teaching students with learning disabilities* (2nd ed.). San Francisco: Jossey-Bass.
*This book is a practical resource for educators and persons interested in learning more about specific learning disabilities. An overview of the disability is provided along with diagnosis and assessment guidelines, strategies, and interventions.*

Swanson, H. L., Harris, K. R., & Graham, S. (2005). *Handbook of learning disabilities.* New York: Guilford Press.
*This handbook provides strategies to support students with learning disabilities in the areas of language arts, math, science, and social studies as well as other inclusive classroom environments.*

## Speech or Language Impairment

Feit, D. (2007). *The parent's guide to speech and language.* New York: McGraw-Hill.
*Advice, medical information, encouragement, and hands-on strategies are provided in this parent-friendly book on supporting children with speech and language difficulties.*

Gravell, R., & Johnson, R. (2002). *Head injury rehabilitation: A community team perspective.* Baltimore, MD: Brookes.
*This resource offers a thorough description of how mild to severe head injuries can impact the individual and caregivers. Strategies are provided for therapists, parents, caregivers, and other professionals who collaborate in the rehabilitation process.*

Kuder, S. K. (2008). *Teaching students with language and communication disabilities.* Upper Saddle River, NJ: Pearson Education.
*Essential and current information on language development and disabilities, with a specific focus on school-age children, is available in this book for educators and other professionals.*

Lash, M., Wolcott, G., & Pearson, S. (2005). *Signs and strategies for educating students with brain injuries* (3rd ed.). Wake Forest, NC: Lash & Associates Publishing/ Training.
*This manual for educators and families provides an overview of brain injuries and strategies for home and school to assist student learning and behavior.*

Martin, D. (2009). *Language disabilities in cultural and linguistic diversity (bilingual education and bilingualism).* Bristol, UK: Multilingual Matters.
*This book is written for teachers, speech and language therapists, and parents to support development of enhanced strategies to assist children with communication disorders and multilingualism.*

Schoenbrodt, L. (2001). *Children with traumatic brain injury: A parent's guide.* Bethesda, MD: Woodbine House.
*This book is directed toward general and special educators working with children who have TBI and their families. Important topics covered in this resource include*

*improving recovery outcomes, coping with the effects of TBI on the child and caregivers, legal issues, medical concerns, and educational needs.*

Schwartz, S. (2004). *The new language of toys: Teaching communication skills to children with special needs* (3rd ed.). Bethesda, MD: Woodbine House.
*This book discusses the use of toys to teach communication skills to children with exceptional education needs. Content includes age-appropriate dialogues along with play and communication strategies. Suggested sources for assistive technology and appropriate toys designed to improve communication are provided.*

## Visual Impairment (Including blindness)

Bishop, V. E. (2004). *Teaching visually impaired children* (3rd ed.). Springfield, IL: Charles C Thomas.
*A best practice strategies and instructional programming resource for special and general educators, other professionals, and parents interested in assisting persons with visual impairments in and out of the classroom setting, this reference guide covers topics such as vision development, assessments, and instructional resources that can be implemented in the classroom.*

Chen, D., & Downing, J. E. (2006). *Tactile strategies for children who have visual impairments and multiple disabilities: Promoting communication and learning skills*. New York: AFB Press.
*This resource provides communication experts, parents, and educators with information and techniques for teaching students to use their sense of touch for skill development, alternative communication, early intervention, and emergent literacy.*

Holbrook, M. C. (2006). *Children with visual impairments: A guide for parents* (2nd ed.). Bethesda, MD: Woodbine House.
*This guide provides concrete information about visual impairments and is directed toward parents and other caregivers. Topics include treatment options, child development, legal issues, orientation and mobility, literacy, and assessment.*

Olmstead, J. E. (2005). *Itinerant teaching: Tricks of the trade for teachers of students with visual impairments* (2nd ed.). New York: AFB Press.
*Specifically addressed toward teachers who travel, this book covers topics such as orientation and mobility, assistive technology, and practical strategies for teachers working with children having visual impairments and multiple disabilities.*

# 2. Electronic Resources

## General Resources in Special Education

### Assessment

*Circle of inclusion.* (n.d.). Retrieved from http://www.circleofinclusion.org
  *Created for early childhood providers and families with young children, this site offers access to lesson plans, sample methods and accommodations, and downloadable resources.*

PACER Center. (2006). *Evaluation: What does it mean for your child?* Retrieved from http://www.pacer.org/parent/php/php-c2.pdf
  *This guide from the PACER center provides information on education evaluations, the purpose and types of evaluations, and analysis and outcome of results.*

### Individualized Education Program Planning

*My child's special needs: A guide to the individualized education program.* (n.d.). Retrieved from http://ed.gov/parents/needs/speced/iepguide/index.html
  *Produced by the U.S. Department of Education at ED.gov, this IEP guide is accessible in MS Word or PDF format. The guide covers all aspects of the IEP to assist educators, parents, and state and local educational agencies in addressing Part B of the law.*

*PEAK parent center.* (n.d.). Retrieved from http://peakparent.org
  *This Web site provides teachers and parents with reference books and resources on IEP development and meetings, with special emphasis on differentiated instruction related to specific academic subjects and inclusion.*

*Wrightslaw.* (n.d.). Retrieved from http://www.wrightslaw.com
  *This Web site provides extensive information on IEP articles, laws and regulations, how to access services, working with schools, IEP cases, and resources.*

### Legal Resources and Advocacy

*Building the legacy/Construyendo el legado: A training curriculum on IDEA.* (2004). Retrieved from http://nichcy.org/laws/idea/legacy
  *These training modules include a slideshow for trainers, trainers' guide, and participant handouts. The modules are in both English and Spanish and address the components of IDEA in an understandable and accessible format.*

*World Institute on disability (WID)*. (n.d.). Retrieved from http://www.wid.org
*Individuals can use this Web site to access numerous electronic publications and resources that provide a global perspective on disability.*

## Research

Nunley, K. F. (1999). *Practical classroom applications of current brain research.* Retrieved from www.brains.org
*This site contains current topic in research related to psychological and neurological research and education.*

## Transition

DCRE Labs. (2007–2010). *Transition from high school to college.* Retrieved from http://dll.ada-podcasts.com/shownotes/DLLPod35.php and http://dll.adapodcasts.com/shownotes/DLLPod36.php
*This two-part podcast includes facts, myths, and tips for students with disabilities planning to go to college, their families, and the professionals who support them.*

Wisconsin Statewide Transition Initiative. (n.d.). *Transition topics A-Z.* Retrieved from http://www.wsti.org/transition_topics.php
*This Web site provides extensive information for students with disabilities and their families and educators on understanding and implementing IDEA transition requirements throughout the life span. Professional development modules are also available for free download.*

# IDEA Categories

## Autism

Child Neurology and Developmental Center. (2000–2004). *Childbrain.com: The pediatric neurology site.* Retrieved from www.childbrain.com
*This Web site has links for families and professional seeking information on pervasive developmental disorders (PDD), autism, and Asperger's syndrome. Specific subjects include the DSMV IV criteria for autistic disorders, assessment and evaluation procedures, behavioral modification, educational and treatment options, and related PDD associations.*

National Institute of Neurological Disorders and Stroke (NINDS). (2009). *Autism fact sheet.* Retrieved from http://www.ninds.nih.gov/disorders/autism/detail_autism.htm
*This Internet fact sheet contains (1) informational links regarding the definition, causes, symptoms, educational options, and current research and (2) numerous links to organizations that focus on autism spectrum disorder.*

## Deaf-Blindness

National Consortium on Deaf-Blindness. (n.d.). *NCDB network*. Retrieved from http://www.nationaldb.org
> *This Web site contains resources for families and professional who are interested in gaining information on deaf-blindness. Numerous articles and resources are available for access, and site materials are provided in Web-based, text only, and Spanish versions.*

Rowland, C. (2009). *Assessing communication and learning in young children who are deaf-blind or who have multiple disabilities*. Portland, OR: Oregon Health & Science University. Retrieved from http://www.ohsu.edu/oidd/d2l/com_pro/DeafBlindAssessmentGuide.pdf
> *This resource is a 59-page guide available for download in pdf format. The guide is written for anyone who is responsible for assessment and program planning for children who are deaf-blind. The strategies and assessment resources are also applicable for professional and families working with children with multiple disabilities.*

## Deafness. See Hearing Impairment (including deafness)

## Emotional Disturbance

Youth Change. (1996–2010). *Youth change: Your problem-kid problem-solver.* Retrieved from http://www.youthchg.com
> *This Web site provides free, practical materials that can be used to address problem behavior in the classroom and at home. Teachers and parents can access management worksheets, posters, newsletters, online workshops, forums, and other resources.*

## Hearing Impairment (including deafness)

Nakamura, K. (1995–2008). *The deaf resource library*. Retrieved from http://www.deaflibrary.org
> *This Web site provides access to a virtual library of online reference materials and links on educating individuals about deaf cultures in Japan and the United States. Resources available include links to deaf-related networks and associations, national and state organizations, deaf culture sites, schools and universities in the United States, Japan, and other countries, interpretive links, and other sites specific to deaf education and culture.*

National Institutes of Health. (n.d.). *National Institute on Deafness and Other Communication Disorders*. Retrieved from http://www.nidcd.nih.gov
> *This site provides information on hearing, ear infections, and deafness. There is also content on diseases and conditions related to hearing impairment, information for new parents regarding hearing and communication development, information regarding communication methods and devices for individuals with hearing loss, and strategies to protect one's hearing.*

West Virginia Department of Education. (2005). *Strategies for teaching students with hearing impairments.* Retrieved from http://www.as.wvu.edu/~scidis/hearing.html
*This link provides practical and easy-to-follow resources on teaching strategies for students with hearing impairments. Topics such as definition of terms, strategies, group interaction and discussion, reading, and assessment are addressed.*

## Mental Retardation

American Association on Intellectual and Developmental Disabilities. (2009). *FAQ on intellectual disabilities.* Retrieved from http://www.aamr.org/content_104.cfm
*Frequently asked questions about intellectual disability are answered in this fact sheet from AAIDD.*

The Arc. (2009). *Introduction to intellectual disabilities—fact sheets.* Retrieved from http://www.thearc.org/NetCommunity/Document.Doc?id=1921
*A downloadable fact sheet about intellectual disability, adaptive behavior, and developmental disability is available from The Arc.*

New York Times. (2009). *Mental retardation—symptoms, diagnosis, treatment of mental retardation.* Retrieved from http://health.nytimes.com/health/guides/disease/mental-retardation/overview.html
*This New York Times health guide provides up-to-date and easily accessible information on intellectual disability, including causes, symptoms, assessment, prognosis, medical terminology, and other links.*

## Multiple Disabilities

Perkins School for the Blind. (n.d.) *Education for students with multiple disabilities.* Retrieved from http://www.perkins.org/resources/scout/students-with-multiple-disabilities
*This Web site provides information for teachers of students with multiple disabilities. Topics include behavioral issues, curriculum, educational planning and assessment, instructional approaches, and learning theory.*

## Orthopedic Impairment

National Association of Special Education Teachers. (2007). *Exceptional students and disability information: Orthopedic impairments.* Retrieved from http://www.naset.org/orthopedicimpairment2.0html
*This Web site provides information and resources on the following orthopedic impairment topic categories: bone diseases, cerebral palsy, muscular dystrophy, scoliosis, spinal cord injury, brachial plexus/Erb's palsy, hydrocephalus, poliomyelitis, spina bifida, and spinal muscular atrophies.*

West Virginia Department of Education. (2005). *Strategies for teaching students with motor/orthopedic impairments.* Retrieved from http://www.as.wvu.edu/~scidis/motor.html
*This Web site offers information on organizations, books, videos, and other resources for educators and other professionals to assist students with orthopedic impairments. The Web site includes specific sections devoted to the areas of epilepsy, cerebral palsy, and autism.*

## Other Health Impairments

National Dissemination Center for Children with Disabilities. (2009). *Other health impairments* (Disability Fact Sheet No. 15). Retrieved from http://www.nichcy.org/Disabilities/Specific/Pages/healthimpairment.aspx
*This Web site provides a thorough description of the "other health impairments" category contained within the Individuals with Disability Education Act (2004), including information and resource links on student eligibility, specific health impairment, medical issues, school accommodations, and transition issues.*

Wisconsin Department of Public Instruction. (2009). *Special education eligibility criteria and evaluation for other health impairments.* Retrieved from http://dpi.wi.gov/SPED/doc/ohi-evaluation-guide.doc
*This document provides a description of "other health impairments" as related to eligibility for services, IEP development, and evaluation and programming for students with OHI. Because Wisconsin criteria for OHI are consistent with the federal criteria and law, this document provides practical and understandable information for educators, parents, and therapists across the United States.*

## Specific Learning Disability

Learning Disabilities Association of America (LDA). (n.d.). *Learning Disabilities Association of America online.* Retrieved from http://www.ldanatl.org
*The LDA Web site has numerous articles and resources that address topics on learning disabilities for teachers, parents, professionals, adults, and children. Full articles are available for download and cover topics such as reading, social/emotional aspects, understanding learning disabilities and ADHD, assessment and evaluation, early childhood, and mental health.*

National Center for Learning Disabilities. (2006). *A parent's guide to Response to Intervention.* Retrieved from http://ncld.org/images/stories/Publications/AdvocacyBriefs/ParentGuide-RTI/ParentsGuidetoRTI.pdf
*Response to Intervention is one of many free downloadable publications available at the National Center for Learning Disabilities Web site. Individuals can access checklists, worksheets, and information guides on learning disabilities for students, teachers, parents, and therapists.*

## Speech or Language Impairment

Children's Speech Care Center (n.d.). *Children's speech care center Web site.* Retrieved from http://www.childspeech.net
*This Web site is organized in four main sections: understanding speech and language impairments and challenges for children, thinking about your child's or student's needs, learning about clinic resources, and discovering and accessing additional resource and support.*

*Communication connects.* (2002). Retrieved from http://www.communicationconnects.com
*This electronic resource is intended for speech/language pathologists, parents, and teachers who are searching for practical information on building speech and communication skills for students with disabilities. The Web site includes classroom and home activities and links to articles and other resources to implement with children.*

## Traumatic Brain Injury

Centre for Neuro Skills. (2009). *TBI resource guide.* Retrieved from http://www.neuroskills.com
*This Web site provides access to resources on brain injury, treatment, publications, and other aspects of TBI.*

*Traumatic brain injury.com.* (n.d). Retrieved from http://www.traumaticbrain injury.com
*This Web site provides detailed content on Traumatic Brain Injury (TBI), including effects, causes, symptoms, treatment options, legal resources, and prevention.*

## Visual Impairment (including blindness)

Perkins School for the Blind. (n.d.). *Teaching resources.* Retrieved from http://www.perkins.org/resources
*This Web site contains training materials and online resources for educators working with learners having visual impairments. Accessible science activities are provided for download along with Webcasts, on-demand educational videos, and other resources.*

University of Buffalo, Center for Assistive Technology. (2000–2005). *Assistive technology training online project.* Retrieved from http://atto.buffalo.edu/registered/ATBasics.php
*This Web site contains online tutorials on assistive technology basics, resources, and technology options for students who are blind, have low vision or visual impairments, or have other disabilities.*

V.I. Guide. (n.d.). *A guide to Internet resources about visual impairments, for parents and teachers.* Retrieved from http://www.viguide.com
> *This site provides links to numerous topics related to vision services, special education services, assistive technology, medical and legal information, reading materials, and research of specific interest to educators and parents of children with visual impairments.*

# 3. Professional Journals

Please note that many of the journals in this section are affiliated with organizations listed in Chapter 6. Journals are listed along with an electronic link to a Web site where more information on the publication, including contact and subscription information, can be found.

*Ability Magazine,* http://www.abilitymagazine.com

*Access World,* http://www.afb.org/afbpress/pub.asp?SectionID=1

*American Annals of the Deaf,* http://gupress.gallaudet.edu/annals

*American Journal of Occupational Therapy,* http://www.aota.org/Pubs/AJOT_1.aspx

*American Journal of Speech Language Pathology,* http://ajslp.asha.org

*American Journal on Intellectual and Developmental Disabilities,* http://www.aaidd journals.org

*Assessment for Effective Intervention (AEI),* http://aei.sagepub.com

*Behavioral Disorders,* http://www.ccbd.net/publication/behavioraldisorders

*Behavior Modification,* http://bmo.sagepub.com

*Beyond Behavior,* http://www.ccbd.net/publication/beyondbehavior

*Braille Forum,* http://www.acb.org/magazine/index.html

*The Braille Monitor,* http://www.nfb.org/nfb/Braille_Monitor.asp

*Career Development for Exceptional Individuals (CDE),* http://cde.sagepub.com

*Communication Disorders Quarterly (CDQ),* http://cdq.sagepub.com

*Education and Training in Autism and Developmental Disabilities,* http://dddcec.org/publications/ETADDJournal.aspx

*Exceptional Children,* www.cec.sped.org/AM/Template.cfm?Section=Publications1

*Exceptionality,* http://www.informaworld.com/smpp/title~content=t775653647~db=all?tab=subscribe

*Exceptional Parent,* http://www.eparent.com

*Focus on Autism and Other Developmental Disabilities,* http://foa.sagepub.com

*Focus on Exceptional Children,* http://www.lovepublishing.com/catalog/focus_on_exceptional_children_31.html

*Information Technology and Disabilities,* http://people.rit.edu/easi/itd.htm

*International Early Childhood Special Education,* http://www.int-jecse.net

*Intervention in School and Clinic,* http://isc.sagepub.com

*Journal of Applied Behavior Analysis,* http://seab.envmed.rochester.edu/jaba

*Journal of Applied School Psychology,* http://www.informaworld.com/smpp/title~content=t792303966~db=all

*Journal of Autism and Developmental Disorders,* http://www.springerlink.com/content/104757

*Journal of Communication Disorders,* http://www.elsevier.com/wps/find/journaldescription.cws_home/505768/description#description

*Journal of Deaf Studies and Deaf Education,* http://jdsde.oxfordjournals.org

*Journal of Developmental Education,* http://www.ncde.appstate.edu/publications/jde

*Journal of Early Intervention,* http://jei.sagepub.com

*Journal of Learning Disabilities,* http://www.proedinc.com

*Journal of Positive Behavior Interventions,* http://pbi.sagepub.com

*Journal of Special Education,* http://sed.sagepub.com

*Journal of Special Education Technology,* http://www.tamcec.org/jset

*Journal of Speech, Language, and Hearing Research,* http://jslhr.asha.org

*Journal of Visual Impairment & Blindness,* http://www.afb.org

*Language, Speech, and Hearing Services in Schools,* http://lshss.asha.org

*LD Online,* http://www.ldonline.org/ldnewsletters

*Learning Disabilities Quarterly,* http://www.cldinternational.org/Index.asp

*Learning Disabilities Research & Practice,* http://www.wiley.com/bw/journal.asp?ref=0938-8982

*Mainstream Online,* http://www.mainstream-mag.com

*Multiple Voices,* http://www.cec.sped.org/content/navigationmenu/aboutcec/communities/divisions/division_for_culturally_and_linguistically_diverse_exceptional_learners__ddel_.htm

*Occupational Therapy Journal of Research,* http://www.otjronline.com

*Palaestra: Forum of Sports, Physical Education & Recreation for Those With Disabilities,* http://www.palaestra.com

*Physical Therapy,* http://ptjournal.apta.org

*Preventing School Failure,* http://www.tandfco.uk/journals/titles/1045988X.asp

*Reading and Writing Quarterly: Overcoming Learning Disabilities,* http://www.tandf.co.uk/journals/tf/10573569.html

*Remedial and Special Education,* http://rse.sagepub.com

*Research and Practice for Persons with Severe Disabilities,* http://www.tash.org/publications

*Research in Developmental Disabilities,* http://www.elsevier.com/wps/find/journaldescription.cws_home/826/description#description

*Rural Special Education Quarterly,* http://www.acres-sped.org/publications

*Sexuality and Disability,* http://www.springer.com/psychology/community+psychology/journal/11195

*Special Ed Advocate Newsletter,* http://wrightslaw.com/subscribe.htm

*Teacher Education and Special Education,* http://tes.sagepub.com

*Teaching Exceptional Children,* www.cec.sped.org/AM/Template.cfm?Section=
Publications1

*Teaching Exceptional Children Plus,* http://escholarship.bc.edu/education/tecplus

*Topics in Early Childhood Special Education,* http://tec.sagepub.com

*Topics in Language Disorders,* http://journals.lww.com/topicsinlanguagedisorders/
pages/default.aspx

*Young Exceptional Children,* http://yec.sagepub.com

# Glossary of Key Terms

**ABA** *See* Applied Behavior Analysis

**ADA** *See* Americans with Disabilities Act of 1990

**Adequate Yearly Progress (AYP)** An accountability measure in the 2001 No Child Left Behind (NCLB) legislation that requires public schools to demonstrate annual gains in reducing performance gaps and meeting specific standards/goals articulated at the federal, state, and local levels.

**ADHD** *See* Attention Deficit Hyperactivity Disorder

*Agostini v. Felton* This 1997 U.S. Supreme Court case reversed a previous ruling that banned the use of public funds to provide special education services for students with disabilities in parochial and other private schools.

**Americans with Disabilities Act of 1990 (ADA)** Also known as P.L. 101-336, this landmark civil rights legislation provides protection against discrimination on the basis of disability in both the public and private sectors in the areas of employment, transportation, public accommodations, and telecommunications.

**Applied Behavior Analysis (ABA)** An approach, a theory, and a group of interventions that attempt to modify behavior and teach skills by examining the events or circumstances that precede behavior (antecedents), and the events or circumstances that follow behavior (consequences).

*Armstrong v. Kline* This 1979 ruling by the U.S. District Court for Eastern Pennsylvania determined that public schools may be required to provide extended school year services to meet the unique needs of children with disabilities as part of a free and appropriate public education.

**ASD** *See* Autism Spectrum Disorders

**Attention Deficit Hyperactivity Disorder (ADHD)** A developmental disorder characterized by chronic and impairing behavior patterns that involve diminished attention, impulsivity, hyperactivity, or their combination.

**Autism Spectrum Disorders (ASD)** A set of five pervasive developmental disorders that appear in early childhood and are characterized by varying degrees of impairment in communication skills and social interactions, as well as by patterns of restricted, repetitive, and stereotyped behavior.

**AYP** *See* Adequate Yearly Progress

***Beattie v. Board of Education*** In this 1919 case, the Wisconsin Supreme Court supported a school district's decision to deny an education to a student of average intelligence with physical disabilities because he had a depressing and nauseating effect on his teachers and fellow students.

**Behavioral Intervention Plan (BIP)** A plan for the implementation of interventions designed to address the needs of students whose behavior impedes their learning, or who have been referred to alternative placement, suspended for more than 10 days, or placed in alternative settings for weapon or drug offenses.

**BIP** *See* Behavioral Intervention Plan

***Board of Education v. Rowley*** In this 1982 case, the U.S. Supreme Court decided that an "appropriate" education is determined by whether or not the student benefits from the education, thus limiting the extent of the services that school districts are obligated to provide to students with disabilities.

***Brown v. Board of Education*** This landmark 1954 U.S. Supreme Court decision outlawed racial segregation in the nation's public schools and declared that all children had a right to an equal education.

*Buck v. Bell*  In this controversial 1927 decision, the U.S. Supreme Court upheld the forced sterilization of people with disabilities.

*Cedar Rapids Community School District v. Garret F.*  This 1999 U.S. Supreme Court decision affirmed that intensive, ongoing health care services qualified as a related service in an individualized education program, as long as those medical services could be provided by trained school staff.

**Child Find**  A mandate of the Education for All Handicapped Children Act (EHA) and Individuals with Disabilities Education Act (IDEA) that requires educational authorities to seek out children in need of a special education.

*Daniel R.R. v. State Board of Education*  This 1989 ruling by the U.S. Fifth Circuit Court of Appeals established a two-part rule for determining compliance with the Least Restrictive Environment mandate of the Education for All Handicapped Children Act (EHA): (1) whether the student is making satisfactory progress in the general education classroom; and (2) whether the student has been included with typical peers to the maximum extent possible.

*Diana v. California*  The consent agreement in this 1970 case said that children must be tested (or retested) in their primary language in order to avoid inappropriate educational placements.

**Disability**  An evolving concept that results from the interaction between persons with impairments and attitudinal and environmental barriers that hinder their full and effective participation in society on an equal basis with others.

**Discrete Trial Training (DTT)**  An instructional method in which tasks and skills are broken into their component parts and taught using an errorless learning approach involving systematic, repeated trials of instruction. Sometimes referred to as Applied Behavior Analysis (ABA).

**Disproportional Representation**  A problem with the distribution of students in special education, or in certain disability categories, in which students from some demographic groups are represented in greater percentages than they are in the total school population.

**DTT** *See* Discrete Trial Training

**EAHCA** *See* Education of All Handicapped Children Act of 1975

**Early Childhood (EC)** Educational programs for eligible children between the ages of 3 and 5 that are designed to improve the children's developmental, social, and learning outcomes; such programs often include speech and language therapy, physical therapy, occupational therapy, and social work.

**Early Intervention (EI)** Educational programs that target children from birth to 3 years old and are designed to improve the children's developmental, social, and learning outcomes; such programs often include speech and language therapy, physical therapy, occupational therapy, and social work.

**EBD** *See* Emotional Behavioral Disabilities

**EC** *See* Early Childhood

**Economic Opportunity Act of 1964** Also known as P.L. 88-452, this legislation launched Head Start, a preschool development program for low-income children as well as children at risk for school failure due to a disability or having a parent with a disability.

**Education for All Handicapped Children Act of 1975 (EHA or EAHCA)** Also known as P.L. 94-142, this was the first federal law ensuring educational opportunity for children with special needs. EHA contained six mandated rights for qualifying students with disabilities: (a) zero reject and child find, (b) nondiscriminatory or unbiased evaluation, (c) individualized and appropriate education, (d) least restrictive environment, (e) procedural due process, and (f) participatory democracy for educational decision making.

**Education of Mentally Retarded Children Act of 1958** Also known as P.L. 85-926, this act provided federal funding to prepare teachers and researchers to improve the education of children with intellectual disabilities.

**Education of the Handicapped Act of 1970** Also known as P.L. 91-230, this legislation created the federal definition of learning disabilities and consolidated all other legislation related to children with disabilities.

**EHA**   *See* Education for All Handicapped Children Act of 1975

**EI**   *See* Early Intervention

**Elementary and Secondary Education Act of 1965 (ESEA)**   Also known as P.L. 89-10, this legislation funded educational programs for economically disadvantaged children and children with disabilities in both elementary and secondary schools, as well as Head Start and Title I programs; in 2001 it was reauthorized as No Child Left Behind (NCLB).

**Emotional Behavioral Disability (EBD)**   Emotional, behavioral, or social functioning that is so different from generally accepted, age-appropriate norms that it adversely affects a child's educational performance, social relationships, classroom adjustment, self-care abilities, or vocational skills.

**ESEA**   *See* Elementary and Secondary Education Act of 1965

**Family Educational Rights and Privacy Act (FERPA)**   A federal law that protects the privacy of students' educational records and gives students and their parents access to records maintained by institutions and educational agencies that receive federal funding.

**FAPE**   *See* Free and Appropriate Public Education

**FBA**   *See* Functional Behavioral Assessment

**FERPA**   *See* Family Educational Rights and Privacy Act

***Florence County School District Four v. Carter***   This 1993 U.S. Supreme Court decision established a precedent that a school district's failure to comply with IDEA could render it financially responsible if a student was then enrolled in a private school.

***Forest Grove School District v. T.A.***   This 2009 U.S. Supreme Court ruling found legal grounds in IDEA to allow financial reimbursement for private education of a child with a disability, even when the student had not been served previously in special education in a public setting.

**Free and Appropriate Public Education (FAPE)**   A right established under Section 504 of the Rehabilitation Act of 1973 for the education of children with disabilities in U.S. public schools; the law defines FAPE as an educational program that is individualized to meet a child's unique needs, provides access to the general curriculum, meets grade-level standards, and confers educational benefit.

**Function**   The normal physiological action or activity of a body part, organ, or system.

**Functional Behavior Assessment (FBA)**   Under the Individuals with Disabilities Education Act (IDEA), this assessment must precede behavior-based decisions related to a change of placement for students in special education; the results determine whether dangerous behavior exhibited by the learner with a disability is related to his or her disability.

*Garland v. Wilks*   In this 1987 case, the U.S. District Court for the Northern District of Texas ruled that when a student does not benefit from the public school program but does benefit from a private extended-day program, the school district must pay for the extended-day programming.

**Goals 2000: Educate America Act of 1994**   Also known as P.L. 103-227, this legislation sought to establish structures and standards/goals that would improve students' post-school outcomes through the development of skills necessary for employment.

**Handicapped Children's Early Education Assistance Act of 1968**   Also known as P.L. 90-538, this legislation led to the establishment of early childhood and preschool special education programs for children with disabilities.

**Handicapped Children's Protection Act of 1986**   Also known as P.L. 99-372, this legislation provided for the payment of attorney fees and court costs to parents who won lawsuits while exercising their due process rights under the Education for All Handicapped Children Act (EHA).

*Hobson v. Hansen*   This 1969 District Court ruling said that it was unconstitutional to use test scores—and specifically IQ tests—to group students into levels or tracks of education, because such practices discriminated on the basis of race and socioeconomic status.

*Honig v. Doe*   In this 1988 decision, the U.S. Supreme Court ruled that the suspension of a student with disabilities for more than 10 consecutive days amounted to a change in placement under EHA and, therefore, was prohibited until the review procedures associated with due process had been completed.

**IDEA**    *See* Individuals with Disabilities Education Act of 1990

**IDEIA**    *See* Individuals with Disabilities Education Improvement Act of 2004

**IEP**    *See* Individualized Education Program

**IFSP**    *See* Individualized Family Service Plan

**Impairment**    Any loss, abnormality, or disturbance of psychological, physiological, or anatomical structure or function that interferes with normal activities and may be temporary or permanent.

**Inclusive Education**    A system that provides instruction and services for students with disabilities in general education settings rather than in separate classrooms to ensure that these students have access to the same educational opportunities as their nondisabled peers.

**Individualized Education Program (IEP)**    Mandated by the Individuals with Disabilities Education Act (IDEA), the IEP documents and guides the process of identifying and referring eligible school-age children for special education services, assessing their needs, planning and implementing individualized programs to meet their needs, and monitoring and evaluating the programs' effectiveness.

**Individualized Family Service Plan (IFSP)**    Mandated by the Individuals with Disabilities Education Act (IDEA), the IFSP documents and guides the early intervention (EI) process for young children with disabilities and their families, with the goal of improving the children's physical, cognitive, social, and emotional growth.

**Individuals with Disabilities Education Act of 1990 (IDEA)**    Also known as P.L. 101-476, this legislation amended and updated the Education for All Handicapped Children Act (EHA or EAHCA) and established the legal definition of disability used in special education law. Major changes in IDEA included the use of person-first language, the introduction of transition planning for students aged 16 years and older, the creation of two new categories of disability (autism and traumatic brain injury), and the addition of new related services.

**Individuals with Disabilities Education Improvement Act of 2004 (IDEIA)**    Also known as P.L. 108-446, this legislation amended IDEA and aligned it with the accountability measures introduced in No Child Left Behind (NCLB); major changes included adding attention deficit hyperactivity disorder (ADHD) to the disability category of Other Health Impairments, creating new disciplinary requirements for special education students, and revising how individualized education programs (IEPs) were developed and monitored.

**Job Training Partnership Act of 1982 (JTPA)**    Also known as P.L. 97-300, this act funded programs that provided job training to individuals who were economically disadvantaged and faced barriers to employment; special education and vocational education teachers used JTPA funds to find and support work experiences for students with disabilities.

**JPTA**    *See* Job Training Partnership Act of 1982

***Larry P. v. Riles***    This 1972 decision by the U.S. District Court for the Northern District of California required schools to use unbiased assessments that did not discriminate on the basis of race in determining whether to place students in special education.

**Learning Disability**    A general term that applies to various disorders that are intrinsic to the individual, adversely affect the individual's educational performance, and are characterized by significant difficulties in the acquisition and use of speaking, listening, reading, writing, mathematical, or reasoning abilities, despite average to above average IQ.

**Least Restrictive Environment (LRE)**    A mandate of the Education for All Handicapped Children Act (EHA) and Individuals with Disabilities Education Act (IDEA) that requires children with disabilities to receive their special education in settings that provide greatest participation in the regular classroom while ensuring maximum educational benefit.

**LRE**    *See* Least Restrictive Environment

*Mills v. District of Columbia Board of Education*   This 1972 U.S. District Court ruling said that the needs of the individual student with disabilities, rather than the cost, should determine the educational services provided by the public school.

**National Defense Education Act of 1958 (NDEA)**   Also known as P.L. 85-864, this act promoted the security of the United States by increasing the educational opportunities and developing the technical skills of American youth; it also established a precedent for federal involvement in education that eventually led to federal intervention in special education.

**National Longitudinal Transition Study (NLTS I and II)**   A long-term research project, funded by the U.S. Department of Education, that gathers data on students with disabilities related to their school experiences, academic performance, post-secondary education and training, and transition into employment and adult roles.

**National Vocational Education Act of 1917**   Also known as the Smith-Hughes Act (P.L. 64-347), this measure enables states to receive matching federal money for vocational education programs and provides the foundation for later employment training programs for youth with disabilities.

**NCLB**   *See* No Child Left Behind Act of 2001

**NDEA**   *See* National Defense Education Act of 1958

**NLTS**   *See* National Longitudinal Transition Study

**No Child Left Behind Act of 2001 (NCLB)**   Also known as P.L. 107-110, this sweeping education legislation established accountability measures, academic standards, and high-stakes testing designed to ensure that all students gained the skills needed to succeed in college and the workforce; schools are required to report to the state educational authority (SEA) and demonstrate adequate yearly progress (AYP) toward a goal of 100% proficiency of all tested students by 2014.

**Normalization**   The concept that people with disabilities should have as much access as possible to mainstream society and culture; the fields of special education and disability rights have used this concept to create curricular content, provide the rationale for educating students with disabilities in general education settings, and promote self-advocacy and self-determination.

*Oberti v. Board of Education of the Borough of Clementon School District*   This 1993 decision by the U.S. Third Circuit Court of Appeals reaffirmed the judicial preference for providing instruction to students with disabilities in general education classrooms over separate special education classrooms.

*PARC (Pennsylvania Association for Retarded Children) v. Commonwealth of Pennsylvania*   The consent decree in this 1972 case affirmed that all children with intellectual disabilities are entitled to a free and appropriate public education, and that educating students with disabilities in a general education classroom is preferable to doing so in a segregated setting.

**Perkins Act (Carl D. Perkins Vocational Education Act) of 1984**   Also known as P.L. 98-524, this legislation established economic and social goals related to improving labor force skills and equalizing opportunities for at-risk populations, which included students with disabilities.

**Rehabilitation Act of 1973**   This landmark civil rights legislation, also known as P.L. 93-112, prohibits discrimination on the basis of disability in programs conducted by the federal government or receiving federal funding, as well as in their employment practices.

**Response to Intervention (RTI)**   Recognized as an alternative method of identifying students with learning disabilities under the 2004 amendments to IDEA, RTI employs a three-tiered approach which measures children's responses to increasingly intensive levels of intervention.

**RTI**   *See* Response to Intervention

*Sacramento City School District v. Rachel H.*   This groundbreaking 1994 ruling by the U.S. District Court for eastern California identified four factors for schools to consider in determining whether to educate a child with disabilities in a general education setting: the educational benefits to the child, the non-academic benefits to the child, the effects of the child's presence on the teacher and fellow students, and the costs associated with the child's presence.

*Schaffer v. Weast*   In this 2005 case, the U.S. Supreme Court ruled that in a due process hearing to decide whether or not an IEP is appropriate, the burden of proof rests with the party seeking to change the plan.

**School to Work Opportunities Act of 1994**   Also known as P.L. 103-239, this legislation sought to establish structures and standards/goals that would improve students' post-school outcomes through the development of skills necessary for employment.

**Section 504**   This section of the Rehabilitation Act of 1973 required programs, services, and entities that receive federal funding to make reasonable accommodations and promote accessibility for people with disabilities.

**SLD**   *See* Specific Learning Disabilities

**Smith-Hughes Act**   *See* National Vocational Education Act of 1917

**Smith-Sears Veterans Vocational Rehabilitation Act of 1918**   Also known as the Soldier's Rehabilitation Act (P.L. 65-178), this measure created a vocational rehabilitation program for disabled World War I veterans; as amended in 1920, the act includes American citizens with disabilities and provides the groundwork for later programs designed to prepare youth with disabilities to transition from school to employment.

**Special Education**   A field and discipline devoted to the education of children with disabilities, as well as the system for delivering such education services in public schools.

**Specific Learning Disabilities (SLD)**   A disability category under IDEA that applies to children with normal intelligence who exhibit patterns of severe learning problems over time, including severe difficulties in acquisition, storage, organization, retrieval, manipulation, and expression of information.

**Stay-Put Provision**   A requirement incorporated in EHA that prohibits schools from changing the educational placement of children with disabilities until the review procedures associated with due process have been completed.

***Stuart v. Nappi***    This 1978 decision by the U.S. District Court for Connecticut said that schools may suspend students with disabilities for disruptive behavior, but that such disciplinary measures must follow due process procedures because they effectively represent a change of placement under EHA.

***Tatro v. State of Texas***    This 1984 U.S. Supreme Court ruling required schools to provide medical and health services necessary to allow students with disabilities to access and/or benefit from education, as long as those services could be provided by trained school personnel rather than a physician.

**Teachers of the Deaf Act of 1961**    This legislation, also known as P.L. 87-276, authorized training for teachers of students who were classified as hard of hearing or deaf; it also lays the groundwork for future legislation to support students with disabilities in school.

**Technology-Related Assistance for Individuals with Disabilities Act of 1988**    Also known as P.L. 100-407, this measure supported the development of assistive technology (AT) for children and adults with disabilities to create greater access to and involvement in their communities.

***Timothy W. v. Rochester School District***    This 1989 decision by the U.S. First Circuit Court of Appeals affirmed that all children—even those with severe disabilities—are entitled to a free and appropriate education, regardless of whether or not the parents can prove the child is benefiting from the education.

**Vocational Education Act of 1963**    This law (P.L. 88-210) and its 1968 amendments (P.L. 90-576) appropriated millions of dollars to vocational education and specified that the funds could be used for persons with mental retardation, hearing impairments, or other disabilities.

**Vocational Rehabilitation Act Amendments of 1954**    Also known as P.L. 83-565, this act significantly increased funding for vocational rehabilitation services, made programs available to individuals with intellectual disabilities and mental health needs, and ultimately resulted in the creation of more than 100 university-based disabled student services programs.

**WIA**    *See* Workforce Investment Act of 1998

*Winkelman v. Parma City School District* This 2007 U.S. Supreme Court ruling said that parents of children with disabilities have the right to represent the interests of their children in court and are not required to have legal representation.

**Workforce Investment Act of 1998 (WIA)** Also known as P.L. 105-220, this legislation targeted the creation of accessible job services and employment training for adults and youth by providing a variety of services, including assessment, academic skill instruction and support, occupational training, and work experiences.

*Wyatt v. Stickney* This 1972 federal court ruling established minimum standards for appropriate treatment of persons with disabilities in an institutional setting, which included access to education.

**Zero Reject** A mandate of EHA and IDEA that says no child may be denied an education, regardless of the type or severity of his or her disability.

# Index